A DIFFERENT SHADE
OF JUSTICE

JUSTICE, POWER, AND POLITICS

Coeditors

Heather Ann Thompson
Rhonda Y. Williams

Editorial Advisory Board

Peniel E. Joseph
Matthew D. Lassiter
Daryl Maeda
Barbara Ransby
Vicki L. Ruiz
Marc Stein

The Justice, Power, and Politics series publishes new works in history that explore the myriad struggles for justice, battles for power, and shifts in politics that have shaped the United States over time. Through the lenses of justice, power, and politics, the series seeks to broaden scholarly debates about America's past as well as to inform public discussions about its future.

More information on the series, including a complete list of books published, is available at http://justicepowerandpolitics.com/.

A DIFFERENT SHADE OF JUSTICE

Asian American Civil Rights in the South

STEPHANIE HINNERSHITZ

THE UNIVERSITY OF NORTH CAROLINA PRESS

Chapel Hill

This book was published with the assistance of the
Fred W. Morrison Fund of the University of North Carolina Press.

© 2017 The University of North Carolina Press

All rights reserved

The University of North Carolina Press has been a member
of the Green Press Initiative since 2003.

Cover photo courtesy of the State Archives of Florida

Portions of Chapter 3 appeared previously in Stephanie Hinnershitz,
"The 'Little Brown Brother' in the Jim Crow South: Race, Sex, and Empire
in *State of Georgia v. Fortunatio Annunciatio* (1932)," *Journal of Southern
History* 82, no. 3 (August 2016): 549–78. Reprinted with permission.

LIBRARY OF CONGRESS CATALOGING-IN-PUBLICATION DATA
Names: Hinnershitz, Stephanie, 1984– author.
Title: A different shade of justice : Asian American civil rights
in the South / by Stephanie Hinnershitz.
Other titles: Justice, power, and politics.
Description: Chapel Hill : The University of North Carolina Press, [2017] |
Series: Justice, power, and politics | Includes bibliographical references and index.
Identifiers: LCCN 2017003592 | ISBN 9781469633695 (cloth : alk. paper) |
ISBN 9781469661506 (pbk. : alk. paper) | ISBN 9781469633701 (ebook)
Subjects: LCSH: Asian Americans—Southern States—History—20th century. |
Asian Americans—Civil rights—Southern States—History—20th century. |
Civil rights—Southern States—History—20th century.
Classification: LCC E184.A75 H56 2017 | DDC 323.1195/073075—dc23
LC record available at https://lccn.loc.gov/2017003592

CONTENTS

Acknowledgments ix

Introduction 1

1 The Oriental Menace Comes to the South: Anti-Alien Property Laws 27

2 Black or White? Asian Americans' Challenges to Segregated Schools 70

3 A Love That Could Not Be Known: Sex, Marriage, and Southern Law 114

Post-1965 Changes in Asian America 155

4 From the Gulf to the Courts: Vietnamese Americans and Human Rights in Texas 158

5 Getting Down to Business in Dixie: Indian American Hotel Owners and Entrepreneurial Rights 195

Conclusion 232

Notes 237

Select Bibliography 265

Index 273

ILLUSTRATIONS

Japanese American farmers and their families at Yamato Colony 37

George Morikami and Japanese American farmers at Yamato Colony 38

Chinese American students in Greenville, Mississippi 83

Chinese American students in Sunday school
in Bolivar County, Mississippi 85

"Philippine yo-yo experts" in Jacksonville, Florida 121

Solicitor General E. A. Stephens in Atlanta 135

Map of fishing towns in the Gulf of Mexico region 163

Klan calling card from Texas 173

Remains of a Vietnamese American fisherman's boat in Texas 176

American-owned-and-operated advertisement in Valdosta, Georgia 205

American-owned-and-operated advertisement
on U.S. Highway 84 in Georgia 231

ACKNOWLEDGMENTS

In many ways writing the second book was both challenging and a welcome change from writing the first. Many people have played important roles in seeing this project from beginning to end, and although I cannot mention everyone in these acknowledgments, this is an undertaking that I could not have completed without the help that I received along the way. Also, when I moved to Georgia from Maryland in 2013, I never would have imagined that I would be writing a book on Asian Americans in the South. While in graduate school and working on my dissertation, I always thought that if I were fortunate enough to receive a job offer, it would be from a school on the West Coast, considering my interests in Asian American history. As fate would have it, I ended up in Valdosta, Georgia, and, during my first semester there, I worried about funding for traveling to West Coast archives to work on a second project. When I took a gamble on searching through LexisNexis for court cases involving Asian Americans in the South, I began a journey that would take me through multiple southern states in search of Asian Americans who fought against southern discrimination and racism in the past.

First and foremost, the members of the editorial team at the University of North Carolina Press made this process as easy as possible and were always there to help talk through ideas and read multiple drafts. From day one, Brandon Proia made sure that the manuscript moved along and offered insight and help in the publishing process, and I am grateful for his support. The anonymous reviewers for the press also offered excellent and much-needed feedback that in the end made the book more complete and analytically sharp, and I thank them for their time and care in reading my work. I also would like to thank the editors of the Justice, Power, and Politics series,

Heather Ann Thompson and Rhonda Williams, for their interest in my work and for their roles in creating an amazing series.

A team of scholars also contributed to this project either through reading drafts, offering comments, or providing friendly support. At the annual Southern Historical Association meeting, Francoise Hamilton changed my view of the project and helped me to get out of a conceptual rut by suggesting that I reconsider how I defined a civil rights movement. Similarly, audience members at the Association for Asian American Studies annual conference offered interesting questions and comments on what would become the third chapter of this book. And, as always, Julie Greene, Eiichiro Azuma, and Lisa Mar wrote letters of support and offered critical advice for moving the project along.

I am obligated to thank Valdosta State University for funding to complete research for this project, nothing more and nothing less.

I'd like to thank the archivists and librarians at the Arkansas State Library, the Georgia Archives, the Hill Memorial Library Special Collections at Louisiana State University, the Mississippi Department of Archives and History, Delta State University's special collections, the State Archives of Florida, the Dolph Briscoe Center for American History at the University of Texas at Austin, the Austin History Center, the Nashville Public Library, the staff at the Portsmouth Circuit Court in Virginia, Benjamin Almoite at the Virginia State Law Library, and Judy Bruno at the Southern Poverty Law Center. I'd also like to especially thank Morris Dees, Lee Duschoff, Michael Leven, H. P. Rama, and Ravi Patel for allowing me to conduct interviews with them for the final chapter. Your time was greatly appreciated, and I absolutely could not have written this book without you.

The *Journal of Southern History* graciously allowed me to reprint portions of Chapter 3 that were previously published in their journal.

As always, a big shout out to all of my family and friends who supported me along the way, but I'd like to especially thank Bob and Rhonda Hutchinson for helping to pay for the permissions costs for the images found in Chapter 4.

And last, but not least, Rob Hutchinson deserves a mountain of praise for (once again) putting up with me as I wrote this book.

A DIFFERENT SHADE
OF JUSTICE

INTRODUCTION

"I've never heard a political opinion from a Chinaman," African American civil rights activist and Mississippi Delta entrepreneur Amzie Moore recounted in a 1967 interview. Although Congress passed and enacted major pieces of legislation, including the Civil Rights Act of 1964 and the Voting Rights Act of 1965, Moore understood that there was still a long way to go on the road to equality and was more than a bit flustered over what he identified as Asian Americans' lack of participation in the civil rights movement. A native of the Mississippi Delta born to sharecropping parents on a plantation near the small town of Grenada and later a store owner in Cleveland, Mississippi, Moore became a leader in the Regional Council of Negro Leadership, an organization that encouraged self-help and entrepreneurship among African Americans in Mississippi. While the 1955 murder of Emmett Till spurred Moore to action in the search for Till's body (where Moore and others learned that there were hundreds of unknown Emmett Tills whom whites had murdered and dumped in the swamps, bayous, and murky, slow-winding rivers of the Delta for decades and probably centuries), Moore was most comfortable in the economic arena of civil rights. Moore believed deeply in the value of small business and property ownership in uplifting black southerners and placing them on the path to equality. This was often difficult to accomplish in the Delta, the "most southern place on earth," as journalists described the flat, cotton-bespeckled landscape of the area. Since the immediate post–Civil War years, however, Chinese migrating to the region from the West Coast in search of business opportunities or to join other family members who lingered after brief stints as plantation workers during the early days of Reconstruction had a strong foothold in the small business scene in the Delta.

Both African Americans and Chinese Americans shared this southern space and attempted to find their place in a racialized society as entrepreneurs and, more generally, as ethnic and racial minorities.

As Moore's perception of the "Chinaman" illuminates, African Americans and Chinese Americans often lived in the same area but did not always share the same experiences within that space. Antagonisms, such as a black boycott of a Chinese grocery store in Grenada, Mississippi, erupted when African Americans perceived that Chinese Americans became too accepting of white racism and benefited from shunning and refusing to intermingle with African Americans. However, the distance between African Americans and Chinese Americans was often greater than antagonisms; they simply did not intersect. The experiences of these two marginalized and often ostracized groups living in a white, racist society were different and created a silence reflected in Moore's experience that he had never heard a political idea or witnessed civil rights activism from the Chinese Americans in Mississippi. If African Americans rarely acknowledged the presence or the voices of Chinese Americans (and vice versa) in Mississippi, whites often did the same. This biracial framework creates the notion that Chinese Americans were an anomaly in Mississippi and that their presence had little impact on the battles for racial justice and equality that shaped the southern civil rights movement of the twentieth century.

But about half an hour up the road from Grenada in the Delta town of Rosedale lived Jeu Gong Lum, a "Chinaman" grocery owner who would have been puzzled by Moore's characterization of him and his fellow countrymen. True, Gong Lum did not join in the protests or picket lines of the African American Civil Rights Movement, and maybe he didn't discuss politics over coffee at the local diner; but he had political opinions, particularly when it came to the well-being of his American-born daughters, Martha and Berda. In 1925 (decades before *Brown v. Board of Education*, *McLaurin v. Oklahoma State Regents*, and *Sweatt v. Painter*), Gong Lum fought against the local school district's decision to deny Martha admittance to the white school, and he appealed his case to the U.S. Supreme Court in 1927. Although Gong Lum would not win his case, here was a "Chinaman" who challenged segregation through the legal system and accidentally became involved in the racial politics of the South. Instead of participating in protests and sit-ins, he pursued a steady fight against Jim Crow in the local, state, and federal courts, and perhaps unbeknownst to Moore, there were other Asian Americans like Gong Lum across the South who fought just as steadfastly for their rights by using the law.

Moore's description of the Mississippi Chinese Americans as politically mute was a gross mischaracterization that continues to shape the narrative of civil rights history in the South. Chinese Americans did have political opinions on their place in a largely biracial society, as did other Asian Americans living in Dixie during the long twentieth century. Similar to African Americans, Chinese Americans, Filipino Americans, Japanese Americans, and later, Vietnamese Americans and Indian Americans faced legal and social discrimination under Jim Crow and its aftereffects. Like African Americans, they often used the courts and advocacy organizations to fight for justice; to disrupt school segregation, antimiscegenation laws, and business discrimination; and to combat racial violence. Unlike African Americans, however, Asian immigrants were subjected to unique discriminatory legislation (including the prohibition of landownership) that rested on their immigrant status as well as international politics and relations between the United States and Asian nations. As a result, Asian Americans utilized a variety of legal strategies in the courts by claiming status as American citizens, exercising special privileges as foreign nationals and (in the case of Filipinos) colonial subjects, emphasizing their liminal racial position via the black/white color line, and later, moving from judicial to legislative lobbying. Despite Moore not hearing it, Chinese Americans did have a political voice, even if it did not intermingle with those of black activists. This book uncovers the political voices of Asian American activists from the 1880s to the late twentieth century and places them within the context of southern and civil rights history.

Why are Asian Americans largely absent from this rich history? As I discovered during frequent research trips and through conversations with friends, family, and other scholars, there is a pervasive belief that because Asian Americans were not present in large numbers in the South for most of American history, their influence on policy must have been minuscule. My mentioning of this project either thoroughly fascinated students in my immigration history course ("Chinese? In the South? That's so random!") or elicited genuine confusion. "Asians" and "the South" are two subjects that do not often go hand in hand, despite Asian Americans representing a rapidly growing demographic in Houston, Atlanta, and other southern cities and their long, if not prolific, presence in this region. A group of Filipino sailors who leapt from a Spanish galleon docked in New Orleans in the late 1700s formed a small fishing village, St. Malo, near current-day St. Bernard Parish, which existed well into the twentieth century and was perhaps the first Asian settlement in the South. Similarly, New Orleans's cosmopolitan atmosphere boasted of its own Chinatown and Japanese quarters during the nineteenth and twentieth centuries, while Chinese Americans began to make their homes in Macon, Savannah, and Augusta, Georgia, during the early twentieth century. Elsewhere, southerners often encountered the one or two Asian families or entrepreneurs in town, such as Chinese Americans in Mississippi and Arkansas. Asian Americans were (and are) part of the fabric of the South, yet have been overlooked in the southern historical narrative.[1]

The absence of Asian Americans in southern and civil rights history is due not to a physical absence in the region but to the idea that because Asian Americans were, as Leslie Bow explains, "racial anomalies," they existed on the margins of southern society.[2] This separation of Asian Americans from the larger narratives of American history is not limited to historical studies of the South. While Asian Americans are front and center in the historiography of West Coast student movements and the Asian American Movement of the late 1960s, their roles in other social and political events nationwide, if we rely on the majority of the existing literature, are minuscule. The political and activist presence of Asian Americans is confined to the historical, geographical, and conceptual boundaries of "Asian America," primarily West Coast based and dating from the late 1960s forward. The lack of engagement among scholars of Asian American and civil rights history more broadly contributes to an incomplete picture of both narratives. More recently, studies of multiracial, interethnic, and panethnic civil rights movements of the West Coast are bringing Asian Americans into the fold of histories that were previously sketched in black and white. However, when we look at the South, the historically low numbers of Asian Americans in the region lead us to believe that they lacked an activist presence or, really, any presence at all.[3]

White southerners, however, identified even the smallest community of Asian Americans as a threat to racial order and stability. Although small pockets of Chinese Americans and Japanese Americans were initially tolerated in Florida, Louisiana, Mississippi, and Texas during the early twentieth century, white southerners viewed Filipinos in the 1930s and Vietnamese and Indians during the 1970s and 1980s with more suspicion. Asian Americans did not fit easily into "colored" or "black" and "white" categories, and even their small numbers posed a challenge to Jim Crow hallmarks such as school segregation and antimiscegenation laws. However, Asian immigrants' noncitizen status (under the 1906 Naturalization Act, Asians were unable to naturalize in America) as well as their social and cultural otherness as "Orientals" led to questions of property rights and legal status. White southerners and southern legislatures viewed these challenges and questions as threats and fired back with a slew of discriminatory court rulings, acts, and even constitutional amendments to limit the potential of Asian Americans to maneuver their position in southern society. The presence of Asian Americans revealed the xenophobia that was rampant in southern racism. From segregation to denial of property and other basic rights to outright violence and intimidation, whites welcomed Asians with codified racism, forcing them to assimilate to the Jim Crow social, cultural, and legal system or to challenge it.

Contrary to Moore's statements and the absence of Asian American activism in works of southern history, Chinese Americans, Filipino Americans, Japanese Americans, Vietnamese Americans, and Indian Americans made political statements by using the courts as well as their noncitizen status and identity to push back against racial inequality. Over the years, Asian American identity in the racially binary South has become a growing subfield of Asian American studies and Asian American history. The experience of Asian Americans with civil rights activism in the South is often overshadowed in the existing literature by a distinct division of the region between "black" and "white."[4] Scholarship on the Mississippi Chinese and their struggles with acceptance and assimilation dominate our understanding of the Asian American experience in the South, but more recently scholars have pushed historians to grapple with the larger conceptual problems and issues of what Leslie Bow has described as the "interstitial" identity of Asian Americans residing in the South.[5] Instead of merely existing between two racial identities (black and white), Asian Americans inhabited a unique space in southern society that was not easily defined and presented opportunities as well as setbacks in maneuvering this racial landscape without necessarily having to strive for or proclaim "whiteness" to thrive and function. Far too often, scholars and the few historians who have focused on Asian Americans in the South characterized them as seeking to become white socially, culturally, and politically to distance themselves as far as possible from the "black" or "colored" categories.[6] Bow challenged historians to move beyond this "yellow to white" framework and instead focus on the unique space and identity that Asian Americans inhabited in Dixie. I build on Bow's foundational work and argue that Asian Americans used their interstitial identity and alien status in court to actively challenge segregation and discrimination. The presence of the interstitial Asian American in the legal realm of the South and its consequences on race relations guide this study.

Because I focus largely on Asian Americans' legal strategies, *A Different Shade of Justice* also brings nuance to the study of southern history and civil rights through applications of critical race theory and Asian American studies. In a black-and-white society, there is no better example of what critical race theorists Michael Omi and Howard Winant identify as the unstable social category of race than the experiences of Asian Americans with southern laws.[7] In many ways, this is as much a story of the variables and gray areas of Jim Crow law and racialized southern courts as it is of Asian American civil rights. Since Asian Americans were neither colored nor white, they were often defined as either colored or "not colored" (a category different from "white"), depending on what state, county, or even city they inhabited. Legal scholar Angelo Ancheta's study of the experiences of Asian Americans with the law as racial minorities and immigrants and the resulting questions of citizenship and its definition in the United States informs this study. Many studies of Asian American legal activity are centered on the West Coast or at the very least west of the Mississippi River, where larger Asian American populations existed before the mid- to late twentieth century. As such, Asian American legal battles in this region moved in cycles, largely corresponding to larger events such as mob violence targeting Chinese during the late nineteenth century (which resulted in Chinese suits for property damages in local and state courts) and, later, during and after World War II, cases against Japanese American incarceration and forced removal (*Korematsu v. United States* in 1944 and *Hirabayashi v. United States* in 1943) and anti-alien land laws (*Sei Fujii v. State of California* in 1952 and *Oyama v. State of California* in 1948). Other cases that went before the Supreme Court and originating from the West, including the 1886 *Yick Wo v. Hopkins* case (where the Supreme Court ruled that seemingly race-neutral laws can still violate Fourteenth Amendment rights) and the 1898 *United States v. Wong Kim Ark* case, which affirmed birthright citizenship, centered on violations of Fourteenth Amendment rights. In contrast, the cases presented in this book originated from the South and dealt with specific day-to-day encounters with Jim Crow segregation and other forms of anti-Asian violence in an area where often few Asian Americans lived. The Asian American plaintiffs from the South used the Fourteenth Amendment's guarantees of life, liberty, and property in conjunction with their status as noncitizens (as many were recent immigrants when they went into the courts) to work around a binary black-and-white, segregated legal system. However, legal strategies among Asian Americans varied throughout the South as well, representing an often personal approach to defining and fighting for civil rights. While Asian Americans faced discrimination on the West Coast as a result of their racial and immigrant status, the fluidity of their racial identity in the South as well as questions surrounding their rights as noncitizens created a more legally convoluted approach to civil rights in the southern U.S. I build on existing works of civil rights and southern history by exposing the complexities that Asian Americans brought to the southern legal system through their racially complex and shifting identities.[8]

A *Different Shade of Justice* restores Asian Americans to a multicultural and diverse legal system in the South. Native Americans and Mexican Americans who called the South their home for either centuries or decades also participated in rights movements that intertwined with the African American Civil Rights Movement, but they faced their own unique forms of discrimination and racism that shaped their strategies for justice and equality. Southern Native American tribes skillfully used federal Indian affairs commissioners to push for reforms in education, poverty, and unemployment in tribal communities, while Mexican immigrants often looked to the Mexican government to intervene on their behalf in fighting Jim Crow racial constructions during the twentieth century.[9] I argue that Asian Americans shared a space as "marginalized" individuals with Native Americans, Mexican Americans, and other groups that fell outside the black/white framework, but their varied ethnic representations and complex legal relationship to naturalization and immigration laws unfold in a complex history of rights, racism, and discrimination in the South. In this sense, *A Different Shade of Justice* joins other scholarly studies of Mexican Americans and Native Americans that challenge the black-and-white story of race in the South during the twentieth century, but I argue for the importance of Asian immigrants for shaping southern laws and presenting crucial legal battles before the bar, often preceding corresponding African American challenges to Jim Crow.

In addition to their racially anomalous status, Asian Americans also walked a fine line between tacit acceptance in southern communities and perpetual otherness. So long as Asian Americans played by the rules of Jim Crow and accepted southern life as dictated by local laws and customs, they were tolerated. Once they pushed too hard for equality, however, their troubles increased and their otherness was highlighted. Lisa Lowe's concept of Asian Americans as perpetual "foreigners within" regardless of citizenship status rings true in the experiences of Asian Americans in the South.[10] From the late nineteenth century through the late twentieth century, whites viewed Asian immigrants as a form of labor in either positive or negative terms. From plantation laborers who filled a need following the emancipation of slaves to Japanese who were expected to rebuild and transform southern land to Chinese American merchants, Vietnamese American fishermen, and Indian American hoteliers, Asian laborers were an integral part of the regional economy but were not often seen as full members of society. Because the identities of Asian Americans were tied to their labor, their acceptance and even racial status varied depending on whether or not the South needed them. Japanese Americans were "model citizens" when assisting southern farmers with new technology; Chinese Americans, "celestial brothers" when assisting with plantation labor; Filipino Americans, a unique and harmless oddity so long as they worked in the fields or in the entertainment industry; Vietnamese Americans and Indian Americans, acceptable if they did not compete with whites, but instantly transformed into a "yellow peril" once whites perceived them as an economic or social threat.

THE "IMPERIAL HEATHENS" ARRIVE: CHINESE LABORERS AND THE POST-CIVIL WAR SOUTH

Understanding the history of Asian Americans in the South requires an examination of their relationship to whites, employment, and property during the late nineteenth century within the broader context of Reconstruction. Land and labor had always shaped southern economic, social, and political life. Following the Civil War, many southern planters came to see Chinese migrants as a valuable tool in the struggle to restore prewar economic prosperity. Reactions to the Chinese from white southerners would set the stage for later receptions of Asian immigrants and lead to questions of the place of Asian Americans in southern society and their respective rights (or lack thereof) as noncitizens.

During the antebellum years, slavery shaped agricultural production and economics in the South. Those who did not own slaves depended on the system for trade and for the accompanying feelings of white supremacy that came from knowing that an entire racial underclass supported and protected the few social and political rights nonslaveowners possessed. After the Civil War destroyed property and land and precipitated the end of slavery, both white and black southerners struggled to understand the transformative changes in the world around them. For Republicans in Congress, the end of the war and the death of slavery represented an opportunity to reconstruct the South in the image of free labor, rights for the newly freed slaves, and industry. The sweeping visions of social, political, and economic change that Radical Republicans and their followers supported created the tumultuous Reconstruction era in the South. From the end of the war through the withdrawal of federal troops from the South in 1877, northern businessmen, politicians, educators, and military officials traveled south to oversee and create the transformation of southern society they desired for collective or individual gains. Programs such as the Freedmen's Bureau assisted newly free slaves with gaining their footing in society, while legislation such as the Civil Rights Act of 1866 and the Fourteenth and Fifteenth Amendments redefined citizenship and the rights therein.[11]

Many white southerners, however, held their own visions for Reconstruction. The rights of newly freed slaves came under fire from white Democrats who feared disorder, racial mixing, and political subversion from African Americans. Hysteria over the potential implosion of the traditional, race-based societal order resulted in discriminatory acts at the local and state levels known as Black Codes. These measures forbade African Americans from a number of activities, including owning firearms and intermarrying with whites, and severely curtailed the citizenship rights of freed blacks. Paramilitary terrorist groups such as the Ku Klux Klan (KKK) represented these sentiments and fueled a social and political movement to redeem the South from outsiders who did not understand and did not care to understand the importance of racial hierarchy for harmony and efficiency. Reconstruction, both formally and informally, came to represent a second civil war for southerners seeking to regain control of their homes and their lives.[12]

Yet southerners did not reject all aspects of Reconstruction. In fact, many embraced the same goals of economic restructuring and progression that northerners held for the region. Planters desired to return their cotton, sugar, and tobacco fields to the glory days before the Civil War, while industrial-minded merchants and businessmen turned to new innovations in factories, steel plants, textile mills, and railroads to either regain or establish their economic prowess. Southerners turned to ventures in agriculture, industry, and capital in order to rebuild Dixie.[13]

But the question of whose labor would rebuild the South preoccupied the minds of planters and entrepreneurs. Both whites and blacks struggled to adjust to the concept of free labor, and the transition was far from smooth. For planters, sharecropping became a new labor system for the cotton and tobacco industries and represented the most efficient relationship between a planter and his tenant farmers. The system was not perfect, as debts could accumulate quickly on harvested crops, but it helped in adapting to new times. Another option was convict lease labor, a system that took advantage of the growing number of young black men arrested for violating the Black Codes. In northern Florida, eastern Alabama, and southwestern Georgia, sheriffs leased convicts to turpentine and sugarcane planters as needed. This was by no means free labor, as the convicts had no rights and the working conditions were typically no better than slavery, but it was again an attempt to fill the need for cheap labor following the war while resisting treating blacks as free workers.[14]

Early on, though, some planters and industrialists turned to an alternate source of labor: the Chinese. During the 1840s and 1850s, Chinese men arrived in the United States in large numbers, fleeing political unrest in their homeland and for employment in mining or railroad construction in the American West, arranged through friend or family contacts or labor contractors. Despite the reputation of the Chinese for being diligent, "docile," and unassuming workers, white backlash against them rose throughout the 1860s as labor unions and the Democratic Party of California decried the Chinese, their "heathen" ways, and their desire to steal American jobs and depreciate wages. A growing global disapproval of the "coolie" trade also soured Americans' opinions on Chinese laborers by the Civil War. Long before southern planters became interested in the Chinese, a coolie trade in Chinese and other Asian labor existed worldwide. Coolies (a term that stemmed from a Mandarin word for "bitterly hard use of strength" or labor) were workers originating from southern China or India recruited for manual labor in various regions around the world, including mining in Peru and other South American nations, but particularly for working on the sugarcane fields in Cuba and the wider Caribbean. The coolie labor system was a form of indentured servitude: Workers signed contracts either through labor brokers or directly through their employers and agreed to work a specific number of years in order to cover transportation expenses. By the early nineteenth century, coolies were shipped around the world and engaged in a variety of labor activities, but in many cases the working conditions resembled slavery more than free labor. Sickness, violence, and death characterized the lives of the many men who became coolies. In other cases, labor contractors obtained coolies through kidnapping or other illegal and/or unethical means. By the 1840s, amid the growing international abolitionist movement, the British and others around the world recognized that coolie labor was rarely free labor. The British shut down ports that oversaw the trading of coolies by the 1840s and 1850s, but coolie labor continued under the auspices of other nations, including Portugal and Spain.[15]

At the height of anti–coolie trade activism, Americans came to associate the Chinese living in their country with enslavement. Although these laborers were free and not coolies, Americans worried about the threat to free labor that any slave or indentured servant would hold. Concerns over the entry of coolies into America to work in mines grew until Congress passed the Anti-Coolie Act in 1862 and banned any ships carrying coolies from entering the United States, while dealing harsh penalties to Americans who aided the importation of coolies. Chinese workers who came to the United States were voluntary laborers, but the U.S. government grew concerned over the possibility that Chinese coolies would further undermine wages. With formal coolie arrangements outlawed in the United States, "coolie" became an unofficial term for any Chinese laborer who came to America to work.[16]

Despite the growing distaste for Chinese in America, by the end of the Civil War, the "celestials" appeared to be an acceptable labor option. But the turn to Chinese labor was more than an attempt to find a simple substitute for slaves or black labor. Planters identified the Chinese as apolitical and less likely than African Americans to challenge their employers. After the Civil War, planters and other whites argued that African Americans were lazy, insolent, and too demanding after they received their citizenship and rights. When southern planters and industrialists first considered importing Chinese labor for their own version of Reconstruction, they opened the South to Asian immigrants and set a precedent for how Chinese and other Asian ethnic groups would be viewed from then on. The Chinese were an odd addition to southern society: They were a commodity (labor), but a commodity with rights as immigrants and Chinese. Under the newly established Fourteenth Amendment, even noncitizens had access to due process and equal protection, establishing a basis for rights that transcended American citizenship. Employers who sought Chinese labor were forced to consider the place of Chinese in the southern economy, the political rights of the Chinese, and the reshaping of the southern racial landscape. These ambitious planters envisioned that when traveling through the cotton or cane fields, one would see Chinese cheaply and efficiently performing the duties that once belonged to blacks. Chinese labor was to be the cornerstone of a New South.[17]

In order to achieve their lofty goals and visions, a group of planters from Mississippi, Arkansas, Tennessee, and Louisiana met in Memphis in July 1869 to discuss the possibilities and potential benefits and liabilities of importing Chinese laborers. Those in attendance from Mississippi, Tennessee, and Arkansas expressed their deep desires to import Chinese but were also concerned about how this desire intersected with the Anti-Coolie Act.[18] Those who were knowledgeable of Chinese labor assured planters that using Chinese already in the United States and living on the West Coast was perfectly legal and more advisable than searching for Chinese overseas. A special transportation committee reported that Chinese could easily be "brought from the Pacific to Memphis in lots of fifty and over for $60 each" in transportation costs.[19] With the cost and mode of transportation more fully explained, others asked about the exact nature of the Chinese and their suitability for labor in the South. Fortunately for the curious planters, there were many West Coast representatives and labor contractors on hand at the convention to assuage any fears that the Chinese might be potential problems. Kim Orr, a Chinese immigrant who spent time as a missionary among Chinese sugar workers in British Guiana and later came to New Orleans as a labor contractor with a boat of Chinese laborers, assured those in attendance that the "habits and peculiarities" of the Chinese made them "well adapted to the southern plantations, the products of China being in many ways similar to the Southern States."[20] "The mighty reservoir of labor," as one attendee described Chinese migration, "is ready to flow into your rich lands."[21] True, Chinese are "heathens," but if a planter "wants cotton, sugar, or tobacco—[he] will get them from the Chinese."[22]

When the discussions of the merits of Chinese labor were through, those in attendance turned to the logistics of importing Chinese to the South. Paying for the passage of Chinese directly from China was expensive. In order to curtail the costs, organizers suggested forming a joint stock company and pooling resources to bring Chinese from the West Coast to designated entry points, including New Orleans, Houston, and St. Louis. Then employers could either send for the workers that they had previously contracted or work with labor agents (some of whom, such as Orr, were Chinese themselves) to hire new laborers. The average contract for a Chinese laborer was between three and five years, and wages often varied. Following the advice to respect the workers and treat them better than African Americans, planters often included extra bonuses such as holidays, opportunities for additional pay, or commodities such as opium in the deals. The planters and employers who sought Chinese labor worked hard to strike a balance between using their new workers as efficiently as possible and respecting their status as free laborers.[23]

Although many of the Chinese who came to the South worked in the sugarcane fields of Louisiana, others scattered across the region where needed. Cotton planters in the Mississippi Delta sought Chinese labor, as did entrepreneurs who entered the high-stakes and lucrative railroad construction industry. Railroads became both a necessity for the expanding markets of the South and an enticing business venture. In order to construct the regional railroads, capitalists turned to the cheap and skilled Chinese, many of whom had recently finished jobs on the Transcontinental Railroad (completed in 1869) and other lines in the West. In 1870, approximately 300 Chinese arrived in New Orleans from the West Coast to begin work on the Houston and Texas Central Railroad, while 700 Chinese arrived in Birmingham and Gadsden, Alabama, from New Orleans and St. Louis to labor on the Alabama Chattanooga Rail Road. The *Daily Alta California* received reports of Chinese arriving in New Orleans and described the fascination and awe for "these strange people" and their "Mongolian habits of shaving."[24] Those of the "colored races" were particularly interested to get a glimpse of their "replacements."[25] Initially, Chinese laborers were welcomed by employers and inspired intrigue in other southerners who caught glimpses of them in the fields, on the rails, or waiting for employment in port cities. Initially, the decision to import Chinese labor to remake the land was promising.

Not all planters rushed to join the new trend in labor. Cotton planters in Arkansas were not immediately convinced of the virtues of Chinese workers, and state officials were even less impressed. Arkansas was devastated in the aftermath of the Civil War and had little state money for rebuilding. Arkansas cotton planters desperately wanted to get back on their feet and only begrudgingly attempted to hire their former slaves as free labor. Racial tensions during Reconstruction as well as corrupt state-level politics did little to restore faith in Arkansas's potential for rebuilding after the war. To make matters worse for white planters, by the time of the Chinese Labor Convention in 1869, Powell Clayton, a former Union brigadier general who was born in Pennsylvania but moved to Arkansas after the war, gained control of the governorship in 1868. Clayton's policies of higher taxes, promotion of rights for freed blacks, and devotion to keeping former Confederates out of the state capitol created rifts between him and his constituents.[26]

Arguments over the importation of Chinese labor to reconstruct Arkansas were complex and did not fall neatly along party lines. Following the Memphis convention, smaller planters went back to Arkansas to engage in their own discussions of Chinese labor and how it related to their state. Governor Clayton paid rapt attention to these discussions and carefully recorded them (along with newspaper reprints) in his memoirs, which provide an in-depth overview of the topic of immigration, Chinese labor, and agriculture in post–Civil War Arkansas. Although both Republicans and Democrats in Arkansas favored immigration for labor, they were "widely divergent as to the character of the immigrants sought and the rights and immunities of the newcomers as compared to the old citizen."[27] "Immigrants" in this sense were those coming from the American North and East as well as Europeans. Clayton argued in an 1869 address to the state legislature that "it is of vital importance for the growth and development of our state that every encouragement be given to the introduction of settlers from abroad . . . in order to restore, all over the state . . . law and order" and rebuild Arkansas's economy.[28] Clayton also praised Arkansas for its "soil unsurpassed for productiveness, a delightful climate and immense amount of cheap land" and called for the establishment of a state immigration bureau overseen by the State Office of Land and Migrations, created by the legislature a few months thereafter. Arkansas could only balance out the "influx of desperadoes and outlaws" coming in from nearby states like Texas and Louisiana by encouraging migrants to make stable homes and reconstruct the state. There was hope that "welcoming immigrants will make [Arkansas] recipients of these elements of wealth—prosperity which by the old order of things were effectually barred."[29]

Many members of the Democratic Party, however, were not enthusiastic over the use of immigrants to rebuild the land and denounced Clayton's approach to immigration. What they were looking for was not a reconstruction like that of Clayton's but, rather, a return to the old agricultural system. As early as 1866, the Democratic *Arkansas Gazette* explained that in the aftermath of the war, "our people are particularly attached to the plantation system which has prevailed heretofore among us. . . . The introduction of foreign elements as laborers will tend to destroy this ancient system."[30] Also, "it is to be desired that the ownership of soil of our state remain for the greater part in our ancient population and their descendants as the proprietors of the soil give the tone to the people of the community."[31] The land of Arkansas was to be that of Arkansans, and laborers should be natives of the state, not outsiders or those who would not settle permanently and invest in the land. For opponents of immigration to Arkansas, land and labor were sacred and essential gifts to the deserving "ancient" populations of the state. Only natives would "give the [correct] tone to the character of the people of a community."[32]

There were also fears that immigrants would bring too much political baggage to Arkansas, adding to an already unstable and volatile atmosphere. Democrats in Arkansas were clear that "we want them [immigrants] to bring with them labor and capital, and not a stock of political morality to force down the throats of supposed barbarians. We desire the greatest amount of industrious energy with the least amount of politics."[33] Possibly referring to the Radical Reconstruction politics that migrants from the North might bring to the state and/or the more radical socialist elements found among some European immigrants, many Democrats feared the instability that new waves of immigrants would present to the people of Arkansas.

When it came to Chinese immigration, the topic became more complex still. Democrats were particularly incensed by Clayton's desire to promote African American settlement in Arkansas as a way to propel the state forward in progressive racial politics and relations. In retaliation, Democratic planters who attended the Arkansas conferences on Chinese labor in 1869 decided that if Republicans wanted immigrants, they would get them in the form of cheap Chinese labor to rebuild the old plantations. In 1870, planters and businessmen formed the Arkansas Valley Immigration Company to import Chinese workers from California and China directly (when applicable) to work on cotton fields in Lincoln, Jefferson, and current-day Pulaski Counties in the Mississippi Delta. Shortly thereafter, approximately 100 Chinese arrived in Arkansas and went to work. Clayton, observing the workings of the immigration company from his office, worried that this was little more than a scheme to "punish the negro for having abandoned the control of his master, and to regulate the conditions of his employment and the scale of wages to be paid to him."[34]

The arrival of the Chinese prompted questions of labor and immigrant rights in the new Arkansas. Since Chinese were not black but were free laborers with protections guaranteed under the Fourteenth Amendment and the Burlingame Treaty of 1868 that granted "first nation" status and basic civil rights to Chinese living in America, how were they to be received and treated on the job? While Democrats supported them for their labor, others in Arkansas worried that, given these freedoms, the Chinese may become too political and that the Republican government would eventually grant them the right to vote in state and local elections. The Republican-controlled *Pine-Bluff Express*, however, was clear in that "a Chinaman . . . has the right to live, he has a right to earn his livelihood wherever he can best find work and wages. Knowing that of all the countries on earth America offers the greatest advantages to working men, he has a right to come hither and take his chances with the rest. Being here he has the right to be treated with the same justice and generosity as we show to other men. And that is the sum of the Chinese question."[35]

Chinese laborers forced Clayton and others to test the bounds of rights in Arkansas following the Civil War. The presence of Chinese migrants in Arkansas brought debates over the relationship between free labor and immigration to the forefront. The politics of the state made this labor system more than just a substitution for slavery. Arkansans had heated discussions over the threat of Chinese labor before the Chinese question would induce debates in Congress on whether or not Chinese were threats to American labor more generally. The in-between status of the Chinese as nonblack laborers and racial others, but also immigrants with rights, would set the stage for later treatment of Asian Americans across the South. In Louisiana, as historian

Moon-Ho Jung explains, the importation of Chinese labor complicated new national ideas of free labor, race, and citizenship, but as the experiences in Arkansas demonstrate, the Chinese also brought up more pointed questions about immigrants, Asian Americans, and their roles and rights in the South. Although the number of Chinese laborers in Arkansas was small, their very presence challenged Arkansans to consider whether or not the laborers had rights as noncitizens.

By the mid-1870s, Arkansas employers learned as others in the South also did that the Chinese were not the answers to their Reconstruction prayers. In many ways, this understanding was a product of the labor and civil rights that Chinese workers often demanded. As early as 1870, 140 Chinese laborers at the Maullauden Plantation in Louisiana grew weary of watching their black counterparts supposedly take frequent breaks and went on strike in retaliation to demand better wages. The plantation overseers were dismayed by the "crowd of infuriated Chinese laborers" and their lack of deference to their employers or even Cum Wing, the Chinese labor contractor who brought them to Louisiana and checked in on them from time to time to see that their needs were met. A year later, Chinese on plantations in Iberville Parish, Louisiana, protested fines deducted from their pay for failing to meet arbitrary quotas by running away. The planters enlisted the help of local law officials and even the state troops to maintain order, but to little avail: The Chinese scattered and refused to return to work. During the late 1870s, Chinese laborers frequently went on strike to protest low wages and left their jobs, transforming themselves from contract laborers to migrant workers who moved across the South in search of better pay and working conditions. Cotton planters in Arkansas also realized that perhaps their plan for using Chinese labor as a substitute for African American slave labor was ill conceived. Chinese on the cotton plantations eventually became dissatisfied with their working conditions and pay, and despite planters' attempts to assuage them by offering an extra half-pound of opium on top of their weekly wages, the laborers left the fields and broke their contracts. "The efforts to utilize Chinese labor proved a disastrous failure," Clayton observed. "Planters soon learned that after all the negroes, as laborers in the cotton fields, were better in all respects then [sic] the men of any other race, and in a little while the Chinamen sagaciously learned the purposes for which they were introduced."[36]

Chinese workers demonstrated that they were free laborers with rights. In Arkansas, where the Republican government was adamant on protecting immigrants, the hands of the planters were tied. Following the failure of Chinese labor, working-class Arkansans were able to take refuge in the increasing number of white European immigrants coming into the state, "thrifty Germans . . . and the hardy sons of toil, who come to work and make a living and build up the fortune of the state."[37] In other words, white working- and middle-class Arkansans celebrated Anglo-Saxons who were there to work the land and reconstruct Arkansas rather than Chinese sojourners who were meant to prop up the old planter classes.

The experiment with Chinese labor across the South was short lived, lasting only a little under a decade. As early as 1873, when an economic depression beset the United States, planters in Louisiana were already releasing their Chinese laborers from their contracts. With a shrinking market and reduced tariffs on imported sugarcane from Hawaii and Cuba, the Louisiana planters could no longer afford to keep the Chinese. The venture had proven too costly and not nearly as efficient as they had hoped. Rather than a magic cure for the "insolent Negro," the Chinese turned out to be anything but "docile Celestials." Planters returned to recruiting poor blacks and whites for sharecropping, while dreams of reviving the old plantation system or re-creating the antebellum economic South on the backs of Chinese laborers evaporated.

Just as southern whites were losing patience with the Chinese, Americans nationwide became more suspicious of the immigrants by the late 1870s. Violent clashes between working-class whites and blacks and Chinese laborers in California, Washington, and throughout the Rockies were physical manifestations of the "Chinese problem" that plagued labor union leaders and West Coast politicians. The Knights of Labor, the Democratic Party of California, and various nativist groups, including the Native Sons of the Gold West, decried not only the unfair competition from Chinese but also the criminality, diseases, and disloyalty that the Chinese supposedly brought to the United States. The Chinese were not racially fit for citizenship under the Naturalization Act of 1790, which prohibited Asians from naturalizing; their culture and "heathen mannerisms" made them unassimilable. Others, including northern Republicans, worried that the Chinese were undermining free labor through their willingness to work for low wages. Both Republican and Democratic politicians assumed that all Chinese were coolies (despite coolie labor being banned in 1862 and the absence of any evidence that Chinese in the United States arrived as part of the coolie trade) and therefore a threat to freedom. Although some, such as Frederick Douglass, who argued that the Chinese were merely practicing their human right to migration by living in the United States, did speak out against anti-Chinese sentiments, calls for exclusion grew louder and more numerous.[38]

Southerners also joined in the fight for Chinese exclusion. In 1879, a bill limiting Chinese immigrants to the United States to fifteen per ship passed Congress but was later vetoed by President Benjamin Harrison, who did not want the bill to sour diplomatic and trade relations with China. Nonplussed, West Coast Democratic politicians, labor leaders, and their supporters crafted another piece of legislation, this time with support from southern politicians, who identified with the West Coast and its racial problems with the Chinese. Democratic representative (and later senator) John Sharp Williams from Mississippi frequently expressed his understanding of the problems of the West Coast with the Chinese. "Although your problem out on the Pacific Coast is not as serious as that with which we are struggling in the South," Williams explained in a House speech, "it may in time become so." "There will be a time, if the influx of Chinamen goes on upon the Pacific slope, when the demagogue will, in order to bolster up party purposes, demand that the Mongolian be equipped with the suffrage 'in order that he may defend himself.'"[39] White southerners, who battled their own "race problem" with African Americans, understood the problems Californians faced with the Chinese. "My friends on the Pacific slope, we [southerners] alone can understand you," Williams assured fellow representatives from the West, "and . . . I think we can not cultivate the acquaintance and knowledge of one another any better than by uniting frankly and fearlessly whenever these questions are presented to do the right thing, trusting our white brethren elsewhere also to do the right thing."[40] After having experienced firsthand the uselessness and threats of the Chinese while facing its own racial problems with African Americans, the South had a connection with the West Coast, and southerners like Williams saw the Californian calls for exclusion as an extension of states' rights to demand change from the federal government.

In 1882, the anti-Chinese backers achieved their goals when Congress passed the Chinese Exclusion Act, which denied entrance to all Chinese manual laborers and required Chinese already in the United States to apply for passports and carry papers with them at all times to prove their legal entry. The Exclusion Act marked an important turning point in American history by engendering a massive immigration bureaucracy, an increase in illegal immigration, further racialization of immigration law, and the struggle of legal Chinese residents and those who were born in the United States to protect themselves and their property from racism and discriminatory measures. The act was also significant for the South in that it cemented planters' and employers' beliefs that the Chinese were incapable of contributing their labor to reshaping and rebuilding the land. If they were not fit for labor, then they were not fit to be in the South or have rights. By extension, most whites would come to see all Asian Americans in the same light, as failed commodities with a perplexing political status living on the margins of society. Asian Americans' apparent lack of commitment to labor made them an interstitial people, not black enough for black jobs but not white enough for white work or landownership.

After the failed labor experiment with the importation of Chinese labor to the South following the Civil War, many of the Chinese who came returned to the West Coast or scattered elsewhere across the country, but others chose to stay in Texas, Mississippi, Arkansas, Louisiana, and Tennessee. Those who lingered went on to establish Chinese communities in rural and urban areas of the states and eventually encountered Jim Crow throughout the early twentieth century. The attempts to use Chinese laborers in the fields and on the rails were quickly forgotten as whites turned their attention toward the growing racial and political tensions of the Jim Crow era.[41]

The troubled legacy of early Chinese laborers in the South would shape white southerners' perceptions of Asian Americans for decades to come. As laborers, they were intractable. As a people, they were perpetually other: dangerous, shady, unwholesome, and incapable of proving their worth or becoming American citizens. They were not white but they were not black, and employers were not comfortable treating federally protected immigrants the same as African Americans. If the Chinese were not suitable for labor in a white-dominated society, then what was their purpose in the South? The Chinese did not "fit" with the labor or racial schema, making them outsiders and creating a pattern of abuse for future Asian migrant groups. The racialization of labor in the South following the Civil War affected Asian Americans as much as African Americans. Japanese, Filipinos, Vietnamese, and Indians would later face similar circumstances, resulting in a variety of legal cases and forms of activism centered on access to civil rights for Asian Americans and noncitizens. Did Asian immigrants have rights as noncitizens, when African Americans themselves often struggled for access to their basic civil rights as citizens? This question would characterize the legal activism of Asian Americans for decades to come.

A CIVIL RIGHTS MOVEMENT OR CIVIL RIGHTS MOVEMENTS?

Because the populations of Asian Americans were so varied and far-flung throughout the South for most of the twentieth century, defining the civil rights activism of Asian Americans as a "movement" belies its fragmented and individualistic nature. There were no large-scale national organizations, such as the National Association for the Advancement of Colored People, the Student Nonviolent Coordinating Committee, the Congress of Racial Equality, or the Southern Christian Leadership Conference, or even large-scale labor unions to represent Asian Americans living in the South. Not only were they racial minorities, but Asian Americans were also minorities in the overall population when compared with African Americans, Latinos, and Native Americans. When Gong Lum fought against school segregation in Mississippi and Lum Jung Luke battled anti-alien land laws in Arkansas, although they were both Chinese Americans, they were not fighting for Chinese American rights or even Asian American rights but, rather, their own civil rights as individuals. Gong Lum wanted his daughter to be able to attend white schools, and Lum Jung Luke simply wanted to own property. Class and gender also played large roles in Gong Lum's and Lum Jung Luke's decisions to battle discrimination: They were economically successful men who had the means to hire the best lawyers to defend their rights and their reputations. Gong Lum and Lum Jung Luke were not representative of all Asian Americans living in the South, but they do provide an idea of who was willing and able to tackle discrimination and take on southern law. In the process of using the courts, however, the two men indirectly challenged Jim Crow for all Asian Americans, as would other individual Chinese Americans and Filipino Americans struggling against miscegenation laws from the 1930s to the 1950s and, later, Vietnamese Americans and Indian Americans who battled de facto segregation and discrimination in the 1980s and 1990s.

Asian Americans in the South generally did not band together across regions and ethnic lines but, rather, engaged in microlegal battles at the state level that at times went up to federal courts—apart from Indian hoteliers who would break this pattern later in the twentieth century by reaching across regional and racial boundaries. This is not dissimilar to the smaller battles for property rights and civil disputes found in courts between whites and blacks from Reconstruction up through the major landmark Supreme Court cases of the post–World War II era. They fought for their own specific rights as Chinese Americans or refugees or colonial subjects or immigrants—not because they were "Asian." Southern and U.S. law may have grouped all "yellow" people under the category of "Oriental" or "Asian," but in the South (as elsewhere) their identities varied, as did their approaches to fighting discrimination. This was not a panethnic movement as would be seen along the West Coast before, during, and after World War II but, rather, a series of individual battles against discrimination in the South that, when taken together, weave a tapestry of legal activism that paralleled, and in some cases anticipated, the landmark African American civil rights cases of the twentieth century.

As Asian Americans attempted to distance themselves from "blacks" or "coloreds" (knowing the repercussions of being identified as either in the South), racial and ethnic tensions between Asian Americans and African Americans flared periodically. As a result, though the two groups were fighting against similar forms of discrimination, their movements would never merge to create an interracial or multicultural movement as they often did along the West Coast. The issues of citizenship and immigrant status often defined Asian American battles for civil rights and separated them from African American legal battles. Jim Crow's powerful effect on assimilation for Asian immigrants had a stronger hold on a black-and-white based society than along the multiethnic West Coast, which would produce an interracial, interethnic, and panethnic movement later after World War II. As a result, historians have generally overlooked the individuated civil rights struggles of Asian Americans in the South. Their battles challenge the legal and historical narrative of civil rights in the South as dominated by African Americans and, later, by large-scale national and regional African American civil rights organizations.

NOTE ON DEFINING THE SOUTH

Defining the South culturally, politically, and even geographically has proven to be a difficult task for historians, as "the South" is often a moving target. Depending on the topic, time period, and methodology, the South can mean different things to different scholars. Many historians geographically define the South as consisting of the former slaveholding states prior to the Civil War as well as those that later seceded from the Union to form the Confederacy. Culturally, the South can also include the Bible Belt (stretching from Virginia to Texas) and is interchangeable with terms such as "Old South" or "Deep South." The official U.S. Census definition of the South is similar to those above except for the inclusion of West Virginia, Oklahoma, and Washington, D.C. Other scholars, such as Khyati Y. Joshi and Jigna Desai, provide a more fluid definition of the South as a "historical, cultural, and geopolitical space that is both understood to be a region of the United States and a space connected to and part of other transnational spaces such as the Atlantic World . . . a coherent region and place as it is associated with a distinct and authentic Southern culture and history" stemming form shared pasts of "slavery, Jim Crow, segregation, and White supremacy."[42] Joshi and Desai also call attention to the "discrepancies in Dixie," or the variations in cultural, political, social, and racial aspects of life that break down the "solid South," yet leave intact "an understanding of the South as a geopolitical place." "Oriental," "yellow," and even "colored" as identifiers for Asian Americans in the South varied from state to state and even town to town, making the definition of the South as a geopolitical region with broad variations essential for my work. More specifically, while small groupings of Asian Americans could be found in all of the traditionally defined southern states, I focus on the regions where they had a profound impact on local and state law regardless of the size of their population. This book does not include discussions of every southern state but, rather, looks closely at Arkansas, Florida, Georgia, Louisiana, Mississippi, Tennessee, and Texas as battle sites for Asian American civil rights and the insight they provide on how Asian Americans maneuvered Jim Crow law and society.

ORGANIZATION

In order to uncover Asian legal activism in the South and the forms it assumed as well as trace how it changed over time, this book is organized thematically and largely chronologically (although some chapters move beyond more limited time frames in order to fully explore a specific form of discrimination and the resulting response from Asian Americans and southerners). In many ways, this book uses cycles of Asian migration to examine legal battles and activism throughout the twentieth century as different ethnic groups encountered different aspects of southern racism and discrimination. I also use 1965 as a pivotal turning point for this history, as the Immigration Act of 1965 as well as other social, political, economic, and cultural factors that developed out of the civil rights movement, the Vietnam War, and changes in American economy and business had a significant impact on Asian American activism in the South. Not only did new Asian immigrants (primarily Vietnamese refugees and Indian hoteliers) first arrive in the South in larger numbers after 1965, but the southern prejudices that they encountered were a peculiar, post–civil rights era blend of racism, economic anxieties, and nativism that created new and challenging forms of discrimination as well as new forms of activism.

Chapter 1 builds on the brief history of Chinese Americans in Arkansas provided in this introduction by moving into the twentieth century and analyzing new forms of property discrimination in the South. Following the failed experimentation with Chinese plantation labor, Japanese American settlers began to look to the South during the early 1900s for agricultural opportunities (particularly in Florida, Louisiana, and Texas) that were denied or difficult to obtain on the West Coast. Initially, whites welcomed Japanese Americans for their ability to revive faltering agricultural industries that did not recover following the Civil War. By the years leading up to World War I, small yet successful colonies of a few hundred Japanese Americans growing citrus fruits and rice blossomed in Florida, Louisiana, and Texas. However, although small in number, the very presence of Chinese Americans and Japanese Americans in the South triggered a fear among southerners of a "yellow invasion." In response, the distaste of whites for Asian settlers gave way to laws and state constitutional amendments prohibiting aliens ineligible for citizenship (Asians) from owning property in their states. The vague wording of the laws and lack of enforcement made mounting a battle against these legal forms of discrimination difficult, but one Chinese American property owner in Arkansas would finally do so in 1927. This chapter forms a foundation for examining the unique experiences of Asian Americans in the majority-black-and-white framework of the Jim Crow South.

Chapter 2 explores the experiences of Asian Americans with school segregation in the South. Focusing primarily on Chinese Americans and Filipino Americans, I compare and contrast the experiences of both groups in different southern states to expose the complicated relationships between Asian Americans and racial segregation in education. More than other aspects of southern society, segregated schools forced Asian Americans to face the binary nature of southern identity. While southern society typically grouped Asian Americans under "colored" and prevented them from attending white schools, Asian Americans often fought this racial classification by stressing their "nonblack" status in their communities, local courts, and federal courts. This strategy often further distanced them from African Americans and highlighted the uneasy relationships between the two groups, but it also showed the dedication of Asian Americans to staking a claim in the South and fighting for their children's right to an education. The experiences of Chinese Americans in Augusta, Georgia, with city plans to segregate their children from whites in the early twentieth century, the challenges to easy racial classification presented by a group of Filipino students and a Chinese boy to a Kentucky school board in the early 1900s, and Gong Lum's unsuccessful fight against school segregation in Mississippi form the core of this chapter. Taken together, these examples serve as an understudied component of civil rights history before the landmark *Brown v. Board of Education* case of 1954 and underline the complex racial and legal statuses of Asian Americans in the South.

While studies of antimiscegenation laws and interracial sex in the South tend to focus on white/black relationships, Asian Americans were also subjected to Jim Crow discrimination in prohibitions on interracial sex and marriage. Antimiscegenation laws pertaining to Asian and white relationships varied from state to state. Some were explicit in barring "Mongoloids," "Malays," or "Orientals/Asiatics" from intermarrying with whites, while others did not specifically mention Asians. Regardless, Asian men often experienced similar suspicions and prejudice from white southerners as African American men did regarding their sexual behaviors. However, the in-between racial and political status of Asian Americans challenged the social, sexual, and legal order of the South. Chapter 3 focuses on two court cases that highlight the complexities of Asian-initiated battles against sexual and racial laws and norms in southern states: the 1932 *State of Georgia v. Fortunatio Annunciatio* case and the 1955 *Han Say Naim v. Ruby Elaine Naim* Supreme Court appeal that originated in Virginia. In *State v. Annunciatio,* Fortunatio Annunciatio (a Filipino man) was accused and convicted of raping a fifteen-year-old white Atlanta girl. He later attempted to appeal his verdict to the supreme court of Georgia by arguing that his basic Fourteenth Amendment rights had been violated by unconstitutional and illegal procedures during the investigation and trial. Han Say Naim was a Chinese sailor who defied Virginia antimiscegenation law by traveling to North Carolina to marry his white fiancée, Ruby. Unfortunately for Naim, Ruby later filed for divorce in a local Virginia court, and the judge annulled the marriage, arguing that the union was void because it was not recognized under Virginia law. In order to keep his marriage and access to a spousal visa intact, Naim appealed his case to the U.S. Supreme Court, initially using his immigrant status to argue that certain rights granted to him through treaties between China and America were violated by the lower court's decision. Both men attempted to use their noncitizen status in courts but repeatedly encountered obstacles to arguing for their rights when faced with southern sexual beliefs and laws in relation to race.

The 1960s and 1970s were a transformative time for Asian Americans across the country, and such changes did not escape the South. Although Asian Americans were assumed to be more successful and integrated than other minorities, the Immigration Act of 1965 and, later, the Vietnam War brought a new wave of immigrants to the United States. While the 1965 act removed decades-old race- and nationality-based quotas that severely restricted the number of Asian Americans allowed to migrate to the U.S., the wreckage of the Vietnam War and new American polices geared toward resettling refugees brought thousands of Vietnamese to America. Although many Vietnamese refugees settled on the West Coast and in the Great Lakes region, thousands more came to the Gulf of Mexico area through sponsors or established family connections seeking work in the shrimping or oil industries of Alabama, Louisiana, Mississippi, and Texas. From the late 1960s through the 1970s, the Galveston Bay area of Texas received hundreds of Vietnamese who were eager to build small, family-owned fishing businesses. But as the Vietnamese soon discovered, they were not welcomed by southern whites who feared economic competition and mistrusted racial outsiders. The Vietnamese faced prejudice, boycotts, and threats but also more hostile and violent encounters with paramilitary white supremacist organizations. When the Galveston Ku Klux Klan burnt Vietnamese ships one night in 1981, the Vietnamese fought back in the Houston District Court, filing a civil rights suit against the Klan with the assistance of the Southern Poverty Law Center. Chapter 4 analyzes the experiences of Vietnamese in the South as a case study in the continued civil and human rights struggles faced by Asian immigrants and minorities in the "post–civil rights" South. With Reconstruction-era elements including violence, the Klan, and southern communities beset with sudden social changes, the Vietnamese proved that the civil rights movement was far from finished by the late 1970s.

Finally, through oral histories and private papers and publications, Chapter 5 uncovers the more recent history of Indian American hoteliers and their battles with discrimination in the hospitality industry. During the 1980s and 1990s, the South experienced yet another demographic shift as an increasing number of Indian immigrants and their families relocated to southern states for business opportunities. As in other regions across the country, Indian American–owned hotels and motels (or "Patel Motels") became a growing phenomenon as migrants took advantage of affordable operating costs and tourism across the American South. While many Indian Americans maintained successful businesses and became a driving force in the southern hospitality industry, such success did not come without a price. As they did with Vietnamese Americans and Japanese Americans in previous decades, many whites resented another possible "Asian invasion" of "un-American" outsiders set on making profits by driving Americans out of business. Specifically, Indian Americans often faced entrepreneurial discrimination from southern bankers and insurance agents who would refuse loans and coverage. As a result, Indian American hotel owners from Tennessee formed the Mid-South Indemnity Association (later the Indo-American Hospitality Association) in 1985 and later merged with hoteliers from Atlanta in 1989 to create the Asian American Hotel Owners Association (AAHOA), an advocacy group that gained national prominence. The fact that AAHOA had its roots in the South was no coincidence: Indian Americans were part of a larger history of discrimination against Asian Americans in this region, and their responses were part of a larger civil rights movement. By using the records of AAHOA as well as oral histories from some of the founding members of the organization, I argue in this chapter that the experiences of Indians with business discrimination are an indication of the complex "postracial" history of the South and its treatment of immigrants and Asian Americans. Unlike previous Asian Americans who used the courts, however, Indian Americans avoided legal action as much as possible. Rather than attempting to work an in-between or interstitial identity to their advantage, Indian American hoteliers relied on the notion of Asian Americans as the "model minority" and "good" immigrants in search of the American entrepreneurial dream to band together and make their case against racism and prejudice. Indian American identity and nonlegal activism during the 1980s and 1990s presents a new look at the evolution of interstitial identities for Asian Americans in the South over time.

From Gong Lum to Indian American hoteliers, *A Different Shade of Justice* uncovers Asian American activism in the South and a more nuanced understanding of civil rights and social justice in this region of the United States. This book is not an exhaustive account of the history of Asian Americans or Asian American activism in the South. Other groups, including Korean American store owners, Japanese American auto-plant workers in Tennessee, or the more recent Asian American settlers in and around Atlanta and parts of Virginia, for example, are not discussed at length here. *A Different Shade of Justice* should serve as a starting point for further exploration of the intersections of Asian American identity and politics and justice in the South. The ways in which Asian Americans used their interstitial identities as well as their resident status to fight for equality with whites challenged southern law and brought immigrant and human rights into the fold of civil rights, creating a legal tradition that is distinct from that of African Americans in the civil rights movement. The xenophobia inherent in southern racism, the importance of citizenship, and the impact of international and immigrant politics on discrimination come to the surface in an analysis of the place of Asian Americans in the South during the twentieth century. Asian Americans did have political opinions, and in the pages that follow, their opinions and their voices challenge Moore's characterizations as well as the standard histories of civil rights, Asian America, and the South.

ONE

THE ORIENTAL MENACE COMES TO THE SOUTH

Anti-Alien Property Laws

Although his name was Lue Gim Gong, Floridians knew him as the "wonder grower" or "citrus wizard." A Chinese immigrant, Lue arrived in San Francisco in 1872 when he was twelve years old and quickly went to work with his uncle, an established merchant and labor contractor in the city. When Lue was sixteen, his uncle sent him to North Adams, Massachusetts, to work in a shoe factory. Lue's easy demeanor and quick embrace of Christianity won him the affection of the powerful Burlingame family, who attended church with Lue. Solomon Burlingame offered Lue a job translating Chinese documents for his business, allowing Lue to strengthen his English language skills and become close friends with Solomon's spinster daughter, Fanny Burlingame. Fanny became a mother figure to Lue and encouraged him to convert to Christianity and even assisted him with becoming an American citizen in 1877. In 1886, Fanny bequeathed five acres of land in Deland, Florida (near Daytona Beach), to Lue.[1]

Lue thrived in Florida, making good use of Fanny's investment. Lue diligently worked at developing hardier strands of citrus that could withstand the sometimes unpredictable Florida climate, and in 1888, he created the Lue Lim Gong orange. By 1911, the Lue Gim Gong orange was a nationwide success. Lue was well respected by the white population of Deland and surrounding areas in Florida, a significant achievement for a Chinese man after the Chinese Exclusion Act of 1882. Perhaps, in the midst of a nation growing increasingly anti-Asian by the 1920s, Florida and more generally the South could be seen as an island of relative tolerance.[2]

Or perhaps Lue's success and popularity among Florida whites were the result of him merely being in the right place at the right time, before the state would join in a national attempt to limit Asian American property rights. In 1926, one year after Lue died, the state of Florida amended its constitution to include a passage barring aliens ineligible for citizenship from owning land. Although "aliens ineligible for citizenship" was a broad category, by 1925 the phrase was racially coded in American political discourse as generally referring to Asian immigrants barred from entering the United States under the Immigration Acts of 1917 and 1924 and prohibited from naturalizing under the Naturalization Act of 1906. If Lue had arrived in Florida in 1927, his ability to become a landowner would have been questionable: He was an American citizen, but he was associated with a racial group "ineligible for citizenship." It is difficult to tell how he would have been received by Florida residents at this time and if he would have easily been able to own property and become the citrus king. Lue's case is exceptional, but it raises questions of the position of Asian Americans in the South vis-à-vis their immigrant status and highlights the xenophobia present in southern racism and its connections to discriminatory movements against Asian immigrants in the West.

Rather than a significant turning point, Florida's radical change in its constitution was a culmination of growing southern fears of a "yellow invasion" during the late nineteenth and early twentieth centuries. The Chinese labor experiment was short lived in southern states such as Mississippi, Louisiana, and Arkansas, but as soon as the fear of labor competition died down by the turn of the century, a new wave of fear over Japanese encroachment on land washed over the South in the early twentieth century. As Japanese immigrants settled in California, Washington, and Oregon following Chinese exclusion in the early 1900s and found work as migrant laborers or later became successful farmers and business owners, West Coast residents feared a Japanese takeover of their land. In response, California and Washington passed laws that barred aliens ineligible for citizenship from owning property in 1913 and 1921, respectively. As a result, whites in the South worried that a "yellow horde" of Japanese was headed their way, fleeing the racism and discrimination in the West. True, more Japanese and Chinese did begin to come to some southern states during the early twentieth century, but they were not refugees from western land laws and they did not come in larger numbers. However, southerners interpreted this small stream as the forerunners to a deluge. In response, southern states enacted their own anti-alien land laws or went so far as to amend their constitutions to deter Japanese Americans from settling within their borders.[3] While the measures targeted Japanese, all Asian Americans became suspect in the South regardless of ethnicity.

Typical stereotypes of both Chinese Americans and Japanese Americans as heathens, dirty, diseased, shifty, and greedy also did little to convince southerners that Asian Americans would not drastically alter the racial or economic landscape of the South. When southern states passed laws that barred Asian Americans from owning property, they were not only protecting their land; they were protecting basic ideas of citizenship and defining the term in their own ways. Although the Fourteenth Amendment guaranteed the right to landownership for anyone living in the United States, southern states argued that such rights were basic tenets of American citizenship alone and not fit for Asian immigrants. Although African Americans were not the ideal citizens that whites had in mind, they were at least born in the United States, and unlike the heathen Chinese or the shifty Japanese, land and protection of property were guaranteed to them. In response, white southerners shaped the anti-Asian legal action in a region of the United States that actually held few Asian Americans.[4]

But Asian immigrants in the South, although few in number, did not easily accept this infringement on their property rights. From the late nineteenth through the early twentieth century, Asian immigrants in Mississippi, Arkansas, Louisiana, Texas, and Florida faced a form of legal discrimination that no other group faced in attacks on their rights to property and earning a living. While historians have pointed to the challenges of leasing land under the sharecropping system and restrictive housing covenants, Asian immigrants also faced violations of property rights, as southern states used landownership to define and codify citizenship as "white." In response, some Asian American groups defied the laws by continuing to operate as usual, while others launched successful legal battles against state governments and their anti-alien laws.

Asian Americans faced unique legal challenges in the South, and the anti-alien land laws were not merely another form of Jim Crow for another race. Asian Americans were not separate but theoretically equal; the discrimination Chinese Americans and Japanese Americans faced in the South with landownership was a statement of their perpetual racial otherness and inability to assimilate and naturalize. The fear of what Asian immigrants *could* do as racial menaces more than what they actually *did* in the South shaped southern law. The amendments and laws were vague and problematic and did not immediately impact many Chinese American or Japanese American landowners; however, the anti-alien legislation discussed here codified Asian Americans as racial outsiders without citizenship rights, setting the stage for future legal activism.

MODEL CITIZENS: JAPANESE AMERICANS IN THE SOUTH AT THE TURN OF THE CENTURY

Following the Chinese labor fiasco of the post–Civil War years, whites were content to watch from afar as another "race problem" unfolded on the West Coast, this time involving Japanese immigrants. Beginning in 1868, the Japanese Meiji Dynasty encouraged migration to Western nations to help Japan modernize and industrialize when Japanese citizens eventually returned home. Japanese who agreed with their government's plan or small-market farmers who could not compete with the rise of commercial agriculture and resulting high land taxes in Japan settled in California and Hawaii. While many Japanese laborers went to Hawaii seeking job opportunities in the sugarcane fields, others came to the West Coast for migrant labor or were later able to use savings to invest in land and business ventures. Truck farming, or small-scale farming with produce hauled to markets, became a profitable form of income for Japanese living in California's inland valleys. Japanese Americans took advantage of California's temperate climate and extended growing seasons to harvest a virtual cornucopia of vegetables and fruits and used their expertise in irrigation to grow asparagus and lettuce. Eventually, Japanese Americans would come to own 450,000 acres of land in California and contribute 10 percent to the state's revenue from agriculture. When farming failed to live up to income expectations, Japanese Americans turned to migrant labor, following the harvesting of different crops along the West Coast. With their nation encouraging them to serve as "pioneers" by crossing the Pacific and settling in the United States combined with the bountiful opportunities for economic growth, Japanese immigrants made their way to the West Coast by the thousands during the late nineteenth and early twentieth centuries. By 1920, there were more than 100,000 Japanese Americans living in the United States, mostly in California.[5]

Initially, Californians and others along the West Coast tolerated Japanese Americans, but this attitude quickly changed by the early 1900s. Whites at first granted Japanese Americans certain leeway, seeing them as a more worthy and respectable class of immigrants than the Chinese. Japanese Americans did not appear to be an immediate economic threat as they focused primarily on small businesses and farming in areas where few others dared to invest money and time in order to make the soil profitable. As a result of the business acumen of Japanese Americans, there was also little fear of labor competition with the working class, a resounding difference between the reception of Japanese Americans and Chinese Americans earlier on.

However, West Coast residents changed their opinions of the Japanese immigrants when Japan secured a stunning defeat of the Russians in the Russo-Japanese War of 1905. Americans and indeed the world were shocked that a small, "yellow" nation could overpower the mighty Russian empire. The Japanese themselves viewed their victory as a foundation for the rise of Asian power, but Americans on the West Coast feared that Japan's muscular foreign policy would serve as the impetus for further Japanese "infiltration" of the United States. Suddenly, Japanese Americans were transformed from an industrious and talented people willing to work hard to transform the California landscape to land-hungry, ruthlessly imperial, and "shifty" immigrants bent on dominating the white race.[6]

Californians engaged in an extensive campaign to discriminate against Japanese Americans in hopes of dissuading them from permanently settling in their state and to prevent a "second Asiatic invasion" of America more generally. Groups such as the American Legion and the Asiatic Exclusion League distrusted Japanese Americans and saw them as little more than subversive agents working on behalf of the Japanese government, while Democratic senator James D. Phelan became known throughout the country for his passionate devotion to Japanese exclusion. Phelan explained that Japanese immigrants were not in America to create new lives for themselves but, rather, to "colonize" the United States, and "a Japanese colony under the American Flag is not compatible with the growth of America."[7] With the urging of Phelan, the American Legion and similar organizations compiled reports based largely on anecdotal evidence that Japanese farmers routinely had belligerent encounters with white land-seekers and were in the process of establishing a monopoly on California's agriculture industry. Many labor unions also feared that more Japanese would replicate the downward pressure on white wages caused by the influx of Chinese labor in the previous century and create unwanted job competition. The legion, anti-Asian organizations, West Coast politicians, and American Federation of Labor leader Samuel Gompers pleaded with Congress for an exclusion act for the Japanese and made numerous trips to Capitol Hill to testify to the ongoing battle between whites and Japanese along the West Coast. Congress, however, hesitated to engage in such measures and jeopardize diplomatic and economic relations with Japan. Dismayed by the lack of federal action, Californians and local leaders turned to their state legislatures and local governments to discourage Japanese immigration. In 1906, the San Francisco school board attempted to segregate Japanese from white children in city schools, prompting a backlash from both the Japanese government and U.S. federal officials. When violent white mobs attacked both Chinese and Japanese homes and businesses in Vancouver, Canada, later in 1907, both the United States and Canada agreed that some measure was to be taken to gain control of Japanese immigration. In order to ease tensions between Tokyo and Washington, D.C., as well as stem the tide of Japanese migrants, President Theodore Roosevelt met with representatives of the Japanese government in 1907 to work out a compromise. The resulting Gentlemen's Agreement of 1907 was a bargain between the United States and Japan: America promised not to discriminate against Japanese immigrants, and in return, the Japanese government agreed to stop issuing passports for manual laborers to come to the United States. Both governments recognized the agreement as a suitable compromise, but Californians and others along the West Coast who vehemently opposed further Japanese settlement viewed it as a setback for American interests.[8]

Despite the rising tensions between Japanese Americans and whites in California, the Japanese government continued to encourage its subjects to settle in America. Japan closely monitored immigration and provided much support for those who chose to settle in the United States. Although the American Legion and anti-Japanese groups found a grain of truth in Japan's use of the words "colonies" and "colonization" to describe immigration to America, Japanese American farming colonies were conceived of as an economic form of expansion as opposed to a political takeover of the United States. Similar to other immigrant groups who established cooperative farming communities in the United States, such as the Swedes in southern Florida during the late nineteenth century, Japanese emigrants often pulled their resources, sought investments from American or Japanese businessmen, and/or received financial or administrative support from the Japanese government. The colony model established a pattern of settlement in California, and cooperative farming was a way for Japanese immigrants to raise the money for irrigation and supplies. Japanese American colonies, such as the Yamato Colony in Livingston, California, raised the suspicions of whites more than the activities of smaller family farmers because the colonies were often self-contained, with their own stores, schools, and even post offices. Word traveled that the Japanese were supposedly isolationist and unassimilable with little desire to acculturate or interact with Americans.[9]

Meanwhile, Japanese immigrants who were merchants or otherwise not engaged in manual labor looked to the rich soil of the South for land opportunities far from the virulent anti-Asianism and discrimination of California. By the early 1900s, the South was well past Reconstruction and into the New South era. Attempts to bring the southern states up to the industrial and productivity level of the North shaped the southern economy. Many planters and farmers sought to reinvigorate some of the lagging agricultural industries, including rice and sugarcane, by learning more modern farming methods. Fortunately for white southerners, Japanese Americans were eager to stake out a claim to land unsettled and generally underused in the South and rejuvenate and/or establish new crops and agricultural practices there. Early on, there was a mutual interest between Japanese Americans and southerners in one another that created the potential for a profitable relationship, a scenario that was different from and more inviting than the racial backlash that plagued the West Coast.

Japanese Americans turned their attention to the Gulf of Mexico region of the South and its rice industry. Until the Civil War, most rice in America was produced in South Carolina, with only small-scale farmers cultivating the crop in Louisiana, Texas, Mississippi, and the plains of Arkansas. However, when the war decimated the Carolina rice industry and the growth of railroads opened up more markets in southwestern Louisiana and the Texas Gulf region, investors and farmers scrambled to capitalize on new opportunities. In 1899, Louisiana rice planter Seamann A. Knapp turned to Japan to learn more efficient ways of growing rice and, with the assistance of the U.S. Department of Agriculture, traveled to Japan to consult with rice farmers there. Seamann later imported to southwestern Louisiana the Kyushu strain of rice, or "Jap rice," which was heartier and more resilient to the new, industrialized milling process of the postwar era, as well as a small group of Japanese planters with experience in more sophisticated irrigation and planting methods. Both Seamann and the Japanese rice planters benefited from the previous efforts of Japanese cotton grower Jokichi Takamine in establishing a productive business relationship between Japan and Louisiana in the 1880s. Eventually, more Japanese turned to rice production in Louisiana and Texas as new opportunities for colonies.[10]

Many Louisianans were initially excited about the possibility of Japanese settlement in their state. Newspapers reported Japanese interest in Texas during the early 1900s, and authors wistfully yearned to see Japanese establish themselves in Louisiana instead. In 1904 the *Houston Chronicle* noted that a "Mr. Akioki, a Japanese of distinction," visited San Antonio to investigate the climate and resources of a 10,000-acre tract of land he purchased with the intent of bringing 300 families from Japan and the West Coast to Texas to form a "colony of his countrymen" to grow tea and produce silk.[11] The article noted that whites in Texas "expected that the newcomers will make good citizens and intermarry and coalesce with Texas neighbors" and wondered if the same could be possible for Louisiana—a far cry from the belief among West Coast whites that the Japanese could never acculturate. Another article commended Akioki for his attempts to locate his colony on rich soil that until recently had been used only as grazing land for cattle, highlighting the innovation and gumption of the Japanese.[12] Louisianans were so enamored with the reputation of the Japanese as skilled agriculturists and horticulturists that when a court in Houston declared in 1905 that Japanese were ineligible for citizenship (well before the Supreme Court decided the same in 1922), an article in the *Shreveport Caucasian* bemoaned the decision as "a serious one" because it had the potential to dissuade Japanese from colonizing in the state and elsewhere in the Gulf region. The author argued that the Japanese "are to be preferred to the Italians and others who are being brought in rather large numbers" to perform manual labor in the fields. "The experience with the Japanese in Texas is that they make model citizens, whereas many of the Italians and Polanders do not. The Polanders are clannish and unwilling to change any of their customs." The author's views on the Italians reflected an incident earlier in 1891 when a large mob of New Orleans citizens stormed the Orleans Parish Prison and lynched eleven Sicilian men who had been charged with the murder of a police chief but acquitted of the crime and were being held in the prison for safekeeping. When compared with the undesirable Italian immigrants and the chaos they brought with them, the Japanese were a welcome ethnic addition to the state's varied demographics.[13]

In November 1904, Masahi Takenouchi, vice commissioner of Japan's agricultural department, and Tetsutaro Inumara, imperial commissioner to Louisiana, traveled to the small town of Welsh in Calcasieu Parish in southwest Louisiana to investigate the growing conditions for rice. Baton Rouge commissioner William C. Stubbs, a classmate of Inumara's when they studied together at Tulane University, had invited the duo to the state to discuss trade relations between Japan and Louisiana. Stubbs placed Takenouchi and Inumara in touch with Welsh planter Paul W. Daniels, who agreed to lease 300 acres of land to thirty Japanese farmers set to arrive in March 1905. Rather than grow only rice, the proposed colony would cultivate potatoes, cotton, and an assortment of vegetables to test the depth and fecundity of the Louisiana soil. Locals were intrigued by the prospect, believing that "experimentation with a new crop could prove a boon to the entire rice-growing section of the South."[14] Although citizens looked forward to watching the "outcome with interest," they were sorely disappointed when they learned in February 1905 that "the experiment will be delayed a year," a decision "regretted by many who were anxious to see the outcome of the Japs' efforts."[15] Residents also religiously followed the travels of Japanese officials and representatives who came to Louisiana searching for profitable land, cheering when the delegations declared their state's rice belt more favorable than that of Texas. When the official representative for all Japanese colonies in America, H. Kito, came to St. Landry Parish and was "highly impressed with the lands and conditions found here, saying that our irrigation system and lands looked better to [him] than any [he] had seen anywhere," the citizens of St. Landry reveled in the fact that their home might attract Japanese colonies like those in other states.[16]

Florida became another site of bright opportunity for Japanese colonists at the turn of the century. Like Lue Gim Gong, who used the Florida soil to revolutionize citrus growing, Japanese Americans looked to the Sunshine State's endless tracts of undeveloped and underused land for colonization sites. From the eastern coast of Florida to the central region known for its citrus groves, the land in this region could be a veritable agricultural gold mine—for those who were willing to undertake the work of clearing out scrub or swampland and going through the trial-and-error process of discovering which crops were most suited for the climate and earth. Few small farmers in Florida were willing to take the chance on such financially risky ventures, but larger industrialists, particularly railroad barons, were interested in developing land to expand markets and tracks. The stretch of coastal land between Jacksonville and Miami (still a "backwater" town at this time) was relatively untouched and underdeveloped, but it caught the eye of railroad magnate Henry Flagler in the early 1900s. Flagler, head of the Florida East Coast Rail Road, was interested in extending the lines down the coast to increase use through tourism and agriculture, but he needed individuals or groups who were willing to do the hard work for him. Flagler established the Model Land Company in 1903 to subsidize the cost of land and provide shipping discounts for those hardy settlers with the dedication to carve out a potentially profitable living on Florida's east coast.

Flagler placed his business associate, James E. Ingraham, in charge of recruiting settlers. Ingraham took out ads in Florida newspapers and other periodicals across the country to entice farmers and reached out to business professor William Clark at New York University (Ingraham's alma mater) for more advice. Clark provided Ingraham with contact information for Joseph Sakai, a graduate of New York University who was currently conducting business on the West Coast. Sakai eagerly responded but wanted to investigate potential sites for the project beforehand and arrived in Jacksonville in 1903 to speak directly to the stockholders of the Model Land Company. The company directed Sakai to land outside Boca Raton, a small community near Fort Lauderdale that served as a shipping center for the small numbers of winter vegetables and peppers grown by local farmers. Sakai traveled to Boca Raton with Ingraham and other representatives from the Model Land Company and was pleased with the soil and climate, foreseeing opportunities for growing citrus fruits and other more exotic products such as pineapples. Soon thereafter, Sakai entered into an agreement with Ingraham whereby Sakai would return to Boca Raton to begin farming no later than August 1904 and the Model Land Company would subsidize the Japanese for the cost of equipment and housing (which would later be repaid by the Japanese as soon as their colony gained footing).[17]

Later that year, Sakai returned to Japan to enlist ambitious families who would come to Florida's Yamato Colony. Sixteen Japanese farmers came with Sakai, and Flagler agreed to pay for their passage from California to Florida. Initially, running the colony and turning a profit was difficult: The Japanese settlers were unaccustomed to Florida's often muggy and oppressive tropical climate, illnesses such as malaria wracked the settlers, and blight decimated the early pineapple crops in 1905. However, in 1906, despite Sakai's sudden death from tuberculosis, the colony prospered as the Japanese learned which crops grew more efficiently (tomatoes and cucumbers) and became more skilled at pineapple cultivation. Once established, the Japanese men sent for their families and turned Yamato from a bachelor's society of "lonely farmers who would gather in a packing shed on Saturday night to socialize after their week's work in the fields" into a "cluster of two-story frame houses, a general store ... and some packing houses where pineapples and tomatoes were taken before being shipped north" on the Florida East Coast Rail Road.[18] Nearby residents took note of the thriving Yamato Colony and reported on the "two cars of pineapples exported to England" and the "800 crates of tomatoes, which netted ... $2 a crate."[19] Nearby white Florida residents initially congratulated the Japanese at Yamato on their "enterprise, ambition, and hard work" as well as their fields, which were "as handsome as any to be found on the East Coast, and the cultivation under which they are kept is a marvel to the ordinary grower."[20] One Florida resident who heard through the rumor mill that the Yamato Colony was looking to expand further into Dade County succinctly summed up the positive effects of the Japanese undertakings: "A hard surface road will be built out to the new settlement, and then watch the country around here develop."[21]

The clear success of Japanese Americans in cultivating the difficult land earned them early respect from many Floridians. Because Yamato was a prosperous colony and the colonists there introduced new forms of agriculture

Japanese American farmers and their families at the depot of the Florida East Coast Rail Road at Yamato Colony, ca. 1909. *Courtesy of the State Archives of Florida.*

that could easily be adapted by other farmers, the Japanese, though "yellow," had proven that they could meaningfully contribute to society. The *Florida Farmer*, a popular statewide periodical for agricultural news, described the colony as "intensely patriotic" and the Japanese there as "working everyday to advance the general welfare of the state." The Yamato Colony's creed demonstrated that these were no temporary settlers like the Chinese or other groups but, rather, people who had "the interests of the state of Florida . . . really at heart." In addition to "encouraging and developing the spirit of colonization among our people of Japan toward the United States" and "building upon our ideal colony to inculcate the highest principles and honor as a Japanese colony," the people at Yamato also made it their duty to "study and improve local farm work" and to "introduce Japanese industries which we can adapt to the place and which may tend to advance the industries of Florida and secure mutual benefits."[22] Floridians who became familiar with the purpose of the colony came to see the Japanese as friends rather than foes in economic and business relations. So long as Japanese Americans were working to help revive agriculture and remained respectful, they were welcomed.

Following the success of Yamato, many Floridians cried out for more Japanese colonies in their state. Dollar signs and the potential for agricultural diversity created an atmosphere in Florida different from that in California for Japanese Americans. Residents of Madison County in northern Florida

George Morikami (*far right*) with two Japanese American farmers in a pineapple field at Yamato Colony, ca. 1906. *Courtesy of the State Archives of Florida.*

(near Tallahassee) wistfully hoped that more Japanese would move farther north. "Again, we rise to remark that a Japanese colony in Madison County would be a good thing. We believe they would make excellent citizens and we'd like to see a colony of them located in the county, wouldn't you?"[23] Powerful businessmen in north Florida agreed that Japanese migration to the state was not only desirable but necessary. In February 1903, well before Sakai established the Yamato Colony, the Jacksonville Board of Trustees hosted a meeting of area businessmen to discuss the potential for Japanese settlement in Florida. Chamber of Commerce president Charles E. Garner delivered the keynote address and spoke out against the rising anti-Japanese attitudes on the Pacific Coast. Garner argued that an exclusion act for the Japanese similar to that of the Chinese Exclusion Act "would injure Florida" and deny the state the benefits of welcoming the Japanese who were "well-versed in advanced horticulture" and other agricultural practices. "As laborers in our mines and turpentine farms, we need them—as domestics they are unsurpassed. Florida and the south need such workmen." Similar to first impressions of the Chinese after the Civil War, the presumed racial characteristics of the Japanese were more favorable than those of African Americans, and the Japanese would ameliorate rather than contribute to race problems in the South. Although the experiment with Chinese labor failed during Reconstruction, here was another opportunity to economically benefit from a new group of laborers and entrepreneurs.[24]

Others emphasized that Floridians did not share Californians' opinion of Japanese Americans and welcomed them to their state. Unlike Californians, northern "Floridians are gratified to hear of [Japanese] success and applaud their desire to draw more of their kind. The little brown men are doing a good work for themselves and for us—it is still true that Florida is not California."[25]

A resident of Pensacola insisted that "unlike the conditions existing upon the Pacific Coast, these thrifty little Japs are highly respected by their American neighbors," and "the people of Florida ... are much pleased with the little Orientals and hope that more may decide to immigrate to the state."[26] This indeed appeared to be true at Yamato, where the Japanese and locals mingled at festivals and celebrations. Sakai's Japanese wife (who was eighteen at the time) was even granted permission to attend the local white high school.[27] When the Japanese consul general Chozo Oikee traveled to inspect the conditions for his countrymen at Yamato, "he expressed great pleasure at the friendly spirit shown by American neighbors."[28] In general, the prosperity and agricultural knowledge the Japanese brought with them made many Floridians feel grateful that there were colonies established across the South and insistent that "a warm welcome await[ed] them [Japanese] in Florida."[29]

Rather than expressing angry hyperbole or virulent attacks on the character of Japanese Americans as seen in California papers, Floridians initially spoke highly of what they saw as the innate, racially bound traits of the Japanese. The *Gainesville Daily Sun*'s editor was proud of the "little Japan down the East Coast that is much better than an Oriental colony in a big city" and reported that "the people of the surrounding county think well of the Japanese, for the latter are a sociable, well-mannered set and would not for any consideration pass you on the road without waving their arms in salutation."[30] In living with Floridians, Japanese Americans had earned the respect of the natives by engaging in southern hospitality and charm and displaying their affable nature. The *Florida Farmer* cheerfully confirmed that "there is not a lazy bone in the body of these people and they have a way of working that makes every effort count."[31] Floridians were happy to report that "their Japanese" were hard working, honest, and friendly people who were more than willing to adapt "themselves to American ideas in their manner of living and dress."[32] Overall, many in Florida agreed that the Japanese, far from posing a threat, were instead a "desirable class of settlers."[33] Just a few decades after southerners rejected Chinese labor, the South led the nation in affection for Japanese Americans.

Floridians went so far as to claim that the Japanese would one day make excellent American citizens, a fairly radical concept at a time of anti-Asian hysteria on the West Coast. Most of the arguments for citizenship for the Japanese rested on their profitability and demonstrated American work ethic. These were not "shady" or greedy individuals but a race devoted to personal fulfillment and achievement while contributing to the growth of their communities. Citizens in Punta Gorda on the Gulf shore of the state marveled at "a Jap who came to this country less than four years ago" and who raised rice on a 230-acre farm in Texas, noting that the Japanese "are a thrifty lot, and making good citizens" in the country.[34] Holly Hill residents buzzed with excitement when rumors that a group of Japanese had purchased a large tract of land nearby to build a colony. The Japanese "while not likely to prove of social benefit, would enhance property values and ... prove good citizens."[35] Floridians near the Yamato Colony noted that the Japanese were already "fully imbued with the American spirit" and that their "highest ambition is to be called Americans and citizens of this country, which they greatly admire."[36]

In the early 1900s, there were more newspaper articles and opinion pieces from supporters of Japanese colonization and citizenship than from individuals who opposed it in Louisiana and Florida. Not only did Japanese Americans bring their knowledge and skills to the South to reinvigorate agriculture and contribute to economic development following the Civil War, but Japanese Americans, by virtue of their desire to farm, were deserving of American citizenship. Whereas many on the West Coast argued that the innate racial characteristics of Japanese Americans prevented them from assimilating and therefore disqualified them for citizenship, southern whites argued the opposite. Japanese Americans did have distinct racial characteristics, but those characteristics made them hardworking, honest, and model American citizens. When Japanese Americans formed colonies in the South, there were few objections to their landownership. The fact that the Japanese were willing to purchase and develop the land that no one else wanted made them more suited for acceptance in American political, economic, and to a degree, social life. There was no question that landownership was nothing less than a right for those willing to work for it, and if southern states could benefit from Japanese settlement, all the better. White southerners not only welcomed Asian immigrants but actively sought out their agricultural expertise. Japanese Americans had more to offer to the New South than African Americans. Respecting the rights to landownership and access to basic civil rights went hand in hand with expecting Japanese Americans to give back to the South. It was a reciprocal relationship that was uncommon for Asian immigrants outside the South.

FROM MODEL CITIZENS TO YELLOW PERIL

But the generally positive attitudes toward Japanese Americans did not last. Following the Gentlemen's Agreement and the failure of Congress to pass a bill that would place a restriction on the number of Japanese entering the

United States, West Coast legislatures devised their own methods of discouraging the arrival and settlement of Japanese. West Coast residents worried that a growth in American-born Japanese children meant a new threat to property ownership and the American way of life. Knowing that truck farming was a profitable enterprise for many Japanese immigrants, politicians decided to attack what they identified as the root of the problem. If they could prohibit Japanese from owning or leasing property, then theoretically the West Coast would become a less desirable place for the "yellow menace." Let the Japanese go elsewhere in the country if they must, but if the West Coast were less attractive, then there might be a chance to exclude Japanese immigrants from owning land if not exclude them from coming to the United States entirely. In other words, if the federal government would not pass a Japanese exclusion act, then the states, relying on creative interpretations of their constitutional rights to self-regulation, would take matters into their own hands.[37]

California and Washington became the earliest states to pass specific laws prohibiting aliens ineligible for citizenship from owning and leasing property. Such measures were not entirely new. Long before the arrival of Japanese immigrants, California, Oregon, and Washington had amended their state constitutions to exclude specifically "Chinamen" (Oregon), anyone who was not either white or of "African descent" (California), and those who were not willing to sign an intent to "naturalize in good faith"—effectively Chinese who could not become U.S. citizens—as part of a land deal (Washington). Other states, including Minnesota, Nebraska, and Texas, placed restrictions on the number of years an alien could own property or limited special government benefits for settling land to citizens or those who could naturalize. Discriminatory land measures were already in place and targeted primarily Chinese immigrants before the early twentieth century, but the new laws coming out of California, Oregon, and Washington in the early 1900s were more specific. The politicians who proposed and supported the acts or amendments to constitutions were not shy about making their intentions known: Despite the vague language concerning "aliens ineligible for citizenship," their main purpose was preventing the Japanese from settling within their states. Washington Democratic state representative Miller Freemen unabashedly proclaimed, "I have noticed the alarming situation by reason of the foothold that aliens, and especially Japanese, are acquiring our agricultural lands. For the purpose of prohibiting and stopping this evil I have drawn a measure which prevents aliens owning land."[38] The newer proposed laws, unlike the constitutional amendments, also laid out more specific language prohibiting business transactions between citizens and aliens ineligible for citizenship (and making those that already existed void), the inheritance of property by American-born children, and most importantly, the leasing of land. For Japanese who could not afford to purchase property outright or who were migrant farmers with dreams of eventually becoming property owners, renting farmland from larger planters was a way to make a decent living on the West Coast. West Coast politicians detested such opportunities and sought to prevent all classes of Japanese from seeking a new start in their states.[39]

California was at the helm of a legislative trend when the state legislature passed the Alien Land Law in 1913. Since there were still some legal and anthropological debates on whether or not Japanese could be classified as "whites," the 1913 act went further than the amendment to the California constitution by mentioning specifically aliens who were ineligible for citizenship. The act prohibited noncitizens who could not naturalize from owning property and also from leasing land for longer than three years. The law did not prohibit the children of Japanese immigrants from owning property, however, prompting California citizens to fear that the act would not be effective. Although there was no legal or constitutional way to prohibit American citizens from owning property under the Fourteenth Amendment, the California legislature passed a new land law in 1920 that completely banned any lease agreement with ineligible aliens and required the sons and daughters of immigrants who held property to fill out yearly reports detailing their business activities. These measures were an attempt to undermine all Japanese American truck farming. The American Legion, anti-Asian associations, and various politicians along the West Coast and in other parts of the nation supported California's measures and sought to bring similar legislation to fruition in other states. Washington passed its own alien land law in 1921, and Oregon followed in 1923. By the mid-1920s, Arizona, Arkansas, Idaho, Minnesota, Montana, Nebraska, New Mexico, Oregon, Utah, Washington, and Wyoming had passed anti-alien land laws with language similar to that of California's.[40]

It did not take long for some southern states to turn on Japanese Americans and pass their own versions of California's law. Although the population of Japanese Americans in the South did not rapidly increase between the early 1900s, when many whites first welcomed the Japanese with open arms, and the later advent of alien land laws, Florida, Louisiana, Texas (the three states with the largest Japanese American colonization populations—153, 219, and 449, respectively), and Arkansas would either pass their own anti-Japanese legislation or, in a more dramatic measure, amend their constitutions to prohibit aliens from owning property. What had transpired in such a short period of time to make whites turn on their "little yellow brothers" who once held such promise? While each southern state had its own problems with Japanese Americans living within it, an imagined fear of Japanese invasion from the West Coast fueled more reactionary measures from state legislators and southern citizens.

There were Louisianans who warned of the impending doom arriving in the form of the Japanese well before the rise of anti-alien land laws. In 1906, a group of 200 Japanese families purchased land for growing rice in Crowley, today the "Rice Capital of the World." Although most of the local businessmen and residents supported the colony, some residents watched what they saw as an unabashed embrace of an "Oriental Host of Mongolian cheap labor" from afar.[41] Rather than see Japanese Americans as motivated entrepreneurs, some in Crowley saw them for what they believed the immigrants really were: "pauper hoards" who were only shipped into Louisiana to benefit a "few large landholders who will be enabled to dispose of a little more land, or farm a little more with this form of cheap labor."[42] An article published in the *Rice Belt Journal* touched briefly on common themes of racial difference between Japanese Americans and "caucasians," wondering why Louisianans should view the Japanese so differently from the Chinese when the basic problem was the same—"Japanese can never be amalgamated."[43] But the bulk of the author's displeasure with his community's welcoming of the Japanese settlers rested with their inability to see that "Japanese immigration . . . will swell the hords [sic] of cheap labor with which our country is already burdened" and "add to the overproduction of our great staple crop [rice]." This was a direct rebuttal to those who sang the praises of Japanese Americans as a vehicle for economic growth and crop diversification. Ultimately, Japanese immigrants would be responsible for placing "the American farmer on the same plane as the Oriental" and "add[ing] a new element of complication to our social problem, cheap labor, and debas[ing] the high standards of American living."[44] These were early warnings of a potential flood of Japanese Americans who would arrive in Louisiana and drastically alter the social, racial, and economic order of the state in disastrous and terrifying ways. "Louisiana already has one race problem," one resident explained in the *New Iberia Enterprise*, "which presents itself everyday of the year and which is ever a costly one in many respects—to introduce a yellow peril . . . would be [to] court disaster, to offer a premium of annoyances of every sort, to invite trouble as a permanent guest for future years."[45] How could inviting more "yellow" Japanese Americans into the state possibly simplify the existing "race problem" between whites and blacks?

The author was begging his or her neighbors to understand that "California's experience with its Oriental problem should be an object lesson, sufficiently convincing to protest any other white community from encouraging the presence of Japanese in numbers, *however small*."[46] There was the key to how this resident and others in Louisiana and across the South would come to view the presence of Japanese Americans in their states. No matter the size of the existing Japanese American population, be it 5 or 500, Japanese Americans challenged the order and structure of southern life. This was not a matter of numbers but, rather, a fear of what Japanese Americans could do. Plus, there was always the possibility that even the smallest number of successful and profitable Japanese Americans would attract more to Louisiana from California. "The press and people must unite in insisting that no Japs are wanted in LA, for as badly as the state needs development, it were better that its farms should become a garden of nettles, its swamps remain unclaimed and its virgin forests un-cleared [than] that a foothold be given within its borders to this pestiferous people who can only be compared with ants—undeviatingly a pest wherever they appear," one resident from Shreveport declared.[47] Like blight, Japanese Americans would sweep into Louisiana and destroy whites' economic basis for survival. Another author from St. Tammany Parish near Baton Rouge bemoaned the continued support of the Japanese, arguing that " if these lands are so valuable and so productive, then surely they must soon be settled by capable and energetic farmers of the white race."[48] "If Louisiana fills her land with Japanese, which she ultimately will do if this colonizing is allowed to get a foothold," the author warned, "she will dig her grave politically and shut herself off from the prosperous states of the Union. . . . Drudgery, cheap labor, and hoarded slaves will never help us."[49] The ability of Japanese Americans to damage economic relations with other states was a grave prediction and reflected the fears of what effect the colonizers would have on Louisiana and southern society.

In 1913, James Taylor, a real estate agent from the Natchez sugar district, submitted an article to the aptly named *Caucasian* that ignited a push for legislative action in Louisiana to prevent Japanese American settlement. In "The Japs Invasion," Taylor, who sold land to "white farmers only," gathered information from rumors and his own discussions with other landowners and real estate agents and compiled a report that he submitted to the *Caucasian*. Taylor warned that with other real estate agents willingly entering into agreements with Japanese colonists and a "tide of Japanese immigration" coming to Louisiana as a result of the California laws, white Louisianans may be forced to sell their land at cutthroat prices to escape the "menace," a form of white-planter flight. Taylor surmised that with its "fertile lands" and cheap prices, "Louisiana is the natural field to which those people might turn following the laws excluding them from owning land in California."[50] As a real estate agent, Taylor was well informed to report that when Louisiana attracted enough Japanese, citizens would see a fate similar to that of California: "When the Japanese farmers move in, American farmers move out." Because "Americans have no neighborly feelings for Japs," they flee to other areas, and as a result, land prices become depressed.[51] Taylor freely admitted that "Southern people are, by nature and environment, reared with the feeling of aversion for races of a different color; and any encroachment by outsiders who are regarded undesirable for this reason is quickly resented by them."[52] Japanese immigrants had learned a valuable less in California that if they settled in greater numbers near whites, the whites would flee, giving Japanese Americans access to cheap land and resources. "High prices will not keep the Jap out of Louisiana," Taylor warned readers. California's history might well be repeated in Louisiana unless "the real estate men ... take some steps to meet and forestall any conditions that would result form an influx of Japanese into this state" or if the Louisiana legislature passed an act similar to California's.[53]

Debates over whether or not to oppose Japanese American colonization diminished in the Louisiana press and among residents during World War I, when Japan allied with Britain, France, and Russia and general war troubles pervaded the country, but reached a fever pitch again in 1921. A year earlier, California amended its earlier anti-alien land law to prohibit the leasing of land in addition to ownership for aliens ineligible for citizenship. Although residents in Louisiana's rice belt, where most Japanese Americans settled, were generally welcoming, those in the northern part of the state near Arkansas worried that if they didn't follow California's lead, they might be faced with the type of problem that Taylor had described. What Louisiana desperately needed was its own anti-alien land law, and Jonathan S. Dykes, a furniture store owner in Union Parish who also had businesses and cotton land in Arkansas, became the voice of those who held similar views. In 1920, Dykes advocated among local business owners in northern Louisiana for an anti-alien land law to safeguard against the settlement of refugee Japanese in his state. The strongest supporters of such a law were the cotton planters who straddled the borders of Louisiana, Mississippi, and Arkansas and feared Japanese Americans leaving the rice belt and settling in cotton country. Considering Taylor's dire warnings, there were concerns that this may be the case if whites fled the land and Japanese Americans gained more power.

The push for anti-alien land legislation in Louisiana revealed an interesting and complex view of Japanese Americans in the South. Although words of anti-Japanese sentiment filled local newspapers in the state, land laws became a form of political opportunism that would benefit mainly farmers and landowners from specific agricultural industries such as cotton or rice. The relationship of Louisianans to their idea of the Japanese—created from negative media portrayals and generalized Orientalist stereotypes—was often different from their relationship to the Japanese Americans within their state, who were brought to help rebuild agriculture and the economy. On the ground, no actions were taken in the southern rice colonies of the state to drive out Japanese (despite boisterous claims from some newspapers), while in the north, where cotton was king, those invested in the crop spoke the loudest against potential Japanese Americans moving into their industry.

Fortunately for Dykes, his opportunity to prevent Japanese encroachment on Louisiana territory came later in 1921 when Louisiana held a constitutional convention in Baton Rouge. Following World War I, questions of taxation, minimum wages for women and children, the relationship between the burgeoning oil industry and the state, and the parish system of local government begged attention from both citizens and the legislature. More importantly, many argued that the most current constitution from 1913 was still too heavily influenced by the constitution from 1879, which was ratified during the days of tumultuous Reconstruction and considered a product of carpetbagger malfeasance.[54] Under Louisiana law, a constitutional convention cannot be called by the state legislature unless the question of whether or not one is needed is put up to public vote. Governor John Parker proposed the idea of a convention to the people in November 1920, and they approved. The residents of Union County voted for Dykes to represent their interests at the convention, and the newly elected delegate was more than eager to serve. By the time the convention delegates descended on Baton Rouge in March 1921 to begin their work, there were a variety of committees and topics, including those mentioned above as well as income tax rates and the election of legislative representatives. Not mentioned was any sort of restriction on alien landownership, but Dykes went into the convention with this goal in mind.[55]

On March 22, a few weeks into the convention, Dykes—who served on the Committee on Co-Ordination—introduced Ordinance 245, a motion to amend Article I, Section 4, to prohibit Japanese immigrants from owning property. Knowing that despite cultural and social anti-Asian sentiment there was not overwhelming support statewide to create an anti-alien *act*, Dykes worked with William Chappius—an opponent of Japanese settlement from the Acadia Parish—to create an anti-alien *amendment* to the constitution. Such a measure would be a strong statement that the constitution of Louisiana did not recognize Japanese as deserving of property rights and the civil rights that accompanied them. In effect, any change to Article I, the basic bill of rights, would change the way the state defined general rights and state citizens. While the article previously did not mention aliens or citizenship in relation to property rights, Dykes's amendment read, "No alien who is ineligible for citizenship of the United States or of the State of Louisiana shall be permitted or allowed to acquire or own, directly or indirectly, in his or her name, or by means of any kind or character whatsoever within The State of Louisiana." Similar to the anti-alien laws of West Coast states, the vague mention of "aliens ineligible for citizenship" could technically have included other groups for criminal or medical purposes, but the intention was clear: to discourage Japanese from settling in Louisiana. Asians were the only racial group that could not naturalize at this time.[56]

Discussions on other matters consumed much of the convention delegates' time and energy between March and the late spring, but the anti-alien amendment did not go away. Walter Burke, a Democratic representative from Iberia Parish and an attorney with a progressive streak, served on the Committee for Co-Ordination with Dykes but was far more interested in his own ordinances on education and employer liability. Burke grew weary of Dykes's attempts to redirect attention away from Burke's needs and urged other committee members to be more specific about the proposed target of the amendment. On June 14, Burke proposed more specific language in the proposed amendment. "If it was the intention of the Convention," Burke began, "to exclude from the right of ownership of property any alien who, because of personal and particular reasons, may be ineligible for citizenship in common with those excluded as a class as for example a European, who, because of his mental ailment, or because of his doctrine upon government might not be admissible to citizenship, then there is no suggestion to offer." However, "if it was the intention to exclude those because of race or nationality are ineligible, then the suggestion made that the ordinance be amended by inserting ... 'by reason of race or nationality.'" If the point was to exclude Japanese and other Asians from owning property in the state, as Dykes had so clearly stated in the press and in personal conversations many times before, then the amendment should reflect this in order to avoid bureaucratic confusion. Burke's suggestion would have made the amendment different from some of the other anti-alien land acts by mentioning race and nationality specifically. Eventually, the convention voted to table the discussion of Burke's suggestion, but it represented a moment when the discussions of race, nationality, and immigration were brought to bear directly on Louisiana's constitution.[57]

Ultimately, Dykes's ordinance was approved by a majority of the delegates of the convention, and the amendment was placed in the new constitution. The general attitude of citizens toward their most recent governing document was not one of jubilant approval but one of weariness and suspicion. The convention lasted nearly five months, prompting many to worry about the tax dollars being wasted. Also, the legislators had to defend the convention against "rumors that the convention was merely a puppet of Standard Oil to dictate a severance tax law," rather than an attempt to revamp the constitution.[58] The biggest controversies of the convention for the average Louisiana citizen were the possibility of turning the parish governing system into a county system and the fact that the delegates decided in May that French would no longer be used in conventions.[59] When all was said and done, 802 amendments were proposed by delegates; 536 were ultimately approved in an up-down vote, including Dykes's. The anti-alien amendment went under Article XIX (General Provisions), Section 21. It not only prohibited aliens ineligible for citizenship from owning property in a variety of forms, including leasing and receiving land through inheritances, but it also gave the Louisiana legislature the power to create any additional laws as needed to support the amendment. The *Donaldson Chief* explained to readers that "this article is in line with the law of California . . . and is intended to prevent all Asians who are not eligible for citizenship of this country from owning any land in the state."[60] Because the legislature was not required to submit the new constitution to the people (as the delegates were elected by the people), it was adopted on June 18, 1921, by the convention and became the law of the land for the next five decades.[61]

The overwhelming details and amendments to the constitution allowed the anti-alien amendment to be somewhat overlooked by the public. In the press, there were few reactions to the new amendment apart from articles explaining how it was similar to California's and that, yes, it did specifically target Japanese Americans. Even Louisianans who opposed Japanese settlement in their state were relatively quiet. Talk of Japanese Americans in newspapers went from discussions of agriculture and colonization to American and Japanese diplomatic relations and arms negotiations. The amendment to Louisiana's constitution pertaining to land, a significant change in property rights, the application of the Fourteenth Amendment, and conceptions of citizenship went largely unnoticed by the populace. Without the need for public approval, Dykes and those northern landholders as well as those in the southern part of the state who supported him received what they had been searching for. The presence of small communities of Japanese Americans and the politics of a few planters shaped the constitution, while Japanese Americans and their interstitial status continued to puzzle Louisianans and create a mix of reactions to the amendment across the state.

The place of Japanese Americans living in Louisiana well before the amended constitution took effect was uncertain. There was no massive backlash against Japanese Americans following the amendment as there was in California after the enactment of its alien land law. Also, it was not clear if the amendment would be retroactive and Japanese Americans who had purchased land before the new constitution would lose their property. Despite the new restrictions, many Japanese Americans continued to live in Louisiana on the land they had previously purchased, or they migrated to New Orleans for new employment opportunities. Like so many Jim Crow laws across the South that were amorphous to a degree that maneuverability was possible, the new Louisiana constitution was vague on how it applied to Japanese Americans and others. The fact that Dykes and others like him so feared even the smallest number of Japanese Americans in their state that they were able to alter the constitution was an impressive feat that reflected the South's fear of Asian immigrants, a new racial minority that Louisianans were unsure of.

FLORIDA JOINS THE ANTI-ALIEN CRUSADE

Despite the initial welcome of Japanese in various parts of the state, by 1912 the same anti-Japanese attitudes that swept through Louisiana also made their way to Florida. Many of the negative descriptions of Japanese Americans were similar to those that originated elsewhere and reflected a growing concern that more Japanese migrants would arrive from the West Coast. According to southerners, their land was a waiting bounty for the ruthless Japanese looking to steal it from white citizens. Almost overnight, the same characteristics of Japanese Americans that many admired became their faults. Japanese Americans went from being "fine farmers" with "agricultural methods that will be a desirable object lesson to their white neighbors" to "ferocious and land hungry" people with no desire to assimilate or discard their "clannish" ways. "In small numbers," an *Ocala Evening Star* editorial warned in 1913, "they constitute no menace, but a thin stream of them trickling into Florida, lured by the success of those now here, might in time swell to a volume that would gives us more Japanese than we needed . . . another California problem."[62] Although President William Howard Taft attempted to "smash the bugaboo of Japanese invasion" in an address given in 1912 by explaining that "there has never been any intention on the part of Japan to attempt to gain a foothold in North America," this did little to assuage a growing number of Floridians who believed that the few Japanese Americans in their state could potentially turn into multitudes.[63] Whereas hardworking Japanese immigrants were once seen as a way to make Florida prosper, now that same work ethic rendered them undesirable.

In addition to blaming the land-hungry and ferocious Japanese immigrants coming from the West Coast for supposed increased competition for land, some Floridians turned their ire toward politicians and leaders for importing competition and cheap labor. In 1913, a group of Japanese horticulturists arrived in Jacksonville "direct from California" to strike up a deal with real estate agents for swampy, unwanted land in Clay County closer to Gainesville than the coast. However, when the *Ocala Evening Star* editors learned of the proposed deal, they lashed out at the "undesirable immigrants" as well as Governor William Sherman Jennings, whom they accused of engaging in underhanded deals in order to recruit Japanese migrants to help Florida compete with the California citrus growers.[64] In Jacksonville, the president of the Chamber of Commerce incensed one resident with a speech openly urging Japanese Americans to settle in Florida. "Just why the businessmen of Jacksonville would import cheap heathen labor to compete with the white farmers and growers of Florida is not plain to us . . . when there are thousands of honest, hard-working white men north of Florida who can be induced to settle in Florida and help develop it."[65] Although "cheap labor may be alright for corporations," it did not sit well with the author. Now Japanese Americans were not only threats to landownership but also threats to the general well-being of all Floridians. The article ended with a rousing call for the farmers and fruit growers of Florida to "join the AFL in asking Congress to exclude Japanese immigrants, the same as it does the Chinese."[66]

An author known only as "The Korokan" also responded negatively to Garner's Chamber of Commerce speech by discussing the devastating impact that further Japanese colonization would have on race relations in Florida. Speaking as a "seasoned traveller" with extensive knowledge of Japanese behavior, The Korokan argued that because "Japanese women keep having babies" (which was also the cause of the Russo-Japanese War and a "scientific and cultural fact") and the "islands of Japan are not big enough to hold the Japanese people . . . they must go somewhere." Should that somewhere be Florida? Although there were already Japanese in the state and "Florida is a cosmopolitan state whose arms are extended to welcome the peoples of the earth ... the line ought to be drawn somewhere." Floridians were already forced to contend with the "colored man," but the Japanese were a different kind of colored. A black man was like an "old, faithful dog" who had adapted to the Jim Crow laws of the South, while the Japanese were "a serpent—subtle, scheming ... and conscious-less [sic]." If Floridians were to "harbor any colored race, let it be the black man," for at least the black man was innately subservient and generally harmless. The Korokan couldn't fathom why businessmen in Jacksonville would be willing to "throw open our gates to another colored race" when the South was still reeling from Reconstruction. "It is strange, but nevertheless true that we never seem to take warning from the plain lesson of history," The Korokan ruminated. The Japanese, though "his civilization [is] higher, his business instincts sharper, and his skin a shade lighter" than an African American's, would only invite more racial turmoil into the state. If Japanese colonization was encouraged in Florida, The Korokan feared that the state would be overrun with Japanese, displacing African Americans and creating a far worse racial scenario. "Let Florida beware the yellow peril," The Korokan grimly warned before concluding his dark and gloomy prediction of the Sunshine State's future.[67]

Florida Democratic representative Frank Clark spearheaded the anti-alien land law movement in his state. Clark, a former district attorney and representative in the state legislature for Jacksonville, was a U.S. representative by the time he began to speak out against Japanese colonization in his state. Well before Japanese Americans arrived, however, Clark had gained a reputation in Florida and throughout the South for his passionate devotion to white purity and Jim Crow. In 1911, Clark proposed a bill before the House of Representatives prohibiting marriages between whites and blacks in Washington, D.C. The bill never passed, but Clark's reputation as a staunch segregationist benefited. Clark's views on the Japanese in his state were relatively subdued before 1913. He shared his time between two homes, one in Jacksonville and one in Gainesville, both near Japanese American settlements. Clark was undoubtedly aware of the presence of Japanese Americans but never publicly took up the crusade against them in the early 1900s. By 1913, however, Clark suddenly became a leader in the state's growing anti-Japanese movement, which was particularly strong in the northern and central counties, far from where the Japanese American colonies were actually located. Some of Clark's critics wondered if his sudden interest in the Japanese problem was merely a ploy to win reelection as representative, but others admired, as one Fort Meyers resident did, his ability to "bravely stand up and object to colonization by other than white people.... We are with him on the side of the race or immigration problem."⁶⁸ Clark exclaimed his passionate anti-Japanese hatred in the press during the summer and fall of 1913 and held up California's alien land law as an example of what should be done in Florida.

In October 1913, Clark issued a statement to the press that would link his name to the Japanese debate. Clark explained that he was "outraged that the proposition for more Japanese colonization did not receive more attention" and stated firmly that "Florida must always be a white man's country and we cannot preserve our civilization if we propose to allow Japanese, Chinese or other races with whom the Caucasians cannot assimilate to become landowners and citizens in our midst."⁶⁹ Clark had other backers, including Mayor Van C. Swearingen of Jacksonville, who had earlier proclaimed, "I know nothing of the Japanese personally, but it would seem from all reports that they have not been acceptable to people on the Pacific Coast" and, with the assistance of the Florida Southern Settlement and Development Organization, advocated for bringing white settlers from Europe and the North to the state instead.⁷⁰ Democratic representative from Jacksonville Claude L'Engle also agreed with Clark's views on the Japanese, explaining that "the Japanese are incapable of being assimilated with Caucasian civilization and as laborers cannot be handled tractably like the whites."⁷¹

The idea of a law that would prevent Japanese Americans from settling in Florida gained support throughout 1913. If California could do it, why couldn't Florida? That was a question easier asked than answered. Clark proposed that perhaps the best way to solve the problem with "the little brown people" was to "institute ... the enactment of a law by the next legislature of Florida that will forever prohibit the Japanese, or other races which cannot assimilate with the white race, from owning lands within the boundary of our commonwealth."⁷² The idea of an anti-alien land law appealed to many of Clark's followers, and Governor Park Trammell assured Clark that he would "investigate" the matter of Japanese colonization further to see if there were any underhanded deals or a few individuals getting wealthy by exploiting either the Japanese themselves or the land.⁷³ Clark grew weary of waiting for Trammel's reports and instead pressured the governor for an extra legislative session in the fall of 1913 to pass an act that would "prevent Asiatics from owning land in Florida." Trammel listened to Clark's request but explained that "there would be no extra session" because under the present state constitution, the Japanese "have the same right to colonize and acquire property in Florida that is guaranteed to the most favored foreigners" and Florida citizens.⁷⁴ Constitutionally speaking, passing such a piece of legislation would be illegal. While Trammel and Clark sparred over the constitutionality of the extra session, the push for an anti-alien land law lay dormant during World War I.

The anti-Japanese feelings emerged again, however, when more speculators became interested in developing and selling Florida land during the 1920s. With the addition of more railroads and better highways as well as the proliferation of the automobile after Henry Ford's efficient mechanization, investors saw great potential in Florida as a haven for tourists. Many wealthy visitors already vacationed in areas near Palm Beach and Boca Raton during the fall and winter to escape the harsh winters of the North, but the affordability of the automobile opened Florida to more tourists who might seek refuge in the Sunshine State. The undeveloped land near the coast offered opportunities to clear out scrub or stabilize marshy swamps to build vacation homes or sites of industry and farming. The development of Florida became one of the largest speculation opportunities during the 1920s as land was cheap and plentiful. There was a general belief that Florida, with its favorable climate and excellent growing conditions, would be the new miracle story of the twentieth century.[75]

With the increase of interest in Florida land, the desire to prevent Japanese American settlement peaked. Although Congress had passed the Immigration Act of 1924, which finally included the Japanese in the group of Asians excluded from migrating to the United States, by 1925 this did little to quell concerns among northern and central Florida farmers, property owners, and laborers that Japanese Americans would come in large numbers to their state. Suddenly, Clark's call for an exclusionary land law seemed more fitting. Although Clark was out of office by this point and practicing law in Miami, there was a growing movement for an exclusion act at the state level in Leon County (where Tallahassee, the state capitol, is located) and in central Florida near present-day Orlando. Representatives Robert Davis (D-Leon) and Timothy Mackenzie (D-Lake County in central Florida) were acolytes of Clark and firmly believed that an anti-alien land law was the best way to prevent Japanese Americans from seeking refuge in Florida following the new acts along the West Coast. Rather than attempt to pass a piece of legislation that might not have enough support, Davis and Mackenzie decided to propose an amendment to the state constitution to prohibit aliens ineligible for citizenship from owning property, taking a cue from Louisiana. Davis and Mackenzie believed that the amendment should be proposed to the public, because the chances of them voting for it would be greater than the chances of passing a bill in the state legislature.

During the 1925 legislative session, Davis and Mackenzie proposed Joint Resolution 750 to amend Section 18 of the constitution to formally exclude Japanese from owning property. Other resolutions, including one for county school funding and the appointment of Supreme Court justices, were more hotly contested, but resolution 750 became one of the legacies of the June 1925 legislative session in shaping the constitution and the state's official views of Asian immigrants. The amendment that Davis and Mackenzie sponsored, however, was different from that of Louisiana's. Section 18 of the Florida constitution, or the Declaration of Rights, dealt with property rights and stated, "Foreigners shall have the same rights as to the ownership, inheritance and disposition of property in this State as citizens of the State." This was a generous statement (only Arkansas's constitution had a more direct clause granting property rights to noncitizens), one that was, according to Davis and Mackenzie, a bit too generous. On June 3, 1925, the two representatives proposed that Section 18 be amended to read, "Foreigners who are eligible to become citizens of the United States under the provisions of the laws and treaties of the United States shall have the same rights as to the ownership, inheritance and disposition of property in the State as citizens of the State, but the Legislature shall have power to limit, regulate and prohibit the ownership, inheritance, disposition, possession and enjoyment of real estate in the State of Florida by foreigners who are not eligible to become citizens of the United States under the provisions of the laws and treaties of the United States." This amendment broadcasted Florida's welcoming of white immigrants rather than the Japanese to help settle the land. However, the "aliens ineligible for citizenship" clause that was prevalent in the anti-alien land acts made its way into the closing sentences of the proposition. Were foreigners who were ineligible to become citizens barred from owning property through the amendment? Not technically, but the message was clear, and the proposed amendment gave the Florida legislature the right to pass any legislation it deemed necessary to stem the tide of Japanese colonization and settlement.[76]

On June 8, 1925, Davis, Mackenzie, and by virtue of association, Clark received what they had hoped for: The house passed the proposed amendment without a single "nay." The fact that not one representative opposed the amendment speaks to the sense of complacency in many states surrounding amendments or proposed legislation to prevent Japanese and other Asians from settling and owning property. Such measures might be necessary to preserve resources and protect citizens, and surely, if other states were engaging in these practices, then far be it from Florida to run the risk of absorbing the fleeing Japanese. As in Louisiana, the fears of a specific group of Floridians over the small population of Japanese shaped the constitutional definition of citizenship and land rights. The senate approved the amendment a few weeks later and placed it on the ballot for the people to vote on in the 1926 elections.

The new amendment did not receive much attention from the general public. The few papers that did cover the amendment expressed confusion over what it was meant to accomplish. The *Miami Herald* editors expressed dissatisfaction, describing it as "constitutional tinkering" and unable "to accomplish any good." "Nobody knows at just what class of people this amendment is aimed at. In all probability, it is intended to exclude Japanese from ownership of land in Florida," the editors explained, adding that "if that is all there is to be accomplished by this solemn measure, it is almost foolish to ask the people of Florida to give it consideration." The number of Japanese Americans in the state was "negligible," and "there is not the slightest ground for the belief that a single Japanese will ever be barred by the amendment if it should become law."[77] Similarly, G. B. Wells from Plant City, Florida, wrote to the *Tampa Times* expressing his displeasure with the proposition. Wells feared that "the adoption of such an amendment will not remedy any existing evil ... and if it is adopted it may be the opening wedge for more far-reaching amendments to come later" that might further restrict property rights for others.[78] The only "favorable" reports of the amendment came from the Jacksonville and Tallahassee newspapers and merely described the proposed amendment.

Despite the warnings, voters approved the provision to deny property rights for aliens ineligible for citizenship. The new constitution produced no discernible changes in the lives of Japanese Americans, however, as Florida never passed a piece of legislation barring them from owning property. The Yamato Colony eventually died out in the late 1920s, but the few Japanese Americans who remained credited competition from Cuban pineapple growers as well as the "big farmers and trucks" that arrived in the area to begin large-scale commercial farming after 1924 with encouraging them to abandon the colony. Although there are no reports that the Japanese Americans of Yamato received ill treatment from their neighbors following the creation of the new constitution, many left Yamato and other colonies to either return to Japan or seek business ventures in other states. Although there are no accounts of direct conflicts between the Japanese Americans who made Florida their home (whether permanently or temporarily) and the native residents, the 1926 amendment to the constitution was a verbalization of the few who opposed them and a more complacent public who approved it. Although the population of Japanese Americans was small, their in-between identity in Florida and the confusion over rights produced legal changes in the basic governing principles of the state. Not all southern states passed anti-alien laws or changed their constitutions because not all southern states had even a minuscule Japanese American or Asian American population. Japanese American and Asian American settlement more generally baffled whites and produced often convoluted and confusing, yet racist and discriminatory, pieces of legislation designed to prevent a "yellow invasion" that never came even when Japanese Americans lived amongst southern residents.[79]

FIGHTING BACK: THE STRUGGLE AGAINST ANTI-ALIEN MEASURES

Because not all southern states amended their constitutions to prevent Asian Americans from owning property, resistance from Asian Americans against property rights violations assumed different forms from state to state. Sometimes the battles occurred in an official legal arena, while others were carried out on a day-to-day basis. The struggles of Asian Americans against restrictions on their property and, as a result, their economic rights and livelihood challenged these discriminatory measures.

In 1921, Texas became the first southern state to pass an anti-alien land law, but it was not entirely new and it was not directed against Asians. The Texas legislature amended its constitution in 1891 to completely prohibit alien-owned corporations from owning or leasing property and to limit to six years the amount of time that an alien or an alien-owned company could own or lease land. When the six years was up, the company was to surrender the land to either a buyer or the state government. The amendment was designed to prevent speculation in Texas land by foreign (namely Mexican) corporations, but in December 1891, the Texas Supreme Court declared the measure unconstitutional. Undeterred, the Texas legislature passed a new law one year later that placed no limitations on alien corporations and increased the number of years that alien or alien-owned companies could lease or own land from six to ten years. The 1892 law remained in effect until a new law was created in 1921 that returned to the 1891 provisions of prohibiting alien corporations from owning property in Texas and decreased the number of years that aliens or alien-owned companies could lease or own land from the original six years to five. There was no mention of aliens who were ineligible for citizenship; all aliens were considered equally undesirable when it came to property ownership in the eyes of Texas law at the time. Unlike in other southern states, the targets were not Asians but, rather, Mexican-owned mining corporations or speculators who attempted to make a profit from Texas land.[80]

There were, however, small communities of Chinese Americans throughout Texas at the time who were directly affected by these laws. Chinese Americans first appeared in Texas in 1869 when approximately 300 Chinese men from the West came to help build a railroad from Calvert in east Texas to Dallas. The Chinese laborers entered into three-year contracts with their employers for monthly pay, but only six months later, the employers terminated the contracts because of a labor dispute over wages. Many of the Chinese laborers returned to California, but about 100 remained and settled in El Paso, San Antonio, and Houston and eventually sent for their wives and families from China. Like their brethren elsewhere in the South, the Chinese Americans of Texas made a living running groceries or laundries, family-run businesses or sole proprietorships that helped them eke out a living in some cases or comfortably attain middle-class status in others. By 1920, there were 265 Chinese Americans living in Texas.[81]

Despite their small numbers, Chinese Americans frequently encountered problems when they attempted to purchase land or establish a business. Although there was no mention of "aliens ineligible for citizenship" in the 1921 law and all aliens were entitled to own or lease property for five years, many white Texans used the law to intimidate Chinese Americans and prevent them from settling in their towns and cities. Fred Wong, an American-born Chinese man who was twenty-one at the time, came to San Antonio with his wife and child and his immigrant father from California in 1927 in order to open a business. Wong's father had heard that there was a small but thriving Chinese American community in San Antonio, and although he was correct, he did not take into consideration that his business opportunities would be limited as a result of his race. Wong suggested that perhaps they could do better if they went outside San Antonio, and they eventually found themselves two hours away in Corpus Christi. Once there, Wong learned of a storefront for rent that would be perfect and affordable for their grocery. Wong was appraising the building one day when local white residents heard of his intentions to open a business in their city. The locals were, to say the least, nonplussed and generally suspicious of the Wongs' intentions. A group of Syrians had settled earlier in Corpus Christi and dominated the grocery business there, and whites "did not want Orientals to come and bring more of their kind" to create further unwanted competition. As in Louisiana and Florida, even a small number of Chinese Americans could induce alarm concerning a forthcoming Asiatic invasion. Before Wong could inquire about the property, a member of the local retail association "saw that there was a Chinese person looking around to open a store and they got wind of it, so they sent someone and contacted me if I were going to open a store there and I kind of said that I was intended to." This did not sit well with the retail association, which replied by letting Wong know that "it was not a good idea for a Chinese to open a store in Corpus Christi." Wong was a bit shocked but took them at their word and did not press the issue. Wong "was very green and naive" and did not realize that he had every legal right to own a store in Corpus Christi, and he signed a contract with the local retail association promising that he would not open a business in their town. Wong realized later that he "could have brought suit, but when you're young... you don't realize these things." The Wongs relocated to Austin and were able to start a successful grocery and help the Chinese American population in the city blossom, but Texans in San Antonio were not pleased with the prospect of "Orientals" trying to establish their business nearby. Sam Handy, owner of a growing chain of local Handy Grocery Stores based in San Antonio, attempted to push the Texas legislature to pass an anti-alien land law that specifically targeted Chinese, but such a law never materialized.[82]

Although Wong and his family did not stay in Corpus Christi, they did continue to make their home in the state of Texas. While it was clear that in many towns and cities in Texas, Chinese Americans were tolerated at best or openly intimidated using illegal measures at worst, families like the Wongs did what they could to earn a living despite the hostility. Chinese Americans and Japanese Americans across the South often defied social or even legal discrimination and racism by remaining on their land or in their stores. They may not have fully understood that there were often no teeth in the constitutional amendments in Louisiana or Florida or that the Texas law did not prevent them from owning property, so they may not have been openly defiant. However, as with other racial groups in the South who were marginalized, the everyday and mundane acts of Asian Americans amidst racism were revolutionary in their own regard, whether they led to legal change or not.

Just north in Arkansas, however, a legal battle waged by a Chinese American man against the state's anti-alien land law was brewing in 1927, the same year the Wongs arrived in Texas. Although Chinese laborers were no longer in demand after the late nineteenth century, small communities of Chinese who lingered in the Mississippi Delta region became fairly profitable and self-sustaining grocery and laundry proprietors by the early twentieth century. Initially, the general attitude of Arkansas residents toward their "celestial neighbors" was one of cautious tolerance, as Chinese Americans typically lived near the black parts of town and developed a primarily black clientele.[83]

Some Chinese immigrants, like Lum Jung Luke, went beyond small business enterprises. Lum arrived in Arkansas during the early 1900s from the West

Coast to work on a former cotton plantation, but he was able to save up enough money to purchase a small storefront building in the town of Elaine, Arkansas, near the Mississippi border in 1910. Like other Chinese American grocers, Lum catered primarily to black neighbors, but he also garnered respect for his thrift and work ethic. Lum's reputation was so well established in the years before World War I that he entered into business deals with prominent whites in Elaine and other nearby towns and cities. Lum became a major buyer and seller of real estate, which he would then rent or lease to sawmill workers.[84]

Lum's experience in Arkansas was not typical, but the state offered some safeguards and reassurances for his business. Arkansas's constitution was atypical in providing special land rights and protections for all residents. In 1874, following a tumultuous and chaotic fight for state power between two rival factions of the Republican Party, Arkansas drafted and approved a new constitution to replace the 1868 version. Building on the state government's desire to see Arkansas agriculturally and economically reborn after the Civil War, the new constitution included a specific section relating to property rights for migrants seeking opportunities: "No distinction shall ever be made by law, between resident aliens and citizens, in regard to the possession, enjoyment, or descent of property." Property owners were property owners in Arkansas, and that right was protected under state law for aliens—whether they were eligible for naturalization or not—and citizens alike. While other states amended their constitutions to include prohibitory passages about property rights for Asians, Arkansas explicitly guaranteed the opportunity for aliens to engage in business activities.[85]

But amid nationwide paranoia of a yellow invasion, Arkansas passed an anti-alien land law in 1925 that reversed the constitution's protection for people like Lum. Despite there being only twelve Japanese in Arkansas, the fevered scurry to protect land from yellow invaders reached the Arkansas legislature, where representatives unanimously passed the state's own version of California's law. Following on the heels of legislators from northern Louisiana, cotton planters in Arkansas clamored for an anti-alien land law to prevent any Japanese Americans from Louisiana from moving into their state. General Act 249, or the Alien Land Law, as it was more commonly referred to, "denied to aliens incapable of becoming citizens and not protected by treaty the right to acquire, possess, use, occupy or transfer real estate." If an alien ineligible for citizenship somehow obtained land after 1925, that property would then "escheat to the State, and the violators become guilty of a felony." This new act was a clear path to depriving resident aliens like Lum of their property rights guaranteed under the Arkansas constitution.[86]

However, few respected the new law. Many Arkansas residents maintained their business ties with Chinese Americans, and Lum ignored the act and continued making his land deals. In the winter of 1926, E. M. Allen, a prosperous white landowner from Elaine, agreed to purchase some of Lum's land near the local sawmill. The transaction was routine (Lum had entered into business agreements of a similar nature dozens of times before) until Charles Yingling, the prosecuting attorney for the First Judicial District, caught wind of the deal after it was filed in the local Phillips County Court. Yingling reported to state attorney general W. H. Applegate that an illegal transaction had occurred according to the new anti-alien land law. Applegate responded by initiating escheat proceedings to confiscate the land that Lum had sold to Allen. In turn, Allen and Lum filed for an injunction against Yingling and Applegate in the Phillips County Chancery Court. Lum hired local attorney Brewer Cracraft to represent him and argued that by attempting to confiscate the land, Applegate and Yingling violated his property rights under Section 20 of the state constitution.[87]

Lum's suit was well outside the realm of cases brought before the chancery court, which typically dealt with bank loans and foreclosures. Technically, Lum and Allen violated the Alien Land Law when they entered into their agreement, and Applegate and Yingling, who demurred on the case, were merely following legal procedure. However, the local court directly challenged the attorney general and his actions when Chancellor A. L. Hutchins declared the Alien Land Law unconstitutional and void, arguing that the act did indeed violate basic provisions in the state constitution. The chancery court issued an injunction against Applegate and Yingling to prevent them from confiscating the land, but more importantly, a small "country court" set a precedent for legal interpretations of anti-alien land laws. In the eyes of Hutchins, this was a cut-and-dry ruling, and Lum successfully used the legal system to his advantage.[88]

But Applegate and Yingling did not accept the lower court's ruling and appealed the decision to the state supreme court in the fall of 1926. Lum's victory not only presented a challenge to the anti-alien land law as well as Applegate's office, but it was also a rare case of a lower court deciding that an Arkansas state law was unconstitutional. Applegate could not sit idly by while a Chinese immigrant and a county court attempted to shape property law and legislation. As the state attorney general, Applegate had a duty to uphold the law, and the local court had challenged that duty in order to protect the rights of a noncitizen.

Unfortunately for Applegate, in March 1927 the Arkansas Supreme Court swiftly and unanimously upheld the lower court's decision in the *Applegate v.*

Luke appeal. The case presented to the superior court was relatively straightforward: "The constitutionality of the alien land act, is the sole question presented by this appeal for determination." This case had little to do with power or the office of the attorney general but, rather, centered on very basic questions relating specifically to the Arkansas constitution. Lum argued that the anti-alien act violated many of his basic rights as an immigrant and that the act was discriminatory, but the court was not convinced by Lum's attempts to prove that Applegate had discriminated against him because of his racial and migrant status. In response to Lum's arguments, the Arkansas Supreme Court cited the *Terrace v. Thompson* and *Porterfield v. Webb* U.S. Supreme Court cases, which ruled that states were able to deny Japanese the right to own property because that right was not guaranteed under any specific international or immigration treaty. The Arkansas court respected the *Terrace* and *Porterfield* decisions and did not rule that *all* anti-alien land laws, by nature, were unconstitutional. However, in this particular instance, the Arkansas land law *was* unconstitutional because it explicitly violated the Arkansas state constitution. The court explained, "The act in question . . . seems to be in direct conflict with section 20, article 2, of the Constitution of the State which states that no distinction shall ever be made by law between resident aliens and citizens in regard to property." The lack of distinction between noncitizens and citizens and the lack of specific mention of those ineligible for citizenship were "peculiar to [the Arkansas] Constitution. It seems that other Constitutions do not contain such a provision." It was clear to the court, as it was to Lum, that the wording of Section 20 was "unambiguous" and "the manifest and only intent which can be extracted from this language is that all resident aliens in Arkansas, whether eligible to naturalization and citizenship or not, have the same right to acquire and enjoy the possession of property in this State that any natural citizen has." The court formally ruled in favor of Lum and declared the 1925 Alien Land Law to be void and unconstitutional, upholding the chancery court's decision.[89]

For the first time in a southern state, an Asian immigrant directly challenged the anti-alien land laws using the courts. Other Chinese immigrants had previously sued for damages (successfully and not) in local courts in West Coast states, using Fourteenth Amendment protections after mobs attacked and/or destroyed their property during anti-Chinese riots. Likewise, representatives of the Japanese government and Japanese immigrants fought against Washington and California anti-alien land laws during the early 1920s, arguing that such acts violated their rights as well as diplomatic agreements for fair treatment between the United States and Japan. Lum was also involved in this larger legal movement; however, his case was tied to the South in that he was not challenging all anti-alien land laws on the grounds of the Fourteenth Amendment but, rather, was using his state-sanctioned civil and property rights to specifically challenge Arkansas's land law. It was clear to both the lower and higher courts that the law was in violation of the Arkansas constitution and that Section 20 provided Lum with solid legal ground for his case. But Lum was lucky in this regard, since not all constitutions were as liberal in defining property rights for noncitizens. Still, Lum's direct challenge to Arkansas's racist act demonstrates the different tactics that Asian Americans used to pursue justice. For Lum, his fight ended in a victory and the 1925 alien land law was overturned, making Arkansas the first state to do away with such an act.

JAPANESE AMERICAN INCARCERATION AND ANTI-ALIEN LAND LAWS IN ARKANSAS

Lum's victory over the Arkansas legislature would continue to resonate during World War II when Arkansas received Japanese American incarcerees from the West Coast. Once again, Arkansas—ignoring the lessons of the past—would turn to anti-alien land laws in an attempt to prevent Japanese Americans from remaining in Arkansas after the war and creating unwanted land competition. Arkansas housed two concentration camps during the war, one in Jerome near the Mississippi border and the other in Rohwer, approximately half an hour northeast of Jerome. Eli B. Whitaker, Arkansas's Farm Security Administration (FSA) chief, ordered the camps' placement on acres of desolate, underdeveloped, and marshy land near the Mississippi Delta. The use of these less-than-desirable lands for construction of the camps was beneficial for both the War Relocation Authority (WRA) (the government agency in charge of incarceration) and Arkansas: The WRA received secure camps far from the West, while Whitaker was able to get some use out of a region of Arkansas that offered little apart from a delinquent tax base. The WRA allotted 10,000 acres each for both camps, and the federal government pumped $9,503,905 into the Arkansas economy in 1942 when more than 5,000 men (many from Arkansas and others from neighboring states) were hired to clear the land, construct the barracks for families and WRA personnel to live in, and pave roads for easy access to and from the town centers. Rohwer, which opened in September 1942, held 8,475 prisoners until its closure in November 1945, while approximately 7,932 Japanese Americans were imprisoned in Jerome between October 1942 and June 1944 (when Jerome closed and prisoners were merged with those in Rohwer). In a state that had always strived, at least from the government's approach, to embrace and encourage immigrants to its territory, World War II and incarceration brought one of the largest waves of migration to the state.[90]

The immediate reaction of Arkansans to the establishment of "enemy camps" in their backyard was unfavorable, to say the least. Governor Homer Adkins was opposed to the building of the camps in his state, not only fearing the presence of the "enemy" in Arkansas but also opposing the idea of the Japanese Americans possibly remaining in Arkansas when the prisons closed. Adkins insisted when the camps were constructed that there should be a "gentlemen's agreement" between the state, the WRA, and local employers that no Japanese Americans would be resettled in Arkansas and they would have to return to where they came from.[91] William F. Norrell, a congressional representative from Arkansas's Sixth District, supported Adkins, declaring in a September 1943 speech before a group of senators from Portland, Oregon, that "we've got 20,000 of your Pacific Coast Japs back in my state and they ain't going to stay there after the war, I'll tell you that right now."[92] Apart from the Arkansas FSA officials who saw promise in the camps for developing undesirable land, the Arkansas state government at first opposed and then begrudgingly accepted Japanese resettlement. Racial fears and heightened wartime hysteria no doubt shaped their responses, but men like Adkins and Norrell also opposed the possible labor competition and economic and social upheaval that one more racial group would add to the existing problems of the state—familiar concerns of white southerners stretching back to the use of Chinese as laborers and the purchase of land by Japanese.[93]

As in other concentration camps, the Japanese Americans incarcerated at Rohwer and Jerome were put to work. Many Japanese Americans in Arkansas, apart from the day-to-day custodian jobs, were engaged in agricultural work. The Arkansas FSA, seeking to diversify the Arkansas crops and move away from a cotton-centered economy, tapped into Japanese Americans' knowledge of planting and agriculture with various crops to test out relatively rough-and-tumble land in the Delta. Primarily, the Arkansas FSA was interested to see if the "delta land could produce high quality vegetables" beyond soybeans, the second most important crop in the region.[94] The "Orientals'... knowledge of irrigation" for vegetable growing was of particular interest for agricultural officials, as was the Japanese experiences with the use of smaller plots of land for truck farming a variety of crops.[95] At Jerome and Rohwer, Japanese Americans had great success in "the conversion of land, not previously used for commercial vegetables, into truck gardens" for strawberries, chrysanthemums, cucumbers, carrots, peppers, and a variety of shrubs.[96] In 1943 alone, Japanese Americans in both Rohwer and Jerome successfully raised 542,981 pounds of produce, none of which was the traditional cotton or soybean crops that Arkansas had come to depend on.[97] As one incarceree pointed out, the success of Japanese Americans in raising a large variety of crops "demonstrates the richness of the Arkansas soil and paves the way for the people of Arkansas to develop large scale and diversified agriculture."[98] Some local residents in Desha County took note as well: "We are presently thinking about the success of the Japanese American evacuees . . . in truck farming. This cotton-conscious county will have to turn to diversification soon if the people here expect to enjoy continued prosperity. In Arkansas as a whole, great gains have been made in vegetable production. Inspiration for a great future in truck farming for the county has been given by the Japanese Americans. County farmers could take the hint."[99] Japanese Americans were more than just prisoners in Arkansas. In some ways, the Japanese Americans at Rohwer and Jerome were agricultural saviors who had something to offer by remaking the Arkansas land and teaching local farmers how to make the most of the Delta. Japanese Americans in Arkansas were so successful and gained such an excellent reputation for hard work and agricultural innovation that small and larger farmers throughout the South wrote to the WRA requesting the release of Japanese Americans to come to work on their land. Not only did Arkansans make requests for farmhands when labor was scarce during the war, but Henry Ford's Richmond Hill Plantation in Georgia sought Japanese American labor, as did farmers in Florida, other parts of Georgia, and Louisiana.[100] States were not allowed to "loan" Japanese Americans out of state for labor purposes under the WRA codes (and many incarcerees were not thrilled about the prospects for fear that they would be underpaid, overworked, and treated no better than sharecroppers or African American workers), but the demand for the skills and labor of Japanese Americans reflected the success of the prisoners in revolutionizing Arkansas agriculture and laying a foundation for further development.

Not everyone viewed Japanese American success with farming in Arkansas as a net benefit, however, and a variety of blatantly racist and discriminatory laws and measures were passed at the state level. Governor Homer Adkins was the state's largest and most powerful opponent of Japanese Americans and was not shy about making his opinions known in the media and in the legislature. Adkins became incensed in 1943 when he discovered that out-of-state employers were seeking Japanese American labor and that there was discussion of using the Japanese Americans for in-state projects. Adkins referred to the "gentlemen's agreement" between the WRA and Arkansas and fired off a telegram to Washington, D.C., officials to protest against the proposed labor plans, reminding them that they promised Arkansas that "these Japanese... would remain in camps under military guard, would not compete with local labor, and would not be allowed to purchase land and would be removed after the war is over."[101] It was precisely the fear of labor competition and the possibility that Japanese Americans would purchase land and remain in Arkansas when the camps closed that pushed Adkins and his supporters over the edge.

In January 1943 (a little over four months after the Japanese Americans arrived in Arkansas), the state legislature once again proposed a bill that would prevent Japanese Americans from owning property. This bill was a throwback to the state's 1925 Alien Land Law but targeted Japanese Americans specifically and also included those born in the United States with U.S. citizenship. Senator Frank B. Williams (whose constituents were mainly large cotton planters) introduced the bill to the senate and stressed that its purpose was to "safeguard the real property of the state of Arkansas and citizens thereof... because on account of the standards of living of the Japanese people, a white person can not profitably compete with the Japanese either in Agriculture or Business."[102] As late as 1943, the lingering stereotypes of Japanese Americans as land hungry and unscrupulous and responsible for creating a hostile labor and business environment for whites in the South prevailed. In this case, the Japanese Americans at Rohwer and Jerome did themselves no favors by successfully aiding Arkansans with developing their land for profit. Williams shaped his bill on such concerns, ensuring that no aliens ineligible for citizenship "shall ever purchase or hold title to any lands in the State of Arkansas," serve as trustees, or rent property for more than a year, and that any previous deals that violated the proposed bill would be void. The initial bill was almost word-for-word identical to the unconstitutional 1925 act. This alarmed Senator Willis B. Smith, who objected to the bill not because he cared about protecting the rights of Japanese Americans (just the opposite, he "favored denying Japanese property rights") but because he was concerned that the measure would "violate the state constitution and penalize Chinese residents."[103] Smith was right. The bill did violate Arkansas's unique constitution, which would ultimately prevent the legislation from passing it. However, Senator C. B. Raggsdale, who sponsored the bill, explained that no bill that would prevent the Japanese from settling in Arkansas was too harsh. After all, "if I had it my way, I'd put them all on a ship and have the ship torpedoed," he remarked. Raggsdale also claimed the act would not retroactively punish Chinese Americans who were already property owners in the state. In the midst of the war when China was an ally of the United States, the last thing many Americans wanted to do was offend the Chinese, as was evident in the repeal of the Chinese Exclusion Act in 1943. However, others pushed Raggsdale on the constitutional issues, with one senator informing his fellow legislators that "we are monkeying with the fundamental principles of democracy," landownership and rights.[104] Raggsdale tried to reassure the senate that nothing would happen to Chinese American property owners and that only Japanese Americans would be affected. Although there were no friends of the Japanese Americans in the senate, many respected the basic rights of property ownership and protection that were enshrined in the Arkansas constitution and previously upheld by the Arkansas Supreme Court.

Because Raggsdale worked so diligently to specifically target Japanese Americans and to ensure that Chinese Americans would not be affected, the bill was unique among other anti-alien land acts in that it applied to Japanese Americans rather than just "aliens ineligible for citizenship." The functional premises of the bill were kept the same as in the previous anti-alien land law, but Raggsdale substituted "Japanese people" for "aliens ineligible for citizenship." Section 1 of the bill was most revealing in that it specified that "no Japanese or a descendant of a Japanese shall ever purchase or hold title to any lands in the State of Arkansas."[105] The specific mention of Japanese Americans won over the senate, which passed with only one nay (Senator Willis Smith, who objected earlier) on February 13, 1943. Governor Adkins, who had written to California legislators a year earlier seeking advice on an anti-alien land law, happily signed Act 47 into action and accomplished his goal of sending a strong message that the Japanese would not be welcomed in his state.[106]

The act was met with the approval of many Arkansans but merely confused the imprisoned Japanese Americans themselves. In an editorial for the Rohwer weekly newspaper, the *Outpost*, one prisoner wrote that "very few if any of the persons of Japanese ancestry have had any intention of staying in the boundaries of this state after the war, so it appears that the legislature should reconsider their decision."[107] Many wanted to return home to the West Coast or, at the very least, avoid the "peonage" of sharecropping or agricultural life in Arkansas. "Is it worth going against the fundamental tenets of the U.S. Constitution in order to satisfy the unsubstantiated fears of conquest from fellow Americans who have no intentions of staying in this state?" the author asked. Others at Rowher and Jerome expressed concern with the act's specific language on Japanese Americans and worried that far greater restrictions of basic civil rights could materialize in the midst of wartime hysteria. Imprisonment without due process in the camps was already a massive civil rights violation that possibly opened the door for more, particularly in the South, where systematic rights violations of African American citizens had been commonplace since Reconstruction. Others also spoke to the injustice done to the state of Arkansas by the anti-Japanese act. "We—Arkansas with its past discrimination that has prevented it from attaining the development that is rightfully hers and the Japanese Americans who have suffered discrimination along racial lines—look forward to the future when we may gain a higher niche in the American dream."[108] The Arkansas act was not only a product of wartime anti-Japanese hysteria but also part of a longer history of anti-Asian discrimination in the state and a large piece of the historical puzzle of anti-Asian land laws in the South that, by the 1940s, had become a staple of southern civil rights violations. Although Pearl Harbor intensified and realized the suspicions of the "treacherous" Japanese, the wartime attempt by Arkansas to limit the civil rights of Japanese Americans stemmed from a longer history. Decades and a world war separated the 1927 Arkansas Supreme Court decision on the first anti-alien land law and the 1943 act, but at their cores, the two acts demonstrated that time stood still in terms of how southerners perceived Asian Americans.

Although the Japanese could only write letters to outside activists who agreed to work on their behalf to protest the anti-alien land law and publish editorials in local newspapers, their work fueled Arkansans who, if nothing else, opposed the law on constitutional rather than racial grounds. In March 1943, Attorney General Guy E. Williams (who had scuffled with Adkins in the past over jurisdiction issues concerning the Jerome and Rohwer camps) reviewed the act and held that under the state constitution, Arkansas "has no restrictions on land or other property, ownership, or its use by Japanese, Chinese, or Indians."[109] Exactly one month after the legislature passed the act, Williams held that, once again, "all aliens shall be capable of taking by deed or will lands and tenements," regardless of their ability to naturalize. Property rights of Arkansas citizens were also, under the constitution, the property rights of immigrants. Williams did not comment on the portion of the act that forbade Japanese Americans from owning property in Arkansas and approached the act as a violation of basic property rights for all as opposed to a specific civil rights violation for Japanese Americans. Williams echoed the ruling of the supreme court in 1927 and assured Arkansans that such land laws were, and would always be, unconstitutional.[110] The Arkansas anti-alien land act was more than a national story of anti-Japanese sentiment running rampant from West to East after Pearl Harbor. This was a piece of legislation that had southern roots.

When it came to property ownership, for many white southerners, Asian immigrants did not have an "in-between" status. While they were desirable resources at first for their agricultural expertise, they quickly gained a reputation as dangerous "others," more threatening than even African Americans. The relationship of Asian immigrants to the traditional themes of land and labor in the post–Civil War South is largely unknown but is necessary for understanding how civil rights violations against Asian Americans unfolded throughout the twentieth century as they became a more visible and, therefore, more problematic group for southerners.

Furthermore, the differences in treatment during World War II for Japanese Americans and Chinese Americans living in the South deserve discussion. Although both were Asian American, international politics and relations during the war created different receptions and reactions to Chinese and Japanese. While white southerners began to welcome (or at the very least to begrudgingly accept) Chinese Americans into their schools (as discussed in the following chapter), Arkansas was attempting to prevent not just Japanese immigrants but also American-born Japanese from owning property—stripping citizens and immigrants alike of basic rights. Anti-Asian sentiment became more specifically anti-Japanese sentiment, as reflected in the proposed prohibition of Japanese American landownership. America's relations to China (ally) and Japan (enemy) during the war helps to explain the reasoning behind differing treatments and experiences, but foreign relations also complicated the racial status of Asian Americans in the South. Ethnicity and nationality mattered more than race in this case and reflected the malleable and complex relationship of Asian Americans to southern laws, particularly in terms of segregation and property. As the twentieth century unfolded, international politics would continue to play a role in shaping southern reactions to Asian Americans.

Had he lived to see the end of World War II, Lue Gim Gong, the miracle grower, would have witnessed a series of changes in how whites viewed Asian Americans. Racism did not vanish, but Asian advocacy groups and other Americans who believed that Asian Americans had "proven" themselves through their service in the war and their patriotism openly challenged the various forms of legal discrimination they encountered throughout the country. The rise of the Cold War also prompted the United States to revisit embarrassing and antiquated laws aimed at Asian Americans and other minorities. In the 1952 *Fujii v. California* case, the U.S. Supreme Court ruled that the California anti-alien land laws violated Fourteenth and Fifth Amendment rights to life, liberty, and property, effectively invalidating such measures for all time. While issues of housing discrimination and restrictive housing covenants persisted, legally the painful legacy of civil rights violations in terms of enforceable anti-alien land laws and amendments came to an end. Not all states immediately revoked the laws, however, and they would eventually be phased out only as new constitutions were ratified throughout the years. Some (such as Florida's amendment) remain as reminders of Asian discrimination with no legal recourse.

TWO

BLACK OR WHITE?

Asian Americans' Challenges to Segregated Schools

In the summer of 1904, the Kentucky state school board found itself faced with an unprecedented question: Are Filipinos "Negroes"? This legal quandary was not part of the conversation earlier in the year when the DuPont Manual Training High School in Louisville agreed to admit four Filipino students into its engineering program. However, come July, the question of Filipinos' racial classification loomed large over the approaching school year. Based on Kentucky segregation laws, "coloreds" (synonymous at this time in Kentucky with "Negroes") were not permitted to attend school with whites. That much was clear, but whether or not Filipinos were colored was not so easy to discern. The school board agreed that Filipinos were certainly not white, but did that make them legally black? Throughout the early twentieth century, the state of Kentucky was not alone in its puzzlement over the racial classification of Asian Americans when it came to education.

The interstitial identity of Asian Americans living in the Jim Crow South often created unique challenges and obstacles to their achieving an education. While southern schools were often segregated along the lines of "colored" or "Negro" and "white," Asian Americans did not always fall neatly into one of these categories.[1] As more Asian Americans began to populate areas of the South during the 1920s and 1930s as families grew, the question of which school they should legally attend became more prominent and pressing. Although Asian Americans did not identify as black, southern law often lumped them together with "coloreds," barring them from attending white schools. However, determining whether or not Asian Americans were colored was also problematic considering the wide range of racial categories, including "Mongoloids," "Malays," "Orientals," or simply "yellows." These classifications were certainly not "white," but did they warrant Asian Americans sending their children to all-black schools?[2]

The answers to this question varied, making southern school segregation both challenging and malleable for Asian Americans. Some (particularly Chinese Americans) who lived in the South used a strategy of "white accommodation" to attempt to gain access to white schools and other areas of white life, sometimes successfully and other times not.[3] In many ways, the experiences of Chinese Americans and other Asian Americans in the South were similar to those of other immigrant groups, such as the Italians, who could be simultaneously "white" and "immigrant other," depending on their location.[4] However, flattening the legal strategies and tactics of Asian Americans for attacking school segregation diminishes the complex challenges that Asian Americans presented to school districts, local and state law officials, and even the Supreme Court. "White" was often a murky concept, and Asian Americans living in the South tried to capitalize on the often fluctuating definitions of racial categories. Rather than argue for their whiteness, Asian Americans more often sought to prove their "Orientalness" or strove for a noncolored status, working with their "other" identity rather than fighting against it. Asian Americans believed that access to white schools was a fundamental right, and they challenged the binary racial system by attempting to fashion a third category defined by ethnicity rather than race.

Appealing to their foreign national status was also a legal strategy used by Chinese Americans to avoid sending their children to colored or black schools. In this case, not being an American citizen had benefits, as the Chinese claimed that they were protected under special privileges granted by treaties between the United States and China. Arguing that they were *nationally* Chinese was in some ways a more straightforward tactic supported with legal documents. Adding immigrant status to the study of school segregation further complicates a history of racism and discrimination that is usually summed up with *Brown v. Board of Education*. Discrimination in education was never simply about skin color or racial conceptions, but the legal status of Chinese immigrants brought questions of citizenship, national belonging, and political identity into debates surrounding race and ethnicity in southern schools.

The most notable example of Asian Americans' run-ins with southern segregation is the 1927 *Lum v. Rice* Supreme Court case. In 1924, Jeu Gong Lum, a Chinese immigrant merchant living in the Mississippi Delta, sent his two daughters, Martha and Berda (the oldest), to the school closest to his house, Bolivar County's Rosedale Consolidated High School, as he had done the previous year. When the school refused to admit Martha and Berda that year, Gong Lum launched a fight against the local school board, arguing that his daughters were "pure Chinese" and therefore not subject to the local segregation laws because they were neither white nor colored. The case eventually worked its way through the legal system to the U.S. Supreme Court, where the judges declared that Chinese Americans are indeed colored and should attend colored schools in Mississippi.

While the Gong Lum case remains the most cited Asian American experience with school segregation in the South, a companion appeal, the 1927 *Bond, State Superintendent of Education v. Tij Fung* case is equally important in defining the varied experiences of Asian Americans with Jim Crow education. In 1927, Joe Tin Lun, an American-born boy of Chinese descent, was denied admission to a whites-only school in Dublin, Mississippi, prompting his guardians to sue the school district for denying him his immigrant rights as guaranteed in special treaties between China and the United States. The Mississippi Supreme Court dismissed Lun's appeal on the grounds that ethnic and immigrant status meant little in terms of racial classifications. The Lun case is often overlooked, but it reveals an interesting point of comparison and contrast with *Lum*, as do the legal battles of Chinese Americans and other ethnic groups across the South before *Brown v. Board*.

Placing the legal strategies found in the Lum and the Lun cases alongside those of other Asian Americans in the South exposes the complex picture of ethnicity, immigration, and otherness brought to light by school segregation. Rather than focusing on one group, such as Chinese Americans in Mississippi (the standard example in the existing literature), this chapter places Chinese Americans in Mississippi in a broader context through comparisons with the experiences of Chinese Americans in Georgia, Filipino Americans in Kentucky, and Japanese Americans and Chinese Americans in New Orleans, Texas, and parts of Florida. In some instances, Asian American students attended white schools and colleges without much resistance, even when the law demanded otherwise. In others, Asian Americans chose to construct their own private schools instead of being drawn into the identity games of choosing which "side" to fight on. However, as the Lum and Lun cases as well as the experiences of Chinese Americans of Georgia demonstrate, others emphasized either their "nonblackness" (rather than "whiteness") or their Chinese ethnicity and/or immigrant status to protest laws that required their children to attend the underfunded colored schools. If Chinese American students were forced to attend the colored schools by law, then Chinese Americans would be classified as colored, threatening the distance that Chinese Americans attempted to maintain between themselves and African

Americans. Unlike *Brown v. Board*, the legal fight against discrimination in education determined the racial status of Asian Americans and cast doubt on their ability to dictate their own identity in the black-and-white South.

THE FLUIDITY OF RACE IN SCHOOL SEGREGATION

Although segregation was certainly not unheard of in other parts of the nation, southern states ardently codified and enforced their Jim Crow laws in education. In the decades before and even after *Brown v. Board*, a racial line drawn between blacks and whites characterized the educational experiences of generations of children in the South. Asian Americans were also no strangers to school segregation. While there was often no de jure segregation at the state level along the West Coast, there was also no explicit legislation preventing local school boards from prohibiting Asian American and other minority students from attending white schools. In 1906, Japanese American parents in San Francisco objected when the city attempted to segregate their children from whites in public schools. In response to the outcry, the Japanese government entered into the Gentlemen's Agreement with America in 1907 that secured a guarantee from President Theodore Roosevelt that Japanese in the United States would receive basic rights and protections in exchange for Japan's limiting the number of visas it approved for laborers seeking to enter the United States. This halted legally enforced segregation in San Francisco for Japanese Americans; but other forms of de facto segregation abounded in California, and the agreement did not address discrimination for other Asian Americans across the country. The terrain of segregation in education was varied on the West Coast: Some Asian American students attended public schools that were majority Asian, others received their education from private tutors or from Chinese- or Japanese-language schools, and many attended integrated schools where possible. However, the stigma of being "Oriental" affected the educational experiences of many students.[5]

For Asian Americans living in the South, seeking an education at a segregated school was often a conundrum. Not only did Asian Americans experience extreme fluctuations in school policies from one state to the next, but discrepancies often arose at the local levels even within the same state. Take, for example, the cases of a group of Filipino students and a Chinese student who attempted to enroll in white high schools in two separate cities in Kentucky during the early 1900s. In 1904, four *pensionados* (students from the Philippines invited to attend high schools and colleges in the United States on scholarships from the American colonial government) applied and were initially accepted to the DuPont Manual Training School in Louisville. Filipino and American colonial officials designed the Pensionado Program in 1903 as an opportunity for "Americanization" of Filipinos who chose to pursue their education at American high schools and colleges and universities. In doing so, colonial leaders hoped that Filipinos who took advantage of the government-funded scholarships would develop a deep appreciation of American values, traditions, and democracy and return to the Philippines after their studies in order to assume positions in the colonial bureaucracy. The Pensionado Program was also an attempt to cultivate good relations between the colony and the metropole and overcome lingering revolutionary tendencies after the American victory in the Spanish-American War of 1898 and the subsequent American annexation of the islands. High schools and colleges across the country readily admitted *pensionados* as an opportunity to bring culture and worldliness to their students. In Kentucky, however, the problem of race far outweighed the potential for cultural growth and improved colonial relations.[6]

While the DuPont School initially supported the Pensionado Program and agreed to admit the students earlier in the year, by July 1904 questions of the racial status of the Filipino Americans created distress for the local administration as well as the state school board. Under Kentucky law (as in many other southern states), schools were segregated along lines of "white" and "colored." "Colored" was a catchall term meant to encompass any race that was not considered white. If race was so easily demarcated, then the DuPont administration would have determined the Filipinos to be colored and therefore unfit to attend the white high schools in the state. But such determination was not easy when it came to Filipino Americans. Many southerners in the early 1900s had never before encountered Filipinos beyond pictures and souvenirs sent back from the Philippines or images taken of the "savage" Filipino exhibit at the 1904 St. Louis World's Fair. Filipinos were people to be studied and ogled from afar, and the possibility of them arriving in Kentucky no doubt forced the school board to think carefully about whether or not their decision to admit the students was wise. As the meeting between the colonial subjects and the white students and teachers of DuPont loomed, the administration worried about a potential clash with parents and other white residents.[7]

In an attempt to solve the problem of the *pensionado* students, the school board investigated the racial standing of Filipino Americans in a segregated system. More specifically, the debate over the Filipino Americans' racial status was not whether or not they were white or "colored" but whether or not the *pensionados* were "Negroes." Under the revamped Kentucky segregation law (or the Day Law) of 1904, it was "unlawful to maintain or operate any college, school, or institution where persons of the white and colored races are both allowed to attend," and colored institutions were required to be located at least twenty-five miles from the white schools.[8] The Day Law was clear in stating that African Americans were colored, but it was less so regarding Filipinos Americans. Because the school board associated "colored" with "Negro," it had the task of determining whether or not Filipino Americans were black according to the law. This was no easy undertaking and required the assistance of a professor from the University of Kentucky who investigated the state's Jim Crow laws to decipher the Filipinos Americans' standing.[9]

After analyzing the racial implications of the Day Law, Professor H. Mark declared that while the law ordered schools to separate white from colored or Negro students, "colored" also included "Indians" and "other brown races." The conclusion that Filipinos were a "brown" race was no surprise: Many Americans often referred to Filipinos as "brown brothers" or, more paternally, their "little brown brothers" in describing their colonial relationship to the United States as well as their skin color. However, the "little brown brothers" presented a challenge to the new Day Law. Was there a difference between "brown" and "colored," or "brown" and "Negro"? The Filipino American students forced the state school board and scholars to grapple with this puzzle in the state's segregation and education policies. Apart from Native Americans, the presence of other races besides African Americans was small, with virtually no other Filipinos in the state at the time of the debate over the students' racial status.[10] Essentially, the Filipino American students presented to both the school board and the state of Kentucky the first real technical problem with the supposedly easy segregation of schools between white and colored. However, because the ultimate conclusion was that brown races are indeed colored, the school board refused to admit the Filipino American students and cited the Day Law as justification for their decision. While it is not clear what happened to the four Filipino American students who were turned away from DuPont, the stir they created led to the establishment of a new racial category in Kentucky—other brown races—to be used for any future legal complications that might arise in school policy. The creation of the "brown" race was useful for the school board but lacked any special privileges for the Filipino Americans, who were grouped with African Americans.[11]

But the state school board's decision in the case of the Louisville Filipino Americans did not match the outcome of a later battle between a Chinese American boy and an all-white school in Covington, Kentucky, which demonstrated that not all Asian Americans were "colored" after all.

In 1913, fourteen-year-old American-born Pong Dock sought enrollment in the all-white First District School. What followed after Pong Dock's request was a debate similar to that involving the Filipino Americans in Louisville. Rather than focusing on whether or not the boy was Negro, however, the main goal of the Covington school board entailed deciphering whether or not Pong Dock fell into the category of "colored." The population of Chinese Americans in northern Kentucky during the 1900s was small, and most of the inhabitants were single males. But as the number of American-born Chinese children increased, the question of where they should go to school in the segregated state became an obsession. Although Pong Dock was the first Chinese American to request admission to the white school, white parents and residents of Covington argued that he should attend the colored school because he was not of European descent and therefore not white. On the contrary, Pong Dock's parents argued that he was certainly not black and therefore belonged in the white school rather than the colored school in Covington.[12]

The question of Pong Dock's racial status and its effect on which school he attended grew into a statewide problem. "What shall be done with Pong Dock?" became a concern for not only the Covington school board but also the state of Kentucky. An article in the *Hartford Herald* explained to readers that the "little chubby fellow" was an "oriental" and the first Chinese American to request admission to the Covington public schools. Unlike Pong Dock, other Chinese American parents schooled their own children or sent them to Chinese-language schools in nearby Cincinnati. "Oriental" was a racial category that the author of the news article used and one that, presumably, Kentuckians were aware of, but this classification did little to clarify which school Pong Dock should attend. His background and residential history also added a layer of complexity to his case. While he was born in America, he relocated to China with his parents when he was three years old. In September 1913, his parents sent him back to America to live with family friend Sing Lee so that he would be "brought up and educated as an American citizen." Because Pong Dock spent a good number of his formative years in China, Kentuckians viewed him as being "educated there as a Chinaman," negating his American status and emphasizing his Oriental otherness. Not only was Pong Dock's racial classification up for grabs, but his ethnicity also complicated his educational standing in the state's attempts to determine his legal race. His predicament had "the state of Kentucky scratching its legal head" over whether or not a Chinese boy belongs in a white or colored school.[13]

The official determination of Pong Dock's admission and racial status became a game of hot potato, with various officials eager to avoid ruling on the complicated question. When white parents protested against Pong Dock's potential admission, First Covington's Superintendent Homer O. Sluss elected to defer to the authority of the Covington Board of School Commissioners. Unable to come to an agreement on whether or not they should permit Pong Dock to attend the white school, the board then turned the matter over to the Kentucky attorney general, James Garnett. While Sluss, the school board, and other parties focused heavily on determining Pong Dock's race, the attorney general also concentrated on bringing Pong Dock's citizenship status into the debate. In a letter to Superintendent of Public Instruction Barksdale Hamlett, Garnett explained that "under the laws of the United States, a Chinese immigrant cannot become a citizen of the United States, therefore, he cannot become a citizen of this state. So far as I'm informed, there are only two races that can become citizens of the United States, i.e., the white race and the negro race." Garnett emphasized that "there is no provision whereby a Mongolian may become a citizen of this country."[14] Although Pong Dock was an American citizen based on his birth in the United States, his "Mongolian" race more generally was denied naturalization under existing legislation and was also denied admission to the United States under the Chinese Exclusion Act, passed in 1882 and renewed indefinitely in 1902.

Unlike African Americans who fought against Jim Crow laws that violated their given rights as American citizens, individuals like Pong Dock had to fight to prove that they had citizenship rights in the first place, struggling to overcome generalized stereotypes that all Asian Americans, even those born in America, were racially and legally others. Despite the 1898 Supreme Court ruling in *United States v. Wong Kim Ark* that emphasized that the birthright citizenship component of the Fourteenth Amendment applied to all persons born in the United States, including Chinese Americans, many Americans still doubted the citizenship of Asian Americans because of their racial and ethnic backgrounds.[15] As such, Mongolians were not and could not become American citizens and were only aliens with limited rights and privileges. As Garnett explained, "Generally speaking, we owe to aliens no duty, except to protect their person and their property, and if the State of Kentucky should deny to a person of the Mongolian race, the right to attend public schools, it could not be said that the State was depriving citizens the equal protection of the laws."[16] For Garnett, Pong Dock's citizenship and civil rights were irrelevant; it was Pong Dock's race, specifically his "Mongolian-ness," that gave Garnett pause.[17]

Garnett then moved on to a more convoluted explanation of how Pong Dock's citizenship affected his racial standing in Kentucky by drawing on the significance of states' rights in relation to education. Despite a Mongolian's inability to naturalize, "the State has the right to care for and educate the members of alien races if it so desires." Garnett explained that "it is necessary to consider the Constitution of Kentucky . . . in order to ascertain whether the right to attend the common schools of the State is based upon citizenship or the right to citizenship."[18] In the exceptional case of Pong Dock, who was both a Mongolian and an American citizen, if the state took only his citizenship into consideration rather than his race, then he "would have no right to attend our public schools, because our Legislature has provided for schools only for the white race and the colored race and the word, 'colored,' as used in our Constitution and Statute relates to the negro race."[19] While Pong Dock was a citizen (despite being of Mongolian descent), he was, according to the Kentucky constitution, a member of neither the white nor the black race and therefore was not entitled to an education in the state. There were no state-funded Mongolian or Chinese schools, and although Pong Dock did hold American citizenship, he was not a citizen of the state of Kentucky and therefore the state could decide whether or not it wanted to accommodate him. If he were either white or colored (which is how the Louisville district described the Filipinos), it would be easier to decide which school he should attend. In this case, Pong Dock's in-between racial status and American citizenship did little to advance his case with the attorney general.

Garnett used his labyrinthine reasoning to meditate on the legal puzzles of Pong Dock's position rather than to offer a clear solution to the problem facing the school district. Despite his argument that Pong Dock's race meant that he could not attend either a white or a colored school in the state, Garnett emphasized that in Kentucky, "there is no provision for a separate school for any of the races, except the white race and the negro race. If a child belongs to any race and resides within the State of Kentucky, in good faith, and comes within the provisions of the School Law, it is entitled to the benefits of the public school. . . . Children shall all attend the public school, regardless of race."[20] Because public education was a privilege for all children in Kentucky and Mongolians were not specifically mentioned as colored, then "there is nothing in [the] law that would prevent the Chinese boy to whom you refer, from attending either the white or the colored school, and in my opinion, it is left to the Board of Education as to which school he shall attend."[21] Not only did the attorney general rule that the question be returned to the school board; he also suggested that "if the board should be of the opinion that it was not best for [Pong Dock] to attend either of the schools, I think the board might make some reasonable regulation to have the child privately instructed, so that he would receive the equal benefits of the public school."[22] Unlike the school board in Louisville, the attorney general did not consider Mongolians as part of the colored race because they were not black, and in the state of Kentucky, the education decisions for those who were neither white nor black were to be decided at the local level. The Covington school board agreed to allow Pong Dock to attend the white school, and despite the pushback from parents and other white residents of Covington who attempted to persuade the boy to attend the colored school, other Asian Americans were able to attend white or colored schools after Pong Dock's experience. Although Pong Dock's racial and citizenship status initially presented a roadblock, his "Mongolian-ness" worked in his favor with the attorney general later on.

The above examples of how two different groups of Asian Americans could be considered "brown/colored" and "Mongolian/not black" within the same state raises an interesting point on the perplexing presence of Asian Americans in the South. Even African Americans across the country took note of Pong Dock's case and the ruling that he was not colored and placed it in context with other segregation laws. How could Chinese be "noncolored" enough to attend white schools in Kentucky, while in Nebraska and other states around the country, Chinese were considered "colored" and unable to wed whites?[23] In many cases, the state and local decisions on education did not always line up with decisions on other matters, including miscegenation. A Chinese American boy might be considered noncolored and able to attend a white school, while in the same state a Chinese American man could be classified as colored for the purposes of preventing interracial marriage. Even in terms of education, there was wide variation from state to state. Under state law in Louisiana, schools were segregated along white and colored lines; however, unlike in the state of Kentucky, there was never a challenge to the binary system by Asian Americans. Legally, for educational purposes, Asian Americans were neither colored nor white, and there was no official ruling or discussion of which school the students should attend. As a result, the few Chinese Americans and Japanese Americans living in New Orleans during the early twentieth century often attended white schools or organized their own private institutions for learning. Similarly, in Tennessee and Arkansas, Asian Americans were legally allowed to attend white schools, unlike in neighboring Mississippi, where Asian Americans were considered colored. In the Jacksonville area of Florida and other communities along the Atlantic coast of the state, small Japanese American farming communities created their own schools for Japanese children because under Florida law "the schools for white children and the schools for Negro children shall be conducted separately." In some cases, no mention of Asians, Orientals, or Mongolians meant that Asian American children were free to attend white schools, particularly if the population in a given area was small enough to not raise concern among white residents. Unlike miscegenation, allowing Asian Americans into white schools was often not deemed an immediate threat to white society. Jim Crow laws were clear in stating the limitations for black students, but when it came to Asian Americans, there was more maneuverability and access to white schools throughout the South. Such maneuverability, however, only lasted so long as the population of Asian Americans within larger communities remained low.[24]

The prospect of one or two Chinese American or Japanese American students attending white schools typically did not produce any mass outcries from citizens between the late 1800s and the 1920s, but when the population of Asian Americans in southern communities began to creep up past three or four families and the number of Asian American children grew by the mid-1920s, trouble began for the Asian students. This slight yet noticeable population growth coincided with a growing wave of wariness and suspicion toward Asians and "new" immigrants from southern, central, and eastern Europe. Anti-immigrant sentiment shaped immigration policy between 1917 and 1924, when Congress passed a series of exclusionary and restrictive immigration laws. Although the Chinese Exclusion Act had been in place since 1882, a growing population of Japanese immigrants on the West Coast prompted calls from inhabitants and legislators in California and Washington for exclusion of Japanese and, more generally, Asians. In addition to a variety of acts prohibiting immigrants who were illiterate, suspected of criminal activity, and/or mentally or physical ill from entering the United States, Congress also passed the Immigration Act of 1917, which created the Asiatic Barred Zone and added Indians to a growing list of Asian immigrants who were not permitted to settle in the United States. At that point, Japanese immigrants were exempt from the list due to diplomatic relations between Japan and the United States. In 1924, however, Congress passed the National Origins Act and severely restricted the number of "undesirable" immigrants coming from southern and southeastern Europe in favor of "traditional" immigrants from western and northern European countries. The 1924 act also excluded all Asians (Japanese included) from entering the United States, granting exceptions only for temporary migrants such as students, state officials, and clergy. The rash of exclusionary and restrictive immigration acts following World War I reflected rising anti-immigrant and anti-Asian attitudes across the country that reached the smallest schoolhouses in the South and affected the small bands of Chinese students who attended them.

No greater example of the increasing challenges to Asian Americans pursuing their education in white schools can be found than in the case of Chinese Americans. They were the Asian American group with the largest population across southern states during the early to mid-twentieth century, and their slowly increasing numbers bred growing resentment against their children attending white schools. Chinese Americans were once seen as an acceptable oddity, a group of others who tended to their businesses in the black sections of town and generally kept to themselves, save the one or two children who attended white schools, but their racial identities came under fire during the mid-1920s and early 1930s. Suddenly, school boards began to bar Chinese Americans from attending the schools where they had been fellow students with white children, forcing them into the colored schools for African Americans. Chinese Americans were once racial others, but now local schools and white parents attempted to reclassify them as colored. Although previous skirmishes between students such as Pong Dock and the Kentucky school board were settled informally through reviews by the attorney general or local school boards on a case-by-case basis, in states with larger Asian populations, local, state, and federal courts were increasingly tasked with enumerating the specific legal rights of "in-between" people.[25]

"OF PURE CHINESE DESCENT": MISSISSIPPI CHINESE AMERICANS AND SCHOOL SEGREGATION

Before there was Oliver Brown, the father from Topeka, Kansas, who would become the figurehead in the battle against school segregation with the 1954 *Brown v. Board* Supreme Court case, there was Jeu Gong Lum, a Chinese immigrant grocery store owner from Rosedale, Mississippi. Like other Chinese living in the Mississippi Delta region in the 1920s, Gong Lum had a comfortable life. Gong Lum entered the United States through the Canadian border in the Pacific Northwest in an attempt to avoid immigration officials after the Chinese Exclusion Act and eventually found his way to the Mississippi Delta, where a distant relative lived. Once settled, Gong Lum met and married a Chinese woman, Katherine Wong, who had lived in the Delta since she was a child. Gong Lum traveled a route similar to that of other Chinese looking to leave the West Coast and its stringent anti-alien land laws that prohibited Asians from owning property.[26] No such legislation existed in Mississippi, and Chinese seeking new business ventures in the state (the home of the largest Chinese population in the South at the time) joined other Chinese who were descendants of the hired Chinese laborers who came to Arkansas during the late 1800s to work in agriculture. During the late nineteenth and early twentieth centuries, the Chinese population was low (only 243 Chinese were counted in the entire state of Mississippi, according to the 1900 census), and Chinese were generally tolerated by both white and black residents. They filled an economic niche by living and setting up shop as grocers in the black neighborhoods of Delta towns and earning the toleration if not the outright respect and acceptance of the local white population. So long as the Chinese were not competing for labor or business with whites and abided by the rules and customs of the state and local communities, they were often prosperous and comfortable in their new homes.[27]

The relative economic comfort of Chinese American merchants in the Delta allowed families to grow and raise American-born children, as the Lums did when their daughters, Berda and Martha, were born in Rosedale in 1913 and 1915, respectively. Between 1900 and 1920, the Chinese American population in Mississippi increased to 364, a growth attributed to more settlement but also to a rising number of children born to Chinese immigrants in the state. In accordance with the Mississippi constitution of 1890, all children were to attend public schools, and throughout the early twentieth century the few Chinese Americans in Mississippi towns often attended the local white schools with few objections from white parents. As in other states, Mississippi state law segregated white students from colored students, but residents and school officials presumed "colored" to mean "black." Since Chinese American students were not black, they initially attended white schools throughout the Delta and the state. No school boards or state officials had formally ruled at this point that Chinese Americans were colored, and for Chinese American parents, sending their children to the white schools was not a choice as much as a reaction to Mississippi culture and racism. While the white schools were better-maintained than the colored schools and had obvious advantages for achieving a higher level of education, Chinese American parents' desires to keep their children out of the black schools also reflected the often uneasy tensions between Chinese and blacks in Mississippi. Although blacks were often customers at Chinese groceries and Chinese Americans willingly accepted their money, the relationship between the two races rarely went beyond that of clerk and customer. Chinese Americans were well aware of the stigma that African Americans carried, and, also aware of the prejudice against Asian Americans as demonstrated on the West Coast, they believed

Students and instructor Miss Mary Ethel Dismukes at the Greenville Chinese School, established by Superintendent E. E. Bass following his concern for the lack of education opportunities for Chinese Americans, March 29, 1938. *Courtesy of the Archives and Records Services Division, Mississippi Department of Archives and History.*

that generally avoiding personal interactions with African Americans was a smart strategy in the South. More personal relationships between Chinese Americans and African Americans developed, particularly among the early male Chinese settlers, who intermarried with black women in the Delta, but by the 1920s, such behavior was shunned by the Chinese American community. Chinese Americans who willingly entered into relationships with African Americans could expect to be ostracized by the rest of their small, tight-knit community, a fate that could spell social and economic ruin. One Chinese American woman explained that "there are two circles of Chinese in the town between which a decided line is drawn. The set who are 100 per cent Chinese do not associate with those who mingle with Negroes or intermarry with them."[28] Chinese American parents attempted to maintain the distance between themselves and African Americans by avoiding the colored schools. Their self-segregation was not so much an attempt to classify themselves as white as much as it was a way to be sure that they were not classified as black or colored by the rest of society. For Chinese Americans, their Orientalness took them far in Mississippi, and they tried to hold on to this status and the social and economic benefits it provided for as long as possible, be it through preserving their ethnic purity or by keeping their children away from the colored schools.

As Gong Lum would find out, however, sending his children to white schools became more difficult as the Chinese American population grew in the Delta. When the number of American-born Chinese in Mississippi increased, more whites noticed the subsequent increase in the number of Chinese Americans attending their schools. Although growth was modest, it was noticeable, and white parents grew wary of a potential Asian American population explosion on the model of the West Coast and increased interaction between their children and Chinese American students. White parents began to object to the presence of Chinese Americans in their children's schools, and principals and other school administrators noted the complaints. Rapidly, local schools began to classify Chinese Americans as colored and barred them from attending white institutions. In the case of young Martha Lum, the transformation from Oriental to colored happened not overnight but, rather, within a few hours.[29]

On September 2, 1924, Gong Lum's daughters, nine-year-old Martha and her older sister, Berda, prepared for their first day at the Rosedale Consolidated High School (a combination of elementary, junior high, and high school levels for white Rosedale residents). This was both Martha's and Berda's second year at Rosedale, and upon arriving at the school that morning, they registered and attended their first lessons. The day was uneventful until after lunch, when their teacher sent them to the main office, where Martha and Berda learned that they would have to return home because they could no longer attend Rosedale. Superintendent J. H. Nutt informed Martha and her sister that Rosedale was for white students, and since they were not white, they would have to attend the colored school. Martha and Berda began their school day as Chinese American or Oriental pupils and left as colored students.[30]

When Martha and Berda returned home and explained to their puzzled father and mother what had happened, Gong Lum and his wife became furious. What had changed? Martha and Berda were not colored when they left for school that morning. Also, Gong Lum's daughters had attended Rosedale Consolidated the year before with no problems. Gong Lum was a quiet man who tended to his own affairs and did not go looking for trouble, so he could not imagine any personal reasons for the school sending his children home. Perhaps the newly enacted Immigration Act of 1924, which barred Asians from entering the United States, combined with anti-Asian hysteria on the West Coast convinced the school officials that now Martha and Berda were of

Undated photo from the Works Progress Administration study of Chinese Americans in Mississippi depicting a Chinese Sunday school in Bolivar County, Mississippi. *Courtesy of the Archives and Records Services Division, Mississippi Department of Archives and History.*

a different ethnic or racial class. All he knew was that by kicking Martha and Berda out of the school, Superintendent Nutt declared them to be colored, which was an affront to Martha and Berda, their father, and their family's identity and respectability. While it is difficult to uncover Gong Lum's personal opinions on African Americans, his desire not to be considered colored and to continue sending his children to white schools demonstrates that Gong Lum was content with the level of tolerance that he received from both white and black residents of Rosedale. Now, however, the school's decision to send Martha and Berda home challenged his racial standing in the community and, as he would argue, his and his children's basic civil rights. Gong Lum began his three-year battle against the school's actions in 1924 and initiated a fight for Chinese American rights in the United States by challenging Mississippi's Jim Crow laws.[31]

Unlike later civil rights activists who would argue for school integration, Gong Lum's strategy rested on pursuing his own rights, not those for all minorities. He understood the ramifications for his family if they were designated as on par with African Americans. Gong Lum knew that he could never be seen as white in Mississippi, but he could legally fight to be seen as Chinese, a race not specifically mentioned in statewide segregation laws and unclassifiable according to Mississippi's binary racial system. In order to challenge Rosedale Consolidated, Gong Lum turned to respected law firm Brewer, Brewer, and McGeehee, based in nearby Clarksdale and known for taking on more controversial cases. As a noted merchant, Gong Lum was able to afford his attorneys and work closely with them to file a lawsuit against the Rosedale school board on October 29, 1924. Gong Lum's attorney chose to focus on Martha's right to attend Rosedale Consolidated, as she was the more "gifted" pupil among the two girls.[32]

Gong Lum and his attorneys appeared before Judge William Alcorn Jr. at the Circuit Court of Bolivar County on November 5 and presented an argument against the school board that emphasized Martha's right to attend white schools based on her ethnicity. Martha's citizenship was not in dispute. Both the judge and the Rosedale school board knew that the young girl was a citizen of both the United States and Mississippi and, as such, was entitled to a public education. What was at stake in this case was determining if Rosedale was correct in sending Martha home from the white school because she was supposedly colored. Gong Lum's attorneys argued that Martha was indeed not white, but she was also "not a member of the colored race nor is she of mixed blood, but she is of pure Chinese origin or descent" as well as a "good, clean, moral girl" and deserving of a just education. Because Martha was not colored, she did not belong in the colored school, and there were no schools established and maintained by Bolivar County solely for Chinese American children. By denying Martha admission, the Rosedale school board discriminated against her and denied her an education, which was a violation of the "privileges and immunities" granted to her under both the U.S. and the Mississippi state constitutions. The school board's actions also violated Martha's right to equal protection under the law as guaranteed by the Fourteenth Amendment. As was a Chinese American living in Mississippi, Martha's ethnicity allowed her to attend white schools, and her citizenship ensured her access to an education equal to that of other noncolored residents of Bolivar County and Mississippi. Gong Lum and his attorneys did not argue that Martha should be considered white (which would be impossible to prove) but, rather, that she was of "pure" Chinese descent and unqualified for the colored schools. Gong Lum and his lawyers also avoided using "Oriental" or "Asiatic" or any other terms that would group Martha with others of Asian descent. Her identity rested not on being seen as Oriental but as being seen by the court specifically as Chinese to prevent anyone from classifying her as part of the colored race. Martha's ethnicity bought her options that her race did not. Because "Chinese" was a classification that Mississippi state law did not address, Martha was uncolored. Socially and culturally, Chinese Americans may have desired to blend in with white society, but legally they were well aware that making such an argument for the sake of defying Jim Crow laws was foolish and unpromising.[33]

As Martha's father, Gong Lum also argued that the Rosedale school board violated his own rights and privileges as a Chinese national living in the United States. Although he was not a citizen, the Mississippi constitution, the U.S. Constitution, and previous treaties between China and the United States provided him with the right to send his daughter to school. Since the Rosedale school expelled Martha, Gong Lum was prevented from fulfilling his duty to the state of Mississippi by educating his children. In this instance, not only did Rosedale Consolidated force Gong Lum to violate Mississippi law, but it also denied him rights and privileges guaranteed by the Fourteenth Amendment. Gong Lum argued that he did not receive equal protection under the law when Rosedale Consolidated refused to admit his daughter. Because Rosedale was the only school in the area that Chinese American students could attend (since they were not colored, according to the plaintiffs), Gong Lum was not allowed to practice his fatherly duties and rights as did other parents who lived in Bolivar County.

Gong Lum also argued that as a Chinese immigrant, he held special privileges, beyond constitutional protections and rights, that were also violated by Rosedale Consolidated's decision. Gong Lum referred to rights "guaranteed ... by the treaties of the United States with the Chinese government." Although he did not specify, Gong Lum referenced the Burlingame Treaty, an 1868 agreement between the United States and China that granted "most favored nation" status to Chinese immigrants who came to America. This treaty ensured that like Americans living in China, Chinese in the United States would "enjoy entire liberty of conscience and shall be exempt from all disability or persecution on account of their religious faith or worship." While the religious lines of the treaty were designed to protect Christian missionaries and Americans living in China, there were also guarantees to protect Chinese against discrimination, exploitation, and violence in America. Rosedale Consolidated also violated, along with the general provisions of the Fourteenth Amendment, this treaty by denying specific rights granted to Chinese from the American government. While the Chinese Exclusion Act of 1882 was in effect by the time of the case, Gong Lum argued that the privileges and rights mentioned in the Burlingame Treaty still applied to Chinese who did live in the United States. Rosedale's decision to send Martha home not only went against Gong Lum's citizenship rights and duties but also undermined federal authority over the rights of Chinese immigrants.[34]

Gong Lum's contributions as a taxpayer to the state of Mississippi also played a role in his case. Public schools in Mississippi were funded by a combination of poll taxes, property taxes, and other various taxes at the time. Gong Lum did not vote or pay a poll tax, but he did pay property and business taxes that contributed to the state and local funds for education. Because he was a taxpayer and helped to maintain Rosedale Consolidated, he was entitled to send his daughter there regardless of her ethnicity. As a working and contributing resident, Gong Lum had economic rights for providing Martha with an education. A denial of his right to do so would be to discount the role of Lum in the local economy, which ordinarily few others in Rosedale would object to. Gong Lum was a productive, taxpaying, and law-abiding member of society, an identity that, similar to the emphasis on Martha's good and moral character, Gong Lum and his attorneys emphasized in order to downplay any suspicion or prejudice that might be harbored against the Lums because they were Chinese.[35]

In response to Gong Lum's claims, Superintendent Nutt, the other members of the Rosedale Consolidated school board, and the superintendent of education of the state of Mississippi insisted that they had done nothing wrong or illegal by dismissing Martha. E. C. Sharp, the assistant attorney general of Mississippi, represented the school board in court and argued that "the complainant is a member of the Mongolian, or yellow race, and therefore, not entitled to attend the schools provided by the law in the State of Mississippi for the children of the white, or Caucasian race."[36] Here Martha was not Chinese (as her father hoped she would be seen by the court) but, rather, "Mongolian," making her clearly not white and therefore unqualified to attend Rosedale Consolidated. She may not have been colored in the sense of being black, but according to Sharp and the school board, she was colored as part of the "yellow" race. While Gong Lum was fighting to have his daughter recognized as Chinese rather than colored, Sharp relied on convincing the court that Martha's Chineseness made her colored. Because Martha was colored, the school board's decision to send Martha home and prohibit her return was a "full, complete, and adequate remedy at law," and to do otherwise would be "contrary to the statutes and violation of the constitution of the State of Mississippi."[37] If the school board allowed Martha to go to school at Rosedale, it would be committing an illegal act under Mississippi law that forbade colored children from attending white schools. Plus, there was "within the reach of Martha, and accessible to her, a school of equal facilities and advantages which she might attend."[38] The school board's defense rested on proving that Martha was not Chinese but, rather, colored, and thus the school board simply followed the proper procedure for ensuring segregation.

Judge Alcorn ruled in favor of Martha Lum. The court determined that Martha was not a member of the colored race under Mississippi law, and therefore she was entitled to attend the white school, particularly because there were no publicly funded schools for Chinese American students in the state. Simply put, Rosedale was "the only school conducted in the said district available to her as a pupil," and to deny her admission would be to deny her the rights and privileges guaranteed to her by the Fourteenth Amendment. The court also called into question Rosedale's initial agreement to let Martha attend the school and then their sudden dismissal of the girl, pointing out irregularities in the reasoning of the school board. The Bolivar County Circuit Court recognized that Martha was Chinese American, was not colored, and therefore was allowed to attend Rosedale in spite of the school board's erroneous decision.

Gong Lum's success in Bolivar County was similar to that of the Tape family in 1885. Two Chinese immigrants, Joseph Tape and Mary Tape, became furious when the San Francisco school board prevented their daughter, Mamie Tape, from attending the local white school. In response, the Tapes sued the school board and won their case: Mamie was allowed to attend the white school because California state law only listed "filthy or vicious habits" and "contagious or infection diseases" as reasons for prohibiting a student from attending a school. Mamie Tape possessed neither of these qualities, and when the school board appealed the lower court's decision to the California Supreme Court, the higher court upheld the ruling in favor of the Tapes. Gong Lum's insistence that his daughter was of good character and a pure girl reflected some of the anxieties that Chinese American parents had when it came to their children being perceived as dirty or foul. For Gong Lum, however, his success in proving that his daughter was Chinese and not colored is what led to a favorable ruling.[39]

While the Bolivar County Court's decision was a victory for Gong Lum, it was not a victory for all Chinese Americans in Mississippi and certainly not a victory for all Asian Americans. This case focused specifically on Martha Lum and her right or lack thereof to attend a white school. Geography, demographics, and her father's ability and desire to hire a legal team to fight on her behalf were contributing factors to this case, possibly more so than race. The Chinese American community in Rosedale was small, Gong Lum held a certain amount of economic standing in the community, and the white residents typically tolerated his presence. He had the means to hire an attorney and the social capital to use the court system to his advantage in order to send his daughter to a white school. Gong Lum fought for Martha and his own personal rights and privileges as a Chinese immigrant with an American-born child living in the South; he did not fight for all Asian Americans or even all Chinese. Gong Lum did not so much wish to challenge the system of segregated education in Mississippi as much as he wished to challenge the racial classification of his daughter. Similar to African Americans who initiated lawsuits for private property, educational access, and other rights prior to *Brown v. Board*, Gong Lum was an individual with his own series of complaints directed toward the Rosedale school board. An affront to his daughter's Chineseness was an attack on his own standing in the community. If white schools in Bolivar County continued to admit Chinese American students following Gong Lum's case, then the court's decision might usher in more opportunities for minority students; however, Gong Lum's victory at the moment was his alone.[40]

Unfortunately, Gong Lum's justice would be short lived. Following the decision on the Lum case, state attorney general Rush Knox filed an appeal on the Bolivar County Court decision and was granted a motion to advance before the supreme court of Mississippi in January 1925. Knox argued that Alcorn's decision should be reconsidered as soon as possible because "many children are now being prevented from attending their schools" as a result of Martha's readmission to Rosedale Consolidated.[41] Knox's concern for the white children of Rosedale stemmed from the outrage of white parents over the county court's ruling. An article from the *Bolivar Democrat* described the resentment growing among Rosedale residents not only for the court's trying to "force the white children of Mississippi to share their schools with the Chinese" but also for the colored schools who refused to accept Chinese American students.[42] White parents argued that Assistant Attorney General Sharp's arguments in the original case overruled the Bolivar County Court's decision and that Judge Alcorn had greatly misread the situation and underestimated the potential problems of allowing Chinese American children to attend school with whites. While there are few written sources that fully explain the specific reasons why white parents objected so vehemently to Chinese Americans in white schools, the general arguments rested on upholding the law and a sudden shift in seeing Chinese Americans as colored as soon as their population increased. Few newspapers or other sources reveal anti-Asian sentiments or fears over land or job competition from Chinese Americans. The backlash against the Bolivar County Court's decision was a reaction to a challenge to the white racial, political, and social order in Mississippi. Preventing Martha from attending Rosedale Consolidated was about finally determining the legal and racial standing of Chinese Americans as well as maintaining lily-white schools. The Rosedale school board's decision to pursue an appeal represented the frustrations of the white community as well as the school's disagreement with the lower court's ruling.[43]

When the case finally reached the supreme court of Mississippi in March 1925, the judges issued a unanimous overturn of the lower court's ruling. According to the state supreme court, Judge Alcorn greatly erred in his support of the Lums. Not only did Alcorn expect the Rosedale school board to go against Mississippi law by allowing Martha to attend Rosedale Consolidated, but Alcorn also incorrectly concluded that Martha was not colored. Under the state's miscegenation laws, marriages between whites and persons of at least one-eighth Asian blood were prohibited. Therefore, as the supreme court argued, Chinese Americans were legally colored. This legal racial classification naturally carried over to education, making Martha ineligible to attend Rosedale Consolidated. The purpose of segregated schools was to "preserve the integrity and purity of the white race," and the state was not legally obligated to provide separate schools for all races. The only option for Martha and other Chinese American students in the state was to attend a colored school or be privately tutored. There was no argument that Martha deserved a public education as an American and Mississippi citizen; however, that education, under existing Jim Crow laws, would not be provided in a white school.[44]

Still, Gong Lum would not rest with this decision and appealed the Mississippi Supreme Court's decision to the Supreme Court of the United States in 1927. While Martha was privately tutored by friends of the family in Rosedale, her father worked with local attorneys Earl Brewer (also a former governor of Mississippi) and J. Flowers to craft an argument that would center on Martha's loss of rights and privileges to an education because of the state supreme court's ruling. Brewer was especially interested in cases resting on the Fourteenth Amendment's protections for racial minorities and eagerly took to interrogating and investigating Gong Lum's plight (although Gong Lum was more concerned with how the Fourteenth Amendment upheld *his* rights as a Chinese man living in the South).[45] The goal was to convince the U.S. Supreme Court that the state had violated basic Fourteenth Amendment rights by defining Martha as colored and to prove that Martha was allowed to go to the white school because she was Chinese ethnically. Because there were no publicly funded schools for Chinese Americans, Martha was unable to attend school in Mississippi, forcing Gong Lum to renege on his duties as a parent. Gong Lum and his attorneys presented their appeal to the Court in the hopes that a ruling in favor of Martha and the rights of Chinese Americans to attend white schools would result.[46]

Gong Lum's hopes would once again be short lived. In November 1927, the U.S. Supreme Court upheld the ruling of the Mississippi Supreme Court, establishing a precedent that would shape hearings on school segregation through the *Brown v. Board* decision. Chief Justice William Taft delivered the opinion of the Court and explained, first, that "the right and power of the state to regulate the method of providing for the education of its youth at public expense is clear," drawing on the 1899 *Cumming v. Richmond County Board of Education* decision that affirmed the state's right to oversee its own system of public education.[47] Second, the justices turned to the problem of whether or not the state's classification of Martha as colored denied her rights and privileges accorded by the Fourteenth Amendment. The Court ruled that all Chinese Americans were members of the "yellow" race and, as such, were correctly classified as "colored" in Mississippi, thereby negating the argument that Martha's basic rights to an education were in jeopardy. For the Court, this was a relatively straightforward issue, stemming from *Plessy v. Ferguson* and the separate-but-equal doctrine that governed any disputes that arose over the years in relation to school segregation. The Court did not find the debate over whether or not Martha's classification as colored and its subsequent effect on her education and rights to be unique. "Were this a new question, it would call for very full argument and consideration, but we think that it is the same question which has been many times decided to be within the constitutional power of the state legislature."[48] While Martha's case was different in that it involved a member of the "yellow" race, the Court stated that there was no indication that "the question is any different or that any different result can be reached, assuming the cases above cited to be rightly decided, where the issue is as between white pupils and the pupils of the yellow races." In its decision on the *Lum v. Rice* case, the Supreme Court declared that Chinese Americans were yellow, that they could be classified as colored, and that education was a state's right and the state could deal with its own system of public education accordingly.[49]

With a swift stroke of the pen, Gong Lum's fight came to an end, and the U.S. Supreme Court established a groundbreaking precedent in relation to Asian Americans and school segregation in the South. Prior cases involving Asian Americans had rested on determining issues of citizenship and/or property rights rather than racial status. In 1886, the Supreme Court heard the case of laundry owner Yick Wo, who fell victim to a San Francisco tax targeting Chinese immigrants, and the justices concluded that a law that was "race-neutral" but prejudicially enacted violated basic Fourteenth Amendment rights. Such a ruling did not hold up in Gong Lum's case because segregation was applied equally to all who lived in Mississippi. Although the federal courts previously declared in 1878 that Mongolians were not Caucasians, there was a wide variety of definitions of "Mongolian" that left loopholes and questions pertaining to which groups of Asian Americans fell under this racial classification. The only other cases that specifically addressed the issue of race were *Ozawa v. United States* (1922) and *United States v. Bhagat Singh Thind* (1923). Both Ozawa (a Japanese immigrant) and Thind (an Indian immigrant) argued that Japanese and Hindus were Caucasians and deserved the right to naturalization, a right they were barred from under the Naturalization Act of 1906. However, the Court ruled in both instances that Asians are not white and therefore were ineligible to become citizens. With Gong Lum, the Court once and for all determined that Asians were "yellow" and therefore "colored." As Gong Lum found out, legally there were no "in-between" or "interstitial" identities in this case: For Mississippi and the Supreme Court you were either colored or you were white.[50]

"MOST FAVORED" IMMIGRANTS IN JIM CROW MISSISSIPPI

Following Gong Lum's failed attempts in the courts, another lesser-known case wended its way through the Mississippi court system in 1927. While Gong Lum and his family packed up and moved to Elaine, Arkansas, following the Supreme Court's decision, other Chinese living in Mississippi, including fourteen-year-old Joe Tin Lun and his family, continued to fight for access to white schools. Unlike Martha Lum, Joe Tin Lun was an immigrant from China and had arrived in the United States with his merchant family in the years immediately after World War I. The Luns settled in Dublin, Mississippi (not far from Rosedale in the Delta), and privately tutored their son until the beginning of the 1917 school year, when they wished to enroll him in Dublin Consolidated High School, which was maintained for white students. Undeterred by Gong Lum's failed attempts, the Luns believed that their situation would be different: They lived outside Rosedale and they were Chinese immigrants with basic rights and protections. Regardless of whether or not the state had previously ruled that Chinese were colored, the Luns were immigrants, they were Chinese nationals, and they therefore were governed by a different set of federal policies than Martha Lum. Much to their surprise, Dublin school superintendent H. P. Taylor did not agree with them and immediately dismissed Joe Tin Lun's application for enrollment in late August 1927 and advised him to go to the nearest colored school.[51]

In retaliation, the Luns enlisted Joe Tij Fung, a local legal advisor to the Chinese American community and friend, to file a writ of mandamus forcing the school to admit their son. Whereas Gong Lum only listed his rights as a Chinese immigrant in passing in his appeal, Tij Fung crafted his legal argument for Lun's right to attend Dublin on the centrality of the Burlingame Treaty. Tij Fung argued that Lun was "not granted the privilege of most favored nation in accordance with the Burlingame Treaty," particularly Article 7, which states that "Chinese subjects shall enjoy all . . . of the public educational institutions under the government of the United States."[52] Because the Dublin schools failed to admit Lun, there existed clear proof that Taylor discriminated against Chinese children and failed to uphold the main tenets of international agreements between China and the United States. Unlike the Lum case, Tij Fung maintained that this was an issue that rested on foreign diplomacy, and Lun and other Chinese immigrants were not beholden to the same Jim Crow laws as American-born children such as Martha Lum.[53] Interestingly, the Coahoma County Court granted Tij Fung the mandamus and ordered Taylor to admit Joe Tin Lun.

The county court's decision did not rest well with Taylor. He responded by enlisting the help of Assistant Attorney General Sharp and State Superintendent of Education W. P. Bond in appealing the decision to the supreme court of Mississippi. Taylor dismissed Tij Fung's argument that Lun's rights under the Burlingame Treaty had been violated. Dublin Consolidated did not deny Lun an education; it merely followed previously established laws and procedures when dealing with colored children. Although Taylor admitted that "the type of instruction [at the colored school] is very much inferior to the white school," he explained that this was because Dublin Consolidated benefited from an extra tax levy in addition to regular funding and that, if they chose to do so, colored schools could also consolidate and achieve additional resources. "Negroes were not possessed with such qualifications as whites and therefore their teachers do not rank with white teachers," but at bare minimum, they were licensed and assigned the same books as the white schools. As a result, Lun would be at a minor disadvantage if he attended a colored school, but all things taken equally, he would receive a state- and locally funded education. Lun's rights under the Burlingame Treaty had not been violated because he received the same treatment as colored American citizens. There were perfectly fine schools for colored students to attend, and it would be erroneous to treat Lun differently than other colored children born in the United States.[54]

Tij Fung's rebuttal returned to the issue of the funding of Mississippi schools. As a provision of the Land Ordinance Act of 1785, the federal government provided plots of land to be used for education in what would later become the state of Mississippi. Each plot was 360 acres and became known in Mississippi as Sixteenth Section Lands. These lands were overseen by the Mississippi secretary of state, but school boards served as the trustees. Sixteenth Section schools received their funding from typical sources, including property and poll taxes, but Tij Fung argued that because Dublin Consolidated was a Sixteenth Section institution and such schools were technically a legacy of the 1785 land ordinance, the federal government had the final word in the maintenance and operation of the school. The history of the Sixteenth Section program meant that federal law overrode state and local laws, making the Burlingame Treaty applicable to this situation and Lun qualified to attend Dublin Consolidated as a "most favored" immigrant. Tij Fung also incorrectly claimed that Sixteenth Section schools were the benefactors of federal funding and were beholden to the federal government, not merely the Mississippi state government.[55]

The supreme court of Mississippi was unimpressed by Tij Fung's legal arguments. First, as far as the court was concerned, the question of whether or not Chinese Americans could attend white schools had been settled with *Lum v. Rice*. Chinese Americans, regardless of their citizenship status, were colored and therefore were entitled to an education at the colored schools. The purpose of separate schools for white and colored students in Mississippi was to "prevent amalgamation and to preserve, as far as possible, the social system of race segregation."[56] By refusing to admit Lun, the Dublin Consolidated school board was complying with Mississippi state law, which guaranteed a basic education at either school for citizens. Lun, "as a Chinaman," was certainly entitled to an education under the law, but he was only entitled to a colored education—nothing more, nothing less. If Lun was able to attend a colored school, "then, how can an alien Chinaman complain when he is assigned to a school provided, under our law for the colored races?" Joe Tin Lun was not deprived of any Fourteenth Amendment rights; the state of Mississippi was generous enough to permit him to "enjoy all of the benefits and privileges" accorded to citizens of the United States and Mississippi.[57]

Second, the court found Tij Fung's argument that Lun deserved special treatment because he was a Chinese immigrant to be weak and unfounded. Not only did Lun basically receive special treatment because he benefited from the same rights to an education as colored citizens of Mississippi, but Tij Fung misunderstood the relationship between the state and federal governments. States maintained the right to regulate education under the Tenth Amendment to the U.S. Constitution because it was not specifically mentioned in the document, and under Mississippi law, local governments operated and oversaw the functions of schools. The court corrected Tij Fung's assumption that because Dublin Consolidated was a Sixteenth Section school it was maintained by federal entities. Sixteenth Section schools did not receive federal funding and were the responsibility of local school boards, who could regulate their students as they saw fit. Lun had the right to "institute proper proceedings to require the school authorities to furnish a colored school equal and uniform, in every particular, for the colored race," but that is where his rights ended in terms of challenging the segregated system of education in Mississippi. Lun's status as an immigrant did little to convince the court that he had the right to attend a white school, because the court did not believe that "alien Chinamen" deserved any special treatment above or beyond what colored citizens in the state received. The Burlingame Treaty, created prior to the Chinese Exclusion Act, was not the Gentlemen's Agreement, although it is difficult to determine if the state of Mississippi would have issued a different ruling if this case had involved a Japanese immigrant.[58]

The supreme court of Mississippi did not see a difference between Martha Lum and Joe Tin Lun. Citizenship in this situation meant little, and an American-born child and a Chinese immigrant faced the same fate because they were legally colored. "The testimony of the county superintendent of education in this case shows that equal facilities are furnished to the two races, white and colored, and, in our opinion, that is all that is required under the Fourteenth Amendment. In its main features, this case is on 'all fours' with the case of *Rice v. Gong Lum, supra*."[59] The court also used the Lun case as an opportunity to affirm the opinion that school segregation was "designed to promote the peace, quietude, and happiness of all the races, by eliminating close and intimate contact, during the hot season of youth, between the white and colored races, so that the prejudices and passions engendered by race consciousness might be avoided," as if educating Tij Fung, an alien, on the power and purpose of the Mississippi system that promoted a "higher degree of peace and happiness."[60] Perhaps aware of the failure of Gong Lum's federal Supreme Court case, Tij Fung did not attempt to appeal the state supreme court's overturn of the mandamus granted by the Coahoma County Court, confirming Mississippi's views that Chinese were colored, that attempts to argue for their rights based on ethnicity or immigrant status were futile, and that Asian Americans deserved discrimination at the hands of local school boards.[61]

Gong Lum's and Joe Tin Lun's attempts to fight the segregation of Chinese Americans in southern education were not so much lead-ups to the future battles found in the *Brown v. Board* decision as they were unique results of the meeting of Jim Crow and immigration and ethnicity. Both Lum and Lun tried to argue their way around discrimination by invoking special immigrant privileges (in the Lun case) and citizenship based on birth and "good moral character" (in the Lum case). Martha Lum's citizenship did not work in her favor, just as Joe Tin Lun's special privileges under the Burlingame Treaty did not convince the courts that he deserved to attend the white school. These were not simple cases that came down to the Fourteenth Amendment or even basic rights, but rather, they were complicated scenarios that highlighted the holes in segregation policies as well as the perpetual foreignness of Chinese Americans in the South. Chinese Americans in these cases did not form a united front, choosing instead to take on the system of southern segregation individually through different strategies. As a result, the courts did not rule in favor of Gong Lum and Joe Tin Lun, and these cases would not necessarily pave the way for the later *Brown* decision. However, they served as examples of the limits of citizenship, ethnic identity, and policy privileges for Chinese Americans and the power of southern law over immigration policies.

Following the rulings on the Lum and Lun cases, the options Chinese Americans had for receiving an education in the South were limited. There were reports from Chinese Americans that colored schools would not accept their children, but there were also Chinese parents like the Lums who chose to relocate to nearby Arkansas or Tennessee, where Chinese Americans were allowed to attend white schools. Other parents sent their children to live with friends or other family members farther north or even back West instead of subjecting them to the black schools. A more popular choice, however, was either to hire private tutors if they were affordable and available or to create Chinese American schools for their children to attend. Because Mississippi did not offer any state funding for Chinese schools, members of the Chinese American community would often pool their resources to purchase old buildings and hire teachers. Others in the Delta, such as the Chinese Americans of Greenville, received assistance from the local Baptist churches and created Chinese mission schools. In 1930, Greenville school superintendent E. E. Bass expressed concern for the Chinese verbally (although not enough to admit them into his school), though not financially, and encouraged Chinese parents to establish schools for their children. The Chinese Mission School in

Greenville became one of the most well-known institutions in the region, with Chinese parents from around the Delta sending their children to Greenville to live in dormitories in order to receive what they identified as a proper "white" education. The school in Greenville was staffed by two white teachers who were assigned to different age groups, and the students learned the standard Mississippi curriculum (English composition and reading and basic math skills) in the morning and Chinese language in the afternoon (taught by local community members). Many Chinese Americans joined the Baptist church in Greenville and had good relations with the white members who did not object to lending money if it meant forming a separate school for Chinese Americans. In other instances, Chinese Americans established their own churches and used a designated room for daily school instruction. Although the state of Mississippi and the U.S. Supreme Court ruled that Chinese Americans were colored, Chinese Americans disagreed, formed their own schools, and continued to function in a social state that existed between white and black.[62]

By the late 1930s, however, Chinese Americans living in the Delta had gone through a fascinating racial transformation, from "colored" to "Chinese" in the eyes of Mississippians within just a few years. When fighting between China and Japan broke out in 1937 over the territory of Manchuria, many Americans sympathized with the Chinese and identified them as the benevolent victims of an aggressive, expansionist, and belligerent Japan. American sympathy for China transformed perception of Chinese immigrants and Chinese Americans. Between the 1920s and the 1930s, the Chinese went from being part of a yellow peril to being brave, courageous, and hardworking people attempting to carve out a living for themselves in the United States. Such attitudes did not translate into total acceptance among Americans, but in the Delta, the idea of welcoming Chinese American children into white schools became more appealing and acceptable to some. The small Delta town of Louise was one of the first to integrate schools between whites and Chinese in 1939, and other schools followed suit; but not all white townsfolk were immediately thrilled. In 1941 when the Clarksdale school board members weighed the possibility of admitting the handful of Chinese American students who lived in town, white parents responded with petitions requesting that "no person or child or children of the Chinese or Mongolian race" be allowed to attend school with their white children.[63] The parents were concerned that the school board had forgotten that although the Chinese were suffering at the hands of the Japanese across the Pacific, their friends and family living in the United States were still Mongolian. The petition "respectfully invite[d]" the school board to return its attention to the ruling of the supreme court of Mississippi in the Lum case and questioned whether or not the superintendent remembered the tenets of that decision.[64]

While the white parents argued that the Chinese of Clarksdale were still colored no matter what transpired in Asia, local white clergy counterprotested by writing letters to the school board arguing on behalf of Chinese Americans in their community and their desire to attend white schools. In such letters, the petitioners (similar to the argument Gong Lum presented before the U.S. Supreme Court), argued that their parishioners were *Chinese*, a distinct ethnic, rather than racial, group. N. D. Timmerman, pastor of the Clarksdale Baptist Church, wrote on behalf of Mrs. Henry Jue and her daughter May, who wished to attend the Clarksdale public schools. Timmerman explained that Mrs. Jue and May regularly attended the Clarksdale Baptist Church with other white members and that they "are a distinct and particular Chinese family" that deserved to be in the public schools with white children.[65] When public sympathies for the Chinese were turning as a response to Pacific and rising international tensions in the wake of World War II, Timmerman argued that the Jues and other Chinese in Clarksdale were not colored but ethnic. Their courageous stand against the Japanese proved them to be an honest, strong, and hardworking strain of Orientals. In other words, the ruling of the supreme court of Mississippi was incorrect and out of touch with the present: Chinese Americans were ethnically Chinese. The Clarksdale school board agreed in 1941 to allow Chinese to attend white schools, signifying a shift in the way Mississippi society viewed Chinese Americans when it came to education. Also, in 1938, the Greenville, Mississippi, school district established a public Chinese school (staffed by white teachers) that operated with funds from the state. By the late 1930s, Chinese Americans were no longer colored; they had taken on the distinct ethnic identity of being Chinese, which allowed them to move into white schools or attend state-funded schools that did not serve black or "colored" children. Well before blacks could attend school with whites in Mississippi, Chinese Americans were able to do so (in spite of rulings stating otherwise at the state and federal levels) with the assistance of those who could attest to their ethnically "pure" Chineseness in a segregated society.[66]

It would be far too simple to argue, however, that Mississippians and Mississippi law accepted Chinese American students as white because they could attend white schools in some Delta towns and cities by the late 1930s. The reality was that the Chinese racial and ethnic identity was still somewhat in flux by World War II. Opinions on Chinese Americans did begin to change once the fighting between China and Japan broke out and China allied with the United States during World War II. While Japanese Americans were imprisoned in internment camps following Pearl Harbor and racist political cartoons and propaganda furthered the anti-Japanese hysteria that existed along the West Coast and elsewhere across the country, Chinese Americans in Delta towns like Greenville, Clarksdale, Louise, and Gong Lum's Rosedale became more accepted in certain areas of local life. Japanese Americans imprisoned in the Rohwer and Jerome detention centers in nearby Arkansas received less-than-welcoming receptions from Governor Homer Adkins and other residents who viewed them as dangerous traitors and "Jap fiends." At the same time, Chinese Americans in Greenwood, Mississippi, in 1941 were officially welcomed into the white public schools. But they were not accepted because the school board or the residents considered them any closer to being "white" than they were before the war broke out. In 1942, a Chinese American mother who lived outside Cleveland, Mississippi, petitioned the local school board to let her daughter attend the white school because gas was rationed during the war and she did not have the resources to drive to the nearest Chinese mission school in Greenville. Despite the mother's position, the school board denied admission to her daughter, and the mother became upset: "We were law-abiding people, so we didn't fight them. I just couldn't understand it. The *Bok Guey* [whites] would take our money to build a church or something, but they wouldn't let us go to their schools. It was unfair, that's all. But we had to hold back our bitterness."[67] In other school districts in the Delta and across Mississippi, Chinese valor in the face of Japanese threats across the Pacific did little to help the Chinese Americans living in the South come closer to being considered white. The issue of Chinese American segregation in Mississippi schools became a transpacific concern for the Chinese government during the war. Not only did Chinese consulates across the country petition Mississippi governor Theodore Bilbo to force white schools to admit Chinese students, but Madame Chiang Kai-shek, first lady of the Republic of China, traveled to Jackson to speak before the Mississippi legislature in 1942 to urge school districts statewide to recognize the rights of Chinese Americans to attend white schools.[68] There was no uniformity in policies regarding Chinese Americans attending white schools during the war, and in many cases, Mississippians still considered Chinese Americans as colored.

Even though some white schools admitted Chinese American students during the war, their reasoning does not provide proof that they saw Chinese Americans as being closer to white than they were before. In fact, school boards identified them as more Chinese than ever, an ethnic identity that distinguished them from African Americans but still prevented them from being accepted as white. In 1945, the Greenville school district decided to admit Chinese American students to the white schools after meeting with local Chinese American community and religions leaders. The board made it clear, however, that "Chinese residents of the Greenville district only will be admitted to the schools and a strict understanding was had concerning racial strains, only native children of pure blood being considered. None other will be permitted."[69] President of the school board Henry Starling informed parents and Greenville residents that "the children of native Chinese strain are pupils of high scholastic and character standards" and that "it is purely a matter of democracy" that the Greenville schools admit "pure" Chinese students during a time when America was fighting for liberty and democracy abroad. Starling played upon concepts put forth by proponents of the Double V Campaign, who urged Americans to fight for a victory against fascism abroad and a victory against fascism (in the form of discrimination and racism) at home. For Starling and other school administrators who agreed with him, the war and China's role in it made it difficult for schools to deny access to Chinese American students—but only American-born, ethnically "pure" Chinese would be accommodated. In other words, schools could still deny admission to Chinese immigrants and to Chinese who may be the products of mixed racial relationships, from either white/Chinese or white/black marriages and relationships. Such measures were more than likely meant to work in cooperation with the state antimiscegenation laws that barred interracial marriages, but they also clarified the school board's beliefs that American-born children of pure Chinese stock were scholastically prepared to attend white schools (something akin to a forerunner of the model minority myth).[70]

One could argue that by admitting Chinese Americans to the white schools, the officials and citizens of Greenville accepted Chinese Americans and began the process of "whitening" them; however, to do so overlooks the fact that the designation of "pure" Chinese created yet another ethnic and racial category that further separated Chinese Americans from whites. The pureness of the Greenville Chinese denoted that they were not colored, but that same pureness separated them from Caucasians. Increased tolerance did not translate to a complete assimilation for Chinese or other Asian Americans, despite the new and more inclusive practices in education during World War II. The Greenville school board's decision only reified the "otherness" and Orientalness of Chinese Americans; it did not make them "white." Gong Lum's argument that Martha should attend white Rosedale Consolidated based on her pure Chineseness would, in the end, convince school districts to accept Chinese American students. Gong Lum's reasoning lacked only the war to encourage school boards to see his point of view.

In the Delta, Chinese Americans could only go so far in arguing for their unique position in the South and the accompanying benefits. Outside influences such as the war and changing international relations would help school officials to finally heed the call of Chinese American parents and community leaders to integrate Chinese American students into white schools. By 1950, white schools across Mississippi had opened their doors to Chinese American students, while black students were still relegated to colored schools. However, outside schools, Chinese Americans still faced isolation and stigmas from both black and white neighbors and residents. As more Chinese Americans were born in the Delta and came of age, the level of toleration among whites rose, but discrimination or other more social and cultural forms of segregation did not completely end. Many Chinese Americans who received education degrees from universities such as Delta State in Cleveland, Mississippi, and Mississippi State wanted to work in the Mississippi public education system but were often denied such opportunities. One woman described an interview with a Greenville superintendent for a teaching position in 1956 as a "slap in the face" when he told her that she could not teach in the white schools because those jobs were reserved for Caucasians.[71] Another qualified candidate for a teaching position in Jackson, Mississippi, was denied an opportunity for an interview because despite his special certifications, the Jackson schools would "never hire anyone like [him]" because he was Chinese.[72] In other cases, students who were eventually accepted into white schools during the 1950s remembered "always [being] singled out because of race" and never being fully accepted socially by their white peers and their teachers.[73] "Chineseness" was an evolving racial category that even the Chinese themselves were not entirely capable of defining in the face of Jim Crow segregation and Mississippi law.

BEING NONCOLORED AND NONBLACK IN GEORGIA

Compared with Gong Lum, the Chinese Americans of Augusta, Georgia, serve as an example of the more successful strategy of Chinese Americans assuming a nonblack or noncolored rather than Chinese status. Similar to Mississippi's, Georgia's codes on miscegenation were clear in that the terms "Mongolian" and "Asiatics" were added to a ban on interracial marriage in 1927. However, this language did not extend to school segregation laws. Georgia lawmakers made school segregation official in 1872 when they passed a Jim

Crow law establishing separate white and colored schools. As more Chinese merchants settled in Georgia towns and cities during the late nineteenth and early twentieth centuries, their children presented a new challenge to the ban on integrated schools. At first, local school boards decided for themselves whether or not Chinese American children could attend white schools, but this method created wide variations in allowances for integrated schools with Chinese American and white students. The vagueness of the Georgia laws on school segregation created holes in Jim Crow education in the state that legislators attempted to manipulate and fill. These legal maneuvers came to a head in 1931 when the Augusta school board and state representatives decided to take up the question on whether or not Chinese Americans were colored. White parents, however, urged local school officials to consider the nonblack status of Chinese Americans, rather than their Chineseness as Gong Lum had done, and allow Chinese American children to attend white schools statewide. Remaining isolated from racial or ethnic distinction was the social survival tool of the Chinese Americans in Augusta and enabled them to exist independently of racial classification in Georgia until the 1920s.[74]

During the late nineteenth century, the presence of Chinese in the state of Georgia raised little concern among whites, particularly with regard to education. The earliest wave of Chinese migration to the Peach State followed the Civil War, when investors and merchants in Augusta set about rebuilding an existing canal in 1869. Manual labor was needed, since slaves were not an option, and similar to planters in the Mississippi Delta who acquired Chinese as cheap employees, construction companies sought out Chinese from the West Coast as well as southern cities like New Orleans to come to Augusta.[75] In November 1873, 35 Chinese came from Indianapolis to Augusta with the assistance of labor contractors to begin work on the canal. By 1875, 165 Chinese laborers resided in Augusta, and residents reacted cautiously to the newcomers, intrigued by their "child-like" and "effeminate" appearance and "celestial" customs and culture. Articles in the *Augusta Chronicle* marveled at the ability of the Chinese to be thrifty with their $35-a-month salary and even argued that "some of us 'outside barbarians' could learn to subsist on such sums."[76] Augustans greeted the initial Chinese laborers who arrived in their city with an Orientalist appreciation of their exotic culture and awe at their hardworking and responsible nature.

In Augusta and in other towns and cities in Georgia, the Chinese American population increased slightly through the late 1800s, as did the tensions between whites and the "Asiatics." Workers completed the Augusta canal in 1875, and although many Chinese returned to the West Coast after collecting their pay, others remained in the city. Similar to the Chinese laborers who erected groceries in the Mississippi Delta when planters no longer required their services, Chinese Americans who chose to settle permanently in Augusta turned to business ventures and filled a niche in the local economy. By 1880, there were five Chinese-operated groceries catering to both white and black clientele. Most Chinese Americans lived above their stores by themselves if they were bachelors or with their families if they married in the United States or later brought their wives and/or children from China. The Augusta Chinese Americans resided in the black neighborhoods and therefore generally avoided confrontations with local whites. The Chinese were economically accepted until the 1880s, when more Chinese migrated to cities such as Savannah and Macon to take advantage of business opportunities and a thriving Chinese American community. Many of the new Chinese migrants established groceries in addition to laundries, but their presence became more problematic when William Loo Chong, an immigrant Chinese merchant from Augusta, moved to nearby Waynesboro, Georgia, with his white wife, Denise Fulcher. Loo Chong, a respected and wealthy tea merchant, married Fulcher in Augusta in 1882 and set about enlisting the help of Fulcher's relatives to open a farmer's market and grocery store in Waynesboro. When Waynesboro residents found out that Loo Chong was married to a local white woman, they "Ku Klux Klanned" him by boycotting his business and threatening him with violence.[77] Loo Chong relocated with his wife to Augusta, but his willingness to cross the racial line reflected rising tensions between the white and Chinese American populations of the city and surrounding towns. Although there were only forty-one Chinese Americans in Augusta by the early 1900s, the relatively small increase in Chinese Americans throughout the late nineteenth century incited fear of further interracial mixing. By crossing the racial line, Loo Chong broke the level of tolerance that Augustans had granted to Chinese Americans.

In 1882, legislators in Georgia supported the passage of the Chinese Exclusion Act in hopes that it would stem the tide of the "Mongolian pests" and their tastes for drugs and polygamy. The exclusionary act as well as Loo Chong's marriage inspired, for the first time, negative reactions to Chinese Americans from Georgia residents throughout the 1880s. In 1885, white merchants argued that Chinese American businessmen created unfair competition by catering to the "ignorant" classes (the poor and African Americans) and urged the Augusta city council to stop issuing business permits to Chinese Americans who resided there. The city council denied the request, but reactions to the presence of the Chinese Americans and their attempts to merge into white life resulted in other legal protests. In 1884, legislators (with the backing of Augusta residents) attempted to alter the 1865 Georgia antimiscegenation law that prohibited white and black marriages to include provisions for "marriages between persons of Mongolian descent and persons of the white race."[78] Just like the call for limiting the business ventures of Chinese Americans in Augusta, the bill to include Asian Americans in the antimiscegenation law failed to pass in the Georgia House of Representatives because outside Richmond County (Augusta's location) there were not enough Chinese men to rouse ire or suspicion. The Loo Chong incident and the various legislative efforts to discourage permanent Chinese American settlement in Augusta were representative of national events in anti-Chinese sentiments at the time. By the 1890s, however, the actions taken by Georgia residents and legislators in the previous turbulent decade faded, and Chinese American life in Augusta, Savannah, and Atlanta (the sites of the three largest Chinese communities in Georgia) appeared to return to normal. The Chinese American merchants, so long as they kept to themselves and did not attempt to intervene too directly in white society, were free to thrive and go about their lives as they pleased. This cautious and at times uneasy compromise between Chinese Americans and whites remained until the 1920s.

The education of Chinese American children was an example of the functional social segregation that both Chinese Americans and whites accepted in Georgia through the early twentieth century. Georgia's 1872 Jim Crow law on education established separate schools for whites and "coloreds" and omitted language on where Chinese children were to go for their education. So long as few Chinese American children lived in Georgia, the question of school segregation for Chinese Americans was not a pressing concern. White schools in Savannah barred Chinese American children, but in Augusta and Atlanta they were allowed to attend otherwise all-white schools. There was little concern from white residents when the few Chinese American children who lived in their communities attended schools with their children, and most did not see white/Chinese integrated schools as serious threats to the racial order of Georgia.

Another opportunity for education was found in the Chinese schools operated by the Chinese Benevolent Association. Initially, the only options available for many Chinese American students were Chinese Sunday and vacation Bible schools offered through either Chinese Baptist churches in Augusta and other cities or through affiliations with majority-white Baptist and Methodist churches. These schools were staffed by whites and offered an education anchored in the general curriculum, but in the 1920s, Chinese

American parents in Augusta desired more autonomy in what their children learned, particularly Chinese language instruction. In 1927, the Chinese American community of Augusta formed a chapter of the National Chinese Benevolent Association and established its own Chinese school in the First Baptist Church of Augusta. A local Chinese immigrant who was once a professor in China but who had relocated to Augusta with his family served as the lead instructor for the school and offered courses in Chinese language and Chinese history in addition to arithmetic and a more general English curriculum. Between the Chinese schools like those in Augusta and the opportunity for Chinese American students to attend selected white schools in other cities, both Chinese Americans and whites accepted the Jim Crow situation for what it was in Georgia. So long as Chinese Americans were not classified as "colored" under social and legal definitions, they were able to move relatively easily between white and black society.[79]

As was the case for Chinese Americans and other Asian Americans across the country, the status of the Chinese Americans in Augusta and in Georgia more generally changed during the 1920s as anti-immigrant and especially anti-Asian sentiment resurged. Just as legislators from Georgia approved the Chinese Exclusion Act, they also supported drastically reducing the number of Asian immigrants allowed to enter the country. Increasing nationwide concern over the growing population of Japanese along the West Coast resonated with southerners in general and Georgians who feared a "yellow invasion" of Asian Americans searching for new homes in the South after fleeing the prejudice and discrimination found in California, Oregon, and Washington.

In Georgia, the anti-Asian sentiments of the post–World War I era also manifested in a strengthened antimiscegenation law that included bans on white/Asian marriages. In 1927, Georgia successfully passed a bill that added "Mongolians" and "Asiatics" to the growing list of those who were barred from intermarrying with whites. Unlike the attempt to pass such an act in 1884, this time legislators were successful in garnering more support as the populations of Chinese Americans, Japanese Americans, and Filipino Americans in the state continued to grow in small increments. As more stories of interracial marriages filled the Georgia newspapers, the need for a legislative remedy to the existing noncolored status of Asian Americans became more pronounced. When the 1927 law reclassified Chinese and other Asian Americans as "colored" because of their "Mongolian" and "Oriental" racial makeup, the legal classification of Chinese Americans in Georgia also changed. Now that Chinese Americans were colored, Georgia legislators were eager to follow the lead of antimiscegenation law in prohibiting Chinese/white integrated schools and the potential for more race-mixing.[80]

In Augusta, the question of school segregation and its relationship to local Chinese Americans was influenced by the Lum and Lun cases. Following the Supreme Court's decision, the *Augusta Chronicle* covered the education situation in Mississippi, providing Augustans a view of how another southern state handled Chinese Americans. In October 1927, the *Chronicle* reported on the rulings for both Lum and Lun, carefully describing how and why the state of Mississippi declared Chinese Americans to be colored. Since the Mississippi Supreme Court ruled in both cases that "any race other than Caucasian" was colored, it appeared to be common sense that Chinese Americans were, in fact, colored.[81] The *Chronicle* also noted that "Mississippi was the only state in the South that excludes Chinese from white schools," an interesting fact that raised questions about Chinese Americans in Georgia.[82] Now that Mississippi considered Chinese Americans to be colored and therefore subject to the Jim Crow laws of education, other states like Georgia had an example to follow. The question of the racial status of Chinese Americans was no longer a puzzle; Chinese Americans were "yellow" and belonged in colored schools. Georgia legislators wondered why it had taken them so long to consider revising their own laws and state constitution to define Chinese as colored. Moving between the worlds of black and white on a social or business level was one thing, but schools required more uniformity when it came to ensuring that white children could be properly educated. The Mississippi examples created momentum for other states to redesign their Jim Crow laws and reclassify Chinese Americans as colored.

The changes in views on Chinese Americans in the South directly affected the white and Chinese American citizens of Augusta in 1931 when a proposal to formally segregate white from Chinese American students in the Richmond County schools created a firestorm. In early July, the Georgia House of Representatives introduced a resolution denying funds to schools that admitted both white and colored students. The bill did not specifically mention Chinese Americans or Asian Americans but was more general in its desire to prevent colored children from mingling with whites. Representative Henry Messer argued that integrated schools were unconstitutional according to Georgia law and that there was a widespread problem across the state with individual school districts allowing minority children to attend school with white children. He also explained that the ban on integrated schools was a way to create more uniformity among the various school districts within Richmond County and throughout the state, thereby solving the problems of uneven applications of various policies of taxation and curriculum in addition to segregation. In order to assess the supposed problem of violation of Georgia's rules of segregation in schools and gain more information on Messer's claims, the Georgia House of Representatives created a special committee to investigate the racial composition of school districts.[83]

Despite the atmosphere of suspicion of Asian Americans and the recent changes in state antimiscegenation laws to include Asian Americans, there is little evidence that white Augusta or Georgia citizens more generally supported the proposed legislation. Editorials and letters in the *Augusta Chronicle* indicate that Augustans saw through the bill's vague language on colored students and knew that the bill specifically targeted Chinese American children, and they were not happy with this provision. "Without a doubt," a *Chronicle* editorial from July 10, 1931, began, "this bill . . . is designed to close the doors of the public schools in Augusta and in Atlanta and in Savannah to the Chinese people."[84] Furthermore, after interviewing local school officials, "the authorities have given the testimony that there has been no objection from any of the patrons of the schools to the enrollment of the Chinese children . . . and the pupils have been most sympathetic in their dealing with the little folk."[85] The editors at the *Chronicle* could not find any indication that there was a problem with the approximately twenty Chinese American students enrolled in white schools in Augusta and throughout Richmond County. "The Chinese are taxpayers, own property, and are no trouble to the authorities."[86] Although the Chinese were an extreme racial minority in Augusta, they were the good type of minority—the ones who worked hard and were not involved in any unsavory behavior. The Chinese had "lived in Augusta long enough to have convinced the great majority of Augustans that they are deserving of the privilege of attending our schools on the same basis as always."[87] To deny Chinese American children admission to white schools would be an "injustice" that, as the editors explained, most in Augusta did not support. The editorial disagreed with the bill, not because it was a violation of racial equality, but because it was a violation of the "privilege" to attend white schools that the Chinese had earned. Chinese American children should be allowed to continue their education at white schools because they were not black—neither racially not socially. Chinese were still Chinese and were not accepted socially as white, but their backgrounds and successful history in Augusta convinced white citizens that they were noncolored. Unlike Gong Lum, the editorial did not emphasize the ethnic or immigrant status of the Chinese; there was no need to do so because the Chinese did not engage in significant resistance to Jim Crow. Chinese Americans did not have to distinguish themselves from blacks or coloreds because the rest of the white Augusta community had already made up their minds that they were a respectable minority that understood their place in southern society. Lum was also a taxpayer and upstanding citizen, but he crossed the line when he insisted on defying school segregation by attempting to use his ethnicity and immigrant status to create a new racial classification for Chinese Americans.

Other Augustans agreed with the editorial and voiced their opinions on the negatives of the proposed bill. Local preacher W. M. Rowland submitted a letter to the editor on Sunday, July 12, commending the *Chronicle* for its views on the prohibition of Chinese American students from white schools. Rowland emphasized the "unheathen" nature of the local Chinese and of China in general, calling upon its missionary history and the bravery of the Chinese in defending themselves from the Japanese during the crisis in Manchuria.[88] Rowland urged parents in Augusta to rest assured that they "have nothing to fear from the Chinese children attending our schools" and provided the examples of two Chinese girls who came to study in Georgia and delighted locals in Macon with their "pleasant acquaintance" and "beautiful dress." One of these young women, a "Miss Soong," studied at Wesleyan University in Macon, Georgia, and went on to become Madame Chiang Kai-shek.[89] Rowland railed against the "prejudice and injustice" of the bill but also emphasized in his letter that the Chinese Americans of Augusta and elsewhere were a good, Christian people who deserved access to white schools based on these characteristics, not because segregated schools themselves were wrong. Chinese Americans were on the socially acceptable side of the black/white divide in Augusta and should therefore not be denied permission to attend the white schools. Rowland and others did not argue that Chinese Americans should not attend colored schools, but that the few Chinese Americans living in Augusta and other Georgia cities should not be prohibited from attending white schools.[90]

While the editorials provide a general overview of the position of Augustans on the proposed bill, there are a number of silences that speak volumes and help to create a more complete picture of the situation. First, the voices of the Chinese Americans in response to the bill are practically nonexistent. There are no direct letters or other sources that provide an indication of the responses of Chines Americans to either the legislators or the school board. Why this is so is uncertain, but the fact that many white Augustans jumped to defend Chinese Americans serves as one explanation. Second, although Augustans did not publicly or explicitly state this in any letters or editorials, another reason for supporting the Chinese Americans could be the nature of the bill. The bill was not reclassifying Chinese Americans as colored to send them to colored schools but threatening the funding and operations of white schools that admitted Chinese American children. Georgia had a smaller population of Chinese Americans when compared with towns and cities in the Mississippi Delta, and as a result, many white parents may not have immediately felt threatened by the idea of their children sharing a desk with a Chinese American boy or girl; however, the idea of shutting down a public school that primarily served whites was a more troubling prospect. By railing against the bill and its proposed budget cuts, Augustans cried out against the injustices of denying admission to the good Chinese Americans in order to keep their children's schools open and functioning. Third, based on the tone of the responses as published in the paper, a gulf existed between Augustans and the state legislators and representatives. Although Georgians and legislators agreed on antimiscegenation, school segregation was a separate issue. Following the Lum and Lun decisions, legislators jumped at the opportunity to pass new legislation that would indirectly reclassify Chinese Americans as colored for the sake of dismantling schools that ignored Jim Crow laws. Augustans, however, viewed the matter differently, potentially seeing it as a growing infringement on the local solutions to school segregation. While the ability of Chinese Americans to continue to operate as noncolored was at stake in the debate over the bill, various inhabitants of Georgia were also attached to the outcome.

In the end, the 1931 bill proposing funding cuts to Chinese American and white integrated schools failed. Representative Messer was an undying devotee to the bill, but others (including the original supporters of the bill) became disillusioned with the measure. Passing such a harsh bill would inflict unnecessary harm on Chinese Americans, but more importantly, the legislators' attempts to make a statement on the racial category of the Chinese Americans would end up hurting innocent white children. A local labor association with an anti-immigrant flare, the Junior Mechanics League of Augusta, drafted a resolution to submit to the Richmond County school district, hoping that a more local approach would achieve the goal of classifying Chinese Americans as "colored" and ending the "unconstitutional" practice of integrated schools. Once again, however, the resolution failed, and Chinese Americans continued to attend white schools as the population grew throughout the mid-twentieth century.[91]

Similar to the Chinese Americans in Mississippi, the Chinese American population of Augusta thrived after World War II. As more Chinese Americans were born in the city and in other areas of Georgia, Asian Americans moved toward being accepted as "white" by residents, although this claim is difficult to evaluate, since Chinese Americans were generally allowed to attend white schools in many areas in the state long before the end of the war. Chinese Americans became economically and socially successful by the 1960s in Georgia, but amid the rising civil rights movement, their noncolored status would create problems. African American boycotts of discriminatory businesses in the late 1960s and early 1970s in Augusta often targeted Chinese stores. Chinese Americans were so accomplished at building their noncolored image that other racial and ethnic minorities came to believe it as well. Although Chinese Americans certainly were not white, their desire to distance themselves from African Americans backfired by creating tensions between blacks and Asian Americans in Augusta. And during the late 1960s and 1970s, few whites defended the noncolored status of Chinese Americans. Although Chinese Americans in Augusta and in Georgia succeeded in obtaining a white education for their children and encountered a different trajectory to acceptance and toleration than that of the Lums or the Luns in Mississippi, in the end, much like Chineseness, being noncolored would only get Chinese Americans so far in relation to both blacks and whites in the Peach State.[92]

The differences between the outcomes for the Chinese Americans of Augusta in 1931 and Gong Lum and Joe Tin Lun in the late 1920s with school segregation were based on the success of Chinese Americans in creating working racial classifications for themselves according to southern law. It would seem as though the Augustan Chinese Americans did everything right: They attended white churches, established families and successful businesses, and generally obeyed the laws and kept low profiles. These would be clear reasons explaining why whites in Georgia responded so negatively to a proposed bill to prohibit Chinese American students from attending white schools. However, such explanations do not hold up when we consider Gong Lum or Joe Tin Lun. By and large, Lum and Lun exercised the same strategies but achieved different results. Gong Lum had many of the characteristics of the Augustan Chinese Americans, but he stepped outside the lines when he challenged Mississippi law that defined him and his family as "colored." The Chinese Americans in Augusta, however, did not attempt to create a new ethnic category to avoid Jim Crow in education. They strove to be seen as "noncolored," a category distinct from "Chinese" in this case. Chinese Americans were not accepted as white in Augusta, but they were seen as being separate and different from black. In other words, Chinese Americans in Mississippi were colored regardless of their ethnicity; Chinese Americans in Georgia were not.

School segregation laws provided the first opportunities for southern states to establish a racial classification for Chinese Americans and other Asian Americans, with varied and often confusing results. Chinese Americans, Japanese Americans, and other Asian Americans attended white schools prior to the *Brown v. Board* decision, and 1954 was not a significant turning point for Asian American education. By the 1960s, white Americans identified Japanese Americans and Chinese Americans as the model minorities, and many second- and third-generation Asian Americans reported feeling somewhat uncomfortable at times in their majority-white schools but were generally accepted and had many white friends. But the struggles of Chinese Americans and others to establish the position of their children are central to understanding southern history. *Brown v. Board* is not the only major milestone in the battle against school segregation and leaves out the more complicated issues of citizenship and immigration. Although the 1931 *Roberto Alvarez v. the Board of Trustees of the Lemon Grove School District* case in San Diego (which ruled that Mexican and Mexican American children should be integrated with white students to promote assimilation and "Americanization") and the 1947 federal *Westminster v. Mendez* case (which resulted in a victory for Mexican parents who wanted to send their children to white schools in Orange County, California) followed the Gong Lum and Joe Tin Lun cases and also centered on race, ethnicity, and cultural citizenship and assimilation, these are only a few examples of legal battles against school segregation beyond *Brown*. Although sweeping and controversial, *Brown v. Board* overshadows the legal strategies attempted by men like Gong Lum and Joe Tin Lun.

The landmark 1954 *Brown* decision was not a victory for Chinese Americans in Mississippi and those elsewhere in the South who previously pursued equality with whites on the basis of ethnicity or argued for special treatment based on immigration privileges that were not granted to other minorities in the region. Mexican laborers living in Mississippi (in the same county as the Lums and during the same time period) also used a similar strategy to allow their children to attend white schools by appealing to the Mexican government and the 1848 Treaty of Guadalupe Hildago (which afforded Mexicans "the enjoyment of all the rights of citizens of the United States") for protection and successfully petitioning Mississippi governor Theodore Bilbo to integrate schools for Mexican American children in order to promote good relations between the United States and Mexico. Mexican immigrants appealed to Mexican nationalism and sovereignty as well as to foreign relations just as Chinese Americans in Mississippi appealed to special ethnic and immigrant status. The main difference between the two groups was that the Mexicans in Mississippi were successful in that their children were attending white schools by the 1930s, while Chinese Americans would retain their "other" identity and attend Chinese schools until the post–World War II era, when some stigmas against Asian Americans became outdated.

Examining the experiences of Chinese Americans in Mississippi and in Georgia (where no legal battle ensued) connects the Lums, the Luns, and other Chinese Americans and Asian Americans to other ethnic and racial minorities in the South, thereby forming a web of legal activism that exposes the limits of the *Brown v. Board* decision in helping to understand citizenship, foreign policy, and immigration influences on segregation decisions. Similar to the alien land laws, definitions of racial identity and international politics shaped school segregation policy in the South for Asian Americans and resulting Asian American judicial activism. Asian Americans approached discrimination in schools as an opportunity to fashion an ethnic and racial position in southern society that defied traditional classification, with varying levels of success.[93]

THREE

A LOVE THAT COULD NOT BE KNOWN

Sex, Marriage, and Southern Law

"Come on, hurry!" fourteen-year-old Rosa Mae Clower yelled while grabbing her fifteen-year-old friend Frances Hutcheson's wrist and pulling her through the crowd gathered in front of Atlanta's downtown McCrory's drugstore. On the afternoon of April 11, 1932, the popular Filipino yo-yo exhibitionists Fortunatio Annunciatio and Ambia "Amby" Subia dazzled their audience as their agile fingers performed a litany of tricks with the toy, a craze that was sweeping through the city during the early years of the Great Depression. But the growing economic storm did little to stifle the enthusiasm of the citizens of Atlanta, who handsomely tipped the yo-yo kings. The two girls, who had spent extra money that day to ride the streetcar from Fulton High School to the show, clamored to see Annunciatio and Subia and applauded the talented duo after each trick, clapping until their hands stung.[1]

As the crowd thinned out, Clower and Hutcheson remained at McCrory's, sipping Cokes, stealing glances at the two Filipinos, and catching twenty-five-year-old Subia's eye. Subia and Annunciatio (who was twenty-seven years old) did not exchange words with their fans that day, but the two girls returned to the drugstore two days later to see more yo-yo tricks. At this point, Subia approached Clower and Hutcheson, inviting them to come see a later performance at the convention hall. The girls never made it to the second exhibition, but on the afternoon of April 13, Clower and Hutcheson climbed the stairs in the Tallulah Apartments building and knocked on Annunciatio and Subia's door. What happened after the two entered the apartment that afternoon spurred a unique Georgia court case involving a Filipino American man fighting for his civil rights while encountering the racialized legal system of the Jim Crow South and Clower's accusations that

Annunciatio had raped her. Although sentenced to ten to fifteen years of hard labor at the Georgia State Penitentiary during his trial, Annunciatio appealed the decision to the supreme court of Georgia, arguing that he was denied a fair trial from the moment the police illegally entered and searched his home without a warrant until the assistant solicitor general provided damaging and racist closing remarks to the jury regarding Filipinos.[2]

Twenty years later, another Asian man, Han Say Naim, would attempt to tackle the racism and prejudice inherent in southern laws and mores that governed the relationship between white women and "colored" men. Naim was a Chinese-born sailor who came to New York City during World War II and eventually made his way to Virginia. While there, he became smitten with a local white woman named Ruby Lamberth. Despite the tabloid stories that warned young white women of the dangers of engaging with Asian men, Lamberth also fell in love with Naim, and the two began a whirlwind courtship. Shortly thereafter, in 1952, Naim and Lamberth eloped to North Carolina in order to avoid Virginia's strict ban on interracial marriages. For a little over a year, the Naim marriage was stable. Han Say Naim led a typical seafaring life, leaving from nearby Norfolk to work on various ships for months at a time and sending money home to Ruby to pay the bills. But Ruby eventually grew tired of Han's long absences as well as the endless paperwork and trips to and from Washington, D.C., in order to help him become an American citizen. While Ruby tried to make her growing unhappiness with her marriage and her loss of patience for her husband's immigration troubles known in often cryptic letters, Han was caught off guard by his wife's suit for her "freedom" from their relationship in 1953. The Portsmouth, Virginia, court honored Ruby's request by annulling the marriage, ruling that the couple violated Virginia's antimiscegenation law. However, Han Say Naim would not accept the court's ruling. His access to naturalization as well as his marriage were on the line, and he was not ready to have a discriminatory Jim Crow regulation on the relationship between husband and wife strip his rights as an immigrant in the United States.

The courtroom experiences of Annunciatio and Naim and their status as Asian noncitizens drew them together in the broader history of civil rights, race, and sex in the South. Both men found themselves before southern courts for cases tied to their racial status and their relationships with white women, but their legal strategies were also similar. Rather than denounce the structure of Jim Crow as it affected sexuality and interracial unions, both men argued that their civil rights in the United States depended on their noncitizen status. Colonial subjects and foreign nationals, Annunciatio and Naim claimed, operated above southern segregation and were not subject to the same plight as African Americans and other minorities because they were outsiders disconnected from such political, social, and legal structures. In a region where African Americans fought for the recognition of their citizenship rights, Annunciatio and Naim attempted to use their noncitizen and immigration status to subvert the South's code of legal discrimination. State antimiscegenation laws created new racial identities for Asian immigrants and American-born Asians between the Civil War and the early twentieth century, transforming them from members of once distinct ethnic groups into an Oriental other to be bound and prohibited from interracial contact as other "colored" individuals across America. However, both Annunciatio and Naim fought against their status according to miscegenation law by using the courts.

Annunciatio claimed that as a colonial subject of the United States, his basic rights under the Fourteenth Amendment to due process and equal protection were abridged during the unlawful and unconstitutional procedures of the Atlanta police and Fulton County Circuit Court. In Naim's case, Naim and his attorney (immigration law specialist David Carliner) argued that as a Chinese national, Naim was not subject to Virginia's antimiscegenation laws. Both Annunciatio and Naim appealed their cases to the highest courts possible, resulting in the 1933 Georgia Supreme Court *State of Georgia v. Fortunatio Annunciatio* case and the better-known *Naim v. Naim* case that Naim and Carliner brought before the U.S. Supreme Court in 1955. Annunciatio and Naim did not argue for their whiteness or assimilation but, rather, called on their political status as noncitizen subjects in their quests for justice. Under existing imperial relationships and immigration laws and treaties, there was the possibility that federally guaranteed rights for American subjects and immigrants could trump discriminatory southern laws. However, as the men and their attorneys would find out, their noncitizen status did not provide protection against a legacy of racism and paranoia directed toward these minority men who dared to disturb the sexual and racial boundaries of the South, whether black or Asian, citizen or immigrant.

Annunciatio's and Naim's legal battles prove that race, sex, and miscegenation affected noncitizens and immigrants in the southern states in a variety of ways. Accounts of discriminatory cases, rape accusations, and miscegenation law in the Jim Crow South tend to focus on relations between whites and blacks, particularly white women and black men. However, these cases reveal the political entanglements that sex and race created. Annunciatio clearly wanted to avoid prison, but he was also invested in using his colonial identity to secure his constitutional and human rights. Naim's ability to remain in the

United States depended on challenging the Virginia court's ruling in order to obtain a nonimmigrant spousal visa. Both cases take well-known topics of cultural and legal barriers to racial equality, rape accusations, and antimiscegenation laws and complicate their legacies by adding immigrants' rights and political status. What results is a portrait of attempts by noncitizens to fight against their racial classifications in the South by appealing to their political identities to circumvent discriminatory sexual norms and laws.[3]

THE "LITTLE BROWN BROTHER" IN THE JIM CROW SOUTH

What began as an impromptu visit to Fortunatio Annunciatio and Amby Subia's apartment quickly turned into a legal maelstrom as soon as Rosa Mae Clower initiated the criminal investigation into her charges of rape and the subsequent trial. Newspaper coverage of the case inflamed the passions of Georgians outside Atlanta, with one resident from Thomasville in southwest Georgia declaring that "those Atlanta yo-yo artists ought to be wrapped around some of their necks with their [yo-yo] strings."[4] Annunciatio's appeal marked the first time in Georgia history that a Filipino challenged the state's Jim Crow legal system (and its racist underpinnings). While the details of what exactly happened that April afternoon in the Tallulah Apartments remain unclear, Annunciatio insisted that the way the police, prosecutors, and the Fulton County judge handled the case violated his basic rights as an American subject. Classified as "nationals" under American colonial rule, the "little brown brothers" (as Governor General William Howard Taft described the Filipinos) were allowed to migrate to and from America and, despite not being recognized as U.S. citizens, were afforded full constitutional rights when residing in the United States.[5] The "national" status did have limitations, however, as Filipinos could not vote in U.S. elections or run for political office. Considering that southern states at this time used voter registration lists to create jury pools, most juries were all white, and Asian Americans like Annunciatio, as well as African Americans, were thus deprived of a fair and equal trial. Rather than challenge the racial makeup of the jury system (an uphill and likely unsuccessful battle), Annunciatio and his lawyer carefully constructed an appeal based on broad violations of the Fourth and Fourteenth Amendments. The lack of a proper search warrant and Assistant Solicitor General E. A. Stephens's remarks to the court and jury that the United States should rid itself of Filipinos and the Philippines alike were only the most overt violations of Annunciato's legal rights. By the time he appeared before the Fulton County court, Annunciatio, as both a migrant and an unwelcome racial minority, was well aware of the color line in the United States; that line was embedded in and emboldened by southern courts and legal systems. But when Filipino migrants faced discrimination, racism, and prejudice in the South, their colonial, cultural, and legal identities placed Jim Crow law within the context of imperialism.

Like other Asian Americans, Filipinos actively participated in lawsuits and legal battles for civil rights and protections throughout the twentieth century. In comparison with Chinese Americans and Japanese Americans, who were generally excluded by existing immigration laws, Filipino Americans possessed a unique political status as colonial subjects that they often attempted to use in their favor. Filipino Americans were often at the center of both successful and unsuccessful court battles for citizenship and against antimiscegenation laws both before and after World War II in the West Coast states.[6] Annunciatio's fight was part of this historical trend, but it reveals the special form a legal battle assumed when fought in a southern state. As Annunciatio discovered, his interstitial place in Georgia presented legal opportunities that African American men may have lacked, but his status as a suspicious minority and unwanted colonial subject could not compete with the protection of white womanhood in southern society.[7]

While a charge of rape was the reason Annunciatio found himself in an Atlanta courtroom, why he settled in the city in the first place was the result of broader immigration patterns. After arriving in the United States at some point in the 1920s and spending a few months working odd jobs in New England and Washington, D.C., Annunciatio moved south to Atlanta, where he met Amby Subia and became a permanent resident in the city.[8] Annunciatio's presence in the Peach State was part of a larger migration of unmarried Filipino men to America in the early years of the twentieth century. By the 1930, approximately 45,200 Filipinos lived in the United States, having crossed the Pacific for education or employment opportunities. The majority of Filipino men lived along the West Coast and worked in agriculture as migrant laborers, but others often followed the harvest seasons across the United States, ending up in the Midwest, the Northeast, and the South.[9] The population of Filipino Americans in the South was small (totaling 911 by 1930 and only 29 in Georgia) and comparable to other Asian American groups in the region, but groups of 10 to 20 Filipinos often formed settlements in these areas. Southerners were intrigued by the presence of even small numbers of "the little brown brothers" amid a society that was largely divided along black and white lines.[10]

During the late 1920s, Filipino Americans created a small but noticeable enclave in Atlanta. As a growing city, Atlanta and its environs attracted a number of different immigrant and ethnic groups, including Chinese, Russian and Polish Jews, and Italians. Filipinos possibly used Atlanta as a temporary home between seasons or, as Annunciatio and Subia did, sought business opportunities in the area. In 1929, *Atlanta Constitution* student reporter Marcia Baker described the city's "foreign colonies" as "intriguing" and counted five Filipino migrants in Atlanta as part of the region's growing immigrant population. While port cities like Savannah and New Orleans had more diversity by the early twentieth century, Baker boasted of Atlanta's burgeoning cosmopolitanism and applauded the immigrants' abilities to "keep the best of their native land and adopt as their own the ideals of America."[11]

This praise for the blending of native and American culture and practices manifested in Atlantans' enthusiastic embrace of the yo-yo, a toy with roots in the Philippines and made popular in the city by Annunciatio and Subia. Other Filipino migrants shared their love of this traditional pastime with Americans wherever they settled in the United States. After Filipino migrant Pedro Flores established a manufacturing plant in California in 1928, the yo-yo became more commercialized and swept the nation from coast to coast in the late 1920s and 1930s.[12] However, difficulties with making the yo-yo "do the things it ought to do" and chances for self-injury (as one father experienced while trying to entertain his son) created opportunities for enterprising Filipinos to conduct demonstrations and judge amateur competitions. By 1932, the "yo-yo craze" had arrived in Atlanta, leading to intrigue and fascination, as well as to confusion, regarding the exotic object. Rumors circulated in Atlanta that Filipinos used the yo-yo as a weapon or as "the slogan of insurrection," that the yo-yoers were scam artists who actually used a hidden spring within the object to fool captivated audiences, and for the most misinformed, that "yo-yo" was a code word to procure "dope." In March 1932 the *Atlanta Constitution* ran a series of articles to clear the air surrounding the introduction of the yo-yo, carefully explaining that the trick to the toy is "a matter of string and fling, not spring." The newspaper assured readers that the yo-yo was "not a yodel, a form of greeting, or a sailor's oath, a secret password, a cry of distress, or a drug. It's a game." The new fad, combined with the yo-yo's association with Filipinos, resulted in a form of cultural Orientalism and exoticism that piqued the interest of Atlantans and contributed to the various rumors about the toy. During the spring of 1932, yo-yo demonstrations and contests sponsored by the *Constitution* filled parks and the sidewalks outside popular department stores with potential customers, youngsters eager to learn tricks like "walking the dog" and the "Kentucky Derby," and simply curious individuals who had never laid eyes on either a yo-yo or a Filipino. And at the center of Atlanta's yo-yo craze were Annunciatio and Subia, who were quickly elevated to the status of premier yo-yo exhibitionists by gracing the pages of the *Constitution*.[13]

While Annunciatio and Subia were enjoying fame and popularity in Atlanta, other Filipino Americans in and around Georgia faced different circumstances. At times, this meant greater acceptance or at least tolerance, as was the case with many Chinese American grocers and entrepreneurs in Georgia, Mississippi, and Texas.[14] In other situations, Asian immigrants became part of the so-called colored menace as whites lumped them together with African Americans. The reputation as untethered sojourners that Filipino bachelors gained through their migratory work in California followed them to the South, further contributing to stereotypes of the shifty, dishonest, and predatory Oriental. Unfortunately, reports of a Filipino man who operated a successful "dope selling scheme" in Atlanta by posing as a doctor until his arrest in 1929 did little to ease white Atlanta's suspicions of the newcomers. As migrants, colonial subjects, and racial minorities, Filipinos always posed a threat. Even in small numbers, Filipinos in other parts of the Southeast encountered less-than-welcoming receptions when they moved into the area. Two years after the break of the drug scandal, the *Atlanta Constitution* reported that 200 white residents in a farming community in southern Florida "ordered out" 30 migrant workers from a "Filipino colony" after one of the Filipino men engaged in "an episode" with a white woman from a nearby town. If the sexual transgression were not enough, rumors that 2,000 more Filipinos seeking work were on their way to Florida from California only fueled fears of unwanted labor competition. The Florida incident was reminiscent of more violent attacks by whites in central California when Filipinos crossed established racial and sexual boundaries with white women, and it solidified the place of Filipinos at the margins of society in the South. Atlantans held Annunciatio and Subia in high esteem for their talents, but the two were still Filipinos, strangers whose reputations were inevitably linked to the larger stereotypes of minority men in a southern state.[15]

Defying the accepted practice of holding Filipino Americans at arm's length, the teenage Rosa Mae Clower and her friend Frances Hutcheson violated the codes of racial and sexual behavior by seeking the attention of Annunciatio and Subia in 1932. According to testimonies given by Clower and Hutcheson in the Fulton County court trial, the initial contact among the parties consisted of little more than innocent, consensual flirting and

"Philippine yo-yo experts" traveling through Jacksonville, Florida, in 1931. There is no indication that any of these men were Annunciatio or Subia. *Photo by Jack (John Gordon) Spottswood, courtesy of the State Archives of Florida.*

coy exchanges. After their encounters at the drugstore and during the yo-yo demonstrations, however, Clower and Hutcheson moved from flirtation to indecent behavior by white societal standards when they arrived at Annunciatio and Subia's apartment on April 13. Subia paused his dinner preparations that afternoon to greet Clower and Hutcheson when they knocked on his door, asking if they could come in and visit. After entering the apartment at 225 Washington Street, they split up: Clower found Annunciatio alone in his room, and Hutcheson went with Subia to his quarters. Both Subia's and Annunciatio's rooms were connected by a shared door, which, according to both Hutcheson and Clower, Subia closed behind him when he and Hutcheson separated from Clower and Annunciatio. Before Subia left, however, he and Annunciatio exchanged a few words in "their native language," which Clower did not understand. Simply being unattended in the home of two older, Filipino men was enough for a young, white southern woman to bring opprobrium from white southern society, but Clower was more bold in her decision to place herself in Annunciatio's company behind a closed door.[16]

Clower's account of what happened behind that door confirmed exactly what southern whites feared most from minority men. Although Clower was fourteen and, under Georgia law, of age to consent, her statement about her encounter with Annunciatio cast the Filipino American's advances as seduction with intent to rape. Clower's detailed retelling on the witness stand of that afternoon satisfied the jurors, and it was this narrative that the court privileged in its ruling. Upon entering Annunciatio's room, Clower found him relaxing and reading a paper on his bed. When he roused himself and saw Clower, he invited her to sit down, but as Clower pointed out to him, there were no chairs in the room. Annunciatio then told her to "sit down on the bed" while he grabbed a pencil and a pad of paper from his dresser. Annunciatio sat down next to Clower and asked her a series of questions, including what grade she was in and if she were taking Spanish in school. Clower replied that she did not know the language and asked Annunciatio to "write a few words in Spanish" for her, which he promptly did. Sharing a seat with an older man on his bed was no place for a young girl to be, but the Spanish lesson was innocent enough until Annunciatio reportedly threw Clower on the bed and kissed her. According to Clower, Annunciatio then "felt of [her] parts" and "put [his] hand up under [her] dress." In desperation, she fought Annunciatio until he "put one leg on [her] and took out his private parts and put them against [her] private parts." Despite the fighting and crying, Hutcheson never heard her friend's struggle. When Annunciatio "finished" with the girl, he got up, and Clower noticed "there was nothing on her bloomers but blood" as she prepared to get Hutcheson and leave. Annunciatio and Clower exchanged no words following her assault except when he told her "not to tell Frances."[17] When Hutcheson opened the door between the two bedrooms, Clower was standing next to Annunciatio as he sat on the bed and scribbled on his notepad. With "tears in [her] eyes," Clower left with Hutcheson, and they made their way outside, past a gas station where a friend of Clower's family worked to the streetcar station. After getting on the car, the two girls rode silently back to their respective stops.[18] As the court and jury later learned, Clower's description of that afternoon differed from Annunciatio's statement on his innocence in terms of forced sexual contact.

Bringing to life one of the central fears of white Georgia society, Clower's account of her rape had roots in a longer history of tense racial relations. In the white South, few cross-racial flirtations were ever seen as truly innocent. White southerners were raised to believe that African American men desired nothing more than to ravage white women, supposedly the pinnacles of purity and symbols of the unobtainable for black men. Any interaction between a white woman and a black man could be interpreted as subversive and a violation of the color line, resulting in the ostracism of both parties and/or violent attacks on the African American man involved in the scandal. With this context, a white woman could wield an accusation of rape against a black man as her ultimate weapon—a way to bring "justice" to a black rapist whether or not he committed the crime (although different outcomes for such rape charges did occur throughout the South, depending on local class and race relations). White fears of interracial sexual relations made even the most innocuous of encounters on city streets or in social settings seem to be the first step in sexual crimes perpetrated by black men. Although not African Americans, Filipino Americans and other Asian Americans were racial minorities and therefore also seen as a constant threat to white female virtue. In the view of white southerners, Clower's initial contact with Annunciatio broke the boundaries of acceptability and thus set the stage for her sexual assault at the hands of a nonwhite man.[19]

Clower's interaction with Annunciatio, however, also highlights the fluidity of Asian Americans in the sexual and racial structure of the South. Had Annunciatio been a black man, it is very unlikely that Clower would have gone to his apartment with only her teenage girlfriend to keep her company. In terms of marriages and interracial sexual relations, the initial antimiscegenation laws of southern states like Georgia, North Carolina, Alabama, and Florida did not specifically mention Asians (or "Mongoloids" or "Malays"), but by the time Annunciatio found his way to the United States, Georgia's law grouped Chinese, Japanese, and Mongolians under "colored."[20] Inspired by Virginia's Racial Integrity Act of 1924, Georgia representatives and officials moved to make their existing antimiscegenation law stronger with the end result of an amended law in 1927 focused on preventing "persons of color" from intermarrying with whites, but still relevant for Asian

Americans.²¹ Filipinos, however, did not always identify as "colored," citing their American "national" status or even Spanish heritage (as evident in their surnames) as evidence that the laws did not necessarily apply to them. Also, determining whether Filipinos were Malays or Mongoloids was a question that troubled county clerks and judges across the country, making Filipino Americans' specific racial identification malleable. The fact that Asian Americans were not black but, rather, "brown" or "yellow" provided them with some maneuverability within the binary black-and-white structure as reflected in southern laws.²²

Filipino Americans' potential for maneuverability within Georgia's antimiscegenation law did not mean that free intermingling between "Malays" and whites was acceptable. Asian Americans were still racial minorities perceived according to their own set of accompanying sexual stereotypes. Similar to depictions of the "black beast" who craved nothing more than white female flesh, American newspapers, films, and other forms of media portrayed Asian Americans as purveyors of white women. In this narrative, Asian Americans desired young white women as much as blacks did, but their purposes were more for financial gain and control than a fulfillment of base sexual desires. Numerous articles in tabloids and gossip rags and respected newspapers alike from the early twentieth century luridly described the tragedies white women faced when they succumbed to the wily ways of the Oriental. Using opium and other drugs to seduce and ensnare women, Chinese, Japanese, and Filipino men subjected women to a lifetime of white slavery, forcing innocent young ladies into prostitution and drug addiction. Even when relations were consensual, stories of a woman who entered into a sexual relationship or marriage with an Asian American man usually ended in poverty, prostitution, adultery, or a realization that interracial marriage had driven her away from her disapproving friends and family and soiled her reputation.²³ Such stories on Asian American seduction of white and black women occasionally appeared in the *Baltimore Afro-American*, the leading black newspaper in the country, reflecting a cross-racial form of Orientalism as well as a means for African Americans to distance themselves from a new racial underclass.²⁴ By using white women for financial gain, Asian Americans represented a particularly dangerous threat to the economic, social, and political power structure in America as well as the South.

The American preoccupation with Asian/white stories of interracial tragedy shaped Atlanta's views of Annunciatio long before the rape charges. American media hypersexualized Filipino American men, drawing them as wanderers and seductive predators who preyed on white women who fell for their debonair style. Filipino Americans did have a higher rate of intermarriage with white women in the United States (where not prohibited by anti-miscegenation laws), and many white critics at the time argued that Filipino Americans, in contrast to African Americans, "'who usually understood how to act,'" felt as though they had the right to intermarry whites because of their national status.[25] Seen as rootless, shifty, desirous of sexual control and power, and prone to using white women in prostitution rings, even the few Filipino Americans in Georgia were considered by whites to be a potential threat to Atlanta society and order. In 1931, Atlanta police found Jose Cruz, a Filipino American magician, and nineteen-year-old stenographer Gladys Frix dead in each other's arms in a car parked outside the Asa G. Candler Jr. estate in the Druid Hills neighborhood. In addition to performing amateur magic tricks throughout the city and at parties, Cruz was a butler employed by Candler (son of the Coca-Cola magnate Asa Candler). Cruz had met Frix a few months earlier at a party where "the young Filipino entertained with this magic." Frix's family and friends rejected her developing relationship with Cruz: The couple crossed not only racial boundaries but also those of class, as Frix, the daughter of a middle-class railroad engineer, dared to stoop to the level of a working-class Filipino. Investigating the scene, police found a note from Cruz indicating that the deaths were a suicide pact and that the pair had decided to take their own lives because they "could not find a way to be together in peace."[26] Piecing together evidence from the crime scene as well as testimony from witnesses, the coroner stated that Cruz shot Frix with a pearl-handled, nickel-plated revolver stolen from the Candler estate and then placed the gun to his head and fired. The coroner's jury thus ruled that the incident was a murder-suicide prompted by the refusal of Frix's parents to let their daughter speak to her lover. Her friends and family explained that she had been unhappy in her relationship with Cruz and, as the *Atlanta Constitution* reported, "feared [the] islander," which often resulted in heated arguments between the two. Atlantans focused on the class and racial components of the Frix incident as well as the trope of the unhappy white woman caught in a web of deceit spun by her Asian paramour. For a city still reeling from the 1913 rape and murder of a thirteen-year-old white girl named Mary Phagan and the subsequent mob lynching of her accused murderer/rapist, an entrepreneur and northern Jew named Leo Frank, interracial and even interethnic relationships appeared to be the root causes of such tragedies that befell innocent and vulnerable white southern women such as Clower.[27]

Bearing such preexisting stereotypes of Filipino Americans as threatening and seductive, the police entered Annunciatio and Subia's apartment with suspicions of rape and sexual misconduct. Paul Seymour, a white owner of a small fruit stand situated on a corner by the Tallulah Apartments, warily eyed what he described as an endless parade of young white girls in and out of the Filipino Americans' apartment nearly every day. Of course, Seymour may also have been concerned about the safety of the girls in relation to the older men, but as he explained, it was his duty as an American citizen to keep an eye on the Filipinos as "any white American would have done." Increasingly concerned that "something was happening [up] there and something ought to be done about it," Seymour provided a tip to the police that the Filipinos were seducing young women and taking advantage of them sexually, based solely on his observations of white girls visiting Filipino men.[28] On April 14 (the day after Clower initially went to see Annunciatio and Subia), detective George Pounds and an accompanying officer went to the Tallulah Apartments to investigate. Although Pounds did not have a search warrant, the building superintendent provided a key to Annunciatio and Subia's apartment. When Pounds entered the apartment, he found Hutcheson and another friend, Evelyn Barnett, sitting in the kitchen while Annunciatio and Subia were in their rooms. Pounds rapidly questioned the girls, asking why they were there and what they were doing, while the other officer rifled through cupboards and drawers, inspecting documents and other personal effects that might provide a clue to the Filipino Americans' lifestyle. Upon hearing the cries of the girls and the rummaging of the officers, Annunciatio and Subia emerged from their rooms, puzzled by the presence of the police. Pounds took both men into custody and also took Hutcheson and Barnett to the station for questioning.[29]

The police learned that Annunciatio and Subia had relationships with the girls that were more complex than seduction or assault. Details on the personalities and backgrounds of Hutcheson, Barnett, and Clower are largely missing from the historical record, but a careful analysis of the court transcripts reveals more about the girls' experience with sexuality and race in the South. Hutcheson explained that although Subia had "groped and fondled" her the day before when she was with Clower, she went back to the apartment with Barnett.[30] Subia's actions, while perhaps crude, were not unwelcomed, making Hutcheson a curious case for the police. Hutcheson appeared to have been inappropriately (according to custom) touched by Subia, but she certainly did not resist any further advances. Also, Hutcheson confirmed that neither Subia nor Annunciatio touched the girls inappropriately or made them do anything against their will. Eventually, Hutcheson revealed to the police that Clower had accompanied her to the apartment on April 13 (the day of Clower's alleged rape) and shared Clower's contact information with Pounds.³¹

On April 18 (the Monday after Annunciatio and Subia were arrested), police officers came to Fulton High School to find Clower. At the school, police asked Clower for "the truth," and she provided her account of what happened in the apartment. Initially, Clower insisted that neither Annunciatio nor Subia had harmed her in any way and that she was not "assaulted, struck, [or] beaten in that apartment."³² She went so far as to claim that "nothing had happened" between her and Annunciatio, denying having any physical contact with him. For several minutes the police pushed Clower to reveal the truth of what happened, but the girl remained steadfast that Annunciatio had done nothing "bad" to her that day. Unsatisfied with the line of questioning, Solicitor General John Boykin had the police escort Clower to his office, where his officers continued to grill Clower for an accurate account of the afternoon of her rape. Eventually, Clower confessed "the truth" and gave a detailed description of her assault—the information needed to proceed with a grand jury to indict Annunciatio and Subia on charges of rape and sexual assault.³³

The exchange between Clower and the officers displayed the notions of white female purity and distrust of minority men found in legal proceedings in the South. In the Georgia criminal codes, in rape accusations a woman remained virtuous and innocent until proven otherwise, a protection that was often restricted to white women and created an insurmountable obstacle for African American men charged with sexual assault, rape, or the ambiguous crime of "eye rape" (committed by black men when their gaze lingered too long upon a white woman).³⁴ The officers refused to accept that Annunciatio did not force physical contact on Clower, a young, presumably virtuous woman. Despite Clower's insistence at first in her examination that absolutely nothing had occurred that day, the solicitor general's representatives would not accept this statement. How could they, according to southern customs and legal traditions and given the eyewitness testimony and racial concerns of men like Paul Seymour? In the eyes of the officers, Clower found herself in the Filipino Americans' apartment because Annunciatio seduced her and then had his way with her against her will. Hutcheson maintained in her interview with the police that neither Annunciatio nor Subia had abused her and that she had entered their apartment willingly, but such an explanation of young white women frequenting Annunciatio and Subia's home was unsatisfactory to the white male inquisitors. For her part, Clower, whose friends explained that she had voluntarily visited the apartment, may have initially denied any relationship or physical contact with Annunciatio for fear of tarnishing her reputation or of her parents hearing of her dalliance with an older Filipino American man. Confessing that Annunciatio forced himself upon her relieved her of any charge of societal misconduct. Before the trial, both Clower and the solicitor general's office had a shared interest in having Clower admit to sexual assault. Consensual contact between Clower and Annunciatio defied racial boundaries, sullied the girl's character, and prevented the officers from controlling the suspicious activities of the Filipino Americans who lived at the Tallulah Apartments.

Annunciatio's decision to invite Clower into his bedroom resulted in grand jury proceedings. On April 22, 1932, the Fulton County grand jurors, believing evidence showed that he beat the girl and engaged in forcible carnal knowledge, returned the indictment to charge Annunciatio with the rape of Clower. Clower's testimony before the grand jury, as well as the prosecution's presentation of materials obtained from the apartment during Annunciatio's arrest, convinced the jury that the Filipino had taken Clower's innocence and endangered the "peace and dignity" of Georgia by committing the crime.[35] Annunciatio was taken into custody and, a few weeks later, placed on trial in the Fulton County Superior Court (which oversaw felony cases), where he pleaded not guilty and was represented by local attorney F. Joe Turner.[36] After hearing testimony from Hutcheson, Clower, Clower's doctor and parents, and other witnesses who lived near the Tallulah Apartments, the jury convicted Annunciatio on May 11, 1932, recommending the mercy of the court and fixing his sentence at ten to fifteen years of hard labor at the Georgia State Penitentiary. (In a separate trial, Subia was found guilty of attempted sexual assault and sentenced to two to five years of prison time for his fondling of Hutcheson and his vicinity to Annunciatio and Clower that April afternoon).[37] Annunciatio maintained that he was innocent. With Turner's assistance, Annunciatio filed a motion for retrial by Fulton County Superior Court judge Virlyn B. Moore Sr. (who later gained a reputation among Atlantans for his fairness in hearing cases involving African American defendants and African American lawyers).[38] Annunciatio argued that many of his basic rights had been violated and that he was denied a fair trial as guaranteed by the Constitution. In July 1932, Judge Moore denied Annunciatio's request for a retrial, finding no legal wrongdoings in the superior court case. Annunciatio's demand for a retrial eventually led to the Georgia Supreme Court in 1933, but his detailed explanations of civil rights violations and the proceedings of the superior court case reveal how a Filipino American man attempted to challenge southern law and customs at various stages of the legal process.[39]

With Turner's assistance, Annunciatio not only attacked the operations of the Atlanta legal system but also denounced Clower's accusations and, as a result, her virtuous white womanhood. That he was a colonial subject within the southern metropole of the American empire adds another layer to this fight for justice. Annunciatio was a racial minority and a migrant without American citizenship, but his insistence on his basic right to a fair trial brought an imperial element into this story of racial and sexual scandal, exposing how southern courts responded to this new threat to order and white power. Although Filipinos were nationals, what that status meant in terms of U.S. laws was often unclear. Legal theorist Frederic R. Coudert attempted to decipher the exact legal rights of Filipino Americans in his 1903 article "Our New Peoples: Citizens, Subjects, Nationals, or Aliens." He argued that because Filipino Americans were not aliens but did owe allegiance to the United States, they were guaranteed under the Fourteenth Amendment basic rights (though not political rights such as suffrage).[40] As Rick Baldoz argues, many Filipino Americans along the West Coast argued similar points when defending their legal rights in marriage and property cases, knowing that their "arrival . . . exposed the shifting and uncertain boundaries of the nation's ascriptive hierarchy."[41] Annunciatio, with the assistance of his lawyer, sought to clarify the legal position of Filipinos in the United States by emphasizing the rights and privileges of nationals and by taking advantage of the uncertainties that abounded in American courts. In many ways, Annunciatio's demands reveal challenges that all racial minorities, Asian Americans and African Americans alike, faced when going against legal norms; however, his experience in the appeals process also creates a more complex picture of how southern courts responded to individuals who did not fit within the racial structure or who lacked citizenship.

Some of Annunciatio's objections spoke to the he-said/she-said nature of rape, particularly of those involving interracial sexual assaults in the South. Other witnesses called before the superior court during the trial told a story much different from Clower's account. To begin, Hutcheson (sworn as a witness for Annunciatio) insisted that there was no evidence that Annunciatio assaulted or raped Clower. Although Hutcheson confirmed that the door between Annunciatio's and Subia's rooms was closed, she testified that she "didn't hear any conversation in the other room and did not hear any noise of any kind" and that she "didn't see anything wrong with the conditions in that room" when she checked on the pair.[42] Instead, Hutcheson found Clower calmly seated beside Annunciatio on the bed, which Hutcheson explained "didn't look . . . like it had been disturbed."[43] Clower "made no complaint" when she came out of the room, and she rode the streetcar home as if nothing had happened. Hutcheson added another twist to the account by revealing that the day after the alleged rape, Clower telephoned Annunciatio and "impersonated" Hutcheson on the phone, telling Annunciatio that she was Hutcheson and asking him "how he liked Rosa Mae." To her supposed dismay, Annunciatio told the incognita Clower that he "didn't like Rosa Mae's looks." Clower then confessed to Hutcheson what she had done and refused to return to Annunciatio's apartment "for this reason." Clower's reaction raised questions of whether the rape had occurred or if the accusation was a scorned Clower's irrational reaction to Annunciatio's reply.[44]

Other individuals who testified also revealed holes and inconsistencies in Clower's story. Fruit peddler Paul Seymour recounted that on the afternoon of April 13 he saw Annunciatio and a girl that resembled Clower "tussling in the window" on their feet for about fifteen minutes, whereas Clower previously explained that Annunciatio forced her to remain pinned on the bed.[45] Another witness, Harry Ingram, saw a couple "loving up on eachother [sic]" and then pulling down the shade about fifteen minutes later in the apartment, but that was all.[46] Because Clower waited until her mother discovered her bloodied bloomers in her bedroom to report for a medical examination, evidence of her alleged rape was not apparent. Officer George Pounds brought Clower to the office of Dr. W. A. Arnold, Clower's family doctor, on April 18. Arnold "examined her to see if she had been entered [and] also to see if she had gonorrhea or any such condition," but he found that although "the hymen had been ruptured" and that "she had been entered," there was "no evidence of anything recent" and no clear way of determining if the ruptured hymen was caused by Annunciatio.[47] Clower's sexual indiscretions with men besides Annunciatio may have resulted in her medical loss of virginity, an idea that would have tarnished her reputation as a good girl and aroused her father's noted temper. Also, when cross-examined by Turner, Clower once again proclaimed that minutes before the trial began, she "told Mr. Stephens . . . about everything that happened to [her] up there in that apartment" and that "neither of these boys threatened [her] with physical violence."[48] Although Clower maintained that both Annunciatio and Subia asked her not to tell of whatever occurred that day, she stated that "they didn't threaten to harm me if I told in anyway."[49] Questions regarding whether Annunciatio had made any physical contact with Clower, why Clower had not cried out if he had, and why she wavered on Annunciatio's use of violence to have his way with her complicated the story and cast doubts on her claims.

While Annunciatio did have the opportunity to testify for himself, he argued in his motion for retrial that the court mishandled information and the questioning in ways that damaged his defense before the jury. Annunciatio's account of the incident in his apartment differed dramatically from what Clower told the court. He admitted that Clower did come to his apartment that day, but he had attempted to deflect what he reported as her romantic advances. According to Annunciatio, Clower said she came to his apartment because "she loved [him]"; he told her that she was "too young to know about love," to which she retorted, "You're crazy." When Annunciatio asked her again why she had come to his home, she replied with the perplexing "[I] know what is good and what is bad."[50] Not knowing how to respond to such an odd comment from a young girl, Annunciatio did not ask her to leave but, rather, asked her to sit down on the bed while he showed her pictures from the Philippines and his travels around the United States. Annunciatio asked her if she would like to know more "about the Philippine problems and the United States," and when she said yes, he told her about his "people" and how poor they were. Annunciatio's brief lesson in international relations ended when Hutcheson came in for Clower, who did not want to leave and was only persuaded when Hutcheson reminded her that their streetcar tickets would soon expire. Annunciatio did not see Clower again, but he did confirm Hutcheson's story that Clower called his apartment later that evening pretending to be Hutcheson.[51] Although Annunciatio's statement presented a different take on the evidence and appeared to corroborate Hutcheson's account, Annunciatio argued that the original jury did not take his statement seriously because the prosecuting officers "unjustly discriminated against him . . . in that he had not been furnished with the name of a single witness . . . to testify against him," leaving him without proper means to prepare for his defense. Most concerning for Annunciatio was the fact that one witness, fruit seller Paul Seymour, never appeared before the grand jury and was a convicted criminal (charged with larceny and burglary over the past two years). Had Annunciatio known about Seymour, he might have been able to conduct research for a character statement. The failure of the court to inform Annunciatio of the witnesses for the prosecution presented obstacles for his defense and made his own statement all but irrelevant by the time the jury heard it. As a result, these discriminatory measures denied Annunciatio access to a fair trial.[52]

Annunciatio's objections to court procedure were not new proceedings for the judge and prosecution, but his racial and migrant status shaped the unique characteristics of his appeal. By demanding a retrial, Annunciatio challenged Judge Moore's handling of the case, whereby the court's bungles allowed a young girl's lovesick blues to undermine a man's innocence. Such claims were certainly not unheard of and were hallmarks of many defense strategies in sexual assault cases. However, Annunciatio's argument that the prosecution deliberately discriminated against him by withholding information about witnesses suggested that the problem was more widespread and not limited to this particular incident. Southern law officials did not practice proper procedure in Annunciatio's case, which raised questions of how many other cases were characterized by such inadequacies and how many other defendants were denied equal treatment under the law. Annunciatio's appeal exposed the tensions that arose when his demands as an American imperial subject collided with his image as a dangerous racial minority.

One of the most egregious violations of Annunciatio's civil rights was the illegal search of his apartment and the seizure of materials found within. Despite the constitutional protections in the Fourth Amendment against illegal searches and seizures, many police and law officials saw little value in these protections, arguing that they applied more to federal investigations than to state or local procedures. Illegal searches and seizures more than likely occurred frequently, but few who endured them challenged such occurrences in court. However, Annunciatio pushed back against the standard practice of overlooking the need for a warrant in an arrest and argued that his right to a fair procedure was a federal right that could not be ignored by the states.[53] In the motion for retrial, Annunciatio and Turner placed this complaint at the top of a lengthy list of misconduct. When Pounds and his officers entered Annunciatio's apartment on April 14, they did so without a warrant. Essentially, the officers "broke into and forced their way into the home" and proceeded to "unlawfully and illegally" arrest Annunciatio with little explanation for his placement under custody.[54] While Annunciatio's arrest was problematic from a legal standpoint, even more galling was the officers' illegal seizure of Annunciatio's private papers, books, and effects "with references to addresses of girls and other parties."[55] The prosecution did not provide Annunciatio with any information on the evidence seized, compelling him to "be a witness and furnish evidence against himself."[56] Solicitor General Boykin's office eventually agreed to turn over the evidence to Annunciatio after Turner filed a complaint, but according to the defense, the damage was already done in moving forward with the appeal.[57] The "unlawful and illegal arrest, search, and seizure" were also unreasonable in that officers did not follow proper procedure and only initiated the search based on the sketchy suspicions brought to the police by Harry Ingram, who supposedly saw Annunciatio and Clower "loving up on" each other that April afternoon. While Ingram and Paul Seymour expressed concern that Annunciatio and Subia were scheming to take advantage of young girls, the fact that both men were racial minorities also contributed to the witnesses' compulsion to report any suspicious behavior that occurred in the Filipinos' apartment. Once again, neither Seymour nor Ingram witnessed any illegal activities; they worked only from their suspicions of such based on the age of the girls and the race of the men. Before the police took Hutcheson and Evelyn Barnett down to the station and questioned them on their reasons for being with Annunciatio and Subia, the officers embarked on an illegal search and arrested both men on little more than racially motivated neighborhood gossip.

Annunciatio and Turner did not hesitate to argue that the illegal searches and seizures were glaring civil rights violations. Although Annunciatio was not an American citizen, he was a "subject of the United States" and was guaranteed basic political rights based on his status and his residency in America. Annunciatio correctly claimed that officers were "in contravention to and in violation of . . . the rights guaranteed to him under Articles 4 and 5 of the Fourteenth Amendment of the Constitution of the United States."[58] More so, the police officers' invasion of his home "deprived [Annunciatio] of his liberty and property without due process of law," and his property had been illegally obtained by the police as a result of their invasion of his home.[59] Annunciatio clearly knew his rights as an American subject residing in the United States and was not afraid to claim them. While the racial classifications of Filipinos and other Asian Americans were often up for social or cultural grabs, minority status placed them in a precarious position before the law even when they claimed the most fundamental rights. In the South, where even American citizens were routinely prosecuted for crimes they did not commit and were blatantly denied even the pretense of a trial, Annunciatio was on shaky ground, and his cries for respect as a colonial subject fell on deaf ears. Although his status as a nonblack person and a racial and political oddity afforded him certain privileges and allowed him to go further than many black men in appealing a conviction of rape, there were limits to this legal maneuvering.

It did not take long for Annunciatio to be reminded that in the South he was a racial minority who faced obstacles in fighting for justice. In addition to the objection that they did not know that Paul Seymour would be a witness for the state, Annunciatio and Turner based their demand for a retrial on Seymour's racially tinged remarks during the case. In his testimony when he insisted that he watched the girls go in and out of Annunciatio's apartment "as any white American would do," Seymour reminded the jury that

Annunciatio was an outsider and a potential predator not only because of his supposedly suspicious behavior with young girls but also because of his race. In the motion for retrial, Annunciatio argued that even though Judge Moore had instructed Seymour "to leave that out" after Turner objected, the remark was damaging and prejudicial. It was impossible for Seymour to "leave out" his comment regarding Annunciatio's race when the jury was already exposed to such racial profiling.[60] Race was undoubtedly a factor in most southern cases involving black defendants, with lawyers, prosecutors, judges, and juries relying on preconceived notions and legal conventions to come to verdicts. Atlantans could not neatly define Annunciatio as black, but as Seymour demonstrated, they knew that he was certainly not white. As in the cases of other minority and black men brought before the bar, Annunciatio's race worked against him before he even set foot in the courtroom; Seymour's racialized explanations for what he saw merely reinforced the jurors' notion that nonwhites, regardless of the shade of their skin, deserved suspicion rather than the benefit of the doubt. Whereas historians have elaborated on the identity crises that Asian Americans many times faced in southern states when authorities tried to determine where they fell on the often malleable color line, at least in the Fulton County courts it was clear to all except Annunciatio that his political and nonblack status ultimately provided few favors in the outcome of the case. Nevertheless, Annunciatio pushed the boundaries of southern legal conventions in the Jim Crow era by demanding a retrial for reasons of racial injustice and discrimination under the law.[61]

Annunciatio's political status as a colonial subject and Assistant Solicitor General E. A. Stephens's openly negative remarks regarding the imperial relationship between the United States and the Philippines, however, demonstrate that this was no ordinary, racially defined case in the South. Annunciatio's classification as a national also worked against him during the trial and revealed the complex relationship that southerners had with the "little brown brothers." Along with the illegal search and seizure of Annunciatio's property, Turner listed Stephens's use of the trial to voice his opinions on the Philippines as the prime justification for declaring a mistrial. At one point during the superior court trial, Stephens turned to the jury and unleashed a string of vitriol: "The United States took over the Philippine Islands, and why? God only knows. We got a burden when we took over those islands. We have the Philippines with us and can't get rid of them. There should be some way to get the Filipinoes [sic] back, but there is no way to do so."[62] Annunciatio himself "then and there called the Court's attention to said alleged remarks . . . and asked and insisted upon the Court declaring a mistrial because there had been evidence

Solicitor General E. A. Stephens (*far left*) during the murder trial of George Harsh in 1929 in Atlanta. *Photo by Kenneth Rogers, courtesy of the Kenan Research Center at the Atlanta History Center.*

introduced regarding the acquisition of said islands . . . whether they were an asset or a liability, or whether they had caused the U.S. any trouble, or how much."[63] Rightfully so, Annunciatio demanded a mistrial because "said remark was made for the purpose of prejudice of the jury . . . and said argument was highly prejudicial against [the] defendant . . . because of his race."[64] Annunciatio accused the court of improper conduct for not declaring a mistrial after Stephens's irrelevant and damaging political rant concerning the Philippines and Filipinos.

In response to Annunciatio's objections, however, Stephens argued that his beliefs about the Philippines and their inhabitants were perfectly in line with the trial. He was not attempting to smear the defendant with prejudicial remarks, he explained, but rather, he "merely intended to argue the difference in customs and social status of the defendant and the alleged victim to show that if sexual relations were had the probability was that it was by force."[65] Stephens's questioning of the U.S. purpose and goals in controlling the Philippines was directly related to the case: Now that the Philippines were a colonial possession, Americans like those in Atlanta were forced to deal with the Filipinos who settled in the United States and the racial, legal, and sexual chaos they brought with them. As a young, white, southern American girl, Rosa Mae Clower defined sexual contact differently than Annunciatio. As such, if any sexual contact occurred between the defendant and Clower, it was because Annunciatio's "customs" encouraged him to take what he wanted by force, bringing to fruition all the preconceived notions of Filipino men as sexual predators. Stephens did not go into great detail about a racial predilection for rape among Filipinos and argued that he was merely reminding the jury that the cultural atmosphere of the Philippines might support the use of intimidation and force in sexual relations. Stephens's own experience with crimes of a sexual nature ran deep: He had assisted the prosecution during the Leo Frank case and had served on special committees to clean up the red-light districts of Atlanta's black neighborhoods in order to promote and protect pure womanhood.[66] Stephens's previous experiences with cases such as Annunciato's, combined with his clear opinions on Filipinos and colonization, fueled his political outburst in court. To guard against any undue uses of Stephens's statement, Judge Moore instructed the jury to disregard the assistant solicitor's argument "as to the race of the defendant" and to "try said case as they would any other case irrespective of where the defendant came from or his race."[67] Moore reminded the jury that Annunciatio was "entitled to a fair and impartial trial as any other defendant would be," and Stephens agreed to "not say anything more about that" for the remainder of the case.[68]

In the context of imperialism and racial relations in the South, Stephens's remarks about colonialism are unsurprising. The remarks and Annunciatio's objections to the solicitor general's racial prejudice brought before the Atlanta court the complex relationship between race, sex, and imperialism. Stephens used Annunciatio's political and racial status and played on stereotypes to discredit the Filipino's character. Whereas Stephens was clear in his distaste for the burden that colonization placed on the United States, others in the Atlanta area were more ambivalent about the political connection between America and the Philippines. Returning from a trip to the Philippines, U.S. congressman from Georgia Charles R. Crisp did not hesitate to argue that "Filipinos were a long way away from being ready for self-government" and "that from the viewpoint of the Anglo Saxon, it would be a long time before they reached that point."[69] Another writer for the *Atlanta Constitution* was wary of continued colonization because correcting the primitiveness of the Filipinos was "a problem that promises to cost more trouble and expense than the United States had any idea of when it made the Filipinos its wards."[70] Many anti-imperialists were interested in granting independence not to ensure political freedom for the Filipinos but, rather, to prevent further migration of

Filipinos to the United States.[71] Socially and culturally, the people of Atlanta, as in other areas of the United States, expressed complicated and sometimes contradictory views on Filipinos. In the courts, however, these views crystallized in Annunciatio's racial classification as nonwhite and un-American. Thus, the classification of Filipino Americans had a peculiar and debated role in the legal, racial, and sexual structure of the South. Annunciatio viewed his political status as an advantage, while Stephens argued that Annunciatio's racial and migrant identities, as threats to white womanhood, overruled any legal benefits that his national status might provide.

Unfortunately for Annunciatio, on July 23, 1932, Judge Moore denied the motion for a retrial. (With Turner's assistance, Amby Subia also attempted to argue for a new trial but was denied in August 1932.)[72] Annunciatio's attempts at overturning his conviction by highlighting the errors and civil rights violations during the case failed to convince Moore of the need for a retrial. As far as the superior court was concerned, any discriminatory or prejudicial remarks were handled appropriately, and the outcome of the case was in line with Georgia's punishment for rape. Annunciatio had received a fair trial in the Fulton County Superior Court and therefore had little ground for demanding a revisit to the case.

Annunciatio's setback in Fulton County, however, did not end his fight for justice. While imprisoned at the Georgia State Penitentiary, Annunciatio worked with his attorney on an appeal to take before the Georgia Supreme Court. In March 1933 Annunciatio and Turner went before the state supreme court with the same list of complaints: illegal search and seizure, inflammatory remarks based on race, and Moore's failure to declare a mistrial and order a new hearing. As with Annunciatio's motion for a new trial at the county level, the supreme court denied his appeal, confirming the lower court's decision.[73]

All the justices except Associate Justice Samuel C. Atkinson concurred. Interestingly enough, Atkinson's dissenting opinion rested not on any of the racial or civil rights violations that Annunciatio had raised but, rather, on the definition of rape and the differences between seduction and intimidation that were part of the original trial. Drawing on previous Georgia cases involving similar circumstances, Atkinson argued that there was no evidence presented to support the claim that Annunciatio raped Clower. Not one witness who took the stand during the first trial clearly indicated that penetration (a necessary component to defining rape under Georgia law) had occurred; Clower had described only Annunciatio's placing of his private parts against her private parts. Also, because of Clower's questionable testimony about what occurred that day in the apartment, it was difficult to discern if Annunciatio actually used intimidation to gain carnal knowledge of Clower without her consent. "It follows, plainly and without argument," Atkinson concluded, "that a rape cannot be made on the basis of a prosecution for seduction. The two offenses are so totally different, they cannot be confused, nor can one of them by any possibility . . . be substituted for the other."[74] Annunciatio may have been guilty of seducing a young girl, but there was no solid proof that he had raped Rosa Mae Clower. For Atkinson, Annunciatio deserved a retrial due to legal technicalities, not because of rights violations or evidence of racism displayed in the courtroom.

Despite the loss, however, Annunciatio's little-known legal battle challenged the southern courts to consider, if not fully recognize, the rights of Asian Americans and colonial subjects in relation to Jim Crow. The traditional boundaries of sexual relationships in the South were expanded beyond black/white in this case, and imperial relationships invaded the Fulton County courthouse and southern sexuality. Annunciatio's supposed sexual nature as an Asian American as well as his political status as a noncitizen from an American colony were focal points of the trial. Although Annunciatio attempted to argue that, as an American national, he was entitled to the rights provided under the Constitution regardless of his race, his arguments proved futile. Although it failed in the courtroom, Annunciatio's case was important for drawing attention to the limits of citizenship as a foundation for rights and the potential for Asian Americans to set themselves apart from the southern system of Jim Crow and racial discrimination.

THE TRIALS OF BEING A "CHINAMAN'S WIFE": MARRIAGE, IMMIGRATION, AND MISCEGENATION

Chinese sailor Han Say Naim arrived in the United States in 1942 when he was a sailor on a British vessel docked in New York City and "jumped ship," a tactic that many Chinese sailors used during the war in order to remain in America. But Naim claimed to have done so in order to "make more money on an American ship."[75] While the details of his entry into the United States are not clear, for the next ten years, Naim traveled along the East Coast in search of work, eventually securing employment on the SS *Lipari* as a merchant seaman. Naim frequently went to sea, traveling to India, Korea, and other Asian nations and docking temporarily in New York City, Baltimore, and more often, Norfolk, Virginia. In Norfolk on an extended leave in February 1952, Naim met Ruby Lamberth (originally from Michigan).

In May, Naim and Lamberth decided to get married, but the decision was difficult to carry out in the state of Virginia. While most southern states had some form of antimiscegenation law in place by the mid-twentieth century that targeted black and white couples, some, like Virginia, broadened miscegenation to include marriages between a white resident and anyone who was not white, including Asian Americans and other racial minority groups. Although the Asian American population in Virginia was small compared with other minority groups during the early twentieth century, the threat of any form of interracial relationship and the potential undermining of racial and legal order was enough for Virginia to enact the 1924 Racial Integrity Act, one of the most restrictive and harsh of all antimiscegenation laws in the United States. While the supreme court of California ruled antimiscegenation statutes unconstitutional in 1948 with the *Perez v. Sharp* case (involving a Mexican American woman and an African American man), southern states still upheld the 1883 *Pace v. Alabama* decision that protected bans on interracial sexual relationships and the power of the states to regulate them. With the Racial Integrity Act, Virginia proved to be a stronghold for discriminatory measures against interracial marriage.[76]

Faced with the reality of how difficult it would be to procure a marriage license in Virginia, Lamberth and Naim fled to North Carolina in June 1952. Fortunately for the couple, the question of Chinese/white marriages in North Carolina had already been decided in 1929, when the North Carolina attorney general approved a marriage license for L. W. Moon (a Chinese man) and his white fiancée to marry in Greensboro.[77] Despite North Carolina's generally "loose" antimiscegenation laws in comparison with Virginia's Racial Integrity Act, little is known of the experience the Naims had in North Carolina: Was it relatively easy to obtain a license? Were there difficulties in finding an official to marry the couple? Did Naim and Lamberth face unsympathetic court clerks who knew of Virginia's laws? Unknowns aside, a few days later they were back in Virginia after having married in the small town of Elizabeth City, North Carolina.

By 1953, however, the marriage began to disintegrate. Ruby Naim filed for an absolute divorce, leveling charges of adultery against Han Say Naim and describing their relationship as a "love that could not be known" in Virginia.[78] Although Portsmouth Circuit Court Judge Floyd Kellam did not grant an absolute divorce, he did annul the marriage using the Racial Integrity Act, stating that the marriage was void under Virginia law. In granting the annulment, Judge Kellam followed precedent set during an earlier ruling in 1949 regarding another Chinese/white couple seeking annulment in Virginia, although in this instance it was "Chinaman" Jong Len Yigh of Richmond who asked that his marriage to Laura Anne Wolfe be voided under the Virginia act.[79] In response, Naim began the long appeals process to have the judgment overturned in order to allow him to remain in the United States on a spousal visa. The resulting 1955 *Naim v. Naim* case brought before the U.S. Supreme Court was an early attempt at challenging states' abilities to pass legislation prohibiting interracial marriages.

But Naim was also a Chinese alien and a man eager for citizenship in a nation where for most of its history such a goal was not easy or even possible for Asian Americans to attain. It is easy to group Naim's case with the contemporaneous 1954 *Jackson v. State* case in which the Supreme Court upheld an Alabama court's conviction of a black woman, Linnie Jackson, for violating the state's antimiscegenation law by entering a relationship with a white man. Both *Jackson* and *Naim* were failed yet important attempts at changing miscegenation law in the progression to the Supreme Court's decision in the 1967 *Loving v. Virginia* case in which the laws barring interracial marriage were declared unconstitutional. However, the Naim case is also important for understanding the centrality of citizenship, immigration, and civil rights in southern legal history.[80]

In addition to its role in the chain of antimiscegenation legal challenges of the 1950s and 1960s, *Naim v. Naim* is part of a larger historical battle for immigrant access to protections and rights in the South. Han Say Naim's status as an immigrant suggests that this case speaks as much to immigration rights as to civil rights history.[81] Having lost his chances of achieving residency through spousal relations after the Portsmouth court annulled his marriage to Ruby, Han faced an uncertain future in the United States, dependent on seaman's visas that expired after anywhere from sixty days to six months. The court transcripts and records do not reveal any of Han's emotional reasons for objecting to his wife's demand for a divorce, but legally speaking, his fight was tied to his resident status rather than a desire to remain in a loving relationship that would characterize later antimiscegenation battles, including the *Loving* case. While *Naim* was no lovelorn or romantic tale of passion squelched by prejudice and racism, antimiscegenation laws prevented Han from receiving a full and fair trial in court, thereby unfairly jeopardizing his future. Han Say Naim's situation represents another aspect of *Naim v. Naim*, one rooted in the often-uphill battles for legal justice that immigrants faced while living under discriminatory laws in the United States. As a racial minority and an immigrant residing in the Jim Crow South, Naim was in a situation that was particularly difficult and speaks to the impossible odds stacked against individuals without citizenship. *Naim v. Naim* represents how intricately connected immigrant and civil rights were to antimiscegenation law in the South.[82]

Faced with this predicament, Naim, like other immigrants before him, turned to the law to ensure that he would be guaranteed a fair appeal and enlisted the help of civil rights and immigration lawyer David Carliner in his fight. Naim's attempt to appeal the decision to the U.S. Supreme Court was similar to Annunciatio's in *State v. Annunciatio* in that both men relied on using their noncitizen status to argue for rights. Carliner and Naim, however, would emphasize Naim's status as a Chinese national and specific rights that were guaranteed to him as stated in previous treaties and agreements between China and the United States, arguing that immigrants received special protections that overrode discriminatory state laws.

The fact that Han and Ruby's marriage ended in a contentious trial would not have surprised many Americans at the time. When we think historically of the hostility toward interracial marriages, white and African American relationships have shaped the literature on the subject; however, the fear of Asian American men intermarrying with white women was a widespread concern across the United States during the early to mid-twentieth century as well.[83] Western but also southern states (even where the population of Asian Americans was relatively low) banned marriages between members of the "Mongol" or "Malay" races and whites. While the idea of miscegenation was repulsive for many whites and various state laws prohibiting interracial relationships reflected this opinion, lascivious stories of mixed-race nuptials gone sour nevertheless filled tabloids and popular periodicals. In the tabloid stories, women often sought annulment or divorce after realizing they had been seduced by Asian men into becoming prostitutes or deciding that they could no longer live as a "Chinaman's" wife in the midst of societal scorn and pressure. The marriages often ended when a judge granted an annulment upon the conclusion of a messy court case set on proving that the Asian man in question was a disloyal or abusive husband.[84]

Ruby's suit for divorce did not specifically mention any abuse or maltreatment, but her statements during the hearing indicate that she had grown weary of Han. Despite very loving letters written to her husband in April 1953, Ruby accused Han of adultery in October when she filed the charges, indicating that his time away as part of a ship crew provided him with opportunities to engage in extramarital affairs. However, there was little proof that he had committed such acts. In fact, a letter from Ruby to her mother from August 1953 revealed that Ruby lived with a man named Stan while Han was away on his most recent trip; Ruby even signed the letter "Love, Stan and Ruby." More telling is an emotional letter that Ruby wrote to Han in September in which she expressed her frustration with his legal and immigrant status. Ruby was supposed to meet him in New York City after stopping in Washington, D.C., to meet with his immigration attorney about paperwork for naturalization. Ruby never made it farther than Baltimore, however, explaining to Han her growing frustrations with the immigration process and that she "got exactly nowhere with results" on his forms and papers. Her impatience overcame whatever love she still held for her husband: "Han, this whole mess is just too much for me to try and contend with. I can't take anymore and sincerely feel that it is best to get completely out of the whole situation." She then informed him that the following morning she would be meeting with her own attorneys from the Bangle, Bangle, and Bangle law firm in Portsmouth and that she would "appreciate her freedom" from the marriage.[85]

Ruby's request for an absolute divorce on the grounds of adultery did not work out well for either plaintiff or defendant. While securing a divorce was her first goal, Ruby also asked for alimony payments of $200 a month from Han, the same amount that he sent home to her from his own pay. Although Ruby filed for divorce in October, the hearing was pushed back until February 1954, when Han was set to return from a trip to Korea. The trial itself was relatively uneventful. Ruby, her friends and family, and Han testified during the hearing, where the focus was on determining whether or not both parties were legal residents of Virginia. The court ruled that Ruby was a resident but that Han was not, considering he was an alien and was away on leave more than he was at home in Norfolk. After hearing testimonies and reviewing evidence, Judge Kellam found no proof of Han's adultery and also denied Ruby alimony (noting that she was able to support herself as she had done while married to Han). Because Ruby lacked a clear and consistent reason for demanding an absolute divorce, Kellam chose to void the marriage under Virginia's antimiscegenation law, noting that both parties were fully aware of the state's bans on interracial marriage and had left the state to procure an unlawful relationship. Judge Kellam's decision in granting an annulment left Ruby without the financial security she had hoped to get from her ex-husband, but she did have her freedom. Meanwhile, Han Say Naim's future in America was unclear.[86]

Before the divorce hearing, Virginia-based immigration and civil rights lawyer David Carliner worked with the Naims as the pair poured money, time, and other resources into helping Han become a legal citizen. After the passage of the Immigration and Nationality Act of 1952, Han began the process of naturalizing, acquiring the assistance of Carliner, a recent graduate of law school with an interest in issues of civil and immigrant rights working in Washington, D.C. Despite Carliner's assistance and the somewhat more relaxed immigration and naturalization laws, the slow legal slog through paperwork and bureaucracy took its toll on both Ruby and Han. With his marriage annulled, Han turned to Carliner to guide him in how to proceed. While Carliner recognized an opportunity to carry out his long-held desire to challenge the constitutionality of antimiscegenation laws in the United States, Han required practical and legal advice on how to fight the annulment in hopes of maintaining his residency. If Han hoped to be able to stay in the United States and eventually become a citizen, his only recourse was to challenge Ruby's case by directly tackling the issues of civil rights and antimiscegenation law.

Neither Han Say Naim nor Carliner was surprised by Judge Kellam's annulment and filed an appeal with the Virginia Supreme Court. For Carliner, the annulment was the first step in challenging the Racial Integrity Act at the state level and, hopefully, later challenging antimiscegenation laws at the national level. Carliner knew that the Virginia Supreme Court of Appeals would more than likely not overturn Kellam's decision; this would be the first step in developing a case that would require more attention from the U.S. Supreme Court. In this situation, a failure in securing an appeal would be a victory in challenging the jurisdiction of the Virginia code and moving the case to the federal level. For Naim, however, the appeal was an opportunity to challenge the ruling as well as to insist on his right to equal protection that had been abridged by the state of Virginia and the Racial Integrity Act, demonstrating that civil rights applied to all who resided in the United States regardless of citizenship status.

In attempting to define the Virginia code as a violation of state jurisdictional power, Carliner identified Naim's status as a Chinese citizen living in the United States as an added boost rather than a hindrance to his legal strategy for the case. Naim's position as an immigrant presented Carliner with an opportunity to challenge the Virginia code on the grounds of immigration violations as well as civil rights. Most historical and legal studies of the Naim case and appeal focus on Carliner's use (and later discarding) of the "full faith and credit" clause of the Constitution that protects one state from infringing on the power and decisions of another. Carliner argued in the appeal that by not recognizing a marriage granted by North Carolina, Virginia ultimately violated this clause. Few scholars mention that Carliner also used immigration and Naim's alien status to argue that the code was in violation of a variety of federal treaties and constitutional laws. In addition to highlighting what would later become staples of the case, including the fact that the "Virginia law was so broad that not even ostensibly white persons can tell whether their marriages are illegal" and was particularly "offensive ... and unconstitutional," Carliner also focused on the statute's "violation of the U.S. treaty with China."[87] The Virginia code was inapplicable to the Naims in this instance because Han Say Naim was "a citizen of China without domicile in the state of Virginia," and as such, the code "conflict[ed] with Article II of the Immigration Treaty of 1880 concluded between the United States and China."[88] The 1880 treaty, or the Angell Treaty, granted Chinese immigrants "most favored nation" status and agreed to extend certain rights and privileges to Chinese laborers already living in the United States. The Angell Treaty and other formal agreements between the U.S. and China during the late nineteenth through early twentieth centuries "superseded" the Virginia code and guaranteed that Chinese nationals in the United States would receive equal protection and rights.[89] Within his notes and records, Carliner made no reference to the legacy of the Chinese Exclusion Act of 1882, which prohibited Chinese laborers from entering the United States. Although Chinese exclusion was formally repealed in 1943 following China's alliance with the U.S. during World War II, Carliner did not acknowledge the fact that the Angell Treaty had not had a bearing on the treatment of Chinese in America for the previous seventy years. Such realities did not stop Carliner in developing a legal strategy that would fly in the face of decades of discrimination against Chinese immigrants. Because Naim was a Chinese citizen, the Virginia code did not apply to him, yet the Portsmouth court violated this principle and Naim's basic rights and protections under the Fourteenth Amendment. Carliner evoked the "diversity of citizenship" clause in his appeal, arguing that because Naim was still a citizen of China, the Naim case fell within the jurisdiction of federal authorities rather than state courts. While crafting his legal strategy with the assistance of other American Civil Liberties Union (ACLU) attorneys, including legal counsel head Herb Monte Levy, Carliner paid special attention to Naim's legal status in the United States and used it as a key piece of evidence in seeking an appeal from the Virginia Supreme Court. Expecting the Virginia appeals court to argue for the validity and constitutionality of the Virginia Racial Integrity Act, Carliner used Naim's Chinese citizenship to emphasize the international and foreign policy violations of the statute, making this case one for federal rather than state courts.

In response to Carliner's appeal, Virginia attorney general J. Lindsey Almond Jr. used previous state cases involving Asian Americans to argue in favor of the Virginia code and the Portsmouth court's decision. Carliner compared the Naim case to other Supreme Court decisions concerning immigrants and state laws, particularly those involving racial classifications. Carliner referenced the 1886 *Yick Wo v. Hopkins* case, where the Supreme Court ruled in favor of Yick Wo, a Chinese immigrant who fought against a California law barring Chinese laundries from operating unless the owners paid an additional tax, successfully arguing that his rights to equal protection under the Fourteenth Amendment had been violated. While Carliner argued in the petition that the Supreme Court's decision in the Yick Wo case guaranteed that the Fourteenth Amendment's protections and rights "apply with equal force to persons other than Negroes," the Virginia attorneys general presented a different interpretation of the decision and how it applied to Naim.[90] Almond argued that Carliner never once "in a brief, six page appeal" challenged the racial classifications in the Racial Integrity Act, a fact that set this case apart from others in the past. Almond referenced the 1952 *Sei Fujii v. California* case involving a Japanese immigrant who attempted to challenge the California anti-alien land laws by arguing that they violated the charters and rights guaranteed by the United Nations. In this case, the Supreme Court ruled that while the United Nations treaty did not overrule local laws, the California land laws did, in fact, violate the Fourteenth Amendment, not because the law itself was racist or unconstitutional, but because the law created racial classifications that had "no substantial relation to the health, safety, and welfare of the state and therefore were arbitrary and capricious."[91] In other words, land laws and antimiscegenation laws themselves were not unconstitutional, but the creation of "arbitrary" racial categories under said laws was. One had to prove that the racial categories created by such laws were done so with the health and well-being of state citizens in mind to be constitutional, which the Racial Integrity Act of Virginia did because the legislature created it for the racial benefit and protection of Virginia citizens.[92] Because Carliner did not actually challenge the racial categories laid out in the Racial Integrity Act but, rather, Naim's subjection to the act as an immigrant, Almond maintained that there was no constitutional issue present in the Naim case and the annulment was well within the powers of the state of Virginia.

As Carliner accurately predicted, the Virginia Supreme Court of Appeals rejected Naim's claim in April 1955, standing by the lower court's initial ruling in favor of the annulment. Justice Archibald Buchannan spoke on behalf of the Virginia court when he rebuked Carliner's attempts to apply the recent *Boiling v. Sharpe* ruling (which overturned *Plessy v. Ferguson* and integrated transportation) to the issue of marriage, arguing that school and busing desegregation was one thing, but to attack a state's right to regulate segregation of marriage would be "harmful to good citizenship."[93] The Virginia Supreme Court ruled that the Racial Integrity Act and the state's right to pass such legislation were merely extensions of the state's attempts to protect its own citizens, a right that was not limited by the Fourteenth Amendment and, in fact, was upheld by the Tenth Amendment. Carliner explained in a letter to Levy shortly after the hearing that "there was little question that the Court will uphold the marriage prohibition statute" and "the reaction of the most vocal member of the bench was that rather than a denial of equal protection under the law, a Chinese had more advantages than a Caucasian," for "a Caucasian ... could marry only other Caucasians, but a Chinese could marry freely among other races—Negroes, Indians, et. cetera, and so had more choice."[94] Despite his temptation to "tell the judge that he was being cute," Carliner bit his tongue and instead went back to the drawing board with Naim to develop a more comprehensive argument to take before the federal Supreme Court.

In rethinking his legal strategy, Carliner eventually dropped the full faith and credit issue and instead chose to focus primarily on the relationship between the annulment and the guarantees of the Fourteenth Amendment. Carliner emphasized that the Virginia Racial Integrity Act violated "the equal protection and due process clauses" of the Fourteenth Amendment, including the rights and privileges guaranteed to noncitizens such as Naim. By combining due process and equal protection with the violation of existing treaties between the United States and China, Carliner argued that antimiscegenation codes harmed not only the rights of citizens but also, in this case, the rights of immigrants residing in the U.S.[95] Although Carliner and the ACLU "waived any claim that Virginia could not control marriages outside of its borders in order to try to make sure that the Court would reach the miscegenation issue," by the time the appeal reached the Supreme Court, Carliner's initial legal strategy focused heavily on the violation of Naim's rights as a Chinese citizen residing in the United States.[96]

Following the Virginia Supreme Court's rejection of Naim's appeal, Carliner, Naim, and the ACLU sought to draw wider support from other branches of government and legal entities for the case. Naim's status as a Chinese citizen, in many cases, either hurt or helped Carliner's appeal for outside assistance. In July 1955, Carliner and the ACLU attempted to "get the Department of Justice to join in the appeal, both because of the constitutional question and because of the immigration aspects of the statute."[97] Unfortunately, the Department of Justice rejected the ACLU's request because, according to Carliner, the case was "too hot."[98] While it is difficult to determine precisely what was "too hot" about the Naim case for the Department of Justice, the positioning of the case within the larger, ongoing battle over the 1954 *Brown v. Board* decision may have played a role in the agency's decision to withhold assistance. Also, the burgeoning Cold War climate, the "fall" of China to Communism in 1949, and the general suspicion of migrants, particularly those from Communist nations or with ties to supposedly subversive or leftist organizations, may have also contributed to the Department of Justice's hesitancy in investigating the case.[99] In other instances, the immigration aspect of the case garnered attention from the media, specifically *Time* magazine, which in June 1955 had contacted Levy and the ACLU because the editors identified "some immigration aspects of the case in which we had been asked to intervene" and were interested in running a story on Naim, his marriage, and the ensuing legal battle.[100] Naim's immigration status signified that this was not only a legal battle between races over antimiscegenation laws but a far more complicated struggle involving rights, racism, and immigration laws and policies.

Carliner and the ACLU also looked into other antimiscegenation cases outlining issues similar to the Naim appeal's. Carliner was able to uncover a case from Mississippi where a white wife was "suing a Chinese husband for support for herself and three children, and for an absolute divorce on grounds of a previously existing undissolved [sic] marriage to a wife in China." The trial court dismissed the case "upon the basis of a Mississippi statute declaring the marriage void [on account of miscegenation]" and "refused to grant support for the wife or children—in effect illegitimatizing the children." Carliner, however, explained to Levy in a letter from June 1955 that this was a "very sympathetic case" and could possibly serve either as a framework for Naim's argument if the Court did hear the case or as part of a larger appeal drawing together a number of antimiscegenation cases involving immigrants and white, American-born spouses.[101] Carliner also carefully followed the development of a similar case in Georgia, hopeful that he might "have a batch of cases to take to the Supreme Court" by the end of the year.[102]

Despite Carliner's identification of *Naim* as a prime test case that could possibly trigger a series of trials that had potential for overturning antimiscegenation laws and upholding minority and migrant/white marriages in the South, others were not as convinced of the power of *Naim v. Naim*. Sol Rabkin, a prominent member of and legal advisor to the Jewish Anti-Defamation League, wrote to Carliner in August 1955 expressing his concern in having his organization support the Naim case at the federal level. Rabkin's doubt arose from the case's perceived inability to "excite public sympathy" for Naim.[103] Rabkin correctly described the Naim case as "a civil proceeding in which a white woman is escaping from a marriage to a Chinese man" and explained that "it would certainly seem much better to have this question come before the court in a case involving a criminal proceeding in which the state of Virginia has prosecuted two persons who love each other and are married and wish to remain married."[104] Certainly, as Rabkin countered, it would seem as though Naim would not receive much sympathy from either the court or other whites. With the public already suspicious of Asian/white marriages from scandalous tabloid stories and the details of the case describing a situation where a woman was seeking a divorce rather than fighting against state law to remain married, Rabkin did have a valid point. While the end of World War II typically brought a degree of acceptance for Chinese Americans and other Asian groups in the United States and the South in terms of school integration, as discussed in Chapter 2, such reconciliation did not easily translate to interracial relations in all southern states.[105] A situation where a white woman sought state recognition of her interracial marriage in order to punish her fleeing Chinese husband (as in the case from Mississippi) would probably appear more favorable. Also, as the *Loving* case would eventually show, a couple that was, in fact, fighting to remain married would garner more sympathy.

Rabkin suggested that Carliner and the ACLU wait for what he believed would be a more ideal case, one where "one of our returning veterans, who married a Japanese or Korean bride, is prosecuted and threatened with a jail sentence."[106] "Here, such a defendant would generate much public sympathy with resultant public disapproval of the anti-miscegenation statute"; this was a reference to the rising number of war brides who came with their husbands or fiancés to the United States following changes in immigration policy (primarily the War Brides Acts of 1945 and 1950) after World War II.[107] A large number of brides were from Japan, China, or Korea and had met and married their American servicemen husbands while they were stationed in the Pacific. This was a unique situation where state-level antimiscegenation laws did not reflect the changes in immigration policies at the federal level. Rabkin argued in favor of waiting for such a case to arise because it would create a better opportunity to challenge miscegenation policies than the Naim case.

But Carliner and the ACLU did not agree with Rabkin. They identified the Naim case as a prime opportunity to challenge miscegenation laws as violations of both domestic and foreign policy. Throughout the summer of 1955, Carliner continued to work with Levy to attempt to build support from a variety of civil rights and ethnic rights organizations, particularly those that represented the interests of Asian Americans and immigrants. Levy explained to Roger Baldwin of the ACLU that "since the Court recently denied review on a similar case," he and Carliner were "thinking of bulwarking our case by getting various nationality groups to join with us."[108] In particular, Levy suggested that Baldwin gather "the names and addresses of Indian, Korean, Chinese, Philippine, and Indonesian groups—non-Communist ones, of course—which you think might be interested in lending their names" to Naim's cause.[109] Levy and Carliner focused on gaining support from other Asian and migrant groups that might identify with the Naim appeal and understand Naim's hardships in naturalizing and living under antimiscegenation laws across the United States. A coalition of racial and ethnic minorities supportive of Naim "would indicate the breadth of interest in the interracial marriage issue if the Japanese American Citizens League, Chinese Citizens Association, the Association of Immigration and Nationality Lawyers, the American Jewish Congress ... and so on were to be listed of counsel through their attorneys."[110] Carliner also noted that "the *Afro-American* here by the way has editorialized that the NAACP should file a petition to appear amicus" in the case.[111] By emphasizing both the immigration and interracial marriage issues, Carliner and the ACLU endeavored to highlight the multiple illegalities of the Virginia Racial Integrity Act and other antimiscegenation laws and codes, making the issue of miscegenation as much a multicultural and immigration concern as a fight against racial discrimination in the Jim Crow South. Naim's legal status represented a new challenge to cases involving antimiscegenation laws as well as a new angle to the growing civil rights movement that addressed the wide implications of the term "civil rights" for everyone living in the United States.

Ultimately, Naim would have limited financial and legal support from the proposed ethnic and racial organizations. Although the Japanese American Citizens League, the Association on American Indian Affairs, and despite Sol Rabkin's initial hesitation, the Anti-Defamation League became strong backers of the appeal and filed amicus briefs, other groups were not as willing to support the case. Some explanations were a combination of logistical and practical justifications. The National Association for the Advancement of Colored People explained that its efforts could be better applied to ensuring the success and enforcement of *Brown v. Board*, while Jack Wasserman, who represented the Association of Immigration and Nationality Lawyers, was barely able to convince members of his organization to appear on the brief (and only without being liable for financial contributions).[112] Despite Carliner's and the ACLU's arguments that Naim's situation represented more than a run-in with antimiscegenation law, many other ethnic and racial advocacy groups did not immediately connect the plight of the Chinese immigrant to the larger issues of citizenship and Fourteenth Amendment violations as hoped. For many, the antimiscegenation laws were overwhelmingly matters of black and white in the South, which complicated Naim's position as a Chinese immigrant fighting against such codes.

Newspapers across the country, however, portrayed Naim as part of a growing civil rights battle aimed not only at antimiscegenation laws but also at broad civil rights violations. In the fall of 1955, the *Lubbock Times* reported that Naim, "a Chinese seaman, contended that [marriage restrictions] violate the equal protection and due process law clauses of the Constitution's Fourteenth Amendment."[113] Here, Naim was the lone fighter against Virginia's antimiscegenation law as well as the laws of twenty-eight other states that forbade interracial marriages. What the article correctly identified was Naim's fight for the right to equal protection and due process under the law for *all* who married and lived under the jurisdiction of the U.S. Constitution; it was not just a fight against Virginia's Racial Integrity Act or even antimiscegenation laws in general. Although many Americans may have viewed the Naim case as an oddity or disconnected from larger civil rights battles such as school segregation or issues pertaining specifically to African Americans, others argued that Naim's fight was an important step for securing individual rights and liberties.

Similarly, the *New York Times* declared Naim's fight a leading case in a growing civil rights movement following the *Brown* decision. In his article "Civil Rights Highlight Supreme Court Session: Justices Will Consider Many Issues Involving Individual Freedoms," Luther A. Huston explained that in "the two recent court terms, the major issue has been racial segregation in public schools," with "corollary questions arising from that decision," one of those questions being interracial marriage. "The civil rights category is broad [and] under it the question has been raised for the first time of whether the equal protection and due process clauses of the Fourteenth Amendment inhibit the power of the state to dissolve a marriage upon the sole ground of the races of the married persons." By classifying Naim's legal struggle as a component of a larger movement, Huston situated Naim, a Chinese immigrant, in the midst of other forms of civil rights activism of the time. Rather than just an individual seeking to challenge antimiscegenation law or segregation in the Jim Crow South, Naim was a man who, despite not being a citizen of the United States, challenged the parameters of the definition of "civil rights" and applied this term to the basic protections guaranteed under the Fourteenth Amendment. Although Huston did not go into great depth in describing Naim's past or his situation, his identification of the Naim fight as a part of the growing civil rights struggle in the United States connected Naim to other immigrant activists before him (such as Yick Wo) who expanded "civil rights" to include individuals who were not necessarily citizens.[114]

Eventually, by November 1955, the Supreme Court received Naim's appeal; however, the immediate reactions of the judges were less than promising. After meeting in conference, the judges ultimately vacated the annulment but remanded the decision of the Virginia Supreme Court of Appeals and asked for the case to be sent back to the circuit court in Portsmouth. The reasoning behind the judges' action rested on a variety of points, ranging from the Court's current involvement in other civil rights issues to the supposed clarity of the initial Portsmouth and Virginia Supreme Court ruling. Among the explanations that the judges provided for their decision to pass on the Naim case, the most well-known was their insistence that the then-current school desegregation issue surrounding the contentious *Brown v. Board* decision and *Brown II* follow-up required full attention. The Court refused to hear the case and summarized its decision with a simple phrase: "lack of substantial federal question." For the majority of the judges, there was little in the Naim appeal that applied to federal principles or laws, and Virginia's right in overseeing marriage was not subject to federal intervention.[115]

More specifically, the Court also addressed the issue of Naim's "complicated status" as an immigrant, a factor in their decision to reject the case. While Carliner initially argued that Naim's immigrant status provided enough ground for the Racial Integrity Act to become a federal concern, the Supreme Court justices thought otherwise. Naim's status as a Chinese national who led a transitory life in the United States, rarely settling down to "establish domicile," added another complicated layer to Carliner's theory that the Virginia act did not apply to Naim or this particular marriage. The Court admitted that this presented a particular problem in determining the relation of Han Say Naim to the state of Virginia, potentially creating a loophole in the Racial Integrity Act; however, the Supreme Court justices ultimately decided that Ruby Naim, as the plaintiff, was a resident of Virginia, and therefore the code applied and the appeal was unfounded based on her residency. By using the "diversity of citizenship" issue as justification for their dismissal of the Naim appeal, the Court did not intervene in the complicated issue of antimiscegenation law, but it also limited Han Say Naim's ability to pursue legal justice as a noncitizen. In addition to delaying the fight against laws prohibiting interracial marriage, the Court also exposed the difficulties that immigrants such as Naim faced while attempting to challenge discriminatory laws in the United States.[116]

The Supreme Court's decision to reject the Naim case and return it to Virginia for further review resulted in a joyous outcry from Virginia residents. In January 1956, the Virginia Supreme Court officially rejected the higher Court's suggestion for a new look at the case, once and for all leaving the issues at hand "devoid of a properly presented federal question."[117] As historians have noted and Virginia newspapers proclaimed, the Naim rejection represented a victory for the state of Virginia against any form of potential forced integration. When Supreme Court Justice Harold Durton noted that "in view of the difficulties engendered by the segregation cases, it would be wise judicial policy to duck this question for a time," inhabitants of Virginia and other states reeling from the recent *Brown v. Board* and *Brown II* decisions celebrated the Virginia Supreme Court's own refusal to review the case again as a victory for states' rights. Although school segregation was the major political, social, and cultural topic of the mid-1950s, the challenges of integration as well as the fear and dread of the *Brown* decision affected other areas of life that were traditionally segregated, including marriage. The state of Virginia essentially "nullified" the Supreme Court's call for the Naim appeal to be remanded, with newspapers "trumpeting the action as the first step in the realization of an 'Ordinance of Imposition' against the Brown decision and school desegregation."[118] The *Washington Post and Times Herald*'s Roger Farquar asked in a January 1956 article if Virginia's "open defiance" of the Supreme Court's suggestion to have the case reopened was "a straw in the wind revealing what the State's highest court would do when public school desegregation cases come before it?" Farquar concluded that "only time could tell."[119] Virginia's decision to uphold Ruby Naim's annulment was a political form of support not only for antimiscegenation law but also for segregation in all realms of social and political life.

While traditional historical interpretations of reactions to the *Brown* decision describe white southerners' resistance to school integration and relations between whites and African Americans, Virginia's jubilant reaction to the failure of the Naim appeal also sheds light on another component of this same civil rights history. Not only were interracial marriages at the heart of one of the state's first official rejections of the federal government's attempt to fully integrate southern life, but the case also involved not a white/black couple but a Chinese/white marriage. Han Say Naim's challenges to the Racial Integrity Act represented an attack on a system of segregation and racism across the South, and his actions speak to the intricate connections between migration, citizenship, and civil rights.[120] In February 1956, Carliner again asked the Supreme Court to attempt another hearing on the case but was once again denied on grounds of "inadequacy of information."[121]

Following the Virginia Supreme Court's rejection of the U.S. Supreme Court's suggestion to send the case back to Portsmouth for review, Carliner remarked that the "fact that this was a Chinese-white marriage didn't make any difference; they [the Virginia Supreme Court] saw black all over the place."[122] But perhaps Carliner's statement is too simplistic. Naim's appeal and Carliner's representation of his client reveal that this case touched on issues of immigration, citizenship, and immigrant rights. In the end, the Court may have reduced Naim's complicated position to a matter of black and white, but the appeals process reveals a more complex picture of the impact of southern antimiscegenation laws. Naim's case was peculiar: He was not fighting against the annulment because he necessarily desired to stay with Ruby but, rather, because an annulment granted only on the grounds of race complicated the process of becoming an American citizen and remaining in the United States. Naim and Carliner set out to prove that although antimiscegenation laws prevented couples from entering into sanctioned relationships, these discriminatory measures also wielded power over immigrants, leaving individuals like Han Say Naim at the mercy of local and state courts. Denying Ruby's request for an end to her marriage would have made her life difficult, but Virginia's Racial Purity Act allowed her to easily remove herself form the marriage, using racial reasoning to place the burden of proof on Han for why the marriage should remain intact. In the end, his appeal revealed not only Virginia's insistence on maintaining antimiscegenation laws but also the federal court's general disinterest in his status as an immigrant in fighting against these laws. Immigrant protections provided no reprieve from southern racism and injustice in the courts.

Although many viewed the Naim case as a chance to either challenge the system of Jim Crow in place or uphold a centuries-old system of antimiscegenation law and discrimination, this example of stillborn justice speaks to more than just binary race relations and antimiscegenation. Many view the case as a failure. Legal scholars such as Gregory Dorr have attempted to identify the reasons for the higher Court's refusal to hear the appeal and examine the cultural and social norms surrounding the Racial Integrity Act. Likewise, lawyers and policy scholars use the Court's unwillingness to engage in the issue of miscegenation law so close to the dramatic *Brown v. Board* ruling in 1954 to shed light on the influences of public opinion on the judicial process. Civil rights and legal specialist Richard Delgado has gone so far as to nominate *Naim v. Naim* for inclusion in the "worst Supreme Court decisions" in history, citing the justices' shortsightedness and cruelty in rejecting Naim's appeal. Overall, the Naim decision (or lack thereof) is a painful reminder of our nation's lengthy battle against inequality and discrimination in issues of marriage and civil rights. However, Naim's appeal represents the globalization of miscegenation law following World War II and the intricate connections of sex to issues of citizenship and civil rights.

Little is known of what happened to Fortunatio Annunciatio and Han Say Naim after their failed attempts at overturning discriminatory statutes and legal practices. Annunciatio appears in the Georgia central registry of convicts as having served time at the Forsyth, Georgia, prison and as receiving a conditional pardon from Governor Eugene Tallmadge in June 1936.[123] We know slightly more about his partner Subia, who according to the same registry was listed as "Cuban" and was paroled in October 1935, the same month that he married a Georgia woman, Marie Henry.[124] Meanwhile, Naim's death certificate indicates that he died alone in Brooklyn, New York, at age ninety-one in 1996, hundreds of miles from the reaches of the Virginia law that stripped him of his marriage. It is unknown if Naim obtained legal residency and later naturalized or if he fell into the large group of undocumented immigrants living in the United States. The unknown whereabouts of both Annunciatio and Naim prove that in many cases, silence speaks volumes.

Both men attempted to use their noncitizen status to defy southern law, but both failed. As a result, their names do not typically appear in larger histories of civil rights and sex and antimiscegenation. Their stories and battles do not easily mesh with histories of the interracial marriage and civil rights movements. What their experiences prove, however, is that there were opportunities for noncitizens to attempt to manipulate southern courts, presenting an overlooked strategy for achieving justice. Citizenship was not the only means to arguing for civil rights, and the two men attempted to subvert state law by appealing to federal power in regulating transnational and international relationships between the United States and other countries. Intimate relationships became part of a web of foreign policies, constitutional law, and discriminatory state regulations in the *Annunciatio* and *Naim* cases. Although their attempts did not weaken the southern system of sexual segregation, both Annunciatio and Naim demonstrated to the courts that immigrants and colonial subjects knew of their civil rights and were willing to fight for them in the Jim Crow South.

POST-1965 CHANGES IN ASIAN AMERICA

After World War II and through the 1960s, Asian Americans began a transformative process, from being the "yellow peril" to becoming the model minority, and Asian Americans in the South experienced, to some degree, the same transformation. The war and its mottos of fighting for freedom and democracy at home and abroad affected the way Americans viewed their own hypocrisy toward minorities in the United States. African Americans were the largest minority group to use the aims of the war to demand attention to their plight with Jim Crow, prompting the growth of a nationwide civil rights movement, but Americans also came to view the century-old forms of legal discrimination against Asian immigrants and Asian Americans in a new light. Not only did Congress repeal the Chinese Exclusion Act in 1943 (making it legal for some Chinese to naturalize and allowing a small number of Chinese immigrants to enter the United States), but Filipino Americans and Indian Americans received similar treatment during and after World War II. In 1952, the McCarran-Walter Act (or the Immigration and Nationality Act of 1952), although designed to protect American security during the early Cold War by prohibiting and deporting subversive aliens, also made it possible for Asian immigrants of all ethnicities to become American citizens (while the number of Asians admitted to the United States did not drastically increase). Americans also viewed the ability of Japanese Americans to overcome the massive civil rights violations of wartime imprisonment and achieve economic and educational success as a model for all minorities to follow. Asian Americans came through the fires of World War II and proved that they were loyal Americans and deserving of equal treatment and respect, and while more subtle and sometimes not so subtle forms of racism and discrimination continued, the idea of the model minority shaped American perceptions of Asian Americans in comparison with other groups for decades to come. Southerners also to some degree welcomed Asian Americans into their society after World War II. Following general patterns across the United States at the time, southern schools, more specifically those in Mississippi, began to allow Asian Americans to attend white schools during the war. Similarly, the economic success of Asian Americans, at one point considered a threat to white labor and business, was now a sign of respectability, demonstrating that Asian Americans were not like African Americans (although limits to economic success and acceptability will be discussed later in Chapter 5).[1]

This new model minority identity helped Asian Americans to integrate into some areas of white southern life, but it also created tensions with African Americans. In the larger realm of African American civil rights activism during the 1950s and 1960s, Asian Americans living in southern states were relatively quiet and removed from such activity. While some Asian American students attending southern colleges and universities became involved in campus civil rights protests by the end of the 1960s, the presence of Asian Americans in the African American Civil Rights Movement was minuscule in the South. Although the Chinese in Cleveland and surrounding areas helped black families by letting them borrow more on credit at their stores and addressed them as "Mr. and Mrs.," the Chinese received preferential treatment by local banks for loans over African Americans, "acted like Caucasians," and refused to hire blacks in their groceries and laundries.[2] Despite lingering forms of social discrimination and ostracism, particularly for some Asian American children who attended white schools, Asian Americans gained a reputation for being "white" in the South following World War II and through the civil rights movement, for better or for worse.

The very fabric of Asian America also changed during and after the 1960s with the Immigration and Nationality Act of 1965. Following cries for more liberal immigration policies, the need for family reunification in America, and more visas to fill labor needs, President Lyndon Johnson signed the Hart-Celler Act in October 1965, shedding what many considered to be out-of-date and racist immigration laws. The act lifted the decades-old exclusion on Asian immigrants, created new visa categories for family members and workers, and established a standard ceiling of 290,000 visas per year. Although the act was not entirely liberalizing (provisions in the bill made it appear that the demand for labor outweighed the ideological abandonment of racist and exclusionary practices in immigration policy), it did succeed in bringing more Asian immigrants from a variety of nations to the United States despite

Johnson's belief that the act would not result in significant changes to previously existing migration patterns. Immigrants from India, Southeast Asia, and China flocked to America for business and educational opportunities. In 1965, Asian immigrants made up only 5 percent of the immigrant population in the United States; by 1985, that number increased to 19 percent.[3] Some, like Indian Americans, came to the southern United States to take advantage of business opportunities as whites fled during the late 1960s through the 1980s, and Atlanta's Asian American population grew rapidly through the 1960s and 1990s as technology and computer specialists were needed. The lifting of the old restrictionist national policies as well as the creation of special work-related visas under the Immigration Act of 1965 ensured that southern states, too, would gradually become more ethnically diverse.[4]

But more ethnic diversity did not equal acceptance of all Asian American newcomers to the South. A sharp divide between "older" Asian American groups such as Chinese Americans and Japanese Americans and "new" migrants including Vietnamese refugees and Indian immigrants developed in southern states as elsewhere in the United States; however, this distinction repeated patterns of racism that characterized the arrival of Chinese Americans and Japanese Americans in the South decades before. While Vietnamese Americans and Indian Americans were perhaps not faced with the challenges of becoming part of a Jim Crow–based, binary system, by the 1970s, a struggling economy, America's loss in the Vietnam War, and a general feeling of malaise created new difficulties for Asian Americans to be accepted in the South. Racial and immigrant statuses combined to make Vietnamese Americans and Indian Americans outsiders and, in many cases, enemies for whites. Taken together, the experiences of Vietnamese Americans and Indian Americans as well as their judicial and legislative activism against discrimination and racism serve as examples of changing strategies for justice in a rapidly changing South as refugee and entrepreneurial rights took center stage.

FOUR

FROM THE GULF TO THE COURTS

Vietnamese Americans and Human Rights in Texas

On an overcast March afternoon, members of the Texas Knights of the Ku Klux Klan cruised the Trinity Bay near Seabrook (a small fishing town approximately half an hour south of Houston) on small fishing vessels as part of a "parade." Brandishing guns and effigies of minority fishermen who were creating competition for locals, the Klan sent a clear message: The Galveston Bay belonged to whites and whites alone. Locals suspected the Klan had made good on these threats already, with the burnt-out skeletons of minority-owned buildings and fishing boats in the area serving as a testimonial to white power. The Klan stood for the rights of white fishermen in Texas and sought to reclaim the bay area from minorities the only way they knew how, "with blood." It was an event that shared characteristics with other Klan demonstrations of threats and white supremacy throughout the southern states following the Civil War. White southerners' ways of life were under attack by unwanted racial minorities searching for new opportunities in Texas, and the Klan's tried-and-true tactics of violence and intimidation would not fail them now.[1]

But this Klan demonstration occurred in 1981, not 1881, and Vietnamese American fishermen, rather than African Americans, were the target of the Texas Klan in Galveston. Time stood still in the Galveston Bay area when it came to racial relations and the role of the Klan in local affairs. The gains of the civil rights movement had in no way ameliorated the terrorist organization's hatred of racial and ethnic minorities. The Klan's intimidation of the Vietnamese American fishermen stemmed from the anger of some of the local white fishermen over the newly arrived immigrants and their "hogging" of the shrimp and crab catches. Following American withdrawal from the long, costly, and demoralizing war in Vietnam, Vietnamese refugees arrived in the United States seeking resettlement and an opportunity to rebuild their lives with the assistance of the U.S. government and various social and religious organizations, such as Catholic parishes, across the country. Many working to resettle the refugees believed Vietnamese to be natural fishermen and encouraged them to seek sponsors or find employment opportunities in the Gulf Coast fishing industries in Alabama, Mississippi, Louisiana, and Texas. By the late 1970s, several hundred Vietnamese settled in the Galveston Bay area of Texas near Houston and built small family fishing enterprises, pooling their resources to buy boats and other materials. To the dismay of local white fisherman, many of the Vietnamese experienced initial success in shrimping or crabbing in Galveston Bay or San Antonio Bay. Fear of competition in the already tight fishing industry, a severe economic downturn nationwide and resulting recession, racial tensions, a general distrust of the Vietnamese "enemy," and harsh memories of the Vietnam War shaped the responses of locals to the Vietnamese refugees. Clashes between Vietnamese Americans and the locals were immortalized in a Bruce Springsteen song, "Galveston Bay," as well as the 1985 film *Alamo Bay*, starring Ed Harris as a white fisherman and Vietnam War veteran coming to terms with both his past and the Vietnamese refugees who settled in his town. It was a classic Reconstructionesque story with a new spin.[2]

The involvement of the local chapters of the Klan, however, moved the interactions between the Vietnamese and a number of local white fishermen into the courts in 1981 with the *Vietnamese Fishermen's Association v. The Knights of the Ku Klux Klan* case. Many suspected that Louis Beam, the Grand Dragon of the Texas Klan, and other members of the organization were behind the burning of several Vietnamese boats in Seabrook and Kemah (two fishing towns near Houston) and the firebombing of a Vietnamese home in Seabrook in February 1981. While Beam was never charged or convicted in any of these violent events, his unabashed use of intimidation prompted the Vietnamese Fishermen's Association (VFA) (a group dedicated to representing the Vietnamese in the area) to enlist the help of the Southern Poverty Law Center (SPLC) in filing a civil rights case at a U.S. district court in Houston. The VFA sought an injunction against the Klan before the beginning of the 1981 fishing season in May for protection from violence and threats to their property and their lives. The trial began in 1981 and received national media attention, largely thanks to Beam's incendiary remarks and dramatic behavior inside and outside the courtroom.[3]

Fishermen's Association v. Klan was a watershed moment for civil rights, human rights, and immigrant rights as the three merged together in one case. Not only were civil rights battles far from over in the South after the landmark Supreme Court decisions and legislation of the 1950s and 1960s, but the struggle for civil rights merged with the struggle for refugee rights as the South became more diverse during the late twentieth century. A close legal analysis of the *Fishermen* case reveals that Vietnamese Americans used the courts not only to protect their property as other Asian Americans had done in the South before them but also to fight for their basic human rights to protection and safety. They called upon their status as refugees who fled Vietnam in search of the American Dream and safety to bolster their battles against the Klan, similar to other Asian Americans who often relied upon their noncitizen status in the courtroom. However, unlike Chinese Americans or Filipino Americans before them, Vietnamese Americans argued for the rights of refugees more generally rather than just Vietnamese refugees or members of the VFA. Also, the struggles of Vietnamese Americans were the result of both their unique identity as refugees and their racialization through the actions of the Klan and other whites in Texas. In turn, their identity shaped their legal strategies, which often relied on appealing to existing codes protecting property and commerce rights as much as refugee rights as they navigated the new terrain of refugee legislation. In many ways, the rights of refugees were up for interpretation, and Vietnamese Americans attempted to take advantage of the fuzziness of refugee status in court with mixed results. During the late 1970s through the early 1980s, the new immigrant Vietnamese clashed with the Old South that never died in Texas, resulting in a landmark stand for rights.

SHATTERING THE MODEL MINORITY MYTH: VIETNAMESE REFUGEES ARRIVE IN THE SOUTH

In addition to the Immigration Act of 1965, the Vietnam War also brought a new group of migrants to America and the South that challenged the model minority myth and created new interracial relations between whites and Asian Americans. When Americans withdrew from the war in Vietnam in 1973, chaos and terror soon followed for the South Vietnamese people. Fighting between North and South Vietnamese continued until the People's Army of Vietnam and the National Liberation Front of South Vietnam captured the southern capital of Saigon in April 1975, causing the city to "fall" and many of its inhabitants to flee. Operation Frequent Wind, a plan to evacuate first Americans and, later, Vietnamese via helicopters, planes, and ships, produced iconic images of Vietnamese refugees scrambling to leave the wreckage of Saigon and their uncertain future under the Communist regime. The earliest Vietnamese refugees were high-ranking servicemen, politicians, and other wealthier elite and highly educated individuals, who were assisted in migrating to the United States with the Indochina Migration and Refugee Assistance Act of 1975 (signed by President Gerald Ford). Later, Americans watched thousands of poorer Vietnamese, or "boat people," pile into ramshackle dinghies or commandeer smaller American vessels that remained after the war in order to flee Vietnam, Communist reeducation camps, famine, and poverty. The Vietnamese who managed to escape joined other refugees, including the Hmong people and Laotians in refugee camps in Thailand, Guam, and the Philippines. The future of the refugees once they arrived at the camps was uncertain and often frightening.[4]

The plight of the boat people prompted President Jimmy Carter and Congress to create a federal program to assist refugees in 1980. Although the Vietnamese government established the Orderly Departure Program in 1979 under the guidance of the United Nations to assist persons seeking to reunite with family members, Carter and humanitarians who believed that America should do more to assist those who aided the American effort in Vietnam and the Cold War more generally supported using federal aid to help refugees resettle in the United States. The Refugee Act allowed Carter to make exceptions for refugees in the Immigration Act of 1965 visa quotas and established a uniform system for resettlement in the United States overseen by the State Department and the Department of Health, Education, and Welfare and assisted by religious and charitable organizations. Once brought from the camps in the Philippines and Thailand, refugees were initially placed in refugee camps across the United States, including Fort Indiantown Gap in Pennsylvania, Fort Chaffee in Arkansas, Eglin Air Force Base in Florida, and Camp Pendleton in California. From there, social service agencies and religious organizations worked to secure sponsors for refugees so that they could leave the camps. Sponsors could be potential employers, churches (particularly Catholic churches, as Catholicism had deep roots in previously French Indochina), individuals, or recently resettled family members or friends. Although social workers and agents encouraged individuals or organizations to sponsor refugees, the resettlement program aimed to ensure that Vietnamese refugees would not overwhelm urban areas or create ethnic enclaves that would be isolated through language and cultural barriers and possibly create ethnic and racial tensions and job competition. As a result, refugees were directed toward sponsors in rural areas, including Minnesota, Michigan, Florida, inland

California, and Pennsylvania. Once in their new permanent or temporary homes (depending on how long their sponsors committed to their needs and whether or not there were adequate, long-term employment opportunities), Vietnamese attempted to put their lives back together by obtaining employment, housing, and other basic needs with the assistance of their sponsors. The challenges the refugees faced in America, including language difficulties, poverty, discrimination, and mental health issues stemming from the stress and trauma of the Vietnam War, were overwhelming and tested the notion of successful Asian assimilation in America. Despite the challenges, by 1990, Vietnamese made up 8.9 percent of the Asian immigrant population in the United States; many were refugees or family members of refugees.[5]

Many social workers who assisted refugees often wrongfully assumed that most Vietnamese made their living from fishing in their homeland and sought sponsors from the Gulf of Mexico for their clients. Although the shrimp and crabbing industries along the Gulf in Louisiana, Mississippi, Alabama, and Texas were not as robust as they once were by the 1970s and 1980s due to environmental threats to the native fish populations and state and federal attempts to regulate the hauls each season, social agencies believed that there would be opportunities for the refugees in the small, often more rural towns along the Gulf Coast. Some larger farmers and planters in these rural areas also attempted to use the Vietnamese refugees as cheap labor, in some instances as little more than slaves. One refugee, Kymberli Zamarripa, came to the United States as a young child during the 1980s and was sponsored by a woman from Macon, Georgia, who brought the Zamarripa family to her farm to work. Upon arriving, however, Kymberli and her family were paid nothing for their labor, forced to live in squalor, and threatened with violence if they attempted to leave. They eventually escaped and were able to make it to Palacios, Texas, with the assistance of other sponsors along the way, but there is no telling how many other refugees ended up in similar situations. Fortunately, social workers and agencies were often able to intercept and direct the refugees to legitimate sponsors around the Gulf Coast. In other instances, Catholic dioceses, like that in Austin, encouraged each Catholic parish to sponsor at least one family. By 1980, 80,264 Vietnamese lived in the South, concentrated mainly in Texas and the other Gulf states.[6]

Entering the fishing industry was not easy for the Vietnamese who settled in the Galveston Bay area of Texas, but for many, it became their way of life and shaped their experiences in the South. Many Vietnamese migrated with their families to Texas and pooled their resources once they were settled

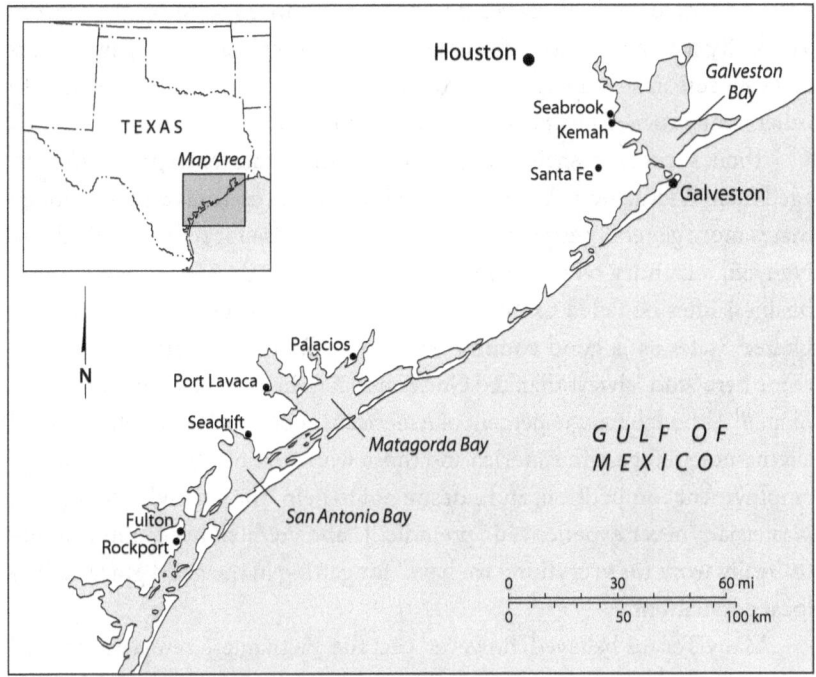

Map of fishing towns in the Gulf of Mexico/Galveston Bay region of Texas where Vietnamese refugees settled.

to purchase boats and other materials needed to shrimp or crab. Although, as one refugee explained, "a lot of these people [Vietnamese] when they came here . . . they [didn't] have the fishing business background," as many social workers believed, they still made a go at shrimping and learned the trade once they arrived in Texas.[7] Hai Trong Nguyen, a refugee who fled from Vietnam by boat in 1976 with his brother, was a prime example of a Vietnamese settler in Texas. When Nguyen arrived in Palacios (a small town about an hour and a half west of Houston on the Matagorda Bay), he and his brother used their pooled resources to build a boat for shrimping. Once they established themselves in the fishing industry, they were able to send for other family members. In other cases, the children left the camps first and moved to Texas before bringing their families with them. Another typical case was that of Thé Nguyen Nasternak, who left Vietnam with her family in 1975 and came to Port Lavaca, Texas, in 1980 with the assistance of the Catholic church of Bloomfield, Michigan (her first stop in resettlement). Nasternak landed a job in a local restaurant and was able to purchase a trailer for her family to live in with savings and loans. After her family joined her in Port Lavaca, her father shrimped there for three years before the family moved on to another nearby Texas city where there were fewer fishermen.[8] After a family achieved moderate success in shrimping or crabbing, they were often able to expand into other family-owned businesses such as restaurants and nail salons.[9]

Their success in shrimping, crabbing, and other enterprises encouraged many Vietnamese Americans to initially think of Texas and the United States more generally as places of boundless promise for refugees. Nghi Van Nguyen, a laundry owner in El Camp, Texas, who decided to try another business after he failed to make a good living in shrimping, described the United States as "a good country with opportunity for people who would come here" and "always thanked God Americans help[ed] us from the beginning."[10] Although only 36 percent of Americans supported the resettlement of Vietnamese refugees in America and those who did not cited overcrowding, employment competition, and a desire not to help "the enemy," Thé Nguyen Nasternak "never experienced [prejudice]" and credited her family's ability to "really work for everything we have" for getting in the good graces of the local populations.

Many Texans believed, however, that the Vietnamese refugees received extra help from the federal government and that their hard-earned tax dollars paid for Vietnamese boats and other fishing materials. At the time, white, working- and middle-class members of what Richard Nixon deemed the "Silent Majority" argued that their tax dollars supported the social and economic reform programs of Lyndon Johnson's Great Society plan, which provided no benefits to them but, rather, supported "moochers" and thankless racial minorities. The belief that the Vietnamese benefited from government assistance more than American citizens was closely related to larger negative perceptions of social safety nets. Nasternak and others understood this sentiment; she explained that her family was never on welfare but that "it's hard because the working class of Americans . . . see certain situations where people are coming over and getting freebies and stuff—I understand if people experience certain prejudice." Nasternak insisted that families who worked hard and worked together did not experience any prejudice from those around them because they proved that they did not depend on the government and were as diligent as Americans. Adopting the Protestant work ethic was a way for Vietnamese refugees to make a living as well as to adapt to American and southern life as racial minorities.[11]

But other reactions from Texans to the new Vietnamese reveal a different, more discriminatory, and more racially charged picture of Vietnamese settlement in the South. There was a potpourri of responses to the arrival of the Vietnamese in Texas, ranging from warm welcomes to reluctant tolerance to general xenophobia and blatant racism. However, the residents in the Gulf region of Texas provided specific economic reasons for their displeasure with the refugees. Whereas many Americans praised Asian Americans for their assumed work ethic, that same characteristic and stereotype made life difficult for the Vietnamese in the Texas fishing industry, proving that hard work and the model minority identity could only go so far. Many fishermen were struggling financially due to environmental and regulatory factors when the Vietnamese settled in Texas, adding extra challenges to an already highly competitive environment. Since the bay shrimp season ran from May to July of each year, there was a weight limit on how much shrimp fishermen could have on their boats.[12] The middlemen who purchased the catches from the fishermen as well as the Coast Guard were charged with reporting and enforcing these limitations; but for decades, such enforcements were lax, and overfishing began to take its toll by the 1970s. Rather than focus their ire on irresponsible federal agencies that failed to regulate the industry, many Texas fishermen blamed the Vietnamese for their woes in the late 1970s and early 1980s, linking the depleted fishing grounds with the arrival of the Vietnamese immigrants. Fishermen in the bay imposed forms of self-regulation or "unofficial codes" of conduct that ensured that no one would infringe on another's catch. Such measures included boundaries to prevent overcrowding in a good shrimping area and threats to report to officials anyone blatantly disobeying catch limits. Some of the earliest complaints made by fishermen against the Vietnamese were that they, according to a Seadrift city council woman and wife of a local fisherman, "pushed their way into the crabbing and shrimping industry with stubborn disrespect for local courtesy."[13] The Vietnamese allegedly placed their crab traps too close to those of other fishermen, but white fishermen also charged the Vietnamese with the illegal purchase and construction of boats to deliberately circumvent the catch limits.[14] Although maritime laws prevented noncitizens from operating boats over a certain weight limit (five net tons of replacement), many fishermen interpreted this rarely enforced law to mean that noncitizens were not allowed to own any vessels regardless of their size.

While some Vietnamese did in fact own boats that were over the weight limit for noncitizens (as revealed by a later investigation by the Coast Guard in 1981), most Vietnamese purchased junk boats from local fishermen at prices far above what they were worth and refashioned them with the help of family and friends—a classic example of one man's junk becoming another man's treasure. As local fisherman and wholesaler Leslie "Lee" Casterline explained, when the Vietnamese started rebuilding the boats that were discarded by local fishermen and became competitive with the locals, "that's where the problem started."[15] "Those American shrimpers sold their old junk boats to the Vietnamese figuring that they wouldn't be able to make any money out of them.... Now the Vietnamese are building ... them lighter, faster, and with better navigational aids."[16]

Vietnamese American leaders attempted to explain that the roots of the problem were simple misunderstandings of the laws and cultural differences (Vietnamese worked as groups in the fishing industry, whereas the local fishermen took a more individualistic approach), but such explanations fell on deaf ears.[17] In 1980, the residents of various bay towns and cities wrote the governor as well as other representatives asking them to intervene against the Vietnamese on their behalf. Concerned citizens of Rockport gathered in the Sacred Heart Parish hall to meet with their local representative and ask for help in "moving these people away from the coast ... because they are overfishing [and] they don't keep the rules of fishing."[18] Father Gregory Dean, who was placed in Rockport by the bishop after the Vietnamese population grew in the town, observed the meeting from the back of the hall, bemusedly listening to the locals "carry on." Dean, who felt the congregation should "always have a soft spot in our hearts for an underdog," became an ally of the Vietnamese in Rockport and challenged the townspeople in attendance at the meeting. When one of the concerned citizens demanded that all of the Vietnamese be arrested because they had broken the shrimping and crabbing rules, Dean retorted, "How about the people that sold those boats to the Vietnamese? Don't you think you should arrest them as well if you're going to go after the Vietnamese?"

Others around the bay demanded government intervention, which they received in early 1981 through a survey of boats by the Coast Guard and the Regional Parks and Wildlife Department commissioned by Governor Bill Clements. Unfortunately for the white fishermen, the survey "debunked yet another persistent, but apparently false claim" that the Vietnamese operated illegally large vessels. Not only did the survey find no evidence of Vietnamese wrongdoings; it also determined that the few boats that were larger than legal limits belonged to white fishermen. Carl Covert, the Wildlife Department director, believed that "this was all stirred up by that bunch down around Seabrook in an effort to get the Viet off the water." There was little substance behind the claim that the Vietnamese were violating laws or even fishing customs, and the only motivating factors, according to the *Houston Post*, which reported on the issue, were "sour grapes" among the fishermen who were desperate to drive the Vietnamese out of town. But the Vietnamese were holding steady, or put more simply by Petty Officer Doug Bandos of the Coast Guard, who assisted with the survey, "You may burn these people [Vietnamese] once [by selling them junk boats], but you're ... damned not going to do it twice."[19]

The local fishermen may have genuinely believed that the Vietnamese were violating laws and overfishing the bay, but there were more deep-seated reasons for why the Vietnamese received such a cold reception in Texas. Fear of competition from immigrants was a common trope in American history and had a long legacy in the South; however, an age-old distrust of racial others combined with more specific circumstances during the 1970s to create a unique situation on the Gulf Coast. Many of the local fishermen were also either veterans of the Vietnam War or friends and/or relatives of veterans who had fought and perhaps died overseas. Echoing similar experiences in towns and cities across the country and specifically where other Vietnamese refugees settled, locals who witnessed the Vietnam War either firsthand or through personal loss viewed the Vietnamese with not only suspicion but outright hatred. Racist reactions to outsiders combined with the fact that, as fishermen explained, the Vietnamese "looked the same" as the enemy in Vietnam, "and when you get geared that a person that looks like that has just killed your friend ... you know you can't block that out."[20] In this case, the racial history of the South melded with the negative legacies of the Vietnam War as well as an economic downturn created a perfect storm of interracial tensions. Anti-Vietnamese sentiment combined with the low levels of support for the refugee resettlement program in the United States added a xenophobic layer to the complications between the Vietnamese and the whites in Texas. The Vietnamese arrived at a time when both legal and illegal migration from Mexico was also on the rise following the Immigration Act of 1965 and social, economic, and political changes in Central and South America. Texans did not respond kindly to what they identified as another group of unwanted immigrants here to create labor competition or to "freeload" off the government. The Vietnamese did not possess an interstitial or a model minority identity in Texas; their racial and immigrant status cemented their reputations among the fishermen as "government moochers" and as yet another problem for the United States and Americans to deal with. Racism and xenophobia were couched in traditional anti-immigrant arguments that represented the South's reactions to the changing ethnic and racial makeup of the United States after 1965.[21]

Racism bubbled beneath the surface of the tensions between the Vietnamese and the local fishermen until a violent encounter in Seadrift (about three hours southwest of Houston on the San Antonio Bay) between two young Vietnamese American men and a white shrimper brought the growing racial conflict to an explosive head in 1979. On Friday, August 3, two brothers and fishermen, Chinh Van Nguyen, twenty, and Sau Van Nguyen, twenty-one, were having a few drinks at a local watering hole where Rudy Aplin, a local fisherman, and his brother Billy, who was visiting from Florida, were also celebrating the end of a another workweek. There were conflicting accounts of how the two parties initially engaged (the Nguyen brothers claimed that Billy—"a big guy . . . a KKK member or something like that"—started the trouble by approaching them and threatening them with a knife, while Rudy insisted that the Vietnamese Americans instigated the trouble by "talking big" to Billy), but the incident quickly escalated from a macho barroom brawl to a violent and fatal encounter. Regardless of the particulars, Sau shot and killed Billy and later fled to Louisiana with his girlfriend Lisa, where police eventually arrested him in Port Arthur the following afternoon (Chinh was also arrested but was released on $75,000 bail paid by his family and friends).[22]

Although Billy Aplin's murder at first appeared to be the result of an unfortunate encounter, more information emerged that revealed ongoing conflicts between the Aplin family and Vietnamese American fishermen. Rudy Aplin recounted to *Houston Post* reporters that he ran into trouble with a group of Vietnamese American fishermen a month before the murder when he and his wife were running their crab traps in the San Antonio Bay. When the Vietnamese American fishermen attempted to drop their own traps close to his, Aplin said that he "tried to tell the Vietnamese . . . and show them" that there was a "general understanding—you don't set your traps between someone else's." However, the Vietnamese left and later returned with "six boats with men holding knives and machetes" that began to circle Aplin's vessel, attempting to intimidate him. Aplin immediately called the sheriff and the Coast Guard, who, much to Aplin's dismay, informed him "there was nothing they could do" about the Vietnamese since there were no formal rules for crabbing relating to traps and there was no proof that the Vietnamese men threated him or his wife. This confirmed Aplin's suspicions that the state authorities were giving the Vietnamese special treatment and that "we [white fishermen] need at least equal privileges in our country."[23] Later, Chinh claimed that both Billy and Rudy harassed members of the Vietnamese community regularly while both groups were out setting crab traps months before the incident.

A few days after Billy Aplin's murder, however, Seadrift exploded with violence, igniting a "crab feud" between Vietnamese American and white fishermen. On Saturday, August 4, a Vietnamese home and three Vietnamese boats were burnt and destroyed (the police described the damage as "slight"). Although police investigated the incidents over the weekend, they filed no charges and identified no suspects. For the Vietnamese, this was a travesty and proof that they did not receive special treatment. Tuyen Nguyen, an employee at the Brown and Root crab processing plant in Seadrift, a local leader for the Vietnamese community, and a veteran of the Vietnam War, explained to reporters, "We are very scared. We don't want to get hurt. Anytime there is a problem, we make a report. I don't know why police do nothing. We have been waiting and waiting. I don't know why the government will not help us fight bad people."[24] On Wednesday, August 8, police in Port Lavaca (a small fishing village near Seadrift) responded to an anonymous tip that another attack on the Vietnamese was in the works and discovered explosives in the motel room of three local fishermen, Bommy Vandergriff, Terry Jones, and Lester Sprague. The men were held on a $50,000 bond, but because officials found no dynamite (used in the previous attacks on the Vietnamese Americans), no arrests were made, prompting Nguyen to question why the Vietnamese "have never seen police ignore anybody like this anywhere else."[25] Following up on the violence in Seadrift, Rudy Aplin forewarned that his hometown would "blow up like a powderkeg" unless something was done to rectify the situation.[26]

But rather than blow up, Seadrift witnessed a mass exodus of Vietnamese Americans. As soon as August 8, five days after Aplin's murder, only 2 of the initial 100 Vietnamese families remained in Seadrift. Most fled to Houston or Louisiana looking for similar employment, or they moved to other bay and Gulf towns and cities in Texas to continue fishing. The loss of Vietnamese in Seadrift also meant a loss of labor for the packing plants where Vietnamese American fishermen often worked to supplement their income during off-seasons. Leon Ruthenberg, the owner of a crab-packing plant in Seadrift who lived year-round in Baltimore, became "outraged" over the treatment of his Vietnamese employees as well as their sudden departure. Ruthenberg asked the U.S. Civil Rights Commission to intervene and hopefully "stir up some White House concern."[27] Although Ruthenberg was not a civil rights activist by any means, his desire to see his plant reopened prompted a visit from Dallas-based Department of Justice representative Robert Alexander on August 11. Upon arriving, Alexander first noted that the few Vietnamese Americans who remained in Seadrift were "shot through with fear" and angry for how one incident had completely ravaged their new lives in America.[28] Clearly, this was a problem that extended beyond employment and closed crab-packing plants; this was, as Ruthenberg correctly identified, a civil rights issue involving a group of immigrants who would rather start over again in a new state than risk the violent atmosphere that had engulfed Seadrift.

All eyes were turned to Alexander; residents hoped he would do something, anything, to end the crabbing feud in Seadrift. While Alexander held no authority to impose any restrictions or measures in Seadrift, he could make recommendations and request assistance from the Department of Justice and other agencies in seeing them through. Rather than approach the conflict as a civil rights issue, Alexander joined other local officials to stress that "communication is the core of the problem" in Seadrift and that if both feuding sides could come together in frequent meetings, the tensions could dissipate and life in Seadrift return to "normal."[29] Former mayor Billy Wilson, a shrimper himself, agreed with Alexander's assessment and added that "the feud involved nothing more than the local fishing customs" and that misunderstandings or miscommunications had prevented the Vietnamese refugees from adapting to the fishing culture of Seadrift.[30] Peter Van Tho, a Vietnamese American representative from the U.S. Catholic Conference who arrived in Seadrift with Alexander, met the Vietnamese American and white fishermen to discuss means of ensuring proper communication between both parties in the future. One solution appealed to both the Vietnamese and others: using local Catholic charities to train and select one native Seadrift resident to serve as a go-between and a Vietnamese priest from another diocese who understood the refugees to "live in the village and arbitrate disputes over fishing rights."[31] The Vietnamese representative would also be expected to teach the Vietnamese the "unwritten rules" of crabbing in Seadrift. These suggested measures unintentionally placed the onus on the Vietnamese American fishermen to learn better communication skills and fishing practices and downplayed the potential racial tensions. However, Alexander and the community hoped that these innovations would "reduce fear" and help the Vietnamese Americans to "gravitate back" to Seadrift because "that's home for them and everybody wants to come home," echoing Tuyen Nguyen's earlier plea for Vietnamese American safety in their new residences.[32] Fortunately, news of the attempts to smooth relations between the Vietnamese American and local fishermen reached the families that fled, and by the following week, most of the original refugees were back in Seadrift. The new measures appeared to work. Alexander was happy the Vietnamese Americans returned, Mayor Rayburn Haynie was pleased that his city was moving beyond the negative publicity, the local Vietnamese representatives were relieved that things were safe, and Leon Ruthenberg was thrilled that he was "getting his people back" and reopening the crab-packing plant. By the end of August, the flare-ups between the Vietnamese Americans and the local fishermen died down, and the situation appeared to be "back to normal."

But the calm waters of the San Antonio Bay and the resumption of crabbing hid the racial and civil rights issues that were left unresolved. Even some of the local fishermen interviewed by the *Post* at the height of the crabbing feud spoke in hushed voices of what they considered to be the "racial undertones" of the tensions and the persistent resentment of "a few bad apples" among the native fishermen as a result of the Vietnam War.[33] For example, Lee Casterline owned Casterline Fish Company (a middleman fish wholesaler) in nearby Fulton, Texas, and he and Lou LeBlanc, a wholesaler in Rockport, Texas, were the only two who would purchase the Vietnamese catches each year when others turned them away. Casterline was merely doing business: The Vietnamese usually had the largest catches and accepted the best prices. Casterline paid little attention as to who his clients were until local fishermen began boycotting his business. Locals were unhappy with Casterline for showing the Vietnamese "special consideration" and providing exclusive discounts. The fear of overfishing extended to the practice of buying and selling catches. Local fishermen argued that the Vietnamese were able to drive down prices for crabs because they unfairly competed with local fishermen and got larger hauls through disrespect for the customs of crabbing. Casterline's business did not suffer without the white fishermen as customers, and to the dismay of the locals, he continued doing business with the Vietnamese.

Casterline saw this as simply business rather than as a racial matter, but when he went out of his way to help the Vietnamese Americans rebuild their boats to meet regulations, he pushed the locals over the edge. In 1980, Casterline and his father, who co-owned the business, hired Steve Yates, a naval architect based in Victoria, Texas, to draw plans for reducing the cargo capacity of the Vietnamese shrimp and crab boats. Yates modified the boats to meet regulations by installing subdivisions using deep frames below the deck spaces. Casterline also went one step further and allowed the Vietnamese to dock their boats at his warehouse. When asked why he did something that seemed so revolutionary at the time in terms of relations between the Vietnamese Americans and the locals, Casterline shrugged and said, "We just figured the Vietnamese are getting pushed around unnecessarily" and mentioned that his father hated to see racial minorities treated poorly after he had worked on a ranch in Tivoli, Texas, and witnessed African American workers "treated like slaves."[34]

When the local community learned of Casterline's assistance to the Vietnamese, things started to get, in the words of Casterline, "pretty hot."

Locals accused Casterline of helping the Vietnamese violate boating laws and regulations (despite the previous Coast Guard survey assuring that overall the Vietnamese obeyed the laws) and began to have closed-door meetings on the topic. One parishioner in Seadrift warned Father Gregory Dean that he'd "better watch out" because "there's going to be lead flying very shortly over the Vietnamese, your friends."[35] Casterline, Father Dean, and LeBlanc attempted to reach out to Governor Clements again for assistance in stemming the potential violence, but their efforts were already too late. While few spoke openly of the racial side to the fishing feuds between the Vietnamese and the locals, that was soon to change when the Ku Klux Klan responded to the complaints lodged by the local fishermen against Casterline and LeBlanc. Bullets would indeed fly within a year's time in the bay region.

THE KLAN AND THE VIETNAMESE AMERICAN FISHERMEN CLASH IN TEXAS

Although the Klan was well established in Texas and had attracted members and sympathizers for decades, the organization made its presence known in the shrimping and crabbing feuds in 1980 when members began to leave their "calling cards" at the homes of persons they felt were coddling Vietnamese Americans. Naturally, Casterline was one of the first "traitors" to receive such a greeting from the Klan. Although Casterline never engaged in any direct confrontation with Klan members, one morning he awoke to see a business card taped to his door that read, "You've been paid a friendly visit by the Knights of the Ku Klux Klan. Be careful. Your next visit might not be the same."[36] Others, including LeBlanc and Casterline's father, began to receive similar thinly veiled threats from the Klan. Another woman who lived in the Galveston Bay area received the same calling card because she allowed a Vietnamese American man to dock his boat on her property for two years. Later, she received three threatening phone calls: one asking if she knew where her children were, the other threatening to burn her boat, and the third stating that she "would die that night." Although she couldn't prove that the calls were connected to the Klan, the calling card led her to believe that the organization was behind the threats.[37] Soon enough, Vietnamese American women also discovered the Klan's calling card at their homes while their husbands were away fishing. The women appealed to Casterline for protection, as he had gained a reputation for looking out for the Vietnamese community. Huong Thi Pham viewed Casterline as "like our Dad" who "took care of the Vietnamese" and "protected us during the time the KKK came over to give us a hard time."[38]

You have been paid a **FRIENDLY VISIT** By the Ku Klux Klan . . . Should we pay you a *Real Visit?*

Klan calling card (undated) from Texas submitted by the VFA as evidence during *Vietnamese Fishermen's Association v. Knights of the Ku Klux Klan*. Courtesy of the Southern Poverty Law Center.

Shortly after the appearance of the calling cards, violence similar to what had happened in Seadrift after the Aplin murder engulfed Rockport and Fulton. Corresponding to the introduction of the Klan calling cards was a series of tire slashings and boat burnings across the area. No suspects were ever identified for these crimes, leaving Vietnamese Americans to wonder once again why the police were not assisting them. However, on February 14, 1981, the Ku Klux Klan held an anti-Vietnamese rally in Santa Fe, Texas (approximately twenty-five miles north of Galveston), and many people in the region connected the Klan to the increasing incidents of arson in the area.

Gene Fisher, a swimming pool installer from Kemah, Texas, contacted Louis Beam, Grand Dragon of the Texas Knights of the Ku Klux Klan, and begged for some sort of intervention in the matter of the Vietnamese in order to raise awareness nationwide of the plight of the American-born shrimpers and crabbers.[39] Beam, a Vietnam veteran, native Texan, and longtime member of the Klan, deeply believed in protecting Americans from immigrant invaders through any means necessary, including violence. Beam would go on to an illustrious career in white supremacy and underground militancy, but in the early 1980s in Texas, he devoted himself to training "able-bodied and hardy men" to be part of a militia for "self-defense." Knowing these credentials, Fisher asked Beam to host a Klan rally in Santa Fe, and Fisher's friend and sympathizer Joe Collins offered to let the Klan use wide-open acres of his own land for the event. Fisher and Beam distributed thousands of flyers advertising the rally and fish fry and garnered the attention of both local fishermen and reporters from various Houston and area media outlets.

Ultimately, 200 participants showed up for the rally (including approximately 50 to 75 reporters), falling well below the expected 1,500.

Although the Klan failed to raise the hoped-for amount of money from rally tickets, they certainly, as Beam explained, "got a million dollars worth of publicity."[40] Beam was naturally the star of the show that day, delivering speeches enflamed with racial and pro-American rhetoric. Validating the fishermen's claims that the Vietnamese Americans received preferential treatment from the government even though they were not American citizens, Beam proclaimed that the Klan was giving the federal and state officials ninety days to enforce applicable fishing laws or "the Klan and the fishermen will enforce the laws themselves."[41] If there were any doubts among the crowd as to how the enforcement was to be done, Beam quickly cleared up the confusion. The local fishermen were to "prepare to reclaim this country for white people," and they were "going to have to get it the way the founding fathers got it—blood, blood, blood," Beam shouted to the small but militant crowd before him. The Klan advertised its "training camps" located throughout the Texas countryside, and Beam explained that he was "more than willing to select some of the more hardy fishermen" to be trained in "self-defense," making them "ready for the Vietnamese" by the time they were done.[42] To make sure that attendees knew who the enemy was and which group of nonwhite people they should be most concerned with, Beam then set fire to a small boat once owned by a Vietnamese American family who had fled the area following violence, and he displayed the Klan's signature burning cross in "opposition to the Vietnamese fishermen."[43] A month later, on March 15, Beam held another rally where he hung an effigy of a Vietnamese American fishermen from a boat and set it ablaze before the crowd, a blatant message illustrating who the enemies were and what was to be done with them. Following the display, Klan members piled into boats with their rifles to conduct a "parade" through Clearwater Creek (a commercial waterway with businesses and private residents lining both sides) to demonstrate the presence of the Klan and its purpose.

The nature of the Klan rallies created controversy but also unveiled the racial tensions underlying the crabbing and shrimping feuds. The presence of the Klan was not overlooked. As a historically racist organization bent on promoting and protecting white supremacy, the Klan became a fixture of the fishing scene in Texas during the late 1970s and early 1980s. Beam and the fishermen who came out in his support called on the reputation of the Klan in encouraging others to view Vietnamese Americans not only as an economic threat but also as part of a larger "invasion" of immigrants and nonwhites dedicated to taking control of the country. Likewise, a complicit government was to blame for the deterioration of Texas and the nation and the undermining of the white man. The Vietnamese Americans in Texas were a particular conundrum for the white fishermen. Not only were they immigrants (and largely unwanted at that), economic competition, and a racial minority that did not fit neatly into the image of the Asian model minority, but they also reminded whites of the "enemy" from Vietnam. When Gene Fisher explained that "North Vietnamese soldiers are coming into this country. That's why there were armed men on that boat ride," he identified all Vietnamese immigrants as the enemy, giving them both a racial and a political identity that encouraged harassment and violence.[44] Vietnamese Americans were a new type of "other" in the South following the Vietnam War and prompted a reaction of xenophobia, racism, and working-class disdain for economic competition from minorities who received special privileges from the government. It was a classic outcry from white Americans in the United States during the economic hardships and stagflation of the 1970s under the Richard Nixon, Gerald Ford, and Jimmy Carter administrations. The racial tensions between the two parties already existed before the Klan arrived on the scene; however, Beam pulled the tensions to the surface by drawing on an organization with roots deep in the South. His call to reclaim the United States from the Vietnamese and protect it for white people was not so different from the calls of previous Klan members to redeem the South during Reconstruction and into the twentieth century. And as the Klan had done previously, Beam and his supporters would also turn to violence and intimidation to achieve their goals while racializing Vietnamese Americans.

The following month, more violent acts occurred in Seabrook. At 2:30 in the morning on Sunday, March 29, 1981, two boats belonging to Vietnamese American fisherman Phuong Henderson were set ablaze. The boats had been listed on a public auction notice, since many Vietnamese were attempting to flee Seabrook following the Klan demonstration in February. Once again, police investigated the arson but found no suspects in the case, further frustrating the Vietnamese American fishermen who, at this point, were mainly interested in selling their assets, abandoning their investments in shrimping, and moving to Louisiana, where the fishing industry was more diverse and the demand for labor higher. Few of the white fishermen voiced their suspicions of who set fire to Henderson's boats, but Nam Van "Colonel Nam" Nguyen, a leader of the Vietnamese American community in Seabrook and a former member of the South Vietnamese Army, explained to reporters that the refugees believed the Klan was behind the fires. He pointed to the recent Klan rally and specifically Beam's inflammatory remarks and "lesson on how to burn a boat" as evidence.[45]

Remains of a Vietnamese American fisherman's boat in Seabrook, Texas, 1981.
Photo by Mark Toohey/©Houston Chronicle. Used with Permission.

The response to the concerns of the Vietnamese about the growing power of the Klan resulted in attempts to defuse the situation, mainly by encouraging Vietnamese Americans to relocate. Once again, local charities and religious officials offered a solution to the problem that ultimately would reward the aggressive tactics of men like Beam. Earlier in February, following the Klan rally, a representative of Governor Clements traveled to Seabrook to reassure the fishermen that state officials were looking into ways to resolve the growing tensions between the Vietnamese Americans and the locals. After receiving advice from his staff in attendance at the meeting, Clements "pledged to call on voluntary agencies ... to try to calm hostilities at fishing ports." Such efforts consisted mainly of "helping Indochinese fishermen to go inland for jobs."[46] Clements's pledge appeared to be more supportive of the fishermen than the Vietnamese Americans, but in March, Christian leaders from the Houston area responded by holding a conference on Vietnamese refugees. Presbyterian, Catholic, and other Christian denominations united and wrote an official statement on the tensions and violence occurring in Seabrook and other Gulf towns and cities. Richard Sicilano, presbyter of the Houston-based Presbyterian New Covenant and president of the Texas Conference of Churches, lamented that "while we specifically condemn the slurs and violence-inciting activities of the Ku Klux Klan and similar organization, we also know that as Christians and Americans, we should be speaking up for you and other refugees."[47] Sicilano was concerned that conference attendees were focusing too much on conflict avoidance and not enough on actually getting to the root of the problem. But Paul Doyle, the assistant director of the local Catholic Charities group, spoke for the majority of the conference when he explained that relocation "is a poor solution to the problem, but no better one has been suggested. Something's got to give and the Vietnamese say they'll give."[48] Many Vietnamese Americans were indeed more than willing to flee Texas to protect their families and their property. Doyle reiterated that the Vietnamese refugees were "welcome in the United States" and that the country was a "nation of immigrants," but relocation was, "at best ... a short-term solution to a difficult problem that belongs to all of us."[49] Few of the leaders truly believed that relocation was a good solution, but they argued that getting the Vietnamese Americans out of Texas was the only way to ensure that no more violence would embroil the fishing industry. It was once again a solution that did not address the Klan and the racism and violence that undergirded the current problems.

FROM THE GULF COAST TO THE COURTHOUSE: *VIETNAMESE FISHERMEN'S ASSOCIATION V. THE KNIGHTS OF THE KU KLUX KLAN*

However, not all Vietnamese Americans in Texas wished to flee, and many opted to fight the Klan through the courts. As tensions mounted in Seabrook and other towns and cities, the Klan announced that another rally and parade would be held at Kemah, Texas, on May 9. Fearing yet another wave of violence after the planned rally, members of the VFA, an organization of Vietnamese American fishermen from around the bay who desired to learn more about the local fishing culture and build better relations with white fishermen, joined forces to seek protection from the Klan. Although the Vietnamese refugees were not American citizens and many were frightened refugees with no other options than to either remain in Texas or flee to Louisiana or another nearby Gulf state, they also knew that the Klan used racially incited violence to intimidate them and keep them out of the waters during the shrimping and crabbing seasons. There were no "official" rules on crabbing and shrimping but, rather, only social customs and norms, meaning that Vietnamese Americans were as entitled to their fishing and property rights as any other American citizen or subject. More importantly, the Vietnamese refugees also knew that their civil and human rights to protection of life and property were violated by the Klan and the unknown individuals who torched their boats and property, and that the police had failed to find suspects and press charges.

On April 16, 1981, the VFA filed a civil rights suit for an injunction against the Ku Klux Klan in the Houston Federal District Court, overseen by African American Judge Gabrielle McDonald. The Vietnamese fishermen, led by Colonel Nam, charged that the Klan, together with the Seabrook-Kemah Fishermen's Coalition, Gene Fisher, Louis Beam, James Stanfield (Grand Titan of the Texas Klan), and Joseph and David Collins (the two landowners who hosted Klan events, including the previous rally), "violated their rights under several civil rights statutes ... including the Thirteenth and Fourteenth Amendments, the Sherman Anti-Trust Act, and the common law torts of assault, trespass to personal property, the intentional infliction of emotional stress and intentional interference with contractual relations."[50] In order to regain their rights, the Vietnamese requested that the court "restrain the defendant from undertaking activities undertaken with the purpose of interfering with the rights of the plaintiff class, unlawful acts of violence or intimidation . . . , engaging or inciting others to engage in acts of boat burning, armed boat patrols, assault and battery, or threats of such conduct."[51] The

VFA also argued that the Klan's use of paramilitary techniques and Texas land to conduct their training violated Texas law. The VFA was specific in its insistence that Fisher, the Collins brothers, and other fishermen from Seabrook and Kemah "conspired with the Klan . . . to receive training in the use of automatic and semi-automatic weapons, explosives, and other methods that can cause mass destruction and death" at the Klan paramilitary training camps near Santa Fe, Texas.[52] The fact that Beam had been arraigned in federal court in Dallas a few weeks prior on a misdemeanor trespassing charge pursuant to the fact that he had conducted a paramilitary training camp on federally owned grasslands appeared to support the Vietnamese claims that violence and militancy were tactics that Beam and the Klan embraced.[53]

Morris Dees, a civil rights attorney and founder of the SPLC in 1971, agreed to represent the VFA in court free of charge and identified a potentially powerful and revolutionary case in the litany of civil rights battles that typically focused on African Americans. Although some Vietnamese Americans still insisted that they would agree to leave the Galveston Bay area if an opportunity arose, Dees and those Vietnamese Americans who filed the case believed that the Klan's actions and use of intimidation to protect white business investments should be stopped once and for all. This was a specific instance of Klan violence directed toward the Vietnamese Americans, but a precedent-setting victory against Beam and the others held the potential to redefine civil rights through ending the use of racial intimidation and other de facto forms of discrimination and prejudice nationwide. Earlier in the 1970s, Dees and the SPLC formed a group, Klan Watch (today known as the SPLC's Intelligence Report, which monitors hate groups), to keep track of Klan activity primarily in the South. Dees was surprised to hear of Klan activity in northern Alabama and other southern states as late as the 1970s and 1980s and wanted to help people who were victims of intimidation and violence from the group. Dees began building a reputation for taking on the Klan directly throughout the South when, in 1981, a Vietnamese American fisherman reached out to him to let him know about Klan activity in the Galveston Bay area. The SPLC and VFA fight against the Klan proved that although many considered the organization as a fringe group after the 1970s, the Klan was still real and terrifying. For Dees, this was another example of the Klan clinging to age-old ideas of white supremacy, regardless of the target.[54]

The legal strategies that Dees and the VFA pursued in *Vietnamese Fishermen's Association v. The Knights of the Ku Klux Klan* revealed the changing nature of civil rights battles in the 1970s and beyond. Their claims of Fourteenth Amendment rights violations were more traditional: They argued that the Klan denied them equal protection through intimidation and threats. Dees also used civil rights statutes that Congress passed following the Civil War, and although they were initially meant to protect the rights of African Americans, they were expanded thereafter to include what Dees described as "class-based animosity," rather than just one specific racial group.[55] However, the VFA suit for an injunction rested more on tort law and the Sherman Anti-Trust Act than on constitutional protections. Dees and the VFA included a smattering of Texas civil rights codes in their suit, but it was the argument that the Klan denied the Vietnamese refugees their rights to their livelihood and, as such, their safety and peace of mind by violating business practices that would make the case a unique addition to civil rights battles in southern courts. Previous Asian immigrants (including Lum Jung Luke from Arkansas, discussed in Chapter 1) living on the West Coast also used the courts to fight for property rights with post–Civil War civil rights legislation and the Fourteenth Amendment during the late nineteenth century, and the Vietnamese refugees continued this legacy in the South.[56]

The Klan's alleged use of intimidation and threats to drive the Vietnamese Americans from Texas and the fishing industries became the focus of the case as well as the basis for the argument that the Vietnamese Americans suffered from various tortious interferences. One of the most problematic aspects of the case for the plaintiffs was that there was no hard evidence that Beam, other members of the Klan, or any other white fishermen had directly inflicted violence on the Vietnamese Americans. When Beam provided a deposition to the court before the trial, he was careful to stress that he was not opposed to the Vietnamese people but, rather, that he "stands for white people ... [who] have certain rights."[57] He also clarified that he was against the Vietcong, not the Vietnamese, and often ate dinner with Vietnamese families around Galveston Bay and wished to help them "get their country back" from the Communists.[58] He was adamant that he was a law-abiding citizen (in reality, he had been previously arrested on several accounts for harassing socialist protesters earlier in Houston and threatening Chinese president Deng Xiaoping when he visited Texas) and would never incite violence between the Vietnamese American and the white fishermen. At the previous rallies, Beam did not rail against the Vietnamese but, rather, "the federal government and the state government, who [have] turned their backs on the citizens of this country in favor of non-citizens."[59] It wasn't Beam or the Klan or the white fishermen who were creating tensions but, rather, "out-of-state agitators, anti-Christ Jew persons" like "Demon Dees" (a nickname Beam thought up for Dees in the courtroom—Dees was actually a Baptist) who tried to "stir up foment and discord between them people."⁶⁰ Likewise, Gene Fisher, a convicted felon and leader of the American Fishermen's Association (AFA) who initially reached out to Beam for assistance in dealing with the Vietnamese Americans, swore in his own testimony before the court that the goal of the AFA was merely to limit the number of fishermen on the bay, not to single out the Vietnamese Americans. Fisher only contacted Beam to raise media attention to the plight of the fishermen and to discuss "different forms of protest, different forms of legal protest within the framework of the Constitution of the United States."⁶¹ True, Fisher stated clearly his belief that Vietnamese American fishermen did not have the same rights to livelihood as white fishermen, and he did not deny that he said at the Klan rally that he would make trouble for those who did business with the Vietnamese Americans. He did not deny that he explained that "unless the large influx of Indo-Chinese refugees was halted, there would be continued boat burnings. . . . There would be continued loss of life, loss of property," or that he "was going to keep fishing if he had to run over every gook on the Bay."⁶² But personally, he didn't hate Vietnamese refugees. He was just an average American who grew tired of watching his rights violated by immigrants while a weak government indifferently looked on. In fact, as Fisher claimed, it was the Vietnamese Americans who had killed Billy Aplin and who should be under suspicion, not the Klan or any of the white fishermen.

Other members of the AFA who appeared on the stand confirmed that the Klan was never enlisted to help with terrorizing Vietnamese Americans and that they and the Klan were falsely accused of harassment. The rallies and boat parades were merely media spectacles to get the government involved (Fisher explained that the effigy was of an "Indian," not a Vietnamese refugee, to protest the government's treatment of the white fishermen as they had treated the Native Americans) and limit the number of refugees coming into America. There were no direct threats made to the Vietnamese and no way to connect the boat burnings to the Klan or the white fishermen. According to all of the defendants, the Vietnamese and white fishermen could work together peacefully without "race-baiters" like Dees and the SPLC intervening.

Members of the Vietnamese American community who provided depositions and testimony before the court failed to deliver any proof that they experienced violence from the Klan or the AFA. Samuel Adamo, attorney for Beam, pressed the Vietnamese Americans who took the stand to think carefully about what they considered to be acts of violence. Many of the Vietnamese Americans who testified described instances of intimidation, but not necessarily of direct violence. Tran Van Phu, vice president of the

VFA, explained that following the Klan parade at Clearwater Creek, many whites refused to let Vietnamese fishermen dock their boats and brandished guns in order to emphasize their point.[63] Tran also offered that a house on Road Number 6 near Seadrift flew a KKK flag and displayed a coffin with the Vietnamese flag draped over it that served to intimidate the other Vietnamese in the area and to drive them out.[64] These incidents, combined with the arson demonstration at the Klan rally and Beam's cries to force the Vietnamese Americans from the bay, frightened Tran "because the act of burning the small boat . . . could affect the big boats" and lead to more arson.[65] But when Adamo asked if any of these incidents had been violent enough to keep him from fishing, Tran replied no because he had too many debts to pay.[66] For Beam and Adamo, this was a victory: The Klan's statements may have frightened Tran but not to the extent of actually driving him from the bay.

Colonel Nam's testimony brought into the courts the question of whether or not the actions of Beam and others could be considered "violent." At one point during his examination, Nam told Adamo that the Vietnamese did in fact suffer from violence when a group of white fishermen threw rocks at a Vietnamese boat during the Clearwater Creek parade. However, when Adamo pushed him to more clearly define what he believed to be acts of violence, Nam's certainty dissipated. "Violence, according to me," Nam explained, "I know that men kill people with the gun and with the physical action by weapon. I think that's violent."[67] Adamo picked up on this and provided Nam with different examples of violence, one being the throwing of rocks and the other being "beating someone to a bloody pulp."[68] These were opposite ends of a spectrum of violence, but Nam ultimately agreed with Adamo that throwing rocks was minor when compared with being beaten to a pulp. Because Beam, the Klan, or any of the other defendants had not directly assaulted Vietnamese Americans, there were no acts of violence. If there were no acts of violence and many Vietnamese Americans continued to go about their business as they would have whether or not the Klan parade had occurred, then it was Beam's and the defendants' rights to free speech and assembly that were violated. Intimidation was not the same as violence, but it was difficult for Vietnamese Americans to prove that they were in fact intimidated by white fishermen when they continued with their daily activities. Nam quickly recanted, though, and further explained that intimidation could be violent when considering its potential results. Nam explained that although no Klan member or white fisherman had directly attacked a Vietnamese fisherman that he was aware of, there were still acts of "lawful violence," meetings where the Klan gathered, the parades, the rallies, and other acts that had the intention of inducing fear and provoking later violent actions. "I think act of violence is the KKK," Nam argued, "after the boat ride, we scared, we think that is unfair."[69] He also explained that the boat burnings were not just intimidation, but acts of violence. "The boat burning, this means the damage to the property of the Vietnamese fishermen. I think it's severe because they burn boat today, but more then more, over and over again like this."[70] There would be no end in sight, and the violence could escalate unless the Klan and its supporters were barred from intimidating the Vietnamese Americans at the start of the fishing season. But as Nam and the other Vietnamese Americans discovered, fighting for the right to safety and peace of mind from Klan violence was a long and difficult battle.

Proving that the Klan "intentionally inflicted emotional distress" on the Vietnamese Americans between 1979 and the spring of 1981 was challenging considering the testimony given. However, there was little doubt for the Vietnamese Americans that the actions of Beam and other members and supporters of the Klan created an atmosphere of fear and trepidation around the Galveston Bay area. As Judge McDonald discovered, in some cases, members of the Vietnamese American community were so frightened that they fled their homes. Many witnesses, including Phuong Pham (Colonel Nam's niece), pointed to the March 15 "boat parade" as evidence of Klan intimidation. The parade passed by Colonel Nam's house (where Pham was living), and Pham recalled being shaken when one of the boats slowed down and a Klan member paused to point directly at her home. Pham interpreted this as a silent threat or at least a form of intimidation. Pham explained that "she was so frightened by the sight of armed and robed Ku Klux Klan members... that she ran from Colonel Nam's home and [was]... afraid to spend the night there."[71] Adamo questioned Pham on whether she was more frightened of the man who happened to be in a Klan outfit who had pointed at her house or of the Klan's reputation, to which Pham replied that she had learned all about the history of the Klan in America and she knew that "they against black, you know," and hated minorities.[72] Pham and others were well aware of the Klan's legacy of violence and knew to be worried when the organization set its sights on the Vietnamese Americans. Fisherman Nguyen Luu echoed Pham's concerns following the boat parade, stating, "Out of fear, to this date, I have not bought a license, a permit to go fishing yet."[73] When the defense pushed Luu to explain what he wanted the state of Texas or the federal government to do about the Klan when none of its members had directly attacked or intimidated him personally, Luu stated, "I cannot state what kind of protection

I want, because I don't know, but it's the domain of the government to give protection to me to operate the business I'm in."[74]

Luu's testimony brought the deeper issues of not only the rights of the Vietnamese refugees but the rights of anyone residing in the United States to protection from intimidation in their business affairs, and the question of the government's role in providing this protection, to the surface. Beam and his defense insisted that because the Klan had not been in direct contact with any of the plaintiffs or witnesses and had not directly attacked or intimidated any Vietnamese Americans, then there was no lawful proof of intimidation. Regardless of the intent of the boat parade, connecting the Klan to any of the previous attacks on boats and property or any plan to forcibly drive the Vietnamese Americans from Texas was difficult, and any attempt to do so would violate, Beam argued, the basic civil liberties of American citizens. However, the Vietnamese fishermen were frightened enough that many did not engage in their jobs, or they were unsure of how long they would be able to do so now that the Klan was assisting the white fishermen. Pham was not wrong in connecting the nasty history of the Klan to her current situation; it was a white supremacist organization (as Beam and others made clear) founded to protect white Americans. Colonel Nam summed up these points at one point in his testimony, explaining, "I think the Klan people who took to burning a boat [had] an effect to our psychology. We think the Klan know how to burn boat so that we feel intimidated to our person and our people, but I don't know if this [Klan intimidation] is in United States lawful or not."[75] The Vietnamese Americans were intimidated and claimed emotional distress, but Colonel Nam and those he represented were unsure if the behavior of the Klan was legal. Nam knew that the Vietnamese Americans were entitled to basic protections of safety, but speaking in a court of law, he was unsure if the Klan had *intentionally* inflicted emotional distress on the Vietnamese Americans.

Texas law, however, was more precise on the matter. According to the state, "damages for mental anguish and fright are not recoverable unless they result from or are accompanied by physical injury."[76] Although some Vietnamese Americans had testified to the Klan throwing objects, there was no proof that any of the plaintiffs in the case were physically injured. In Texas, unless there was specific evidence that the acts of an individual inflicted emotional distress or mental anguish, then there was no ground for suit.

The VFA's attempt to charge the Klan with intentional emotional distress represented an attempt to fight for human in addition to civil rights. When Vietnamese refugees came to the United States, they brought with them the trauma of the war. Those who came later escaped the political turmoil and violence that accompanied the fall of Saigon and were often mentally as well as physical and spiritually scarred. A burgeoning Asian American activist movement identified a need for mental health facilities and care to help the new refugees cope with post-traumatic stress disorder as well as the challenging process of adjusting to life in the United States with limited means. Free mental health clinics designed to simultaneously analyze and assist the Vietnamese refugees in Los Angeles, Sacramento, and other areas in California faced often insurmountable financial odds and shortfalls, but they provided the most basic services to the mentally anguished and also established training programs for social workers. Such opportunities and facilities did not exist for refugees who came to the Gulf South. Clinics and mental health care professionals were more available for the refugees who settled in or eventually fled the Gulf for cities like Houston or Austin, but refugees in Port Lavaca, Seadrift, Kemah, Seabrook, or Fulton were left to their own devices, relying on their small communities to help them adapt to their new lives. Local charities and Catholic churches assisted Vietnamese refugees with financial matters and provided social opportunities, but they advised relocating as a coping mechanism for the Klan's intimidation. Many of the Vietnamese were successful in fishing, allowing them a certain level of security, but the actions of the Klan further exacerbated existing stress and trauma from the war and the act of relocating. In the face of intimidation and violence, the only sanctuary for many Vietnamese was to flee to other cities in the Gulf and seek other forms of employment. In the case of the Gulf Coast Vietnamese refugees, fleeing the area in the face of threats was a response to a lack of services as much as it was a response to the Klan.[77]

When read in the context of human rights law, the fight response of the Vietnamese Americans who went to court was a cry for the human right to security and safety for refugees. President Carter argued as part of his Cold War policy that the United States had a responsibility to assist those (like the Vietnamese refugees) who suffered as a result of earlier American actions and a duty to protect and promote basic human rights. This plan brought the Vietnamese refugees to America and led them to believe that their human right to migration, to escape physical and/or mental torture in search of safety, would be protected. As they explained to reporters when the crabbing feuds first broke out in Texas and as they further explained in court, the Vietnamese refugees believed that America was a chance to start fresh, not another place to experience violence and intimidation. Although the VFA used torts and the language of civil rights violations in its suit, when placed within the context of the post–Vietnam War era and the other experiences of

Vietnamese across the country, the push for an injunction against the Klan on the grounds of intentional emotional distress was a plea for human rights. The South's history of violating civil rights was well documented, however, and the VFA in this instance pushed this idea further in its claims. The Klan's power over minorities was evident in the case, as was its intent to deprive the Vietnamese Americans of their human rights and refugee status by destroying their economic safety net as well as their mental state. Previous Supreme Court cases as well as local cases throughout the South argued for civil rights and pointed to violations of the Fourteenth Amendment to equal protection against psychologically damaging racial practices, and in this sense, the VFA's fight was similar.

However, by explicitly referencing mental anguish and intentional emotional distress, this language tied the legacy of racial discrimination to a larger realm of migrant rights, refugee rights, and more importantly, human rights. Technically, the Texas Klan used intimidation to violate Article 14 of the Universal Declaration of Human Rights, the Right to Asylum in Other Countries from Persecution. When this reading is placed alongside the intimidation that the Vietnamese Americans faced, we see that the Klan then prevented many Vietnamese Americans from enjoying the fruits of their labor and essentially caused a high level of emotional distress and mental anguish that forced them to flee. The VFA members argued in court that they did not feel safe in Texas so long as the Klan continued its systematic use of intimidation and violence, echoing the earlier calls of African Americans who lived under the terror of the Klan during Reconstruction and the civil rights movement. However, the VFA members' fight for their basic rights as noncitizens was a new move in the "post–civil rights era" and married the civil rights battles of the past to the social, political, and migrant issues of the time. Their fight for an injunction against the Klan was an age-old fight that became larger and more global at this time and brought the southern battle for civil rights onto the stage of twentieth-century human and immigrant rights.

Unfortunately for the VFA, Judge McDonald rejected the claim of emotional distress. Although the VFA "produced sufficient evidence to establish a substantial likelihood that the defendants intended or at least could have reasonably anticipated that the boat ride would cause . . . severe emotional/mental distress," under Texas law, physical damage must accompany mental or emotional trauma.[78] The same need for physical proof of mental anguish applied to the VFA's claim that the Klan was guilty of assault. Klan members may have brandished weapons on the boat parade; but no one was physically harmed, and the Klan was not close enough to the Vietnamese Americans that day to inflict physical harm. Judge McDonald conceded that "the actions of the defendants created an atmosphere conducive to the commission of violence and that such violent acts were the foreseeable natural cause of the call for violence," but there were no concrete connections between the actions of the Klan members and the boat and home burnings that occurred before and after the rallies and parade.[79] Emotional distress and mental anguish were at the heart of the VFA's pursuit of an injunction against the Klan, and yet there was little members could do to ensure their mental well-being at the time. While the VFA argued that safety and security from threats and intentional emotional distress were basic rights, the court essentially ruled that protection from physical assault and distress were the only rights that were protected under Texas and, in some cases, federal law. The fact that the Klan did clearly create an "atmosphere" of fear for the Vietnamese Americans as they had done for decades meant little when it came to mental trauma.

Although Judge McDonald lacked faith in the VFA's arguments for an injunction based on emotional distress or specific racial intimidation, the association had more success in proving that the Klan had violated VFA members' rights to business and property. In its case, the VFA accused Beam and the Klan of interfering with members' contractual relationships through intimidation and harassment. Not only did Klan members leave their threatening calling cards with the Vietnamese American fishermen, but they also freely distributed them to wholesale owners such as Lee Casterline. When the workers at a Kemah crab plant fled the area after Klan-related violence, the owner was forced to close down the plant and suspend his business operations. The Vietnamese American fishermen became too frightened to continue their business and fulfill their contractual agreement to supply product to wholesalers or to complete their work duties as promised to their employers, and as a result, the wholesalers and employers could not fulfill their own contractual agreements. Although the VFA basically presented the same argument when it argued for emotional distress and assault, the fact that it and Dees used a contractual approach made a difference. As Judge McDonald pointed out, under Texas law alone there was ample ground for the VFA to seek an injunction based on the contractual interference claim. The Vietnamese Americans, like everyone else in Texas, had "the right to be free from malicious interference with the right to conduct negotiations that have a reasonable probability of resulting in a contract."[80] The law also recognized the right to contract as the right to own and/or hold property, making the Klan's intimidation of Vietnamese Americans a violation of property rights. At the federal level, U.S. code 42 guaranteed that "all persons within the jurisdiction of the United States shall have the same right in every state and territory to make and enforce contracts . . . and to the full and equal benefit of all laws and proceedings for the security of persons and property as enjoyed by white citizens." Through its use of intimidation, the Klan had violated a number of basic property rights granted to anyone living in the United States, citizen or noncitizen. Like Asian Americans who earlier battled against the anti-alien land laws, the Vietnamese Americans fought for their basic rights to property. If the human right to safety and mental security as refugees would not win in court, perhaps an appeal to the need for protection of property would secure an injunction against the Klan.

The VFA also pursued its members' basic rights to safety and property by charging that the Klan used its tactics to build a white monopoly in the shrimping and crabbing industries. Dees could not have been more correct in his assessment that "besides outright discrimination . . . trade was at the bottom of things in Galveston Bay."[81] Racism and discrimination directed toward the Vietnamese were major factors, but business violations were also at the heart of the case. The white fishermen's desire to limit the competitiveness of the Vietnamese Americans and the actions of the Klan created a control of the fishing industries that resembled a monopoly. The Vietnamese American fishermen were not allowed to compete in the markets, and the wholesalers who bought their hauls also felt the effects of the Klan's monopolization of crabbing and fishing. During the injunction hearing, Dees questioned a Kemah-Seabrook seafood processor, Henry Huets, on his views of the Vietnamese Americans and their role in fishing. Huets testified that "too many Viet boats [were] on the bay" and confirmed that he had stated earlier that "some Viet boats should be removed." Although Huets's views were not drastically different from the others expressed on the stand, his insistence on the need for the Vietnamese to "go by the wayside" in order to protect the industries confirmed Dees's argument that the Klan and its fishermen supporters formed a trust. When Dees pushed Huets on his statements, asking him if he gave preference to white fishermen in his business practice, Huets boldly stated, "I wouldn't be American if I didn't."[82] It was clear that there were racial, xenophobic, and nativist undercurrents in Huets's statements (as well as those from others who took the stand and shared similar beliefs on the Vietnamese); however, it was also evident that men like Huets and those in the Klan used these beliefs to deny basic economic and property rights to the Vietnamese American fishermen. Earlier in 1981, the Texas legislature had passed new laws limiting the issuance of bay fishing licenses for two years in order to ease tensions and limit the number of shrimpers, but few, particularly the Klan and the local fishermen, believed that this would cure any of the supposed problems of overfishing. The Klan acted to preserve competition on the bay but actually created a recognizable monopoly of the industry that drove out competition and targeted a specific racial group.

While on the stand, Colonel Nam, as spokesperson for the VFA, testified on the matter of economic livelihood and how it related to the safety of Vietnamese Americans. If there were any doubts as to why the VFA filed the suit for an injunction, Nam set about eliminating any confusion. "The defendants know the reason we file the suit, and the federal court know our situation.... We would like to live peacefully in this free country and we would like to do the free trade, free enterprise with the help of the government."[83] Nam was not only requesting protection of personal property but also court protection to participate in free enterprise and the market, in other words, to be able to compete in the fishing industry as freely as any American citizen. Nam admitted that he agreed with Fisher and Beam that there were too many fishermen on the bay, but the Klan's belief that the Vietnamese made things worse was the problem. It was the right of the Vietnamese as protected refugees and individuals living in America to have their property protected and to be able to fully participate in an industry in which they were legally eligible. Nam believed that "the law in this country can enter the problem at the court better than expect to fight or to be killed on water after May 15 [beginning of the shrimping season]"; that is why Nam led the charges on behalf of the members of the VFA. The law existed to sort out these matters so that people would not resort to violence, and the courts had a duty to uphold the human, immigrant, and economic rights of the refugees.[84]

Colonel Nam's argument for economic protection tied in with Dees's strategy to use business law to his advantage in the case. Dees turned to the 1890 Sherman Anti-Trust Act that outlawed trusts or monopolies to argue that the Klan violated the most basic rights of the Vietnamese fishermen to protection, property, and the pursuit of happiness. It was a novel use of the Sherman Anti-Trust Act in a civil rights battle, and Judge McDonald agreed that the Klan did use unfair business practices to target a specific racial group and drive out competition. Other attorneys used business laws such as the Interstate Commerce Act to fight against businesses that refused to integrate following the 1964 Civil Rights Act and purchased business supplies from various states, but the Sherman Anti-Trust Act in this case broadened the concept of a civil right to include the day-to-day protections and human rights that the Vietnamese refugees held while in the United States. There was no way to prove that the Klan inflicted emotional distress on the Vietnamese or that Klan members had assaulted them, but the Klan and its supporters unabashedly proclaimed their intent to drive out competition and were proud of their attempts to make the wholesalers comply with their business tactics as well. Convincing the court that in this case the Klan and others operated as a trust was an important step for enumerating specific civil rights violations. There was no hiding behind the First Amendment or other civil liberties in this case; the Klan sought to establish a monopoly, and its tactics in doing so denied a minority class of its rights.[85] These charges were initiated not by American citizens fighting for their civil rights but by a group of refugees fighting for their human rights.

The economic approach clinched the case for Dees and the Vietnamese Americans. On May 12, the VFA emerged victorious when Judge McDonald granted a permanent injunction against the Klan. The injunction forbade Klan members and "militant U.S. fishermen from carrying guns, wearing Klan robes in groups of two or more people, or burning crosses where Vietnamese American fishermen worked or lived around Galveston Bay."[86] More generally, the act prohibited any activities having "the intended purpose or the reasonably foreseeable effect of intimidating or harassing" Vietnamese Americans, including the boat parades that Beam and the other Klan members were so fond of. Dees's use of the civil rights statutes, the Sherman Anti-Trust Act, and Texas's common law tort of interference with contractual relationships persuaded McDonald that the Klan had systematically committed rights violations. Although McDonald did not grant protection by federal marshals in the Kemah-Seabrook area or order the dismantling of the Klan's paramilitary camps for the Texas Emergency Reserves (TER) at the time, Texas attorney general Mark White agreed to intervene where necessary in order to ensure that the Klan followed the rules of the injunction. Dees and the VFA believed that the suit and injunction "sent the Klan a message that those who enforce federal laws don't intend to put up with Klan harassment of the people."[87] David Berg, co-counsel for the VFA, went further by suggesting that McDonald's injunction was the "death knell" for the Klan. For the Vietnamese, however, the injunction was not so much a victorious battle against a longtime foe of racial equality but, rather, much-needed protection that would allow them to resume their daily lives. Colonel Nam professed to reporters following the announcement of the injunction that he "hoped the defendants respect this rule and cooperate with us in the fishing business in the area."[88]

Nam's wish for a more peaceful relationship with local fishermen appeared to come true when the shrimp season officially began on May 16, 1981. Although Louis Beam was not thrilled with the injunction on the grounds that it violated his freedom of speech, he did not give any indications that he planned to cause trouble at the opening of the season. Beam proclaimed that "he won" in the case because "she [McDonald] didn't order me to do anything I haven't done all along."[89] In fact, when reporters thronged to Seabrook to get a glimpse of any violence that might erupt during the first day of the season, Colonel Nam explained that he actually liked Beam's suggestion of an arbitration board between Vietnamese and white fishermen and that there was nothing to see in the way of violence or fights at the moment: "no more Klan, no more problems."[90] As the *Post* reported, the "windy weather was the only destructive force" in the bay that day, and Vietnamese participated in the annual blessing of the boats by Catholic priests while the U.S. fishermen readied their vessels for their hauls.[91] It appeared as though the injunction was a draw for both sides. The VFA received its injunction, but the TER was allowed to continue its operations. Beam was not happy about the injunction, but he argued that at least the case brought attention to the problems whites faced through competition with the Vietnamese. Although the weather was windy on May 16, relationships among the fishermen were smooth without the presence of the Klan. Just as the *Post* declared, the 1981 shrimping season was the "quietest in years," a welcome reprieve for all residents from the violence and terror of prior years.

But the Vietnamese were not ready to drop their fight for the end of the Klan's paramilitary training camps. In June 1982, Dees and the VFA again sued for an injunction, this time against the TER, the "military arm of the Klan." The Vietnamese claimed that despite the injunction against the Klan, the TER continued to operate with the Klan and train members and civilians for possible retaliatory measures against the Vietnamese. They asserted that "injunctive relief from the military operations of the defendant Ku Klux Klan and its TER is justified and proper" because "Texas law proscribes conduct of the sort in which the defendants have engaged."[92] More specifically, the TER violated Texas Civil Statute 5780, which prohibited private militias and the parading of firearms in public. Beam and other defendants from the first injunction case countered by insisting that operating the camps was not illegal and was, in fact, an acceptable exercise of their First and Second Amendment rights. The VFA once again called upon Judge McDonald to determine if the very existence of the TER violated its civil and human rights as well as state law.

Just as with the previous injunction case, rather than focus on constitutionally guaranteed rights, Dees and the VFA used state law to corner the Klan. McDonald's job in the case, however, was not difficult. She was quick to dismiss Beam's argument that the TER was allowable under the First

Amendment, ruling that "an injunction against the defendant's military training operations in no way hinders defendants' meeting together as a group."[93] "The First Amendment is no defense to a charge of conspiracy even if the act was committed for political or ideological reasons."[94] Also, it was clear that the "Second Amendment does not imply any constitutional right for individuals to bear arms and form private armies."[95] Because Texas law also forbade parading with firearms in public, Beam could not complain that an injunction would violate the right to bear arms more generally.

The final blow to the TER and preservation of Vietnamese rights, however, was Texas Statute 5780, which prohibited private militias. In video evidence presented by Dees to the Court, Beam and other Klan members could be seen conducting training exercises with guns at Camp Puller, Texas. Neal Payne, another member of the Klan and a close friend of Beam's, confirmed that the activities on the tapes were military-style exercises designed to protect private Texas citizens in and around Seabrook-Kemah as well as the Klan bookstore in Pasadena, Texas. Those who participated in the TER were assigned military-style rank and were ordered to dress in military-style uniforms, confirming that the organization was truly paramilitary in nature. Combined with Beam's previous inflammatory remarks of recruiting local fishermen to deal with the Vietnamese "problem" and that the Klan "stands for the rights of white people," the evidence and testimony that the TER was the paramilitary organization of the Klan convinced McDonald that the defendants violated 5780. Not only did the TER violate 5780, which also prohibited a paramilitary group from parading with weapons in public, but it more generally harmed the public through "usurpation of the State's right to the exclusive control of military force within its boarders."[96] McDonald was quick to clarify, though, that "the plaintiffs however are among the few members of the public whom the defendant's private militia has singled out as a target of intimidation and harassment.... Clearly, the plaintiff class' federal civil rights have been deprived as a result of the Klan-TER military operations."[97] Although Beam argued that the TER existed more to defend against a potential Communist attack than to initiate violence toward Vietnamese Americans, McDonald identified only one reason why the Klan would associate and operate with the TER: racial intimidation and potential violence.

After considering all the evidence, McDonald announced her decision in favor of the VFA on June 19, 1982, and delivered a verdict that did not destroy the Klan but challenged its century-old tactics and ability to evade legal justice. It was clear to McDonald that "the Knights of the Ku Klux Klan have operated military training camps in the State of Texas" and that such actions deprived the Vietnamese of their federal civil rights. Although the previous injunction prohibited Klan intimidation, "there [was] no reason to believe that the Vietnamese fishermen [were] ... free of intimidation by the remaining defendants [Beam and the TER]."[98] In the final judgment, McDonald ordered that Louis Beam and the KKK were "permanently enjoined" from continuing to participate in or operate private military organizations, parading in public with firearms, and engaging in any military or paramilitary training, specifically combat-related training. McDonald also ordered the state of Texas to ensure that this measure was carried out. In the end, the TER was disbanded. A few days later, local police officials placed copies of the judgment on bulletin boards and in store windows throughout the Kemah-Seabrook area, signaling the court's stance on the Klan, the victory of the Vietnamese refugees over hatred and prejudice, and what many hoped was an end to the tension that had plagued the Galveston Bay region for so long. What appeared to be the conclusion of a battle between the Vietnamese and the local fishermen was actually a milestone in a longer fight for human rights, safety, and protection from the violence and racial intimidation in the South. The SPLC and other organizations would use this strategy as a template for further action against civil rights violations in decades to come.

In her conclusion to the case, Judge McDonald noted that "over the years, members of the various Klan organizations have engaged in acts of racial intimidation, harassment, and terrorism," tying the fight of the Vietnamese Americans against Louis Beam and his organization to larger trends throughout southern history. For a century, the Klan had terrorized minorities, but the *Vietnamese Fishermen's Association v. The Knights of the Ku Klux Klan* case represented a turning point. The ruling would not, as the attorneys for the VFA believed, be the "death knell" for the Klan. Indeed, racism, xenophobia, and nativism aimed at immigrants would continue to fuel the activities of its members. However, the case pinned tangible acts of harm to the Klan and placed specific restrictions on its activities, sending a message that when the Klan's beliefs manifested in open intimidation, harassment, and violence, they went beyond the realm of civil liberties and violated the civil rights of others.[99]

The fact that it was refugee Vietnamese who brought down justice upon the Klan should not be overlooked in the story of civil rights, human rights, and Asian migration to the United States. This was not a "typical" civil rights case, and Vietnamese Americans called on the court to defend their basic human rights while living in the United States. The case was a test of U.S. commitments to human rights and refugees and how far the federal government would go in defending the rights of noncitizens against nativist racism and violence. While the Vietnamese refugees argued that they had basic rights to protection from violence, harassment, and mental trauma, it was ultimately their right to property and contracts that would result in an injunction against the Klan. The emphasis on property and the ability to enter freely into contracts, rather than broad claims of harassment or mental trauma, was the way to pin the Klan to civil rights violations. The result of the case was both a victory and a loss for refugee and immigrant rights: The injunction was achieved, representing a blow against the Klan and the success of noncitizens in arguing for their basic rights, but the human and refugee rights to freedom from fear and intimidation (with or without property destruction) were not convincing claims in the Houston court. In other words, the legal system protected their rights as minorities, but their rights as refugees were still in question. In bringing elements of the Old South such as the Klan and racism and discrimination into contact with new questions of refugee rights, a more diverse immigrant population, and human rights in the Cold War, the Vietnamese battle represented not only the changing nature of civil rights in the South, but also the continuing presence of xenophobia and international affairs and politics in southern racism.

In the end, the Vietnamese American fishermen resumed their fishing, shrimping, and crabbing in the Galveston Bay area. Others opened family-run businesses, including salons and restaurants, throughout the bay to supplement their incomes during the off-season, while many of their American-born children would migrate to Houston for more economic and educational opportunities. All in all, overt racism and discrimination against Vietnamese Americans seemed to diminish (if not disappear) once the Klan was removed from the scene. As Vietnamese explain, they are proud of the way their community rebounded after the Klan attacks and their courage in fighting, but their overall view of America as a land of opportunity is somewhat skewed by the earliest experiences of the refugee class. The experiences in the courts and with the Klan were examples of justice in the face of white power in the South but also a reminder that the human rights of refugees and other noncitizens were unstable and often enforceable only with a court order in Texas and beyond.

FIVE

GETTING DOWN TO BUSINESS IN DIXIE

Indian American Hotel Owners and Entrepreneurial Rights

In the early 1970s, Harish Pattni, a former bellhop who worked his way into hotel management positions in California, arrived in Rockingham, North Carolina (about an hour and a half east of Charlotte), unsure of what opportunities for business might exist in the small town. Pattni found that buying property in California was nearly impossible without significant financial resources and connections, so he made his way across the country to the Southeast. Pattni's journey was part of a broader wave of migration as Indian American hoteliers left the West Coast's high property values behind and looked to the South for reasonable prices and a solid customer base of weary travelers pulling off highways to stay at hotels and motels. Mom-and-pop motels languished in disrepair throughout the South as sons and daughters refused to continue to operate the family business and fled decaying towns bypassed by the interstate highway system. In Rockingham, Pattni found a small, forty-eight-unit hotel with owners desperate to unload the property. He worked out a deal, acquired the property, and within a few years completely renovated the hotel and expanded his holdings into South Carolina by purchasing other old, run-down lodgings and transforming them into clean and reasonably priced venues. By the early 1980s, the former bellhop was a successful multiproperty business owner.[1]

Pattni and thousands of other recently arrived Indian immigrants who set up shop in the hospitality industry represented a new version of the American Dream found in Georgia, North Carolina, South Carolina, Texas, and other southern states. These migrants enlivened the economic structure of the South when many factories and textile mills closed as the United States increasingly transitioned to a service-sector economy. In many ways, Indian

Americans viewed the southern region of the United States as a cradle of business opportunities (as did other investors after World War II) and appeared to be perfect examples of a new generation of the Asian American model minority. Perhaps this was the true "new" South that many had searched for following the Civil War.

But other Asian Americans had traveled to the South in earlier decades for opportunities, only to be met with discrimination, and old habits died hard. The majority of Indian American hotel owners at the time operated in some region of the South, so it was no coincidence that the majority of the discrimination was centered there. From customers who refused to stay at hotels or motels once they discovered Indians owned them to insurance agents who refused to insure property owned by Indian Americans because of racist stereotypes, Indian Americans faced discriminatory obstacles similar to those of previous waves of Chinese American, Japanese American, Filipino American, and Vietnamese migrants. Indians became socially, culturally, and economically racialized in the South, where even the most successful of the model minorities faced uphill battles in the business world. Like immigrants before them, however, Indian American hoteliers would demand their entrepreneurial rights in the South. Indian American hotel owners in Tennessee would band together in 1985 to fight insurance discrimination, but it was not until Indians experienced difficulties in acquiring franchises from the larger hotel and motel chains that they received outside assistance from business leaders and other associations in organizing for their right to freely enter into contracts, acquire and sell property, and obtain insurance.

In the 1980s, chief executive officers of Days Inn responded to the demands of Indians for fair treatment by assisting financially and strategically with organizing the Asian American Hotel Owners Association (AAHOA), headquartered in Atlanta. The motives of the major hotel corporations for providing aid to Indian hoteliers were complex, but Indians embraced this new form of interracial business activism to achieve their goals and entrepreneurial rights.

AAHOA brought a new look to civil rights organizing in the South in the latter decades of the twentieth century. Although AAHOA represented Indian American hoteliers and not other Asian American ethnic groups, it was one of the first interracial and Asian American–led business organizations in the South. The focus on moving away from judicial activism was the result of the commercialization or privatization of civil rights battles situated within the business climate of the 1980s and early 1990s. While other Asian American activists in the South mainly used the legal system to fight for an end to segregation and discriminatory business practices, Indian American hoteliers argued that ending prejudice, rather than using the courts to force acceptance, was the proper way to build better relations between Indian and white hotel owners. With AAHOA, Asian Americans' battles for civil rights in the South moved into a new realm that relied on respectability politics and entrepreneurial rights to achieve justice through legislative rather than judicial means. The activism of the Indian American hoteliers not only represented a change in Asian American approaches to fighting against discrimination but also challenged the definitions of "civil rights," "equality," and "justice" after the legislative changes of the 1960s.

FROM WEST TO EAST: INDIAN AMERICAN HOTELIERS MOVE TO THE SOUTH

When Indian Americans first arrived in the South, they encountered a changing economic and physical landscape. A combination of domestic and international forces following World War II left their markings on Dixie and created a land of often contradictory financial conditions. The once dominant cotton industry in the South had faded as textile production shifted from the southern United States to the growing "global South" in southeast Asian and other developing nations from the 1960s through the 1980s. It became more cost effective for manufacturers to purchase cotton overseas at cheaper rates and to move production to low-paying sweatshops in Asian nations and Central America. In some respects, the South benefited from the deindustrialization of the Northeast and the rise of the Rust Belt consisting of cities such as Cleveland, Detroit, and Gary, Indiana, when companies moved production to the Southeast in search of tax breaks and cheap pools of labor. However, the general move to a service-sector economy through the 1970s and 1980s left its impact on a region where people typically depended on agricultural and textile industries for employment. An injection of military spending through the proliferation of air force, army, and naval bases as well as defense contracts for private industries created the rapid growth of the Sun Belt, but such windfalls did not touch all southerners who were forced to adapt to the economic changes around them.

For those with the resources, however, the New South of the post–World War II era held boundless opportunities for entrepreneurs. The shift to a service-driven economy helped cities such as Atlanta, Dallas, and Chapel Hill, Raleigh, and Durham (or the Research Triangle of North Carolina) grow in the medical and education fields, but retail was also a new frontier of business. In the early 1980s, Sam Walton expanded his locally based general store into a multibillion-dollar industry by creating one-stop shops known as Walmarts throughout the Midwest and the Southeast. Similarly, small-town restaurants such as Chick-fil-A became regional names as franchises opened throughout the Sun Belt. The projected image of traditional family values combined with low prices and convenience derived from low employee pay and tax breaks allowed businesses like Walmart and Chick-fil-A to flourish during the 1970s and 1980s while redefining entrepreneurship in the South and across the country.[2]

Accompanying the rise of service-sector industries and franchises was a sharp decline in small, family-owned businesses throughout the South, since, when compared with the Sam Waltons and S. Truett Cathys (of Chick-fil-A), small businesses owners often simply could not compete. In small towns across the South, mom-and-pop groceries, gas stations, restaurants, and general stores were able to hold on due to a solid local customer base, but no one was "safe" as the department stores and franchises grew to previously unspoken of levels of wealth and power. It was as if a new wave of Gilded Age tycoons swept through the region, except in service instead of manufacturing sectors and led by faith-based and family-oriented grandfatherly figures who appealed to a wide and growing conservative base in the Sun Belt.

The hotel and lodging industry in the South was hit particularly hard by the rise of corporations and franchises during the 1970s and 1980s. Similar to stores and restaurants, what were once small, single-family-owned hotels such as Days Inn, Comfort Inn, and Quality Inn eventually became mammoths in the industry, with franchises springing up across the country. Large corporations had the resources to become franchises and open hotels and motels in key travel and heavily trafficked areas. Many of these prime lodging locations were located in small towns and cities that were now accessible from the interstates through new exits and extensions. A franchised Days Inn could offer a more modern stay for a better price than smaller, forty- to sixty-unit family-owned motels that were often not as conveniently located. The growth of the interstate system after World War II was both a blessing and a curse to hoteliers in the South: More traffic came through more areas, but the smaller hotels and motels either could not compete with the franchises or were deemed too out-of-the-way by travelers. A once booming location off a two-lane highway often became a less-traveled route for motorists breezing by sleepy southern towns and cities on the new interstates.[3]

Both white and black owners of small hotels and motels suffered with the rise of the corporate-owned franchise. Black-owned hotels and motels had a long history in the South, particularly in cities such as Birmingham, New Orleans, and Atlanta, and represented an area of entrepreneurial opportunity. Jim Crow segregation created a need for black-owned-and-operated lodging, and many African Americans took advantage of a ready-made clientele by advertising in *The Negro Motorist Green Book*, a directory of hotels and motels that accommodated blacks. Stories of African Americans traveling across the country and being denied a room at white-run hotels and motels prompted Martin Luther King Jr. to speak out against this specific form of discrimination and contributed to the push for the 1964 Civil Rights Act, which outlawed segregation and discriminatory treatment in services provided to the public. However, long after the milestone civil rights legislation of the 1960s, hotels and motels in the South were still largely segregated and catered to customers of one race. Black hoteliers often faced uphill financial battles as discrimination in insurance coverage and claims as well as white flight and the decline of southern urban areas caused customer bases to diminish after World War II. By the 1960s and 1970s, however, both black and white owners felt the effects of new franchises and the corporatization of the hotel industry.[4]

Across the South, once stable if not bustling mom-and-pop hotels and motels went out of business. Boarded-up windows or decaying and dilapidated structures became a common sight along the old two-lane highways such as U.S. Route 1 running from Virginia to Florida and U.S. Route 90 from Florida through Texas. Small hotels across the country witnessed similar fates as gas prices rose and longer road trips became more difficult for the average American family, but southerners viewed their experiences with declining customer bases as a regional or local problem and could not easily discard their businesses. Owners expected their children to step up and run the family businesses when they retired, but they found that their sons and daughters had no desire to remain in sleepy southern towns and run failing enterprises. Families became saddled with aging properties that rapidly declined in value and could not be revived or rehabilitated to offer the level of comfort and ease for the prices offered by the new franchises. Small hotels and motels across the area became financial burdens and entrepreneurial nightmares in the new, post–World War II economy of the South.

Just as southern hoteliers were struggling to dump their properties, Indian immigrants were looking for business opportunities in the United States. These two occurrences were far from coincidental and were related as much to changes in immigration patterns after the 1960s as to changes in the southern economy. After the United States allowed Indian immigrants to naturalize with the passing of the Luce-Celler Act in 1946 and following

Indian independence from the British in 1947, more Indians began to arrive in the United States. Most immigrants came from the Gujarat state in western India and were often among the more financially stable and educated classes. Despite the level of education of these Indians, high taxes and endless, labyrinthine levels of bureaucracy made obtaining placement in a professional field or opening a business next to impossible for them in India after World War II. As other migrants before them, many Indians could not resist the siren call of new starts and opportunities from the United States, and as Indian American hotelier H. P. Rama explained, "We traveled thousands of miles to realize the American Dream backed up by hard work, dedication, and faith in this promise land called America."[5] Sikh migrants from Punjab, India, had made their homes in the inland portions of California and became a core labor force in the timber industry of the Pacific Northwest during the early 1900s, but their numbers were low compared with other Asian migrant groups for the first half of the twentieth century. The earliest wave of post–World War II Indian immigrants primarily settled along the West Coast and in pockets in New York City and engaged in small entrepreneurial enterprises such as groceries and hotels and motels. The first Indian American hotel owner in the United States was possibly Kanjibhai Desai, an undocumented migrant who came to San Francisco during the late 1940s and bought the aging Goldfield Hotel. Because only approximately 100 Indian immigrants and their families were allowed into the United States per year through 1965 because of immigration restrictions, the number of hotel owners on the West Coast grew slowly. However, many soon found it difficult to run a successful business while breaking even in California with increasing property taxes through the 1950s and 1960s and climbing operating costs.[6]

Just as Indian Americans living on the West Coast looked eastward for better and more affordable and efficient opportunities, the Immigration Act of 1965 opened avenues for more professional or white-collar laborers to come to the United States from Asian countries as the decades-old race- and nationality-based quotas were abolished. The majority of Indian immigrants who arrived after 1965 were college educated, with degrees in engineering, nursing, mathematics, and computer science, and searching for employment opportunities with the assistance of special labor-based visas. By 1990, 469,000 Indian immigrants came to the United States.[7] Although professionals such as nurses, computer programmers, and engineers were in demand in the United States, there were not enough jobs to accommodate all Indian migrants. As the small hotel and motel industry across the country began to face the consequences of the growing hospitality moguls, Indian immigrants with little experience running businesses identified an economic possibility and became, in their own words, "accidental hoteliers." Many Indian immigrants initially desired to return home to India but stayed in the United States as they succeeded in various business and hospitality ventures. Hotelier Vilpesh Patel described running a hotel as "easy" because you "don't need fluent English, just the will to work long hours."[8] Many Indian Americans had will in ample amounts and were also fluent in English, so they found opportunities for economic stability and entrepreneurship.[9]

The South drew Indian Americans from the West Coast for the same reason that other manufacturers and industries came down to Dixie: affordable property taxes and operating costs. On the West Coast, Indian Americans established their presence in the lodging industry during the 1950s and 1960s in California (particularly in the San Francisco area) by pooling resources with family to buy and operate hotels and motels, a tactic that was not uncommon for many immigrants who migrated as families and worked as a unit for economic stability. However, they soon looked to the more cost-effective opportunities in the Southeast. Many would follow the path of Harish Pattni and migrate to southern states. Not only was the weather more familiar in the southeast portion of the United States, but the desperation of small motel and hotel owners to rid themselves of their money pits created excellent purchasing deals for Indian Americans. Prices were already reasonable, as many owners wanted to sell as quickly as possible, but Indian Americans were also able to enter into special mortgage purchase agreements. Indian Americans often did not have the money to pay the full price (approximately $30,000 at the time) for a small property, but they could put $3,000 down as a payment and in return receive the seller's property and then take responsibility for the seller's mortgage. In essence, it was a win-win situation for both the Indian Americans and the sellers. Indian Americans entered into these transactions across the South during the 1970s, and through wise investment and maintaining low overhead costs by using family members as employees and living on-site, they were able to purchase a number of small motels and hotels in the area and transform the properties as well as the ailing small motel and hotel industry in the South.[10]

Despite eagerness to get rid of run-down properties, not all southern sellers willingly turned their businesses over to Indian Americans. As soon as a seller found out from a broker, realtor, or lawyer that the intended buyer was Indian American and not white, he or she often wanted to rescind the offer. H. P. Rama, who came to Buffalo, Tennessee (near Nashville), in 1974 to purchase a small, sixty-unit motel, experienced such discrimination firsthand when he entered into an agreement with a realtor from Greenville, South Carolina, to purchase another small hotel and begin to expand his holdings. As soon as the buyer discovered that Rama was an Indian American, the lawyer called Rama to explain that the seller was no longer interested in selling his property. Both the lawyer and the seller did not hesitate to credit Rama's "Indianness" with the decision not to sell. Under the 1968 Fair Housing Act, property owners could not refuse to sell based on race or national origin, so the hotel owner's actions were illegal. Rama was "hurt on a personal level" but did not pursue any legal action against the seller. Not only was Rama not interested in buying a hotel from a seller who was not willing to enter into an agreement with an Indian, but he also "was not just buying brick and mortar from this guy. . . . [He] was buying the goodwill behind the hotel," and if the goodwill was not there, Rama did not feel as though he could force the deal on the seller. Three years later, the same seller contacted Rama again and offered the motel at a third of the original price. At this point, Rama happily accepted because he "understood that people do business with people they can trust and feel comfortable [with]," but also because he finally "won him over rather than forced him to sell." Rama credited his "self-confidence without arrogance" for his ability to "overcome this discriminatory transaction," which led to one of his life-long mottos: "I always say, 'Who says discrimination does not pay?'" This belief in the value of the dollar and fair business transactions would go a long way in shaping the activism and responses of Indian Americans to other forms of entrepreneurial discrimination in the South, but in the 1970s and early 1980s, tacitly accepting a seller's desires without legal or other pressure appeared to be the best way to do business.[11]

As more Indian Americans migrated to the South from the West Coast or directly from India through the late 1970s and early 1980s, they added to the changing economic and ethnic landscape of the South. Although Indian Americans were technically "accidental hoteliers," their professionalism, education, and business acumen made them the model minority Asian Americans in the United States. This was a new spin on the classic American Dream story, and Indian Americans were more than happy to seek a new beginning in a New South. Those like Rama recognized the pitfalls of doing business with whites as an Indian, but they also had the desire to become entrepreneurs and attempt to maneuver around the racial roadblocks and obstacles in southern business.

But entering into business deals was always a precarious position for Indian Americans, who often depended on purchase mortgages and special loans through sellers. After Harry Pattni established himself in Rockingham, North Carolina, he saw a special deal on the Baker Motel in Cheraw,

South Carolina, and purchased it in 1981. Pattni and his family poured time and money into renovating the property but failed to attract enough customers to either stay in the rooms or eat at the on-site restaurant. The majority of Pattni's customers were African Americans, and although Pattni saw nothing wrong with this (like other Asian American entrepreneurs in the South before him who developed a large black clientele), when the former owners found out that Pattni was serving and hosting African Americans in their formerly whites-only hotel and restaurant, they moved to initiate foreclosure on Pattni. The sellers, attempting to conceal the racial undertones of the case, sued Pattni in 1981, claiming that he mishandled the property and violated the contract by undergoing drastic and out-of-code renovations. Eventually the court ruled in favor of Pattni and held that the renovations were not harming but, rather, greatly increasing the value of the property and that Pattni was well within his rights to make improvements. This was a rare example of Indian Americans appealing to the southern legal system to defend their property rights at this time, but the seller's rejection of Pattni's misunderstanding of race relations in the South would shape other experiences for Indian hoteliers in the region.[12]

"CURRY PALACES" AND "PATEL HOTELS": DISCRIMINATION IN THE SOUTH

In the case of Indian Americans who came to the South, the "model minority" was perhaps too "model" in its economic success and reflected growing anti-Asian trends. The age-old fear of labor and business competition from Asian immigrants resounded in various industries in America. As Asian car manufacturers such as Toyota and Hyundai outpaced and outperformed American automakers, including Ford and Chevrolet, Americans demonstrated their patriotism by urging others to "Buy American" and lashing out against both the manufacturers and the Asian employees who worked in plants. The presence of Asian-based car plants in the South (particularly in Tennessee, where Nissan was one of the first Asian corporations to take advantage of tax incentives and a climate that was, according to Nissan, "southern, but not too southern") was perplexing to locals, who both desired and welcomed the new plant but also exercised their patriotic inclinations to criticize the competition with American-made autos.[13] The xenophobia and nativism reached a peak with the 1982 murder of Vincent Chin, a Chinese American draftsman who worked at an automotive supplier in Highland Park, Michigan, near Detroit, after he encountered two drunken white supervisors from the nearby

Chrysler plant outside a bar on June 19. The two men were angry at "chinks" for stealing jobs and supposedly initiating a series of layoffs, and they brutally beat Chin (whom they believed to be Japanese) to death. While the Chin murder helped to galvanize a new wave of activism among Asian Americans, it also served as a reminder that despite their economic, educational, and professional success, Asian Americans were still eyed with suspicion and blamed for America's economic woes.[14]

In the South, Indian Americans faced uphill battles with cultural racism and a more insidious form of discrimination in business practices. Interestingly, it was *after* Indian Americans became successful in their ventures that they became racialized and othered in the South. Although Indian Americans and Asian Americans were well educated and professional, cultural stereotypes of them often hindered the ability of "accidental hoteliers" to attract customers and gain recognition in the hospitality industry. One of the more pervasive negative images of Indian Americans related to curry, a staple dish of Indian cuisine. Because Indian American families often lived in or near their hotels and motels when they first bought their businesses, the smell of curry may have greeted some customers when they initially entered the lobbies. The smell of curry would be no different from the odor of any other spice or entrée cooked in a restaurant or home, but whites who were not acquainted with curry were put off by the scent and often immediately associated it with filth and "otherness." As a lawyer who later assisted Indian Americans with fighting against cultural stereotypes explained, "Curry is an aroma that is foreign to Americans. They associated the odor of curry with dirt—the place was dirty."[15] Many whites assumed that if the smell of food permeated the lobby, then cleanliness was an issue with the hotel or motel. From this line of thinking, it did not take long for whites to associate motels and hotels run by Indian Americans and the Indians themselves with dirtiness and uncleanliness. While this was a problem for Indian owners across the country, because the majority of motels and hotels run by Indian Americans were located in the South, this form of prejudice fell within the larger, southern context of distrust of those on the racial margins and a longer history of Orientalism used to ostracize Asian Americans. Other Asian Americans had begun to assimilate into southern society and achieve a level of respect by the 1980s, but Indian Americans were a relatively new presence in the South and were not as easily grouped with the model minority Chinese Americans or Japanese Americans who had called the southern states home for decades. Travelers from across the country who drove through the South may have encountered their first hotel run by Indian Americans and easily adopted the stereotypes and cultural

American-owned-and-operated advertisement in Valdosta, Georgia, 2015. *Photo by the author.*

forms of racism that lingered in the South and deterred them from giving their business to "curry palaces," the derogatory and colloquial term used to describe Indian-run hotels and motels in the 1970s and 1980s. The prejudice against Indian Americans became so great that many owners in the South reported incidents of potential customers walking into the lobby, seeing that the hotel was run by Indian Americans, and immediately getting back on the road to find an "American-owned-and-operated" hotel or motel.[16]

The growing resentment of whites in the South for Indian American–owned hotels and motels inspired an insidious yet successful billboard campaign against Indians. Once white hoteliers discovered that the smell of curry and the presence of Indians in the lobby repulsed travelers and moved them to seek out other establishments, they slapped the phrases "American-owned" or "American-owned-and-operated" on every advertisement possible. Hoteliers displayed signs in their lobbies, on their windows, and particularly on highway billboards as a reassurance to customers that they would not be duped into spending the night in a filthy curry palace. As with other industries and products, the American-owned-and-operated campaign was a coded form of racial and marketing branding, indicating to travelers not that the hotel was owned by Americans but, rather, that it was owned by *whites*. But amid the larger buy-American campaign that applied to everything from

Hotel Owners and Entrepreneurial Rights

appliances to cars, on the surface, this could be interpreted as a form of patriotic consumerism.

Indian American hoteliers, however, like H. P. Rama, knew better and immediately recognized the practice for what it was: a racially charged campaign designed to use prejudice to gain customers. In 1985, Rama was traveling from Atlanta to Nashville on Interstate 75 when he saw a sign for a hotel declaring it American-owned-and-operated. He was intrigued by the sign but thought little of it until later, when he stopped in Commerce, Georgia, on a business trip and saw a hotel marquee that also proclaimed the same message. He was even more shocked a few months later when he went to Arkansas and, while flipping through the yellow pages, counted numerous ads for hotels and motels that proudly displayed "American-owned-and-operated" phrases. "This prompted me to investigate further why they are putting this thing [on their ads] because if the American traveling public started believing in this, I will be out of business," Rama explained.[17] After some inquiries to other Indian American hoteliers, Rama discovered that white hoteliers were "using this tagline to bring customers and the traveling public to their hotel. . . . They were using this as a marketing tool to bring business to their hotel."[18] Rama understood the racially coded messaging behind this ad campaign, but he was perplexed that "people didn't realize that this [Indian American hotel industry] was ran by Americans, built by Americans, and sold to Indians."[19] Other Indian American hoteliers learned to shrug the campaign off; one, who migrated to the United States from Uganda after leader Idi Amin expelled Asians in the 1970s, mentioned that "if we survived Idi Amin, a couple of redneck motel owners aren't going to bother us."[20] Still, the idea that "American-owned-and-operated" implied that Indian Americans were not and could never be "American" reflected a deep-seated xenophobia and anti-Asian sentiment.[21]

The American-owned-and-operated campaign was a visible sign of the persistence of anti-immigrant practices and beliefs in the South and reflected the changing nature of racism and discrimination toward the end of the twentieth century. The marketing campaign was a cultural form of discrimination that sought to disrupt the progress of Indian American hoteliers and prohibit them from entering the white and "American" space of entrepreneurship in the southern economy. By proclaiming "American-owned," white hoteliers were reinforcing the notion among customers that Indian Americans by culture were foreign and other and undeserving of business or respect. Were the hoteliers simply responding to the customers' desires, or did the billboards themselves shape and perpetuate the stereotypes of Indians and their "curry palaces"? Although marketing a brand is a central component of any form of advertising, this particular branding shaped perceptions of the marginal place of Indian Americans in southern and American society. This was a subtler form of racism and anti–Asian American and anti-immigrant sentiments masked by patriotism, coded racial branding, and Orientalism that replaced the openly hostile language and racism of the past. But it was a form of marketing that both white southerners and Indian American hoteliers immediately understood nonetheless.

The cultural stereotypes went beyond unpleasant smells and customer dissatisfaction and influenced how other businesses and agencies negatively viewed Indian Americans as hoteliers. The belief that Indian hotels were dirty or unclean lent credence to the idea that Indian Americans were incapable of properly running their businesses. Such assumptions negatively impacted Indian Americans when they applied for insurance for their properties. If they did not face discrimination from banks or sellers when they initially set out to purchase hotels, they more than likely encountered it from insurance agencies throughout the South. Many insurers identified Indian Americans as poor and therefore risky managers and refused to provide protection for Indian properties. Although Indian Americans were accidental hoteliers, they strove to advance their professionalism and integrity in the industry but continuously ran up against discriminatory barriers from insurance agents. When an Indian American–owned hotel burned down outside Nashville, Tennessee, in 1979, this appeared to confirm insurance agents' and sellers' worst fears about the type of businesspeople that Indian Americans were. The agency that insured the hotel refused to pay benefits because it suspected (without grounds) that the owners themselves had set fire to the hotel as part of a scam to use insurance money to invest in other property. There was no proof or evidence of these claims, and the Indian American owners, out of confusion and a misunderstanding of insurance policies and regulations, decided not to pursue the matter. As a result, insurance agencies across the South increasingly refused to insure more Indian American hoteliers, arguing that Indian Americans as a group were prone to illegal methods of obtaining their insurance benefits. This was not a far cry from the centuries-old Orientalist claims that Asian Americans in general were shifty, shady, and dishonest by nature. To the dismay of the Indian hoteliers who strove for professionalism and respect in the industry, cultural stereotypes shaped not only the customers' responses to their business but also subverted their basic operating and entrepreneurial rights.[22]

When Indian Americans did manage to do well for themselves despite these setbacks, their success was met with derision from others in the industry and from the media as well. Many of the Indian Americans who migrated to the United States after World War II and particularly after 1965 had the surname Patel, a ubiquitous name from the Gujarat region of India that denoted descendants of peasant clans from prior centuries. The name was no different from Smith or Brown in the United States, but the otherness of Patel and its association with Indianness resonated with white Americans. The belief that all Patels were from the same family permeated society and caused many to wonder if a single, giant, Patel family was creating a monopoly in the hotel industry. Concerns of a Patel cartel combined with the fact that many Indian American families did operate as a unit and run a hotel or motel themselves with little help from outside employees created further suspicion of the motives of Indian American hoteliers. Were these individuals following their American Dream, or were they money-hungry immigrants who would do whatever it took to control an entire industry? Many insurance agencies favored the latter stereotype and frequently denied coverage to anyone with the last name Patel. "Patel hotels," like "curry palaces," became a common, derogatory term among the public to refer to Indian-run hotels and motels and did much more than indicate that a certain establishment was not American-owned-and-operated. Perpetuating the fear of Patel hotels as an un-American monopoly was a way to distance Indian American business owners in the South from whites and to strip this new immigrant group of their social and economic capital.[23]

The biases and prejudices against Indian Americans in insurance agencies carried over to corporations and their franchises. When Days Inn began to franchise in the late 1970s, Indian Americans who had built up capital by investing in smaller hotels leapt at the opportunity to branch out and have a degree of financial safety in aligning with larger corporations. However, they ran into continuous problems with Days Inn when they applied for a franchise. Word of shifty Indian Americans who set fire to their own hotels for money and who were uninsurable and dirty carried to the highest reaches of corporate offices. Those in charge of franchising did not deny the Indian Americans a franchise outright; they simply refused to meet with them to discuss options. Other corporations, including Hilton, Holiday Inn, and Marriott, followed suit and shied away from interacting with potential Indian franchisees. By the early 1980s, H. P. Rama was able not only to operate independently owned small motels but also to acquire a franchise from Days Inn. It was an uphill battle, but Rama pooled so much capital for investing in a franchise that Days Inn found it difficult to ignore his request. But this was not a typical trajectory for Indian American hoteliers looking to break into the corporate or franchise sectors of the hospitality industry. Despite being a franchisee, Rama had a difficult time reaching the corporate offices of Days Inn if he had problems or questions. He did not immediately connect this with racial bias or prejudice, but he soon heard of other Indian American hoteliers with franchises from Comfort Inn and Suites who had similar problems. For Rama, it didn't make good business sense to shut out a growing subset of the industry. "We couldn't ever get in to see or even speak to the higher-ups in Comfort or Days Inn.... We built these chains and they were not giving any time of day to the Indian hotel owners ... because they didn't think they would bring much money into the company."[24] And considering the pervasive stereotypes of Indian American hoteliers, it was not a leap of imagination to understand why corporate leaders may have felt this way. For the hotel and motel chains, granting franchises to a few Indian Americans was a way to spread out locations into the more off-the-beaten-path spots throughout the rural South. Otherwise, they were well aware of the American-owned-and-operated campaign and believed that white travelers would not patronize franchises owned or operated by Indian Americans. Days Inn and Comfort Inn not only embraced the stereotypes of Indians but also effectively racialized and ghettoized their own Indian franchisees.

Initially, Indian American hoteliers were unsure of how to approach the prejudice and discrimination they faced from sellers, customers, and corporations. Many, like Rama, were merely trying to learn the trade and build a better economic life for themselves and their families. The deeply embedded racism of the South made this difficult. Even if Indian Americans did manage to secure small properties, their attempts to branch out or buy franchises were met with resistance from a variety of forces. Indian American hoteliers also broke away from traditional Asian American business models in the South in that they did not (as Chinese Americans did) try to serve mainly minority clientele; there was no need for this when they were operating motels and hotels designed to accommodate all travelers regardless of race or ethnicity. And while Indian Americans did manage to secure economic stability and branch out through wise investment, they repeatedly encountered discrimination and a lack of recognition of their entrepreneurial rights. The 1970s and 1980s, however, were supposedly the "post–civil rights" era—the Civil Rights Act of 1964 theoretically ended discrimination in the business world. Thus fighting against de facto segregation and racism was more difficult. There were no laws that prevented Indian Americans from owning property or receiving insurance or buying franchises, but the discrimination, in all of its traditional racial and xenophobic forms, continued nonetheless. The initial response among Indian Americans, as Rama's case demonstrated, was often to buckle down and work hard to further prove their professionalism in keeping with the widespread conviction that the solution to the problem of discrimination lay with individual progress and merit. "We never wanted to have a confrontational attitude with the industry or people who were doing those things because we wanted people to win the hearts and souls, not force them ... because we are minorities," Rama explained. "Because from day one we wanted people to do business with us. . . . We had to rise to on our side to be professional and not just accidental hoteliers."[25] Indian Americans were well aware of their racial place in the South: They were minorities, and they would have to learn how to navigate that identity in the later decades of the twentieth-century business world.

"ACCIDENTAL ACTIVISM"

Other Indian Americans, however, organized to ensure their success in the hospitality industry despite the racism and discrimination they faced in the South. Indian American activism for equality and entrepreneurial rights assumed different forms during the 1980s and 1990s, few of which resembled Asian American civil rights activism in the past. In a "post–civil rights" age and within the realm of private business, the struggle against racism and discrimination in the South and within the industry itself was generally not pursued through the courts. Rather, it was geared toward fighting de facto prejudice and discrimination in the world of business through the education-oriented efforts of professional associations. Indian American activism revealed the limits of civil rights legislation from the 1960s as well as the strategies for fighting discrimination in the post–civil rights era.

Insurance discrimination prompted the first attempt at organization among Indian American hotel owners. By the mid-1980s, approximately 80 percent of the hotels and motels owned by Indian Americans were located in the Southeast. Although Indian American hoteliers faced discrimination from insurance agencies nationwide, the South quickly became the epicenter of the battle. Between 1983 and 1985, a string of Indian American–owned hotels and motels in the Nashville, Tennessee, area burned down. The exact cause of the fires was unknown. Police suspected poor electrical wiring, while Indian American hoteliers feared that arson was at the root of the fires (not surprising, considering the high levels of anti-Indian sentiment and the American-owned-and-operated campaigns). Regardless of the cause, the Indian American hoteliers in Nashville suffered severe economic setbacks as either they were uninsured or their insurance companies refused to pay out on their policies. The stereotype of Indian Americans setting fire to their own property to collect insurance claims undergirded discriminatory practices by insurers. The American Hotel and Lodging Association (the largest nationwide association for those in the hospitality industry) also participated in such practices of discrimination and prejudice in an ancillary way by creating a list of American-owned-and-operated hotels and motels following the fires.[26]

In response, Indian Americans in and around Nashville formed the Mid-South Indemnity Association (MIA) in 1985. Shankur "Big Sam" Patel, a hotelier from Lebanon, Tennessee, whose hotel was one of the properties that burned down earlier that year, led the effort in organizing Indian American motel and hotel owners to ensure their equal participation in the hospitality industry. Identifying the MIA as a civil rights organization with roots in the South is somewhat problematic, however, as it did not fit the mold of a standard civil rights group. The MIA more closely resembled immigrant aid organizations formed by Jewish and Italian communities during the early twentieth century. Rather than pushing back against the insurance agents who openly discriminated against Indian Americans or challenging the American Hotel and Lodging Association through the courts, the MIA was purely for indemnity and did not engage in legal activism or pursue legal solutions to its problems. In other words, it did not directly challenge the prejudice that Indian Americans experienced in the industry. Patel and the others who joined him in 1985 during the early days of the MIA were primarily interested in forming an association to protect Indians and their property when others failed to do so. Members of the MIA joined together and paid a membership fee that would be used to provide insurance if any could not obtain it from a larger insurance agency or if their insurers did not grant a policy that covered enough or refused to pay out on the policy in the event of a disaster or damage (by the mid-1980s, many insurers refused to include fire damage in policies sold to those with the last name Patel). The members and leaders of the MIA did not push for punitive measures against discriminatory agencies and groups and did not directly challenge discriminatory practices. Rather, they engaged in the same type of benevolent activity as so many other immigrant and minority groups had done years before to protect their own when no one else would.[27]

The early organization of Indian Americans against discrimination reflected a longer history of activism from Asian Americans even without the legal action of Chinese Americans, Japanese Americans, Filipino Americans, and Vietnamese Americans who came before them and settled in the South. As with other minority businesspeople (including the Chinese grocers, Japanese farmers, and Vietnamese fishermen, as well as black entrepreneurs), Indian Americans engaged in a financially oriented version of respectability politics in the 1980s. Respectability was often a central component of civil rights activism since the late nineteenth century: appeal to white liberals as well as the upper stratum of minorities to garner respect and acceptance in southern society. For many immigrant groups, the politics of respectability took the form of assimilation and dictated their success based on their ability to fully acculturate to social, political, economic, and cultural aspects of American society.[28]

The model minority myth also dictated the level of acceptance (or lack of it) of Asians Americans among white Americans. Like H. P. Rama, not only did many Indian Americans lack a good working knowledge of the law, but they also did not wish to push back too hard, as they believed deeply in the free market and how the market affected personal relationships between buyers and sellers. Indian Americans and members of the MIA knew that prejudice was at the root of the denial of insurance agencies to accommodate them, but they did not see legal action as an appropriate tool to regulate business relationships. They believed in entrepreneurial rights in that they were entitled to full participation in the hospitality industry, but in a free market system, they would have to protect their own interests. They did not have to challenge the discriminatory agencies and organizations, but they could also not sit idly by and have their economic dreams shattered by racism, prejudice, and discrimination. Indian Americans respected the revered concept of private property in America and the right of owners to oversee their property as they see fit—a concept challenged by the Civil Rights Act of 1964 and other subsequent statutes and laws. Here, entrepreneurial rights meant the right of whites to refuse to do business with Indian Americans, just as it meant the right of Indian American hotel owners to manage their own properties as they wished. Determining whether or not the MIA was a civil rights organization depends not only on how historians define civil rights but also on how activists themselves identified their role in fights against prejudice or discrimination. Indian Americans had a right to be insured and to property protection; but business owners also had their own rights to their own property, and if they did not wish to sell to Indian Americans or insure Indian Americans, then there was nothing that could be done legally. This philosophy was in stark contrast to that of the Asian Americans who used the legal system in previous eras to fight against school segregation and antimiscegenation, while at the same time it was reminiscent of the Japanese and Chinese who chose to defy anti-alien land laws and anti-Asian sentiments against Asian American property owners in the South by continuing with their business practices. As with other minorities in the South, at times, going about day-to-day business while prejudice, racism, and discrimination abounded was often a radical act in and of itself and a statement of rights and equality.

Others in the hospitality industry, including whites and corporate leaders, came to recognize the discrimination the Indian American hoteliers faced as a form of civil rights violations. In the early 1980s, Mike Leven, a relatively young up-and-comer in the hospitality industry, was appointed chief operating officer (COO) of Days Inn, working directly under the president of the corporation. Obtaining the position of COO was a long journey for Leven. Growing up in Boston with his Jewish family during the 1940s, Leven distinctly remembered traveling to Cape Cod one summer for vacation and facing the difficult task of finding a hotel to stay in. The Leven family spotted a pleasant-looking bed-and-breakfast that appeared welcoming but, upon closer inspection, proudly displayed a "No Jews or Dogs Welcome" sign on the lawn.[29] This moment stuck with Leven for his entire life. While it is unclear if the incident influenced his decision to major in business and hospitality at Cornell University, Leven would continuously reference that moment in interviews, and his friends and colleagues would always include it in their descriptions of his character and drive as a businessman. In 1961, Leven first tried his hand at a career in advertising but found that he couldn't climb the corporate ladder because of lingering anti-Semitism in the industry. Later, when he was living in Chicago, a real estate agent outright denied him a home in a well-established neighborhood because the community did not want Jews living there. For a Jewish kid from Boston to begin with a negative view of ethnic discrimination in hotels and motels and later climb to the top of the hospitality industry (Leven would go on to found the Holiday Inn Express and Microtel hotel chains as well as serve as president and chief executive officer of The Sands hotel and casino in Las Vegas) was an impressive feat, and Leven offered a sympathetic ear when he began to hear complaints from Indian owners of Days Inn franchises of the rampant discrimination in the corporation.[30]

In 1987, H. P. Rama, who owned a Days Inn franchise in addition to his other investments across South Carolina and Tennessee, was finally able to schedule a meeting with Leven. As COO, Leven was in charge of overseeing the operations of the franchises and responding to issues, concerns, and complaints as well as making sure that franchises abided by state and federal codes and regulations. The position of COO was relatively new at Days Inn, and Leven was quickly learning how in-depth the job was. Rama had been desperately trying to contact Henry Silverman (chief executive officer of Days Inn) to discuss the various levels of discrimination in the hotel industry and within Days Inn itself, but he was not having much luck. Rama and other franchisees did not fully realize that Leven was the person to contact, but once Silverman heard of Rama's attempts, he placed him in contact with Leven. Rama traveled to Leven's office in Atlanta, where Leven heartily greeted him and the two initiated a conversation about discrimination against Indian hoteliers. Leven initially assumed that Rama had a specific, individual concern about his franchise and asked Rama what he could do to help him improve his business. "No, I don't need anything from you," Rama began, "but this is what I'm facing. This is what I see. And this is what many Asian Indian hotel owners are facing." He then launched into the myriad ways that the hotel industry (including Days Inn) discriminated against Indian American hoteliers and further propagated negative stereotypes and prejudices in American society.[31]

Although Leven was not entirely surprised by what Rama reported, he was taken aback that his own company (where Indian Americans owned 10 percent of the franchises and were mainly located in the South) participated in such discriminatory practices. Leven confided in Rama and recounted his story of growing up Jewish in Boston, and although the two experiences were not the same, Rama and other Indian American hoteliers would identify Leven as a kind of "godfather" who understood their predicament and was an ally in the business world. Rama discovered that Leven "faced the same thing while growing up—dogs and Jews not allowed in hotels—he immediately understood what I was going through . . . and [I understood] why he was so keen to help us."[32] Leven immediately proposed to Rama that he allow Days Inn to conduct a survey of Days Inn personnel at the corporate level and around the country to uncover their perceptions of Indian Americans and Indian American hoteliers and gain a sense of how deep the stereotypes and prejudice were. Rama wholeheartedly agreed, as he believed "there is a big gap between what we do and what is our intention versus what people thought about us."[33]

In 1987, Leven procured funds from Days Inn and hired Lee Duschoff, a young lawyer and consultant to the hospitality industry from Philadelphia, to travel to Days Inn franchises across the South not owned by Indian Americans and survey personnel at the corporate level. Duschoff had a pragmatic view of his role in Leven and Rama's plan to assess discrimination in Days Inn, explaining, "Leven was trying to be responsive to what was already becoming a growing group of Days Inn owners [Indians], so there's policy and profits. And when social policy and profits come together, all good things could happen."[34] Duschoff was not necessarily a high-minded civil rights advocate and recognized (as did many other businesses that chose to integrate after the Civil Rights Act of 1964 rather than lose customers) that discrimination was often bad for profits. Duschoff accepted Leven's task because he did consulting work and had a firm handle on managing large corporation surveys, but also because "obviously ... there wasn't anybody in the Days Inn chain who had the time to do it, so he [Leven] hired an outsider to manage the process."[35] If Indian Americans were "accidental hoteliers," men like Leven, Duschoff, and Rama could be classified as "accidental activists."

Duschoff's survey took approximately four months to complete and revealed that Days Inn employees at all levels confessed to knowing little about the people who owned 10 to 15 percent of the franchises. The little that they knew was rife with generic stereotypes of Indian Americans as dirty, unscrupulous, and unable to speak English. Also surprising to Duschoff was that as he interviewed more Indian American franchisees, he learned that the American Hotel and Lodging Association not only tacitly participated in the American-owned-and-operated campaign but had rejected the membership applications of a number of Indian American hoteliers. When Duschoff shared the results of the survey, Leven and Rama were crushed to see evidence of such prejudice permeating Days Inn and the entire hospitality and lodging industry more generally. As Rama noted, "There was a gap between the reality and the perception [among Days Inn employees] of Indian hoteliers" that was wide and disheartening. It appeared as though racist and xenophobic anti–Indian American sentiment existed at all levels of the industry and that dispelling these myths would be a difficult task. Later that year, Leven held two meetings with small groups of Indian American hoteliers in Charlotte, North Carolina, and Atlanta, where he shared the results of the survey and learned more about the extent of insurance discrimination as well as more general discrimination against Indian Americans in the industry and in larger southern communities. What was to be done with the survey results if they appeared to simply confirm Leven's and Rama's worst suspicions? This would be a question that would pull Days Inn, Leven, and Rama further into the realm of organizing and activism.[36]

In 1988, armed with the results of the survey, Duschoff, Leven, and Rama reported to Days Inn Chief Executive Officer Henry Silverman, who decided that the Indian American franchisees were an asset to his corporation and required organization and representation to make themselves heard. "We knew that Asian Americans had size in the market, but what they needed was political clout," Silverman explained. The discrimination the Indian hoteliers faced was "a civil rights issue for them and a business issue for [Days Inn]," which required "lobbying power" to take on the racism and prejudice inherent in the industry and particularly in the South.[37] Silverman provided Leven with $100,000 to assist the Indian franchisees in joining together and forming an organization that would build solidarity to tackle some of the larger issues, including insurance discrimination and the American-owned-and-operated campaign. Leven, Rama, and Ravi Patel, another Indian hotelier from North Carolina, oversaw a meeting of approximately 300 Indian hotel and motel owners in Atlanta (where Days Inn's headquarters were located at the time) in April 1988. The men kept the purpose of the meeting vague, apart from inviting the attendees to convene in Atlanta to discuss current issues facing Indian American hoteliers in the South and across the United States. Leven agreed not to have any Days Inn sales members attend the meeting so that, according to Duschoff, no one "would think that Days Inn was putting this together in order to sell more franchises."[38] The entire Days Inn team was concerned that outsiders and particularly other chains would believe that their assistance in organizing the Indian hoteliers was purely motivated by business interests—to attract more Indian American hoteliers to their company and saturate the southern hospitality market with "curry palaces" under the guise of altruism. However, Leven and Days Inn had little to worry about in this regard. At the end of the meeting, after breakaway meetings and more personal dinners, lunches, and coffee breaks, a group of twelve Indian hoteliers decided that they needed a formal, visible, and nationwide organization to more fully address the needs of Indian American hotel and motel owners.[39]

As with other groups in their early stages, the initial goals of the organization (yet to be named) were not fully formed. The Mid-South Indemnity Association (formally renamed the Indo-American Hospitality Association in 1987) dealt largely with insurance discrimination but not with other aspects of discrimination, such as the American-owned-and-operated billboard campaign or broader social and cultural instances of anti–Indian American prejudice. Few outside Tennessee knew that the Indo-American Hospitality Association (IAHA) existed, leading hoteliers to believe that a larger, more multifaceted group was needed. Would this be a legally minded organization? Would the group also focus on regional insurance discrimination? How would they go about challenging social and cultural prejudice? What would the new organization look like? Who would lead it? Who would fund it? These were all questions that plagued attendees at the 1988 Atlanta meeting. Although the initial vision for the proposed association was not yet clear, Leven and Days Inn were thrilled with the idea and wholeheartedly supported a group run by Indian hoteliers to assist Indian American hoteliers. Leven and other Days Inn executives and leaders viewed the formation of an Indian hotel association as a means for Indian American motel and hotel owners to integrate into the larger motel and hotel association. As Duschoff explained, "The goal was never to have a permanent separate organization" but to become a fully functioning part of the larger hospitality industry without prejudice or discrimination barring Indian American hoteliers from advancing.[40]

But Indian American hoteliers, not Leven or Days Inn, were in charge of the would-be association, and they would come to dictate their own goals and missions. At the meeting in Atlanta, a small group of Indian American hoteliers, including Rama and Ravi Patel, decided to meet again one year later in Charlotte. Leven suggested that Days Inn representatives not attend the meeting to encourage the hoteliers to independently form the framework for their larger association. Twelve hoteliers met in Charlotte and created a steering committee to form a national association and invite all Indian American motel and hotel owners regardless of whether or not they were Days Inn franchisees. It was to be a membership-based group with annual dues and would serve as the voice of the Indian American hoteliers in the United States. One member of the steering committee suggested that they call themselves the Indian American Hotel Owners Association to advertise that this was a group made by Indian American hoteliers for Indian American hoteliers and that it recognized the problems and opportunities for Indians in the hospitality industry. However, others suggested that not only did this sound similar to the Indo-American Hospitality Association, but it was also not as inclusive. Although there was never any intention to attract hoteliers of various Asian ethnicities beyond Indian Americans, naming the association Asian American Hotel Owners Association was a nod toward the potential expansiveness and reach of the organization and also differentiated its members from Native Americans (a point of confusion for many Americans at the time whenever the term "Indian" or "Indian American" was used).[41]

The steering committee also decided on the goals and mission of the group, which would be the all-inclusive "fighting against discriminatory activities." Organizers did not want to limit their purpose to insurance discrimination (which was the focus of IAHA) and wanted to tackle larger, deep-seated prejudices in the industry and in larger communities that served as the rationale for discriminatory practices. AAHOA would not be a legal group but, rather, an association that sought to build "acceptance in the mainstream hotel and motel industry" through cooperation rather than "coercion." Although "fighting discriminatory activities" was at the center of AAHOA's mission and appeared to be in line with other civil rights and equality organizations, from day one, the Indian American hoteliers never considered themselves as part of a civil rights group. "It's an organization that helped to remove the stereotypes, bias, and ignorance, but, no ... it was not a civil rights organization," according to H. P. Rama, who would go on to be the first chairman of AAHOA and a key founding member. Rama had a very firm definition of a civil right: "Civil rights [means] 'it's my right and I'm enforcing [it] on you.' We already had a right, people were just not treating us on a human basis."[42] For Rama, there were no rights to fight for, just a fight against cultural and social prejudices that led to discrimination in the industry. Prejudice was cultural, not legal, and one "cannot legislate the behavior of people ... but we can educate and we can try to remove bias and stereotypes."[43] AAHOA would be "inclusive" and "not force others to behave a certain way," unlike other civil rights organizations, which founding members of the association were not interested in collaborating with for a larger end to discrimination in the hospitality industry.[44] Using legislation to force insurance agencies to provide coverage and sellers to not rescind agreements if they discovered that their purchasers were Indians was not the goal of the Indian hoteliers. They viewed these problems as rooted in business and a poor understanding of Indian culture and characteristics. You could not force individuals to do something with their property that they did not want to do, and you could not force businesses to perform a duty if they did not want to, no matter the wrong-headed reasons why they did not wish to do it. While the Civil Rights Act of 1964 made many discriminatory activities technically illegal, AAHOA existed to improve relations between the white-dominated hotel industry and white communities and the Indian Americans, not antagonize whites by creating a further poor image of "hostile" Indian American hoteliers. Rama explained the goal of the group succinctly: "I want you to accept me and I accept you and we both feel good about it."[45] Perhaps this attitude could be grouped with the idea of maintaining a model minority identity that at times worked for Asian Americans in the past and sometimes did not; however, overall, the strategy of avoiding legal action was not the same strategy that other Asian Americans previously utilized in the South.

The white corporate officers from Days Inn who provided financial backing to the upstart AAHOA certainly grounded their efforts in the language of civil rights, however, even if they, too, agreed that legal action was not the correct path to follow. "Was it about civil rights? Absolutely! It was about civil rights—the discrimination against the Indians in the industry was terrible," Duschoff exclaimed when describing his efforts in organizing the association. For Duschoff, Leven, and Silverman, the Indian Americans hoteliers did suffer from civil rights violations that were fueled by prejudice, misunderstandings, and racism. Denying insurance coverage was, for Leven, a clear-cut example of a violation of basic business rights. The Indian Americans "needed an advocacy group that would give them a voice in the industry . . . and let the vendors and insurance agents know that they [the Indians] knew what they [the vendors and agents] were doing was wrong and was illegal."[46] Such practices were, as Leven pointed out, also "bad business" for all involved. Silverman agreed with Leven and placed his concerns within a business-oriented context. Silverman viewed the American-owned-and-operated campaign as "a civil rights issue for them [Indian hoteliers] and a business issue for us [Days Inn]."[47] The American-owned campaign, while being detrimental to the Indian Americans' business, was also detrimental to Days Inn when Indian American franchisees took a financial hit when travelers refused to stop. "In the South, where Days Inn grew up, competitors noticed our growth and noticed which franchisees were most responsible for it," Silverman noted, and he condemned "their rather unsavory response" of posting "American-owned" signs and putting up "American-owned" billboards.[48] Duschoff, Silverman, and Leven identified both civil rights and business issues with the ways in which the Indian hoteliers were treated. Unlike the Indian hoteliers who became "accidental activists" once they became involved, the three Days Inn corporate representatives identified the burgeoning AAHOA as a civil rights group and, simply, the "right thing to do" to protect the civil rights of minority members of the Days Inn family. Murmurs throughout the hotel industry that Days Inn was only devoted to the Indian American hoteliers because the franchise wanted to make money and not because it cared about the rights and equality of the Indian Americans angered Leven and Silverman. The two went out of their way to ensure other competitors and Indian American hoteliers that this was not merely about business or profits, but if profits and business increased as a result, then that would be a favorable by-product of their involvement with the group.

The fact that only the white Days Inn executives characterized AAHOA as a civil rights organization creates a complex and problematic place for the organization and Indian American hoteliers in the longer history of Asian American civil rights organizing in the South. Although Asian Americans in the past who had used the courts to fight for their civil rights had often worked with white attorneys and other organizations such as the Southern Poverty Law Center, interracial activism on a group scale was not common. Asian ethnic groups identified their own needs and rights violations and worked to address their individual issues. When Asian Americans used the courts, it was typically to fight for themselves rather than their entire ethnic or nationality group and certainly not for all Asian ethnic groups (the Vietnamese Americans being an exception when they fought for property rights for all Vietnamese refugees). Once Days Inn became involved with the Indian American hoteliers, the goals and characteristics of AAHOA, according to Leven, Duschoff, and Silverman, were broader than simply ending prejudice. These men believed that this was a larger civil rights issue and one that exposed deep-seated prejudices and obstacles in the hospitality industry. If Days Inn had never become involved with the group, it is questionable if AAHOA would ever be classified as a civil rights organization. Ravi Patel differed from the Days Inn executives on the purpose of AAHOA, explaining that "AAHOA is not a civil rights group. We did not witness any civil rights violations, only prejudice. We would never have compared our situation to that of the African Americans."[49] By the post–civil rights era and into the 1980s, the Indian American hoteliers firmly defined civil rights violations as including "not having the right to vote and the right to own property" (as Patel explained), and they defined who suffered from inequality as African Americans. African Americans experienced real civil rights violations from visceral and systematic racism, while Indians were only dealt the glancing blows of cultural prejudice. For Patel, Indian Americans defined themselves not racially but ethnically and did not experience racism (as only African Americans did) but, rather, prejudice—which was not the same. As a result, the Indian American hoteliers' battle was against the effects of prejudice and not civil rights violations. In the South, Indian American hoteliers believed that associating their plight with that of African Americans was not a particularly wise strategy. Meanwhile, the white Days Inn executives had the privilege of viewing what they were doing as civil rights organizing from a position of class, racial, and corporate privilege. It was interracial civil rights activism and organizing for the new corporate climate.

One point on which the Days Inn executives clashed with Indian American leaders during the early days of AAHOA was whether or not to invite other Asian ethnic groups to join the organization. Leven envisioned an organization that was truly all-encompassing, consisting of Indian American, Korean American, and Thai American hotel owners, who were not as prevalent in the hospitality industry but were still Asian American hoteliers.[50] However, Leven's proposal did not receive a favorable reception among either the Indian American hoteliers or other hoteliers of different Asian ethnic groups. "We were the majority in the hotel and motel industry . . . and we wanted to make sure that our interests were addressed and met," Patel explained. "We didn't know of any problems that other Asian Americans experienced with insurance agencies—we may have all suffered because of the [American-owned-and-operated] billboards and signs—so we wouldn't speak for them. That's not what we wanted to do."[51] And hoteliers of different ethnicities apparently agreed with Ravi Patel and the other early leaders of AAHOA. When Leven and Silverman attempted to reach out to a few of their franchisees who were Asian American, there was little interest in the group. Other hoteliers viewed AAHOA as a purely Indian American organization, and the Indian American hoteliers behind the group did not see any problems with this. Hoteliers who were not Indian American did not believe that they would receive any benefits from joining an organization, particularly one that was so young and so outside the mainstream. Leven attempted on a few occasions to continue to push the subject of being truly representative of all Asian American hoteliers, but the idea was not favorable across the industry. In the South, Asian American activism was rarely panethnic, and the Indian American hoteliers were merely following a pattern of self-interest that Leven had difficulty understanding. While organization across various ethnic groups was the hallmark of a burgeoning Asian American movement on the West Coast and other areas of the United States since the late 1960s, organizing was different for Indian American hoteliers in the South, who (as other ethnic groups did) banded together in a region where the Indian population had only recently begun to grow and held an uncertain place in the racial and social order. Unlike the Indian American hoteliers, Leven and Duschoff viewed AAHOA as a way to fully integrate the Indian American hoteliers into the industry, primarily forcing the American Hotel and Lodging Association to fully recognize Indian hoteliers and admit them as members rather than letting them remain as an ethnic association. This was a further example of the divide between the Days Inn executives and the early leaders of AAHOA over whether or not the group was a civil rights organization or an association to end prejudice and protect the business interests of a particular ethnic group. Integration for Leven was a matter of civil rights, and while the Indian American hoteliers did wish to become fully represented and respected in the industry, they chose to do so not with "arrogance" or "force" but through representing their ethnicity with AAHOA.[52]

With the outline of the organization formed, the steering committee for AAHOA planned its first annual convention in Atlanta in 1990. This was to be the association's coming-out party and would be the main platform for attracting dues-paying members to the group. Rama, Leven, and Duschoff sent more than 1,000 invitations to Indian American franchisees not only from Days Inn but also in other chains throughout the United States. Once again, Leven guaranteed AAHOA that while he would put up the money to help finance the cost of the conference, there would be no Days Inn representatives in attendance. However, in attempting to maintain the idea that Days Inn was not involved with AAHOA for money or to attract more franchises, Leven also invited representatives from other corporations to attend the meeting (a move the Indian American hoteliers supported), not only to educate the other chains about the problems that Indian Americans faced in the industry but also, if they desired, to give them the opportunity to assure Indian Americans that the other chains were not discriminatory and were open to doing business with them. However, many of the other corporations were not interested in sending representatives to the meeting, and the majority of the invited Indian American hoteliers did not express much enthusiasm for AAHOA either. A disappointing 200 Indian American hoteliers traveled to Atlanta for the meeting, and Rama was only able to convince about 15 of them to become dues-paying members. Although AAHOA had ambitious goals, it was not clear to the outside world or even to many of the early members of the organization exactly what those goals were.[53]

The major problem that AAHOA faced in its first year was a lack of a clear strategy. It was difficult to pinpoint exactly what AAHOA was going to do to "fight against discriminatory activities." IAHA was already working on helping Indian Americans with insurance, so Rama argued that the new group should not necessarily engage with that mission. It made little sense to early members to battle insurance discrimination on two separate fronts; forming a united coalition might be more effective. Members of AAHOA held several meetings with IAHA in 1989, and both organizations agreed that fighting insurance discrimination was within IAHA's realm. Indian American hoteliers were unsure of what their dues (which were originally suggested to be $100 a year but were lowered to $25 annually) were supporting. What was in it for them? Not only was the mission of the organization vague, but AAHOA also lacked a professional presence as far as organizations go—it did not have a central office and lacked any clear leadership structure. Fighting against discriminatory activities was noble, but there was no explanation on how AAHOA planned to do this and who the targets would be.[54]

AAHOA had a rocky start, but Rama and Patel wasted little time in actively recruiting new members. Later in 1990, Rama and Patel traveled throughout the South at their own expense, stopping in urban and rural areas to speak to Indian American hoteliers on an individual basis. Rama and Patel crisscrossed the South and explained to hoteliers the "challenges we are facing and if someone says we are a bad operator, we should take this as an opportunity to learn from people who are telling you that you are not good. We cannot be arrogant about it."[55] Rama and Patel preached the business-oriented model of fighting against prejudice in a way that appealed to many Indian American hoteliers. Joining a trade organization would help in professionalizing the image of Indians and "build[ing] a bridge to the mainstream." This was not organizing for legal justice but, rather, organizing to help Indian businesses eliminate prejudice. Rama and Patel also offered the concrete goal of working toward membership in the American Hotel and Lodging Association to raise the professional profile of Indian American hoteliers. As a result, "people understood," and Rama sweetened the deal by offering to pay the first year's membership fees (with his own money). If members decided at the end of the year that AAHOA was not for them or was not assisting them in any way, then they would not have wasted any of their money. "They saw the sincerity in our efforts, so they all came around actually. It was maybe right time, rightly orchestrated, rightly articulated and we can validate what we do and what we say."[56] Rama and Patel convinced other early members of AAHOA to travel to other regions, including farther out toward Houston and the Midwest, in order to raise awareness of the group and its activities. Following Rama and Ravi Patel's efforts, Asvlin Patel joined AAHOA "with a passion of belonging" to a group that so represented his needs. Despite being a poor upstart franchisee from New Jersey, he would drive from New Jersey to Atlanta as soon as he was done manning the lobby of his hotel at 7pm, wake up at 8am the next morning to drive around the area drumming up members, and then get back on the road later that same evening so that he could be at his hotel in time to start another business day.[57] In other words, Rama, Ravi Patel, Asvlin Patel, and the other early leaders who traveled became experts at "good communication and good networking" and developed a business-oriented model of grassroots activism that was the hallmark of many other civil rights groups.

Impressed with Rama and Ravi Patel's efforts in recruiting new members, Henry Silverman and Days Inn parent company Hospitality Franchise System contributed to the professionalization of AAHOA. In 1990, Silverman provided AAHOA with an office at Days Inn headquarters in Atlanta and paid

Duschoff and Leven to further assist AAHOA with establishing itself and recruiting more members. A year later, Silverman agreed to provide AAHOA with an endowment of another $100,000, while Days Inn and Hospitality Franchise System donated $1 million to help AAHOA open its own office on Clairmont Road in Atlanta. Competitors refused to believe that Days Inn was supporting an organization simply because of a deep-seated belief in justice and civil rights and not as a means to make more money. However, Leven and Duschoff always maintained that if their actions and their money happened to increase growth while bringing equality for Indian hoteliers, "then the money was a good investment."[58] The members of AAHOA never questioned the motive behind Days Inn's support for their endeavors and actually came to view Leven as a type of "godfather" for their organization and all Indian American hoteliers. Leven traveled to the Gujarat region of India in 1990 to learn more about Indian hospitality culture and came to be seen as a man who, with the assistance of Lee Duschoff, "helped [AAHOA] grow, gave [AAHOA input on] how to grow. Very important contribution by Mike and his team."[59]

The efforts of Rama and Patel in recruitment as well as the assistance of Leven, Silverman, and Days Inn worked. Approximately 600 Indian American hoteliers attended the second annual convention in 1991 at the Opryland Hotel in Nashville, and all 600 signed up to become members of AAHOA. Vendors and representatives from different chains also attended the conference that year and succeeded in selling franchises to many of the Indian American hoteliers in attendance. By the early 1990s, AAHOA was becoming more mainstream. Members created bylaws and elected a board of directors (with a rotating chairman every two years so that one member would not monopolize the position) to further professionalize their organization and create a leadership structure for change and activism. H. P. Rama served as the first chairman of AAHOA (with Ravi Patel as assistant) and oversaw early attempts at putting into practice the organization's ideas to end prejudice and promote equality within the hospitality industry.[60]

THE GROWTH OF AAHOA

The first issue AAHOA tackled was the American-owned-and-operated campaign. The racist and prejudiced billboards and signs inspired a goal that spoke to the organization's tactics of cooperation and outreach to end discrimination rather than using the courtroom or "force." The campaign was a manifestation of a cultural practice that had dire consequences for Indian

American hoteliers' success in obtaining insurance and, in many cases, customers. But more so it was an easy target for the inequality that was prevalent in the industry and supported by the American Hotel and Lodging Association. By 1994, AAHOA had merged with IAHA after leaders of both organizations agreed that they would have more political clout if they formally worked toward the same goals. Also, by the mid-1990s, the American-owned-and-operated campaign that began in the South had garnered national attention, with stories appearing in the *New York Times* highlighting the "absurdity" of such a marketing technique. While many whites still viewed Indian American hoteliers and their curry palaces suspiciously, others identified not a menace but a group of immigrants who were simply living the American Dream. By the mid-1990s, Indian American entrepreneurs were on their way to becoming part of the model minority myth in the business-oriented imagination of America. As a result, AAHOA perceived a prime opportunity for pushing back against the American-owned-and-operated campaign.

In 1995, Silverman, Rama, and Ravi Patel began their own countercampaign against the "American-owned-and-operated" billboards and signs. First, Rama viewed this movement as an opportunity to increase the presence of Indian hoteliers in the larger, nationwide associations and use them to help combat the prejudice apparent on the highways and byways of America through billboards. In dealing with the organizations, Rama and AAHOA took a slightly more forceful approach than they had before, particularly with the American Automobile Association (AAA). Rama believed that the organization, the go-to expert in hotel and motel diamond ratings, had the clout to put pressure on the industry and larger chains to take down the billboards and signs. Recognizing that Indian American hoteliers were a rapidly growing portion of hotel owners in the United States, the AAA pressured participants in the American-owned-and-operated campaigns to realize the discriminatory message behind their marketing strategy and encouraged the larger chains to survey their franchisees and create a corporate policy that would ban such activity. Days Inn was the first chain (under the demands of Silverman) to completely ban any franchisees from displaying "American-owned" or "American-operated" signs on their property (this was part of a signed agreement for all franchisees). Silverman also inquired of local prosecutors in the South if the signs violated any business or civil rights acts. At the time, these measures did not fall into any legal category for action, but Indian American hoteliers were not deterred, as they preferred cultural and social plans of action in any case. Other chains soon followed suit, realizing, as Duschoff previously mentioned, that discrimination and racism could be bad for business. Although smaller mom-and-pop motels and hotels continued to display handwritten "American-owned" signs on the doors of their lobbies, fewer billboards were seen along major highways in the South and in other parts of the nation.[61]

The mid-1990s also saw the elimination of other discriminatory practices in the industry, primarily among the nationwide associations and organizations. The American Hotel and Lodging Association admitted more Indian hoteliers as members, and in 1999 H. P. Rama became secretary and chairman of the association. Similar to the push to do away with the "American-owned-and-operated" signs and billboards, reaching out to the national organization was in line with AAHOA's goals of cooperation and ending prejudice in the industry. "We invited the American Motel and [Lodging Association] to speak at our conventions to help our hotel owners," Rama explained, but these invitations also helped the larger organization. "That's how we created a platform for them and helped them to recruit membership to their organizations, so it was a very collaborative effort from day one. We had started building a bridge to mainstream hotel industry."[62] Rama and the other members of AAHOA viewed building a bridge between Indian hoteliers and the rest of the hospitality industry as a means of business-oriented integration that would also go a long way in deconstructing racist stereotypes of Indians.

As AAHOA's membership grew throughout the 1990s, its political and financial presence did as well. Thousands of Indian American hoteliers throughout the country joined AAHOA as members, and although AAHOA was based in Atlanta and continued to have members primarily from the South, it garnered nationwide attention. AAHOA branched out from cultural and social outreach and became fully engaged in legislative action in 1998 when it developed the "Twelve Points of Fair Franchising," a set of provisions for best practices in franchisor and franchisee relationships spearheaded by Chairman Mike Patel. Indian American hoteliers found it easier to obtain insurance by the late 1990s, but there remained problems with unequal treatment in the relationship of a franchisee to the owner and other middlemen (such as sales agents). Of primary concern were examples of sales fraud wherein larger corporations or regional sales managers would deny certain coverage or benefits to Indian American hoteliers and unfairly terminate the sales contract. Also, franchisees were often bound to purchasing supplies and materials from specified vendors, creating a form of vertical integration and constrained capitalism. Under U.S. business and finance regulations as well as civil rights legislation, AAHOA had some grounds for seeking redress in the courts. However, Mike Patel and AAHOA chose to leave the legal battles to the individual hoteliers and work through the larger legislative process to enact change.

In 1998, Mike Patel and AAHOA authored the "Twelve Points," which consisted of best-practices guidelines that would prevent franchisees from being "profit centers for franchisors." The "Twelve Points" included "fair formulas to protect the franchisees assets and the franchisors interests in cases of economic impact," the belief that "franchisees should enjoy the right to purchase goods and services from any vendor," and the right of franchisees "to be able to exit a relationship without having to pay liquidated damages when a brand does not perform at minimum occupancy," which was a problem for Indian American franchisees who suffered as part of the American-owned-and-operated campaigns earlier in the 1990s.[63] More generally, AAHOA hoped that franchisors would "mandate 'good faith and fair dealing' practices among their sales agents" to limit fraud and deception. These were problems that affected franchisees across the country, but AAHOA, representing a growing number of franchisees, argued that violations of franchisee rights were of special concern to Indian American hoteliers and particularly those who operated in the South.

AAHOA's fair franchising ideas became more than just guidelines. Late in 1998, AAHOA joined with other associations and corporations (including Kentucky Fried Chicken, Domino's Pizza, and The Country's Best Yogurt, among others) to work with Congress on legislation that would make franchisor and franchisee relationships more equitable. Though opponents of the Small Business Franchise Bill, such as McDonald's, Burger King, and David Koch, argued that the proposed bill would give too many rights to the franchisees at the expense of the franchisor (particularly the clause that allowed state attorneys general to become involved in disagreements if they were perceived to hurt the interests of the citizens of the state), the bill's sponsors, Representative Howard Coble (R) of North Carolina and John Conyers Jr. (D) of Michigan, believed that these measures simply leveled the playing field in the partnership. Franchises were small business and the franchisees were technically small business owners; too often, franchisees were grouped with corporations, and few recognized the complete control of the franchisor over all of the franchisee's actions. The bill proposed to reclassify (for legal purposes) franchisees as small business owners to protect their business rights and interests. Apart from inspiring the basic components of the bill, AAHOA also supported the recognition of Indian American hoteliers as small business owners who had begun with nothing and pulled themselves up to become highly visible members of the industry. Through the lobbying efforts of AAHOA, the bill garnered bipartisan support and passed easily in 1999. The Small Business Franchise Act revolutionized the relationship between franchisor and franchisee and pushed AAHOA further into the political and legislative (if not the judicial) realm of activism.[64]

Interestingly enough, AAHOA's turn to using the legislative process to protect small business owners created tensions with other corporations in the hospitality industry. One of AAHOA's earliest supporters and essential founders, Henry Silverman, questioned the organization's motivations for becoming legislatively invested in limiting the power of franchisors. In 1997, Silverman's corporation, Hotel Franchising System, merged with the direct marketing firm CUC International to create Cendant Corporation. Silverman reduced his role in the new corporation, becoming chairman and leaving Chief Executive Officer Walter Forbes in charge of the day-to-day operations. While Cendant initially agreed to honor most of AAHOA's "Twelve Points," the leadership of Cendant became wary of AAHOA's support of the 1999 Small Business Franchise Act and openly spoke out against the association in various trade publications and venues, labeling AAHOA's activities a form of "radicalism."[65] Later in 1999, Cendant cut off support and involvement with AAHOA after expressing fears that the organization would venture further into legislative action to limit the rights and powers of franchisors. What AAHOA viewed as best practices, Cendant and others interpreted as restricting business and operation rights. AAHOA leaders worried that other franchisors would follow suit and suspend their ties and support as well. Fortunately, no other franchisor powerhouses followed Cendant's lead, and one, AmeriHost, strengthened its support of AAHOA. As Indian American hoteliers came to make up 40 percent of the hospitality industry by the late 1990s, they became more difficult to exclude, a fact not lost on franchisors and corporations. Cendant's actions inspired more praise than denouncements of AAHOA, and by the early 2000s, AAHOA fell back into favor with Cendant and continued to receive support from Silverman's corporation. Following the success of the Small Business Franchise Act, AAHOA moved further into political action in 2000 when it held its first legislation action summit and, later, in 2008 when it formed a political action committee to focus on issues of bank lending in the franchise industry. From darlings of the hospitality industry during the mid-1990s to "radicals" and back again, AAHOA experienced growing pains that resulted in the creation of the most powerful association in the hospitality industry and a legislative force to be reckoned with.[66]

The South provided AAHOA and Indian American hoteliers more generally with an opportunity to witness the depths of racism and discrimination but also the means to challenge these forces. For those Chinese Americans, Filipino Americans, and Vietnamese Americans who came before, legal activism produced uneven results. Indian American hoteliers may not have taken into account the many failures or successes of Asian Americans in the courts, but their practically uniform decision not to seek justice through lawsuits against agencies and businesses that discriminated against them was a reflection of how the South and civil rights had evolved through the twentieth century. Indian American hoteliers set up shop in a post–civil rights era, after the passage of the Civil Rights Act of 1964, which was supposed to have leveled the playing field in business operations. As such, identifying discriminatory business practices as racist or in violation of civil rights was difficult for Indian American hoteliers, who largely associated civil rights violations with African Americans. From the formation of AAHOA to the support of legislation for franchisees, Indian American hoteliers engaged in a form of business or entrepreneurial activism that sought to end prejudice rather than racism. Prejudice could only be eradicated through organizational development and outreach; court cases would only lead to antagonistic relations with sellers, buyers, and customers. The fact that Gong Lum almost immediately turned to the local judge to help his daughter gain admission to a white school while H. P. Rama's initial reaction when faced with a racist seller was to avoid a lawsuit at all costs speaks volumes on both the changing nature of Asian American activism over time and how Asian Americans in the South experienced racism and discrimination not as a unified whole but as individual ethnic groups. In many ways, the actions of the Indian American hoteliers resembled the reactions of Japanese American farmers in Florida and Louisiana who chose to tend to their daily businesses in the face of rising anti-Japanese sentiment and racist constitutional amendments during the early twentieth century. Also, Indian American hoteliers worked openly with whites in the industry, beyond the typical interactions between Asian Americans and lawyers in past southern battles for civil rights. The concentration of Indian Americans in the South, the southern roots of the growing hospitality corporations, and respectability politics created an opportunity for Indian hoteliers to grow as activists in this region and approach the issue of civil rights from an entrepreneurial angle in a post–civil rights era.

In 2014, AAHOA celebrated its twenty-fifth anniversary, and leaders and members looked back fondly over its history and its dramatic growth. Today, AAHOA is more than 14,000 members strong, and its annual convention is one of the largest trade association meetings in the country. Indian American hoteliers now make up more than half of the hospitality industry, and many of the early AAHOA members, like H. P. Rama, have moved beyond small motels and into successful corporations and franchises (Rama has done so well that he recently started a university in India to provide students with the know-how for making it in the industry)—accidental hoteliers no more.

While many Indian American hoteliers can look back fondly on their business successes, how can historians track the success of AAHOA as a civil rights organization and Indian American hoteliers as civil rights activists? Perhaps, as Rama and Ravi Patel have explained, it is unfair to classify them and their organization as vehicles for Asian American and Indian American civil rights if their focus was never on civil rights but, rather, equality and an end to prejudice. However, as AAHOA stated in its own mission statement since its earliest days, the goal of fighting "against discriminatory activities" certainly conjures images of civil rights activism. By using stereotypes and racism to deny Indian American hoteliers the same opportunities as others, insurance agencies, customers, and even the large hospitality industry associations denied Indian Americans their basic civil rights and property rights. Also, it was neither an accident nor a coincidence that AAHOA was (and remains) very much a southern-based organization. This was not a national story that just happened to begin and be set in the South; this was part of a larger story and history of racism directed toward Asian Americans in the South and a denial of rights.

But was AAHOA a civil rights organization? That is a difficult question to answer, and as mentioned above, there is division on this even among the organization's leaders. While Leven, Duschoff, and Silverman refer to AAHOA as a civil rights group, Ravi Patel and H. P. Rama see it differently, although Rama has since changed his opinion slightly: "If you consider ending prejudice a part of civil rights, okay, then AAHOA is about civil rights."[67] Leven also admired the association's nonlegal approach to civil rights because, as he explained, "you're never going to do away with prejudice—it's a human condition, it's human and it will always be there." But Leven did consider business rights as civil rights, and he considered AAHOA extraordinarily successful as a civil rights association. During a recent interview, Leven countered that "there is no discrimination in the hospitality industry today—prejudice is still here, but there's no more discrimination."[68] AAHOA *was* a civil rights organization that practiced post–civil rights activism by attempting to end prejudiced practices even if it was not able to do away with prejudice altogether. Without any discrimination, however, perhaps AAHOA is a civil

American-owned-and-operated advertisement on U.S. Highway 84 West outside Valdosta, Georgia, 2015. *Photo by the author.*

rights association no more. The problem lies in how we define civil rights, its boundaries, and its activists when Indian Americans used strategies and tactics to fight against racism that were often different from those of both Asian Americans before them and African Americans.

Driving along Highway 84 in southern Georgia today, going east from Tallahassee toward Valdosta, one would be hard-pressed not to notice a billboard advertising a hotel as American-owned. The original signs can still be found here and there, and new "American-owned-and-operated" signs resurfaced in the wake of anti-Muslim sentiment after the September 11 attacks on the World Trade Center and the Pentagon, with Americans confusing Hindus for Muslims. The prejudice is still here, if perhaps not the more formal means of discrimination that existed in the early days of AAHOA. As time moved on, the model minority myth obscured the previous battles of Asian Americans in the South against de jure forms of discrimination and wiped Asian Americans from the history of civil rights activism in the region. However, prejudice remains as perhaps the most difficult battle yet for Asian American activists, and if Leven is right, then this will be an ongoing battle for years, decades, and centuries to come. As Leven explained in a recent interview, "Prejudice will always be here, you just have to work with it or work against it. Maybe you can end your book on that."

CONCLUSION

In November 2008, Floridians who went to the polls to cast their ballots for the next president of the United States also had the chance to reverse eighty years of institutionalized discrimination against Asian Americans in their state. Asian American rights groups in Florida and nationwide distributed pamphlets, sent emails, and spoke to media outlets to build support for a ballot initiative that proposed removing the "aliens ineligible for citizenship" clause from the state constitution. There was hope that Florida could go the way of states like Kansas and New Mexico and formally remove the lingering anti-Asian language. Although the U.S. Supreme Court rendered legislative measures to prevent aliens ineligible for citizenship from owning land unconstitutional in 1952, the connection between the continued presence of this outdated language in the constitution and the legacy of anti-Asian sentiment was clear—this would be a symbolic victory that would signal a purge of de jure if not de facto prejudice and racism aimed at Asian Americans. Because Florida's anti-alien legislation was enshrined in the constitution, 60 percent of voters would have to approve the initiative in order to remove the discriminatory language from the first amendment and insert neutral language specifying property rights for all. Surely, in the twenty-first century, Floridians would recognize the outdated and discriminatory portion of their constitution and vote to move the law of their land beyond the limits of the past.[1]

But on Election Day, 52 percent of Floridians voted "no" on the proposed Amendment 1, choosing to keep the Florida constitution unaltered. Organizations and Asian American and immigrant rights activists were stunned. Why would the majority of Florida voters choose to maintain discriminatory language against Asian Americans, the supposed model minority? Voters had just elected their first African American president, and 50.91 percent of Florida voters cast their ballots for Barack Obama. It appeared as though America was slowly, but perhaps surely, moving toward a more inclusive and representative nation. However, for those who voted against the measure, the decision was straightforward: Illegal immigrants should not be able to own property in Florida. Latino immigrants and Muslims, rather than Asian immigrants, were the feared minority groups because of increased migration from Central and South America and tensions following the September 11 attacks. While some, such as Citizens of Dade United leader Enos Schera, were "1000%" happy that the amendment didn't pass because "they're buying up all the land," others, such as Representative Dennis Ross, believed that the current amendment provided protection against members of the Taliban buying property in Florida and using the state as a base for the next terrorist attack.[2] More generally, however, the media reported that most Floridians who voted against the amendment confused "aliens ineligible for citizenship" with "illegal aliens." The word "alien" triggered images of illegal immigrants, and anyone who entered the country illegally should not be allowed to own property, like American citizens or those who had naturalized or entered legally. Many media outlets criticized Florida voters for their anti-immigrant views, but the story was largely forgotten amidst the electoral triumph of America's first African American president.

Time and willful ignorance have erased the history of Asian Americans in Florida and the discrimination they faced. The legacy of racism and discrimination against Asian Americans in the South has been subsumed by a larger, black-and-white narrative of racial injustice in the United States. The struggles of Gong Lum, Lum Jung Luke, the unjustly imprisoned Japanese Americans in Arkansas during World War II, the Vietnamese refugees, Han Say Naim, Fortunatio Annunciatio, and the founders and members of the Asian American Hotel Owners Association are not part of the historical memory or are only footnotes in larger studies of civil rights.

The strength of the model minority myth pervades American society and has devastating effects on attempts at political and social change. Average Americans may be familiar with the history of Chinese railroad workers or Japanese American incarceration during the 1940s, but their understanding of Asian American history is shaped more by stereotypes of Asian immigrants. The belief that Asian Americans have worked hard to overcome adversity erases the struggles of the past and creates "two Asian Americas": those who came before 1965 and those who came after, with the struggles of both groups largely forgotten or ignored.[3]

The erasure of Asian Americans from southern legal and civil rights history does more than leave a glaring hole in the historiography. If we forget about the presence of Asian Americans in the South and the legal struggles they faced, racism and discrimination appear to be merely cultural and without a past. However, Asian Americans continue to face discrimination, as in 2014 when they experienced difficulties voting in Georgia.[4] Cultural and social prejudice also continue to shape receptions of Asian Americans. Betty Brown, a Republican representative from North Texas, casually remarked in 2009 that if Asians wanted to make the voting process easier on themselves, then they should just "adopt a name for identification purposes that's easier for Americans to deal with."[5] While Brown's solution to the continued discrimination that Asian Americans face inspired chuckles and exasperated eye-rolls from Americans who viewed her comments as just another example of right-wing, southern attitudes toward minorities (Betty Brown "American name generators" are still available online), they are not simply cultural gaffes but indicators of the long struggle of Asian Americans to overcome prejudice and legal inequality. It appears as though Asian Americans have no claims to a history of civil rights and no place in a history of southern racism and discrimination.

Considering the more recent examples of prejudice and lingering discrimination toward Asian Americans, the history of Asian American activism in the South also raises questions of how successful legal change is in terms of ensuring civil rights. In the racial history of the United States, discrimination and prejudice are intricately connected; however, changes in the law mainly address *open* racism as found in discriminatory actions and deeds and not necessarily prejudicial beliefs or thoughts. As the Indian American hoteliers indicated in their own battles against entrepreneurial discrimination, the law cannot "fix" prejudice. While the Indian American hoteliers were able to achieve a level of success with legislation protecting franchisees and Lum Jung Luke was able to gain property rights by using the courts to fight against anti-alien land laws, legal victories for Asian Americans were in many ways attached to what Derrick Bell Jr. has described as "convergent interests." Legal victories for African Americans (such as the *Brown* decision) only occurred when their interests converged with those of whites. For decades, African Americans had battled against school segregation but had little success in destroying the larger system of "separate, but equal." Once white Americans became concerned for their nation's image during the Cold War, however, they turned to supporting African Americans in order to preserve liberal ideas of freedom and democracy. Despite the *Brown* decision, school segregation as well as prejudice in the United States remained, illustrating the limits of legal measures in addressing racism. Asian Americans were required to convince whites that they were not threatening and that they deserved basic rights and protections, all the while remaining, as Lisa Lowe argues, "othered" through their history of immigration and American Orientalism.[6] Asian Americans were in difficult situations, as many often appealed to their "otherness" (through race, ethnicity, or immigrant status) to demand rights, but were at the mercy of a court system that allowed whites to either recognize their unique position or not, thereby confirming that Asian Americans were perpetual outsiders. At times white Americans embraced this otherness as favorable (such as during World War II and the postwar years), while in other scenarios they identified it as a hindrance. The experiences of Asian Americans in the courts and in promoting legislation are also examples of the connections between the power of white Americans and civil rights laws that apply to immigrants and noncitizens as well as African Americans.[7]

The history of Asian American legal activism in the South sheds light on current problems for both racial and ethnic minorities in this region and immigrants more generally. With the recent string of anti-immigrant laws and practices in Alabama, Georgia (where you must show a social security card to obtain water service), and Texas, a deeper understanding of the history of immigrant and Asian activism would tie the past to the present and provide opportunities for thoroughly examining racist and discriminatory rules and regulations. Asian Americans were not always successful in their individual attempts to combat inequality, but when they banded together, as did the Vietnamese refugees and the Indian American hoteliers later in the twentieth century, and joined with other civil rights organizations (such as the Southern Poverty Law Center and business organizations), they actively participated in the process of pushing the South away from legalized discrimination. However, their experiences also remind us of the limits of the law in addressing a legacy of segregation, racism, prejudice, and discrimination that affected all minorities and created different shades of justice in the South.

NOTES

ABBREVIATIONS

The following abbreviations appear in the notes:

- AAHOA — Asian American Hotel Owners Association
- AF — *Vietnamese Fishermen's Association v. The Knights of the Ku Klux Klan* case files, Southern Poverty Law Center, Montgomery, Ala.
- AR — *State of Georgia v. Fortunatio Annunciatio,* Fulton County Superior Court, Case Number 37315, Supreme Court Criminal Appeal Case Files, 1917–1990, Record Group 92/1/3, Georgia Archives, Morrow
- BCVA — Brief of the Commonwealth of Virginia, Virginia State Law Library, Richmond
- COH — Chinese Oral Histories, Delta State University Special Collections, Cleveland, Miss.
- CR — Carliner Records, American Civil Liberties Union Records, Seeley G. Mudd Manuscript Library, Princeton University, Princeton, N.J.
- LC — Loewen (James W.) Collection, Mississippi Department of Archives and History, Jackson
- Lum Case — *G. P. Rice et al. vs. Gong Lum and Martha Lum,* 1924, case 24773, series 6, box 16951, Mississippi Department of Archives and History, Jackson
- NVAR — *Han Say Naim v. Ruby Elaine Naim,* Record Number 4386 case files, Portsmouth Circuit Court, Richmond, Va.
- VOHP — Vietnamese Oral History Project, Dolph Briscoe Center, University of Texas at Austin
- WFP — Wong Family Papers, Austin History Center, Austin, Tex.

INTRODUCTION

1. Very few in-depth works on St. Malo exist, but Maria F. Espina's *Filipinos in Louisiana* (New Orleans: A. F. Lordes and Sons, 1983) provides an overview of not only Malo but

also the Filipino dry shrimp industry that later developed in Louisiana. The year the settlement was originally established is still in dispute, with historian Malcolm Churchill discovering that all references to the earliest days of St. Malo date to one newspaper article from 1937 that provides no source for the 1765 date provided. See Malcolm Churchill, "Louisiana History and Early Filipino Settlement: Searching for the Story," *Bulletin of the American Historical Collection* 27 (1999): 25–32.

2. Leslie Bow, *Partly Colored: Asian Americans and Racial Anomaly in the Segregated South* (New York: NYU Press, 2011), 11.

3. See William Wei, *The Asian American Movement* (Philadelphia: Temple University Press, 1993); Daryl Maeda, *Chains of Babylon: The Rise of Asian America* (Minneapolis: University of Minnesota Press, 2009); Yen Le Espiritu, *Asian American Panethnicity: Bridging Institutions and Identities* (Philadelphia: Temple University Press, 1993); and Moon-Ho Jung, *The Rising Tide of Color: Race, State Violence, and Radical Movements across the Pacific* (Seattle: University of Washington Press, 2015), for more on Asian American activism more generally.

4. See Cindy I-Fen Cheng, *Citizens of Asian America: Democracy and Race during the Cold War* (New York: NYU Press, 2013); Randall Kennedy, *Interracial Intimacies: Sex, Marriage, Identity, and Adoption* (New York: Vintage, 2004); and Juan F. Perea, "Ethnicity and the Constitution: Beyond the Black and White Binary Constitution," *William and Mary Law Review* 36 (1995): 571–611, for more discussions on the experiences of different racial and ethnic groups with a black/white legal framework.

5. Bow, *Partly Colored*, 8. See also Robert Seto Quan's *Lotus among the Magnolias* (Jackson: University Press of Mississippi, 2007); James W. Loewen, *The Mississippi Chinese: Between Black and White* (Long Grove, Ill.: Waveland Press, 1988); John Jung, *Chopsticks in the Land of Cotton: Lives of Mississippi Delta Chinese Grocers* (New York: Yin and Yang Press, 2011); and Lucy M. Cohen, *Chinese in the Post–Civil War South: A People without a History* (Baton Rouge: Louisiana State University Press, 1999), for more on Chinese in the Mississippi Delta (and the South more generally) and racial, ethnic, and cultural identity.

6. Loewen, *Mississippi Chinese*, 23.

7. See Michael Omi and Howard Winant, *Racial Formation in the United States: From the 1960s to the 1990s* (New York: Routledge, 1994), for more on the foundations of critical race theory and race as a social construction.

8. See Angelo N. Ancheta, *Race, Rights, and the Asian American Experience* (New Brunswick: Rutgers University Press, 1998); Mari J. Matsuda, Charles R. Lawrence III, Richard Delgado, and Kimberlè Williams Crenshaw, *Words That Wound: Critical Race Theory, Assaultive Speech, and the First Amendment* (New York: Westview Press, 1993); and Kennedy, *Interracial Intimacies*.

9. See Denise Bates, *The Other Movement: Indian Rights and Civil Rights in the Deep South* (Tuscaloosa: University of Alabama Press, 2012), for more on Native Americans and southern civil rights history. Julie M. Weise's *Corazón de Dixie: Mexicanos in the U.S. South since 1910* (Chapel Hill: University of North Carolina Press, 2015) examines Mexican migrants and adaptations and challenges to southern society. Brian D. Behnken's *Fighting Their Own Battles: Mexican Americans, African Americans, and the Struggle for Civil Rights in Texas* (Chapel Hill: University of North Carolina Press, 2014) also adds nuance to the study of the civil rights movement in the South during the twentieth century.

10. Lisa Lowe, *Immigrant Acts: On Asian American Cultural Politics* (Durham: Duke University Press, 1996), 5. See also Krystyn Moon's *Yellowface: Creating the Chinese in American Popular Music and Culture* (New Brunswick: Rutgers University Press, 2004) for more on Asians and culture in the United States.

11. Allen C. Guezlo, *Fateful Lightning: A New History of the Civil War and Reconstruction* (New York: Oxford University Press, 2012); Douglas R. Egerton, *The Wars of Reconstruction: The Brief, Violent History of America's Most Progressive Era* (New York: Bloomsbury Press, 2014); Eric Foner, *Reconstruction: America's Unfinished Revolution* (New York: Harper Perennial Modern Classics, 2002); George A. Rutherglen, *Civil Rights in the Shadow of Slavery: The Constitution, Common Law, and the Civil Rights Act of 1868* (New York: Oxford University Press, 2012).

12. See Michael Les Benedict, *A Compromise of Principle: Congressional Republicans and Reconstruction, 1863–1869* (New York: Norton 1974), and George C. Rable, *But There Was No Peace: The Role of Violence in the Politics of Reconstruction* (Athens: University of Georgia Press, 2007).

13. See Edward L. Ayers, *The Promise of the New South: Life after Reconstruction* (New York: Oxford University Press, 2007).

14. See Douglas A. Backmon, *Slavery by Another Name: The Re-Enslavement of Black Americans from the Civil War to World War II* (New York: Anchor, 2009), and Heather Cox Richardson, *The Death of Reconstruction: Race, Labor, and Politics in the Post–Civil War North* (Cambridge: Harvard University Press, 2004).

15. Moon-Ho Jung, *Coolies and Cane: Race, Labor, and Sugar in the Age of Emancipation* (Baltimore: Johns Hopkins University Press, 2008), 37–38.

16. See John Kuo Wei Tchen, *New York before Chinatown: Orientalism and the Shaping of American Culture, 1776–1882* (Baltimore: Johns Hopkins University Press, 1999); Richard Steven Street, *Beasts of the Field: A Narrative History of California Farmworkers, 1769–1913* (Palo Alto: Stanford University Press, 2004); Madeline Y. Hsu, *Dreaming of Gold, Dreaming of Home: Transnationalism and Migration between the United States and South China* (Palo Alto: Stanford University Press, 2000); Jean Pfaelzer, *Driven Out: The Forgotten War against Chinese Americans* (Berkeley: University of California Press, 2007); and Jung, *Coolies and Cane*, 9–17.

17. Richardson, *Death of Reconstruction*, 57–62.

18. Jung, *Coolies and Cane*, 26–37.

19. "Chinese Labor Convention," *Daily Alta California*, July 15, 1869, 2.

20. Ibid.

21. Ibid.

22. Ibid.

23. Jung, *Coolies and Cane*, 1–5.

24. "Sambo's Successor: Arrival of 250 Chinamen at New Orleans—Queer Scenes and Incidents," *Daily Alta California*, January 30, 1870, 2.

25. Ibid. See also Lucy Cohen, "George W. Gift: Chinese Labor Agent in the Post–Civil War South," in *Chinese America: History and Perspectives* (Brisbane, Calif.: Chinese Historical Society of America, 1995), 157–59.

26. See Carl Moneyhon, *Arkansas and the New South, 1874–1929* (Fayetteville: University of Arkansas Press, 1997), and William A. Russ, "The Attempt to Create a

Republican Party in Arkansas during Reconstruction," *Arkansas Historical Quarterly* 1 (September 1942): 206–22.

27. Powell Clayton, *The Aftermath of the Civil War in Arkansas* (New York: Neale Publishing Company, 1915), 207.

28. Ibid., 211.

29. Ibid.

30. Qtd. in. ibid., 207.

31. Qtd. in ibid., 207–8.

32. Qtd. in ibid., 208.

33. Qtd. in ibid., 207.

34. Ibid. 208.

35. Qtd. in ibid., 213–14. See also Shih-shan Henry Tsai, "Chinese in Arkansas," *Amerasia Journal* 8 (1981): 1–18.

36. Clayton, *Aftermath*, 214; Tsai, "Chinese in Arkansas," 12; Jung, *Coolies and Cane*, 204–7.

37. Clayton, *Aftermath*, 215.

38. Jung, *Coolies and Cane*, 221–25; Pfaelzer, *Driven Out*, 54, 94, 133–49, 335. See also Erika Lee, *At America's Gates: Chinese Immigrants during the Exclusion Era, 1882–1943* (Chapel Hill: University of North Carolina Press, 2003), and Lucy E. Salyer, *Laws Harsh as Tigers: Chinese Immigrants and the Shaping of Modern Immigration Law* (Chapel Hill: University of North Carolina Press, 1995).

39. John Sharp Williams, "Speeches of . . . John S. Williams, of Mississippi, in the House of Representatives, Monday, March 31, 1902; Chinese problem on the Pacific; the Negro problem in the South; race problems . . . ," 2, 324.15/W675s c., Mississippi State Archives, Jackson.

40. Ibid.

41. Tsai, "Chinese in Arkansas," 8–10.

42. Khyati Y. Joshi and Jigna Desai, "Discrepancies in Dixie," in *Asian Americans in Dixie: Race and Migration in the South*, ed. Khyati Y. Joshi and Jigna Desai (Champaign: University of Illinois Press, 2013), 4.

CHAPTER 1

1. Him Mark Lai, "Lue Gim Gong: Wonder Grower," *East/West* (1973): 5. See also Virginia Aronson, *Gift of the Unicorn: The Story of Lue Gim Gong, Florida's Citrus Wizard* (Sarasota: Pineapple Press, 2002).

2. Lai, "Lue Gim Gong," 5–6.

3. Moon-Ho Jung, *Coolies and Cane: Race, Labor, and Sugar in the Age of Emancipation* (Baltimore: Johns Hopkins University Press, 2008), 5–12; Heather Cox Richardson, *The Death of Reconstruction: Race, Labor, and Politics in the Post–Civil War North* (Cambridge: Harvard University Press, 2004). See also Lucy M. Cohen, *Chinese in the Post–Civil War South: A People without a History* (Baton Rouge: Louisiana State University Press, 1999), and Ronald Takaki, *Strangers from a Different Shore: A History of Asian Americans* (New York: Little, Brown, 1998), for an overview of both the early Japanese and Chinese immigrant experiences in different regions of the United States.

4. See Khyati Y. Joshi and Jigna Desai, eds., *Asian Americans in Dixie: Race and Migration in the South* (Champaign: University of Illinois Press, 2013), and Krystyn Moon, *Yellowface: Creating the Chinese in American Popular Music and Culture* (New Brunswick: Rutgers University Press, 2004), for a more detailed and interesting discussion of Chinese stereotypes.

5. Eiichiro Azuma, *Between Two Empires: Race, History, and Transnationalism in Japanese America* (New York: Oxford University Press, 2007), 27.

6. Roger Daniels, *The Politics of Prejudice: The Anti-Japanese Movement in California and the Struggle for Japanese Exclusion* (Berkeley: University of California Press, 1999), 26–28.

7. "Pacific Coast Is Excited over Japanese," *Saint Landry Clarion*, February 19, 1921, 3.

8. See Stephanie Hinnershitz, "Demanding an Adequate Solution: The American Legion, the Immigration Act of 1924, and the Politics of Exclusion," *Immigrants and Minorities* 33 (September 2015): 1–21.

9. Azuma, *Between Two Empires*, 22–31.

10. Lawson B. Babineaux, "A History of the Rice Industry of Southwestern Louisiana" (1967), http://ereserves.mcneese.edu/depts/archive/FTBooks/babineaux.html (accessed August 12, 2015).

11. "Japanese in Texas," *Houston Chronicle*, March 12, 1904, 4.

12. "Japanese Colony for Texas," *Houston Chronicle*, March 20, 1904, 3.

13. "Japanese Citizens: Recent Ruling on Naturalization Is Worked On," *Shreveport Caucasian*, March 28, 1905, 5. See also Alan G. Gauthreaux, *Italian Louisiana: History, Heritage, and Tradition* (Mount Pleasant, S.C.: Arcadia Publishing, 2014), and Elizabeth Fussell, "Constructing New Orleans, Constructing Race: A Population History of New Orleans," *Journal of American History* 94 (December 2007): 846–55, for more information on the 1891 lynching as well as Italians in New Orleans and Louisiana.

14. "Welsh Lands Japanese Colony," *Welsh Rice Belt Journal*, November 25, 1904, 1.

15. "Jap Colony Delayed in Coming," *Welsh Rice Belt Journal*, February 10, 1905, 3.

16. "Shell Canal Experiment," *Opelousas Saint Landry Clarion*, November 11, 1925, 3.

17. "Yamato," *Spanish River Papers* 6 (October 1977): 3. See also "Brief History of Bocca Raton," *Spanish River Papers* 2 (May 1973): 6–7.

18. "Yamato and Morikami: The Story of the Japanese Colony and Some of Its Settlers," *Spanish River Papers* 13 (Spring 1985): 7–11.

19. "The Homeseeker," *Florida Farmer*, July 12, 1908, 4.

20. Ibid.

21. "Japs Locate West of Eau Galle," *Florida Star*, August 28, 1908, 1.

22. "The Homeseeker," 4.

23. "News from Around the State," *Madison New Enterprise*, March 16, 1905, 6; "News from Around the State," *Madison New Enterprise*, January 7, 1904, 3.

24. "Florida Needs Japanese Immigration to Develop Her Latent Resources," *Pensacola Journal*, May 26, 1903, 11.

25. "Letters to the Editor," *Live Oak Democrat*, November 11, 1905, 4.

26. "Jap Colony Flourishing," *Pensacola Journal*, September 22, 1907, 4.

27. "Celebration for 350th Anniversary of House of Okudaira," *Ft. Pierce News*, April 17, 1912, 1; "Yamato July 4th Celebration," *Pensacola Journal*, July 15, 1908, 1; "State Gleanings," *San Mateo News*, February 5, 1910; "Yamato," 8–10.

28. "Japanese Official Inspected Colony," *Ocala Evening News Star*, November 18, 1907, 7.
29. "Letters to the Editor," *Gainesville Twice-a-Week*, January 4, 1906, 3.
30. "Editorials," *Gainesville Daily Sun*, September 7, 1907, 3.
31. "The Homeseeker," 3.
32. Ibid.
33. "Japanese Colony," *Madison New Enterprise*, November 17, 1904, 3.
34. "Japanese Flourish in Florida," *Punta Gorda Hardware*, May 2, 1909, 6.
35. Ibid.
36. "The Homeseeker," 3.
37. Hinnershitz, "Demanding an Adequate Solution," 5–6.
38. See Stan Flewelling, *Shiakawa: Stories from a Pacific Northwest Japanese American Community* (Seattle: University of Washington, 2002), for more information on Japanese and early anti-alien land laws.
39. Daniels, *Politics of Prejudice*, 45–48.
40. Ibid., 48–49; Edwin E. Ferguson, "The California Land Law and the Fourteenth Amendment," *California Law Review* 35 (March 1947): 73–75.
41. "Danger from Japanese Migration," *Rice Belt Journal*, April 20, 1906, 3.
42. Ibid.
43. Ibid.
44. Ibid.
45. "LA Can Get Along without the Japs," *New Iberia Enterprise*, April 24, 1915, 5.
46. Ibid.; my emphasis.
47. Ibid.
48. "Japanese Colonies in Louisiana," *St. Tammany Farmer*, April 17, 1915, 5.
49. Ibid.
50. James Taylor, "The Japs Invasion," *Shreveport Caucasian*, August 12, 1913, 1.
51. Ibid.
52. Ibid.
53. Ibid.
54. "Old and New Constitution," *St. Landry Clarion*, January 22, 1921, 1.
55. Ibid.
56. "Seek Alien Land Law in Louisiana," *New York Times*, March 23, 1921, 3.
57. *Official Journal of the Proceedings of the Constitutional Convention of the State of Louisiana* (Baton Rouge: Ramires-Jones Printing Company, 1922), 965.
58. "Legislators Defends [sic] the Constitution," *Opelousas Star-Progress*, October 5, 1921, 3.
59. "Acts Hereafter Only in English," *Opelousas Star-Progress*, May 18, 1921, 4.
60. "Aliens Cannot Own Land," *Donaldson Chief*, April 23, 1921, 5.
61. *Official Journal of the Proceedings of the Constitutional Convention*, 965.
62. Editor's Letters, *Ocala Evening Star*, October 10, 1913, 2.
63. "President Taft Will Smash the Bugaboo of Japanese Invasion," *Pensacola Journal*, April 5, 1912, 1.
64. "Undesirable Immigrants: Colony of Japs Will Probably Settle in Clay County," *Ocala Evening Star*, October 4, 1913, 1.
65. "Protest against Japanese Immigrants," *Jacksonville Star*, April 12, 1913, 6.

66. Ibid.
67. The Korokan, "The Yellow Peril," *Ocala Banner*, October 5, 1913, 3.
68. *Fort Myers Press*, August 19, 1913, 4.
69. "Congressman and Ex-Governor Clash," *Ocala Evening Star*, October 8, 1913, 1.
70. "White Men and Women," *Ocala Evening Star*, October 10, 1913, 1.
71. "Florida's Leading Men Agree with Congressman Clark in His Opposition to Asiatic Immigration," *Ocala Evening Star*, October 10, 1913, 1.
72. "Congressman and Ex-Governor Clash," 1.
73. "Governor Trammel Investigating," *Pensacola Journal*, October 16, 1913, 7.
74. Ibid.
75. Barry Eichengreen, *Hall of Mirrors: The Great Depression, the Great Recession, and the Uses and Misuses of History* (New York: Oxford University Press, 2015), 3–12.
76. *Laws of Florida*, General Index to House Bills and Joint Resolutions (1926), 544.
77. "Defeat All," *Miami Herald*, October 30, 1926, 15.
78. G. B. Wells, "Letters to the Editor: Dangerous," *Tampa Tribune*, October 29, 1926, 7.
79. "Yamato and Morikami," 10–11.
80. T. R. Fehrenbach, *Lone Star: A History of Texas and Texans* (Boston: DaCapo Press, 2007), 434–36.
81. Irwin A. Tang, *Asian Texans: Our Histories and Our Lives* (New York: It Works Publishing, 2008), 112–17. See also "Chinese-Texans," folder 1, box 1, WFP.
82. Fred and R. C. Wong, Oral History Transcript, October 20, 2007, folder 28, box 1, WFP.
83. Shih-shan Henry Tsai, "Chinese in Arkansas," *Amerasia Journal* 8 (1981): 12–13.
84. *Applegate v. Luke*, Supreme Court of Arkansas Opinion delivered March 4, 1927, Supreme Court of Arkansas, 173 Ark. 93.
85. "Arkansas State Constitution," http://arkleg.state.ar.us/assembly/Summary/ArkansasConstitution (accessed July 16, 2015).
86. *Applegate v. Luke*.
87. Ibid.
88. Ibid., 94.
89. Ibid., 95.
90. Dori Felice Moss, "Strangers in Their Own Land: A Cultural History of Japanese American Internment Camps in Arkansas, 1942–1945" (master's thesis, Georgia State University, 2007), 15–17. See also John Howard, *Concentration Camps on the Home Front: Japanese Americans in the House of Jim Crow* (Chicago: University of Chicago Press, 2008).
91. Personal narrative of Ray D. Johnson, September 18, 1942–December 31, 1945, file 6, box 1, 12, Austin Smith Papers, Austin History Center, Austin, Tex.
92. "They'll Have to Get Out after War," *Denson Tribune*, September 17, 1943, 2.
93. See Scott Cashion, "Actions Speak Louder than Words . . . Sometimes: Reactions to the Wartime Evacuation and Internment of Japanese-Americans at Rohwer and Jerome" (master's thesis, University of Arkansas, 2006); Calvin C. Smith, "The Response of Arkansas to Prisoners of War and Japanese Americans in Arkansas, 1942–1945," *Arkansas Historical Quarterly* 53 (1994): 340–64; and William G. Anderson, "Early Reaction in Arkansas to the Relocation of Japanese in the State," *Arkansas Historical Quarterly* 23 (Autumn 1964): 196–211.

94. Eula Wilson, Arkansas Publicity and Parks Commission News Release, Publicity Division, 413 State Capitol, Little Rock, Arkansas, folder 1, box 112, General Miscellaneous Files, Arkansas Studies Institute, Little Rock.

95. Ibid.; "Truck Farming in Desha County," *McGehee Times*, January 3, 1946, 4.

96. "Center Closes as 345 Japs Leave for West," *McGehee Times*, December 6, 1945, 2.

97. "Total Produce for 1943," *Denson Tribune*, January 11, 1944, 3.

98. "Large Scale Farming—Rohwer Enterprise," *Rohwer Outpost*, May 14, 1943, 4.

99. "Truck Farming in Desha County," 2.

100. "Parish Officials Refuse and Rescinded in Louisiana," folder 3, box 1, War Relocation Authority Personal Narratives, Arkansas Studies Institute, Little Rock; "Final Details from Georgia Farm on Way," *Rohwer Outpost*, February 2, 1944, 2; "Enroute for Florida, Georgia," *Rohwer Outpost*, January 19, 1944, 35; "Outside Employment," *Rohwer Outpost*, August 7, 1943; "Japs May Not Leave the State," *McGehee Times*, October 18, 1942, 1.

101. "Jap Colony Brings Stiff Protest—Governor Objects to Use of Japanese Labor," *McGehee Times*, October 22, 1942, 5.

102. Acts of Arkansas, Act 47, p. 74.

103. "Would Prevent Japanese from Buying Land: Bill Introduced in State Senate," *McGehee Times*, January 21, 1943, 1.

104. Ibid.

105. Acts of Arkansas, 75.

106. Calvin C. Smith, *War and Wartime Changes: The Transformation of Arkansas, 1940–1945* (Fayetteville: University of Arkansas Press, 2009), 71–72.

107. "Democracy at Home," *Rohwer Outpost*, March 10, 1943, 27.

108. "To Our Development," *Rohwer Outpost*, April 28, 1943, 46.

109. "Land Act Unconstitutional," *Rohwer Outpost*, March 13, 1945, 7.

110. *Biennial Report of the Attorney General*, Anti-Jap Law (Little Rock, Ark., 1944), chap. 3, "Aliens, S.," 344; "Japanese May Purchase Land: 1943 Act Is Ruled Unconstitutional," *McGehee Times*, March 11, 1943, 5.

CHAPTER 2

1. See Richard Kluger, *Simple Justice: The History of* Brown v. Board of Education *and the Struggle for Equality* (New York: Vintage, 2004); Anders Walker, *The Ghost of Jim Crow: How Southern Moderates Used* Brown v. Board of Education *to Stall Civil Rights* (New York: Oxford University Press, 2009); Vanessa Siddle Walker, *Their Highest Potential: An African American School Community in the Segregated South* (Chapel Hill: University of North Carolina Press, 1996); James D. Anderson, *The Education of Blacks in the South, 1860–1935* (Chapel Hill: University of North Carolina Press, 1988); Tracy E. K'Meyer, *From* Brown *to* Meredith: *The Long Struggle for School Desegregation in Louisville, Kentucky, 1954–2007* (Chapel Hill: University of North Carolina Press, 2013); and William H. Watkins, *The White Architects of Black Education: Ideology and Power in America, 1865–1964* (New York: Teachers College Press, 2001), for more on the history of African American segregation in schools. For a more in-depth discussion of how segregation affected other minorities in the South, see Gilbert G. Gonzalez, *Chicano Education in the*

Era of Segregation (Denton: University of North Texas Press, 2013); Jennifer R. Najera, *The Borderlands of Race: Mexican Segregation in a South Texas Town* (Austin: University of Texas Press, 2015); Carlos Kevin Blanton, *Georgie I. Sanchez: The Long Fight for Mexican American Integration* (New Haven: Yale University Press, 2015); Kim Cary Warren, *The Quest for Citizenship: African American and Native American Education in Kansas, 1880–1935* (Chapel Hill: University of North Carolina Press, 2010); and David Wallace Adams, *Education for Extinction: American Indians and the Boarding School Experience, 1785–1928* (Lawrence: University of Kansas Press, 1995). For a more in-depth discussion of public and private education in early America, see Carl Kaestle's *Pillars of the Republic: Common Schools and American Society, 1780–1860* (New York: Hill and Wang, 1983).

2. See Leslie Bow, *Partly Colored: Asian Americans and Racial Anomaly in the Segregated South* (New York: NYU Press, 2011).

3. See Robert Seto Quan, *Lotus among the Magnolias* (Jackson: University Press of Mississippi, 2007); James W. Loewen, *The Mississippi Chinese: Between Black and White* (Long Grove, Ill.: Waveland Press, 1988); and Bow, *Partly Colored*.

4. See Thomas Guglielmo, *White on Arrival: Italians, Race, Color, and Power in Chicago, 1890–1945* (New York: Oxford University Press, 2003), for more on Italian immigrants and whiteness in American history.

5. See Joyce Kuo, "Excluded, Segregated, and Forgotten: A Historical View of the Discrimination of Chinese in Public Schools," *Asian American Law Journal* 5 (January 1998): 181–212, for a more general discussion of discrimination against Asian American students.

6. See Paul Kramer, *The Blood of Government: Race, Empire, the United States, and the Philippines* (Durham: Duke University Press, 2006), for a more in-depth discussion of the Pensionado Program and its impact on U.S. colonial relations.

7. "Filipino Students," *Louisville Evening Bulletin*, July 11, 1904, 4.

8. See John A. Hardin, *Fifty Years of Segregation: Black Higher Education in Kentucky, 1904–1954* (Lexington: University of Kentucky Press, 2014).

9. "Their Color Bars Them," *Spokane Daily Chronicle*, July 7, 1904, 3.

10. Twelfth Population Census of the United States, reel 539, National Archives and Records Administration, Washington, D.C.

11. "Their Color Bars Them."

12. "Shall Chinese Boy Go to White or Colored Schools, Kentucky Problem," *The Day*, October 9, 1913, 7.

13. "State Officials Ponder Very Vexing Problem: Shall Chinese Boy Go to the White or Colored Schools of State?," *Hartford Herald*, November 12, 1913, 1; "Shall Chinese Boy Go to White or Colored Schools."

14. Office of the Attorney General, *Biennial Report of the Attorney General of the Commonwealth of Kentucky* (1913), 273.

15. See Erika Lee, *At America's Gates: Chinese Immigrants during the Exclusion Era, 1882–1943* (Chapel Hill: University of North Carolina Press, 2003); Angelo N. Ancheta, *Race, Rights, and the Asian American Experience* (New Brunswick: Rutgers University Press, 1998); and Lucy E. Salyer, *Laws Harsh as Tigers: Chinese Immigrants and the Shaping of Modern Immigration Law* (Chapel Hill: University of North Carolina Press, 1995).

16. Office of the Attorney General, *Biennial Report*, 273.

17. Ibid.
18. Ibid.
19. Ibid.
20. Ibid.
21. Ibid., 275.
22. Ibid.
23. Monroe Nathan Walk, *Negro Yearbook and Annual Encyclopedia of the Negro, 1912–1913* (Tuskegee, 1913), 392.
24. See Richard Campanella, "Chinatown, New Orleans," in *Preservation in Print*, Preservation Resource Center of New Orleans (November 2013): 17–18, and *Geographies of New Orleans: Urban Fabrics before the Storm* (New Orleans: Center for Louisiana Studies, 2006).
25. See Ronald Takaki, *Strangers from a Different Shore: A History of Asian Americans* (New York: Little, Brown, 1998); Elmer Sandmeyer, *The Anti-Chinese Movement in America* (Champaign: University of Illinois Press, 1991); Roger Daniels, *The Politics of Prejudice: The Anti-Japanese Movement in California and the Struggle for Japanese Exclusion* (Berkeley: University of California Press, 1999); and Mae M. Ngai, *Impossible Subjects: Illegal Aliens and the Making of Modern America* (Princeton: Princeton University Press, 2006), for more discussion on the rise of anti-Asian sentiment along the West Coast.
26. Adrienne Berard, *Water Tossing Boulders: How a Family of Chinese Immigrants Led the First Fight to Desegregate Schools in the Jim Crow South* (Boston: Beacon Press, 2016), 11.
27. See Chapter 1.
28. Loewen, *Mississippi Chinese*, 44–52; "Abstract of the Chinese in Mississippi: The Test Case for Segregation," folder 1, box 3, LC; "Mississippi Chinese Statistics," folder 3, box 3, LC.
29. Interview with Willa Johnson, November 28, 1938, folder 10, box 3, LC.
30. Loewen, *Mississippi Chinese*, 108–14.
31. Ibid.
32. Berard, *Water Tossing Boulders*, 5.
33. Lum Case.
34. Ibid.
35. Ibid.
36. Petition for Writ of Mandamus, Lum Case.
37. Ibid.
38. Ibid.
39. Suggestion on Error, Lum Case. See also Mae M. Ngai, *The Lucky Ones: One Family and the Extraordinary Invention of Chinese America* (New York: Houghton Mifflin Harcourt, 2010), for more details on the *Tape v. Hurley* case and its implications for Chinese American history.
40. Kluger, *Simple Justice*, 50–84.
41. Motion to Appeal, Lum Case.
42. "Chinese Barred from the Rosedale Schools," *Bolivar Democrat*, November 12, 1924, 7.
43. See Sieglinde Lim de Sánchez, "Crafting a Delta Chinese Community: Education and Acculturation in Twentieth-Century Southern Baptist Missionary Schools," *History*

of Education Quarterly 43 (2003): 74–90; Kit Mui L. Chan, "The Chinese-Americans in the Mississippi Delta," *Journal of Mississippi History* 35 (1973): 29–35; Robert W. O'Brien, "Status of the Chinese in the Mississippi Delta," *Social Forces* 19 (1941): 386–90; and Robert M. Winter, "Rosedale Presbyterians and the Mississippi Chinese: Changing Concepts of Equality in an Aristocratic Southern Town," *Journal of Presbyterian History* 78 (2000): 32–47.

44. Lum Case.

45. Berard, *Water Tossing Boulders*, 84–85.

46. Chan, "Chinese-Americans in the Mississippi Delta," 33–35.

47. *Gong Lum v. Rice*, 275 US 78, Supreme Court, 1927, https://www.law.cornell.edu/supremecourt/text/275/78 (accessed May 13, 2015). For more on the Cumming decision, see James T. Patterson, Brown v. Board of Education: *A Civil Rights Milestone and Its Troubled Legacy* (New York: Oxford University Press, 2002).

48. *Gong Lum v. Rice*, 275 US 78.

49. Ibid.

50. See Ancheta, *Race, Rights, and the Asian American Experience*, 78–110.

51. *Bond, State Superintendent of Education v. Tij Fung et al.*, No. 26333, Supreme Court of Mississippi, Division A., October 10, 1927; Albert Frantz, "Notes on Recent Cases," *Notre Dame Law Review* 3 (1928): 1–3. See also Charles S. Magnum Jr., *The Legal Status of the Negro* (Chapel Hill: University of North Carolina Press, 1940).

52. *Bond v. Tij Fung*.

53. Ibid.

54. Ibid.

55. Ibid.

56. Ibid.

57. Ibid.

58. Ibid.

59. Ibid.

60. Ibid.

61. See Gabriele Chin, Cindy Hwang Chiang, and Shirley S. Park, "The Lost *Brown v. Board of Education* and Immigration Law," *North Carolina Law Review* 91 (2013): 1657–98, for an interesting discussion of the effects of the Tij Fung case on immigration law following *Brown v. Board*.

62. Tev Shepherd, *The Chinese of Greenville, Mississippi* (self-published, 1999), 38–42.

63. Letter to Mr. H. B. Heidelberg, 1941, folder 4, box 3, LC.

64. Ibid.

65. To Clarksdale School Board from N. D. Timmerman, February 1941, folder 4, box 3, LC.

66. Chan, "Chinese-Americans in the Mississippi Delta," 38–40.

67. Qtd. in Shepherd, *Chinese of Greenville*, 43.

68. Ibid.

69. "Local School Privilege Is Given Chinese," *Greenville Delta Democrat Times*, May 27, 1945, 6.

70. See Ellen Wu, *The Color of Success: Asian Americans and the Origins of the Model Minority* (Princeton: Princeton University Press, 2013); Madeline Y. Hsu, *The Good Immigrants: How the Yellow Peril Became the Model Minority* (Princeton: Princeton

University Press, 2015); and K. Scott Wong, *Americans First: Chinese Americans and the Second World War* (Cambridge: Harvard University Press, 2005), for more discussions of the model minority identity before and after World War II.

71. Transcript, Dr. Audrey Sidney Oral History Interview 1, February 4, 2000, by Kimberly Lancaster, 5, COH.

72. Transcript, Edward Joe Oral History Interview 1, May 1, 2000, by Kimberly Lancaster, 5–6, COH.

73. Transcript, Bobby Jue Oral History Interview 2, February 4, 2000, by Kimberly Lancaster, 7, COH.

74. Daniel Bronstein, "Segregation, Exclusion, and the Chinese Communities in Georgia, 1850–1940," in *Asian Americans in Dixie: Race and Migration in the South*, ed. Khyati Y. Joshi and Jigna Desai (Champaign: University of Illinois Press, 2013), 122–23.

75. Ibid., 124–25.

76. Qtd. in Thomas Ganschow, *The Chinese in Augusta: A Historical Sketch* (self-published, 1996), 10–11.

77. Ganschow, *Chinese in Augusta*, 11–12. See also Bess Beatty, "The Loo Chong Case in Waynesboro: A Case of Sinophobia in Georgia," *Georgia Historical Quarterly* 67 (1983): 35–48.

78. Ganschow, *Chinese in Augusta*, 11–12.

79. Sally Ken, "The Chinese Community of Augusta, Georgia, from 1873–1971," *Richmond County History* 4 (1972): 55–56.

80. "Ban on Race Amalgamation to Be Urged in Legislature by DeKalb Representative," *Atlanta Constitution*, June 21, 1925, 7.

81. "Bar Chinese from Attending School in Mississippi," *Augusta Chronicle*, October 11, 1927, 6.

82. Ibid.

83. Ken, "Chinese Community of Augusta," 55–56; "Let Us Be Fair," *Augusta Chronicle*, July 10, 1931, 4.

84. "Let Us Be Fair," 4.

85. Ibid.

86. Ibid.

87. Ibid.

88. "Letters from the People," *Augusta Chronicle*, July 12, 1931, 8B.

89. Ibid.

90. Ibid.

91. "Harmony Urged on Education Board," *Augusta Chronicle*, July 12, 1931, 4.

92. Ken, "Chinese Community of Augusta," 60–61.

93. Julie M. Weise, *Corazón de Dixie: Mexicanos in the U.S. South since 1910* (Chapel Hill: University of North Carolina Press, 2015), 68–71, 73, 75–76.

CHAPTER 3

1. Direct examination of Frances Hutcheson by E. A. Stephens, May 11, 1932, AR, 27–29. Evidence cited throughout this chapter for the case in all its incarnations is found in this supreme court trial record, which is paged continuously.

2. Ibid.

3. See Danielle McGuire, *At the Dark End of the Street: Black Women, Rape, and Resistance—A New History of the Civil Rights Movement from Rosa Parks to the Rise of Black Power* (New York: Vintage, 2010); Phillip Dray, *At the Hands of Persons Unknown: The Lynching of Black America* (New York: Modern Library, 2003); Amy Louise Wood, *Lynching and Spectacle: Witnessing Racial Violence in America, 1890–1940* (Chapel Hill: University of North Carolina Press, 2009); and Dora Apel, *Imagery of Lynching: Black Men, White Women, and the Mob* (New Brunswick: Rutgers University Press, 2004). As W. Fitzhugh Brundage explains, lynching was more common in the cotton belt of Georgia as opposed to the coastal regions (where a variety of factors, including a well-established set of white-paternalist norms and large black communities, often maintained boundaries and tempered violence). See W. Fitzhugh Brundage, *Lynching in the New South: Georgia and Virginia, 1890–1930* (Champaign: University of Illinois Press, 1993), and W. Fitzhugh Brundage, ed., *Under Sentence of Death: Lynching in the South* (Chapel Hill: University of North Carolina Press, 1997).

4. "Filipino Yo-Yo Artists," *Thomasville Times Enterprise*, May 13, 1932, 2.

5. The political status of Filipinos during American rule was a product of the Insular Cases, a series of court cases relating to citizenship in American colonies and territories (primarily Puerto Rico, Hawaii, and the Philippines) brought before the Supreme Court in 1901. The Insular Cases established the general principle that the rights of American citizenship did not necessarily "follow the flag." For discussion of the intersection of imperial policy and American legal and constitutional debates, see Bartholomew H. Sparrow, *The Insular Cases and the Emergence of American Empire* (Lawrence: University of Kansas Press, 2006); Christian Duffy Burnett and Burk Marshall, eds., *Foreign in a Domestic Sense: Puerto Rico, American Expansion, and the Constitution* (Durham: Duke University Press, 2001); and Rick Baldoz, *The Third Asiatic Invasion: Migration and Empire in Filipino America, 1898–1946* (New York: NYU Press, 2011). On Taft and the phrase "little brown brothers," see Stuart Creighton Miller, *"Benevolent Assimilation": The American Conquest of the Philippines, 1899–1903* (New Haven: Yale University Press, 1982), 134, 167.

6. See Baldoz, *Third Asiatic Invasion*; Dorothy Fujita-Rony, *American Workers, Colonial Power: Philippine Seattle and the Transpacific West, 1919–1941* (Berkeley: University of California Press, 2002); and Angelo N. Ancheta, *Race, Rights, and the Asian American Experience* (New Brunswick: Rutgers University Press, 1998). See also Peggy Pascoe, *What Comes Naturally: Miscegenation Law and the Making of Race in America* (New York: Oxford University Press, 2011), for a more in-depth discussion of Filipinos who fought against antimiscegenation laws in the American West.

7. See Leslie Bow, *Partly Colored: Asian Americans and Racial Anomaly in the Segregated South* (New York: NYU Press, 2011), 4–6, for more explanation of her use of the term "interstitiality" to describe the identities of Asian Americans in southern states.

8. Defendant's Statement, AR, 47–48.

9. There were 42,268 Filipino men and 2,940 Filipina women enumerated in the 1930 U.S. Census, vol. 2, table 6, 103. See also Fujita-Rony, *American Workers*, 91.

10. According to the 1930 census, there were 1,869 Chinese in the South Atlantic states and 743 Chinese in the East South Central region, whereas there were 393 Japanese living in the South Atlantic region and only 46 recorded Japanese in the East South Central

region. For the purposes of census data, "the South" means the South Atlantic and East South Central regions (Georgia is enumerated with the South Atlantic region). See U.S. Census Bureau, Fifteenth Census of the United States, 1930, Population by Sex, Color, and Nativity, 1930, with Number of Males per 100 Females, 1900 to 1930, by Divisions and States, 103.

11. Marcia Baker, "Atlanta's Foreign Colonies Prove Intriguing to Visitor: Many People of Other Lands Moving Here," *Atlanta Constitution*, April 15, 1929, 17. On immigrants and ethnic diversity in the South, see Louise Reynes Edwards-Simpson, "Sicilian Immigration to New Orleans, 1870–1910: Ethnicity, Race, and Social Position in the New South" (Ph.D. diss., University of Minnesota, 1996); Andrew Sluyter, Case Watkins, James P. Chaney, and Annie M. Gibson, *Hispanic and Latino New Orleans: Immigration and Identity since the Eighteenth Century* (Baton Rouge: LSU Press, 2015); and George B. Pruden Jr., "History of the Chinese in Savannah, Georgia," in *Georgia's East Asian Connection: Into the Twenty-First Century*, West College Studies in the Social Sciences 28, ed. Jonathan Goldstein (Carrollton, Ga., 1990), 17–34.

12. "Flores Services," *Coshocton Tribune*, January 4, 1964.

13. "Yo-Yo Trick Goes on the Air as Town Goes Crazy on Toy," *Atlanta Constitution*, March 23, 1932, 4; "Yo-Yo Brings Entertainment to Scottish Rite Hospital," *Atlanta Constitution*, March 17, 1932, 5; "Yo-Yo Is No Cry, Oath, Drug, It's Simply a Unique Game," *Atlanta Constitution*, March 14, 1932, 14; "Yo Yo Boys Show Atlantans Elusive Top Game," *Atlanta Constitution*, March 15, 1932, 5; "There Is No Spring in Yo-Yo; Axle and the Discs Do the Trick," *Atlanta Constitution*, March, 25, 1932, 18.

14. Daniel Bronstein, "Segregation, Exclusion, and the Chinese Communities in Georgia, 1850–1940," in *Asian Americans in Dixie: Race and Migration in the South*, ed. Khyati Y. Joshi and Jigna Desai (Champaign: University of Illinois Press, 2013), 107–14.

15. "New Dope Selling Scheme Charged by Federal Agent," *Atlanta Constitution*, October 19, 1929, 8; "Balmori Faces New Narcotics Inquiry," *Atlanta Constitution*, October 8, 1930, 7; "U.S. Circuit Court Opens October Term," *Atlanta Constitution*, October 7, 1930, 9; "White Farmers Oust Filipinos in Florida," *Atlanta Constitution*, July 24, 1932, 12B. See also Paul Kramer, *The Blood of Government: Race, Empire, the United States, and the Philippines* (Durham: Duke University Press, 2006), and Linda Espana-Maram, *Creating Masculinity in Los Angeles's Little Manila: Working-Class Filipinos and Popular Culture, 1920s–1950s* (New York: Columbia University Press, 2006).

16. Direct examination of Frances Hutcheson by E. A. Stephens, May 11, 1932, AR, 28; direct examination of Rosa Mae Clower by E. A. Stephens, May 11, 1932, AR, 34 (quotation).

17. Direct examination of Rosa Mae Clower by E. A. Stephens, May 11, 1932, AR, 35–39 (first quotation on 35; second through seventh quotations on 36; eighth quotation on 39).

18. Recross-examination of Rosa Mae Clower by F. J. Turner, May 11, 1932, AR, 41.

19. See McGuire, *At the Dark End of the Street*, 24–27; Diane Miller Sommerville, *Rape and Race in the Nineteenth-Century South* (Chapel Hill: University of North Carolina Press, 2004); Crystal N. Feimster, *Southern Horrors: Women and the Politics of Rape and Lynching* (Cambridge: Harvard University Press, 2009); and Lisa Lindquist Dorr, *White Women, Rape, and the Power of Race in Virginia, 1900–1960* (Chapel Hill: University of North Carolina Press, 2004). Dorr argues that in Virginia, class factored into accusations

of rape as much as race, creating a complex picture of white female sexuality and respectability in the South.

20. See Peter Wallenstein, *Tell the Court I Love My Wife: Race, Marriage, and Law—An American History* (New York: St. Martin's Griffin, 2004); Rachel F. Moran, *Interracial Intimacy: The Regulation of Race and Romance* (Chicago: University of Chicago Press, 2003); and Gregory Michael Dorr, "Principled Expediency: Eugenics, Naim v. Naim, and the Supreme Court," *American Journal of Legal History* 42 (1998): 119–59. See also Randall Kennedy, *Interracial Intimacies: Sex, Marriage, Identity, and Adoption* (New York: Vintage, 2004), for more on the relationship between interracial relationships and the law more generally.

21. "Ban on Race Amalgamation to be Urged in Legislature by DeKalb Representative," *Atlanta Constitution*, June 21, 1925, 7A; "An Act to define who are persons of color and who are white persons, to prohibit and prevent the intermarriage of such persons . . . ," August 20, 1927, *Acts and Resolutions of the General Assembly of the State of Georgia, 1927* (Atlanta, 1927), esp. 273–77.

22. Michelle Brattain's article "Miscegenation and Competing Definitions of Race in Twentieth-Century Louisiana," *Journal of Southern History* 71 (2005): 558–621, provides an excellent examination of the complexity Filipinos introduced into the Louisiana courts and miscegenation law. See also Hrishi Karthikeyan and Gabriel J. Chin, "Preserving Racial Identity: Population Patterns and the Application of Anti-Miscegenation Statutes to Asian Americans, 1910–1950," *Asian Law Journal* 9 (May 2002): 1–40.

23. For an example from the Atlanta press, see Frank Dallam, "Following the Scarlet Trail of White Slavery in America," *Atlanta Constitution*, August 14, 1921, magazine section, 5. See also Mary Ting Yi Lui, *The Chinatown Trunk Mystery: Murder, Miscegenation, and Other Dangerous Encounters in Turn-of-the-Century New York City* (Princeton: Princeton University Press, 2005); Allison Varzally, *Making a Non-White America: Californians Coloring outside Ethnic Lines, 1925–1955* (Berkeley: University of California Press, 2008); and Elise Chenier, "Sex, Intimacy, and Desire among Men of Chinese Heritage and Women of Non-Asian Heritage in Toronto, 1910–1950," *Urban History Review* 42 (Spring 2014): 29–43.

24. "Miss Sigel Made Love to Two Chinese: Success of Wealthy Rival Drove Leon to Kill Girl," *Baltimore Afro-American*, June 26, 1909, 2; "Enraged Chinese Lover Shoots Girl Friend, Kills Self," *Baltimore Afro-American*, September 10, 1949, 18.

25. Quoted in Baldoz, *Third Asiatic Invasion*, 122. See also John S. W. Park, *Elusive Citizenship: Immigration, Asian Americans, and the Paradox of Civil Rights* (New York: NYU Press, 2004), 118–20.

26. "Suicide Pact Takes Lives of Two in South," *Geneva Daily Times*, January 19, 1931, 1; "Filipino Butler and Girl Found Dead in Automobile on Candler Estate," *Atlanta Constitution*, January 19, 1931, 1–2.

27. On Mary Phagan and Leo Frank, see Matthew Frye Jacobson, *Whiteness of a Different Color: European Immigrants and the Alchemy of Race* (Cambridge: Harvard University Press, 1999), 68–70; Leonard Dinnerstein, *The Leo Frank Case* (rev. ed., Athens: University of Georgia Press, 2008); Steve Oney, *And the Dead Shall Rise: The Murder of Mary Phagan and the Lynching of Leo Frank* (New York: Vintage, 2004); and Jeffrey Melnick, *Black-Jewish Relations on Trial: Leo Frank and Jim Conley in the New South* (Jackson: University Press of Mississippi, 2000).

28. Direct examination of Paul Seymour by E. A. Stephens, May 11, 1932, AR, 51.
29. Direct examination of George Pounds by E. A. Stephens, May 11, 1932, AR, 54.
30. Direct examination of Frances Hutcheson by F. J. Turner, May 11, 1932, AR, 33.
31. Ibid., 34.
32. Defendant's Exceptions Pendente Lite, AR, 15.
33. Ibid.
34. McGuire, *At the Dark End of the Street*, 62.
35. Indictment, April 22, 1932, AR, 2.
36. Turner was a former police reporter for the *Atlanta Constitution* who passed the bar exam in 1928 and practiced law until his death in 1942. See "F. Joe Turner, Lawyer, Dies at Age of 49: Was Police Reporter for Constitution for 10 Years," *Atlanta Constitution*, December, 18, 1942, 27.
37. Charge of the Court, AR, 66.
38. Interestingly, in a 1954 court case Moore declared a mistrial when the well-respected African American and Atlanta-based civil rights attorney Donald L. Hollowell objected to the use of the phrase "that fat nigger" to describe his client. Many Atlantans came to recognize Moore as one of the fairer judges in cases involving African Americans. See Maurice C. Daniels, *Saving the Soul of Georgia: Donald L. Hollowell and the Struggle for Civil Rights* (Athens: University of Georgia Press, 2013), 39–40.
39. Transcript of Record, True Bill, *State of Georgia v. Fortunatio Annunciatio*, Case Number 9249, Supreme Court of Georgia, October 1932 term, AR.
40. Frederic R. Coudert [Sr.], "Our New Peoples: Citizens, Subjects, Nationals, or Aliens," *Columbia Law Review* 3 (January 1903), 13–32.
41. Baldoz, *Third Asiatic Invasion*, 71.
42. Direct examination of Frances Hutcheson by E. A. Stephens, May 11, 1932, AR, 29–31.
43. Cross examination of Frances Hutcheson by F. J. Turner, May 11, 1932, AR, 31.
44. Ibid., 30–31.
45. Direct examination of Paul W. Seymour by E. A. Stephens, May 11, 1932, AR, 49.
46. Harry Ingram, sworn for the state rebuttal, AR, 53.
47. Direct examination of Dr. W. A. Arnold by E. A. Stephens, May 11, 1932, AR, 44.
48. Recross-examination of Rosa Mae by F. J. Turner, May 11, 1932, 41.
49. Ibid.
50. Defendant's Statement, AR, 47.
51. Ibid., 48.
52. Defendant's Exceptions Pendente Lite, AR, 7.
53. The Fourth Amendment's protections against illegal search and seizure did not become prominent parts of criminal investigations until the 1960s when the Supreme Court ruled in *Mapp v. Ohio* (367 U.S. 632 [1961]) that all evidence obtained illegally is inadmissible in a court of law. On the Fourth Amendment, see Cynthia Lee, ed., *Searches and Seizures: The Fourth Amendment, Its Constitutional History and Contemporary Debate* (New York: Prometheus Books, 2011), and William J. Cuddihy, *The Fourth Amendment: Origins and Original Meaning, 602–1791* (New York: Oxford University Press, 2009).
54. Defendant's Exceptions Pendente Lite, AR, 3.
55. Ibid., 6.
56. Ibid.

57. "Crossections of the South," *Atlanta Constitution*, May 15, 1932, 16A; "Cross Sections of the South," *Atlanta Constitution*, May 17, 1932, 8.

58. Defendant's Pendente Lite, at 19–20.

59. Ibid.

60. Motion for Retrial, AR, 17.

61. Ibid.

62. Ibid., 18.

63. Ibid.

64. Ibid.

65. Ibid., 19.

66. *Leo Frank v. State of Georgia*, 142, Ga. 617 (1914); Ray H. Everett, "Failure of Segregation as Protector of Innocent Womanhood," *Social Hygiene* 5 (1919): 529.

67. Motion for Retrial, AR, 19.

68. Ibid.

69. "Filipinos Not Ready for Self-Government, Crisp Says on Return," *Atlanta Constitution*, August 11, 1925, 14.

70. "Uncle Sam's Jekyll-and-Hyde Problem," *Atlanta Sunday Constitution Magazine*, September 14, 1924, 7.

71. Kramer, *Blood of Government*, 397–98.

72. Motion for New Trial, AR, 25. On Subia's hearing for a retrial, see "Cross Sections of Southern Life," *Atlanta Constitution*, August 21, 1932, 3A.

73. *Annunciatio v. State*, 176 Ga. 787 (1933).

74. Ibid., 796.

75. Despite China's relationship with the United States as a wartime ally, the Chinese Exclusion Act (which would be repealed later, in 1943) prohibited many Chinese from entering the United States, resulting in captains and authorities denying leave to Chinese sailors for fear of illegal entry and abandonment. Although attempts were made to find the Chinese sailors who abandoned ship, many fled in hopes of remaining in the United States for more than just a temporary shore leave. See "Chinese Sailors Revolt in N.Y.," *Atlanta Daily World*, June 29, 1942, 2; "Chinese Seamen Win Agreement with British Merchant Marines," *New York Times*, May 10, 1942, F7; and "China Comes Ashore," *New York Times*, August 6, 1942, 18. Little is known about Naim's life either prior to or after his legal battles during the mid-1950s.

76. Pascoe, *What Comes Naturally*, 206, 226–31. See also Julie Lavonne Nokov, *Race Union: Law, Intimacy, and the White State in Alabama, 1865–1954* (Ann Arbor: University of Michigan, 2009); Charles Frank Robinson, *Dangerous Liaisons: Sex and Love in the Segregated South* (Lafayette: University of Louisiana at Lafayette Press, 2003); Lisa Lindquist Dorr, "Arm in Arm: Gender, Eugenics, and Virginia's Racial Integrity Acts of the 1920s," *Journal of Women's History* 11 (1999): 143–67.

77. "Virginia 'Argers' if Girl May Wed Chinese," *Baltimore Afro-American*, December 1, 1928, 1. Maryland was also not an option for Naim and Lamberth. In 1927, a Chinese man, Samuel Moy, and his white fiancée, Turretta Budd, were denied a marriage license in Rockville under the state's existing antimiscegenation code prohibiting marriages between whites and "coloreds." See "Refuse Chinese License to Wed Girl," *Baltimore Afro-American*, April 16, 1927, 20.

78. Ruby's difficulty in securing a divorce via charges of adultery speaks to the nonexistence of no-fault divorces in many states at this time.

79. "Chinese, White Marriage Voided," *Baltimore Afro-American*, July 22, 1950, 19. The newspaper article explained that Yigh was more than likely "pressured" by Wolfe's parents to have the marriage annulled.

80. See Fay Botham, *Almighty God Created the Races: Christianity, Interracial Marriage, and American Law* (Chapel Hill: University of North Carolina Press, 2009), and Peter Wallenstein, "Race, Marriage, and the Law of Freedom: Alabama and Virginia, 1860s–1960s," *Chicago-Kent Law Review* 70 (1994): 371–419.

81. Cathleen Caron, "Continuing to Draw Inspiration from David Carliner," February 15, 2013, http://www.acslaw.org/acsblog/continuing-to-draw-inspiration-from-david-carliner (accessed November 11, 2013).

82. Richard Delgado, "*Naim v. Naim*," *Nevada Law Review* 12 (2012): 526–31; Gabriele Chin, Cindy Hwang Chiang, and Shirley S. Park, "The Lost *Brown v. Board of Education* and Immigration Law," *North Carolina Law Review* 91 (2013): 1657–98; Chandan Reddy, "Time for Rights? Loving, Gay Marriage, and the Limits of Legal Justice," *Fordham Law Review* 76 (2008): 2849–72; Kennedy, *Interracial Intimacies*; Rebecca Schoff, "Deciding on Doctrine: Anti-Miscegenation Statutes and the Development of Equal Protection Analysis," *Virginia Law Review* 95 (May 2009): 627–65.

83. Botham, *Almighty God*, 11–17.

84. "She Weds a Chinese," *Baltimore Afro-American*, April 11, 1925, A17; "Chinese Takes Bride," *Baltimore Afro-American*, August 13, 1920, 1; "Miss Sigel Made Love to Two Chinese: Success of Wealthy Rival Drove Leon to Kill Girl," *Baltimore Afro-American*, June 26, 1909, 2; "Enraged Chinese Lover Shoots Girlfriend, Kills Self," *Baltimore Afro-American*, September 10, 1949, 18; Harry Winston, "Chinese Love: The Story of an Interracial Love That Was Slightly Hampered by an Old Chinese Custom," *Baltimore Afro-American*, June 2, 1934, 24.

85. Ruby Elaine Naim to Han Say Naim, April 17, 1953, NVAR, 1955, Supreme Court of Appeals of the State of Virginia.

86. Ruby Naim to Han Say Naim, September, 29, 1953, NVAR.

87. David Carliner to Edward J. Emis, March 9, 1954, folder 21, box 1106, CR.

88. Memo re: Ruby Naim v. Han Say Naim, CR.

89. Petition for Appeals—Supreme Court of Appeals, CR.

90. See Erika Lee, *At America's Gates: Chinese Immigrants during the Exclusion Era, 1882–1943* (Chapel Hill: University of North Carolina Press, 2003); Madeline Y. Hsu, *Dreaming of Gold, Dreaming of Home: Transnationalism and Migration between the United States and South China* (Palo Alto: Stanford University Press, 2000); Jean Pfaelzer, *Driven Out: The Forgotten War against Chinese Americans* (Berkeley: University of California Press, 2007); and Judy Yung, Gordon Chang, and Mark Him Lai, eds., *Chinese American Voices: From the Gold Rush to the Present* (Berkeley: University of California Press, 2006), for a closer analysis of early Chinese and Chinese American civil rights suits and cases.

91. J. Lindsey Almond, C. F. Hicks, and R. D. McIlwaine, Amicus Curial, Record No. 4368, BCVA, 25–26.

92. Ibid.

93. "Court Upholds Interracial Marriage Ban," *Washington Post and Times Herald*, June 14, 1955, 30.

94. Carliner to Levy, April 29, 1955, CR.

95. Ibid.

96. Memo from Levy, November 21, 1955, CR.

97. Carliner to Levy, July 20, 1955, CR.

98. Ibid.

99. See Cindy I-Fen Cheng, *Citizens of Asian America: Democracy and Race during the Cold War* (New York: NYU Press, 2013); Sucheng Chan and Madeline Y. Hsu, *Chinese Americans and the Politics of Race and Culture* (Philadelphia: Temple University Press, 2008); and Xiaojian Zhao, *Remaking Chinese America: Immigration, Family, and Community, 1940–1965* (New Brunswick: Rutgers University Press, 2002).

100. Levy to Carliner, June 29, 1955, CR.

101. Carliner to Levy, June 1, 1955, CR.

102. Ibid., April 20, 1955, CR.

103. Sol Rabkin to Carliner, August 25, 1955, CR.

104. Ibid.

105. In the years following World War II, the classification of Asian Americans as the "model minority" began to emerge. See Ellen Wu, *The Color of Success: Asian Americans and the Origins of the Model Minority* (Princeton: Princeton University Press, 2013); Cheng, *Citizens of Asian America*; Madeline Y. Hsu, *The Good Immigrants: How the Yellow Peril Became the Model Minority* (Princeton: Princeton University Press, 2015); K. Scott Wong, *Americans First: Chinese Americans and the Second World War* (Cambridge: Harvard University Press, 2005); and Jingyi Song, *Shaping and Reshaping Chinese American Identity: New York's Chinese during the Depression and World War II* (New York: Lexington Books, 2010).

106. Sol Rabkin to Carliner, August 25, 1955, CR.

107. Ibid.

108. Levy to Roger Baldwin, August 2, 1955, CR.

109. Ibid.

110. Carliner to Levy, June 24, 1955, CR.

111. Ibid.

112. Jack Wasserman to Herb Levy, October 24, 1955, CR. See also Dorr, "Principled Expediency," 147, for a more in-depth discussion of the NAACP's reaction to the Naim case.

113. "Virginia Decision Vacated," *Lubbock Times*, November 15, 1955, 5.

114. Luther A. Huston, "Civil Rights Highlight Supreme Court Session: Justices Will Consider Many Issues Involving Individual Freedoms," *New York Times*, October 22, 1955, E6.

115. "Court Calls for More Data on Interracial Marriages," *Los Angeles Times*, November 15, 1955, 7.

116. Dorr, "Principled Expediency," 135.

117. David Carliner to Rowland Watts, Staff Counsel of ACLU, March 13, 1956, CR.

118. Dorr, "Principled Expediency," 156.

119. Roger Farquar, "Virginia Eyes Sailor's Status," *Washington Post and Times Herald*, January 23, 1956, 12.

120. "High Court Hits Vote Racial Tag," *Washington Post and Times Herald*, November 15, 1955, 23.

121. "Racial Marriage Case Reopened," *Washington Post and Times Herald*, February 3, 1956, 42; "Court Shelves Interracial Marriage Case," *Los Angeles Times*, March 13, 1956, 26.

122. As told to Gregory Dorr. See Dorr, "Principled Expediency," 142.

123. Georgia Central Register of Convicts, 1913–1952 (bulk 1930–1938), A–G, 4, Georgia Archives, accessed through subscription database *Georgia Central Register of Convicts, 1817–1976* (Provo, Utah, 2014), images 11–12, via Ancestry.com.

124. Central Register of Convicts, 1913–1938, P–Z, 18, Georgia Archives, accessed through *Georgia Central Register of Convicts, 1817–1796*, images 157–58, via Ancestry.com; marriage record of Amby S. Subia and Marie Henry, October 12, 1935 (recorded October 14, 1935), Paulding County, Ga., Record of Marriages, Book E, 1922–1936, 567, County Marriage Records, 1828–1978, Georgia Archives, accessed via subscription database *Georgia Marriage Records from Select Counties, 1828–1978* (Provo, Utah, 2013), image 326, via Ancestry.com.

POST-1965 CHANGES IN ASIAN AMERICA

1. See Ellen Wu, *The Color of Success: Asian Americans and the Origins of the Model Minority* (Princeton: Princeton University Press, 2013); Madeline Y. Hsu, *The Good Immigrants: How the Yellow Peril Became the Model Minority* (Princeton: Princeton University Press, 2015); and Cindy I-Fen Cheng, *Citizens of Asian America: Democracy and Race during the Cold War* (New York: NYU Press, 2013). See also Charlotte Brooks, *Between Mao and McCarthy: Chinese American Politics in the Cold War Years* (Chicago: University of Chicago Press, 2015) and *Alien Neighbors, Foreign Friends: Asian Americans, Housing, and the Transformation of Urban California* (Chicago: University of Chicago Press, 2009), for a more general look at the social and political changes that Chinese Americans and other Asian American groups faced following World War II.

2. See Leslie Bow, *Partly Colored: Asian Americans and Racial Anomaly in the Segregated South* (New York: NYU Press, 2011), and interview with Amzie Moore, 1967, folder 22, box 3, LC.

3. Pew Research Center, "Modern Immigration Wave Brings 59 Million to U.S., Driving Population Growth and Change through 1965," http://www.pewhispanic.org/2015/09/28/modern-immigration-wave-brings-59-million-to-u-s-driving-population-growth-and-change-through-2065/ (accessed September 28, 2015).

4. Mae M. Ngai, *Impossible Subjects: Illegal Aliens and the Making of Modern America* (Princeton: Princeton University Press, 2006), 257–62.

CHAPTER 4

1. Steve Olafson and Glenn Lewis, "Klan Chief Tells Rally Country Must Be Reclaimed by 'Blood,'" *Houston Post*, February 15, 1981, 10A.

2. Roy Vu, "Natives of a Ghost Country: The Vietnamese in Houston and Their Construction of a Postwar Community," in *Asian Americans in Dixie: Race and Migration in the South*, ed. Khyati Y. Joshi and Jigna Desai (Champaign: University of Illinois Press,

2013), 165–67. See also Fred R. Von der Mehden, *The Ethnic Groups of Houston* (College Station: Texas A&M Press, 1984), and Irwin A. Tang, *Asian Texans: Our Histories and Our Lives* (New York: It Works Publishing, 2008), for more in-depth discussions of the Vietnamese, their communities, and their culture in Houston. See also Sucheng Chan's *The Vietnamese American 1.5 Generation: Stories of War, Revolution, Fight, and New Beginnings* (Philadelphia: Temple University Press, 2006) for a more general description and analysis of the Vietnamese refugee experience in the United States.

3. Olafson and Lewis, "Klan Chief," 10A.

4. Ronald Takaki, *Strangers from a Different Shore: A History of Asian Americans* (New York: Little, Brown, 1998), 452–54, 481, 491.

5. United States Census Bureau, 1980 Census of Population, General Population Characteristics, pt. 1, United States Summary, 137; U.S. Department of Commerce, *We the Americans: Asians* (Washington, D.C.: U.S. Government Printing Office, 1993), 4.

6. United States Census Bureau, 1980 Census of Population, General Population Characteristics, pt. 1, United States Summary, 137; "From Vietnam to Austin," folder 3, box 1, Austin History Center, Austin, Tex.; interview with Kimberli Zamarripa, June 10, 2008, folder 29, VOHP.

7. Interview with Hue Nguyen, November 15, 1992, folder 20, VOHP.

8. Interview with Thé Nguyen Nasternak, June 24, 2008, folder 11, VOHP.

9. Interview with Nancy Hoang Dan, June 1, 2008, folder 3, VOHP.

10. Interview with Ngai Van Nguyen, June 6, 2008, folder 25, VOHP.

11. Interview with Nasternak.

12. Interview with Vuong V. Nguyen, May 29, 2008, folder 31, VOHP.

13. "3 More Men Arrested, Justice Department to Mediate Dispute in Seadrift," *Houston Post*, August, 9, 1979, 4.

14. Interview with Father Gregory Dean, June 13, 2008, folder 2, VOHP.

15. Interview with Leslie Casterline, June 12, 2008, folder 2, VOHP.

16. "Shrimpers Conflict: Survey Finds More Sour Grapes Than Illegal Boats," *Houston Post*, March 29, 1981, 1.

17. Interview with Judge Linh Van Chau, May 23, 2006, folder 47, VOHP.

18. Interview with Dean.

19. "Shrimpers Conflict," 1.

20. Interview with Casterline.

21. See Jefferson R. Cowie, *Stayin' Alive: The 1970s and the Last Days of the Working Class* (New York: New Press, 2011); Thomas Borstelmann, *The 1970s: A New Global History from Civil Rights to Economic Inequality* (Princeton: Princeton University Press, 2013); and Rick Perlstein, *Nixonland: The Rise of a President and the Fracturing of America* (New York: Scribner, 2009), for more on the rise of the Silent Majority and the economic downturn and rise of conservatism in the 1970s. See also Matthew D. Lassiter, *The Silent Majority: Suburban Politics in the Sunbelt South* (Princeton: Princeton University Press, 2007), for a more specific discussion of the Silent Majority and suburbanization politics in "new" southern cities.

22. Interview with The Van Nguyen, March 30, 2008, folder 2, VOHP.

23. Mike Avalos, "Crab Fishing Feud Called 'Powderkeg,'" *Houston Post*, August 6, 1979, 1, 23A.

24. Ibid.
25. Ibid. "Federal Peacemaker Meets Feuding Factions in Seadrift," *Houston Post*, August 11, 1979, 8C.
26. Avalos, "Crab Fishing Feud," 23A.
27. "Feud Driving Vietnamese out of Seadrift, Spokesman Says," *Houston Post*, August 8, 1979, 7A.
28. "Federal Peacemaker Meets Feuding Factions," 8C.
29. Ibid., 10.
30. "Seadrift: Most of 100 Vietnamese Return after Fleeing in Fear," *Houston Post*, August 12, 1979, 7.
31. "Pair to Settle Dispute in Fishing Rights Feud," *Houston Post*, August 15, 1979, 4A.
32. "3 More Men Arrested," 4.
33. "Seadrift: Most of 100 Vietnamese Return," 7.
34. Interview with Casterline.
35. Interview with Dean.
36. Interview with Casterline.
37. Judge Gabrielle McDonald, Memorandum Opinion and Order, *Vietnamese Fishermen's Association v. The Knights of the Ku Klux Klan* (1981), 4, http://www2.law.columbia.edu/faculty_franke/Torts/kkk.pdf (accessed July 12, 2015).
38. Interview with Huong Thi Pham, April 29, 2008, folder 21, VOHP.
39. The Knights of the Ku Klux Klan was a separate organization from the nationwide Ku Klux Klan. Following FBI investigations into the Klan during the 1970s, members determined that a new organization was needed to avoid further suspicions and broke with the dwindling original Klan. The Knights were based in Metairie, Louisiana, and granted Beam a charter for Texas in 1975. The Knights attempted to distance themselves from the drastic violent and racist measures associated with the "old" Klan of the South.
40. Olafson and Lewis, "Klan Chief," 10.
41. Ibid.
42. Ibid.
43. Ibid.
44. "Witness Says Defendant Told Vietnamese Boats Easy to Burn," *Houston Post*, May 12, 1981, 22A.
45. "2 Vietnamese-Owned Boats Burn; Seabrook Police Seek Cause," *Houston Post*, March 20, 1981, 2A.
46. "Assurances Given in Shrimpers' Dispute," *Houston Post*, February 18, 1981, 2A.
47. "Religious Leaders Support Viet Refugees," *Houston Post*, March 19, 1981, 10.
48. Ibid.
49. Ibid.
50. McDonald, Memorandum Opinion and Order, 4.
51. Ibid.
52. "Suit Filed to Protect Area Vietnamese Fishermen," *Houston Post*, April 17, 1981, 15A.
53. Ibid.
54. Author's telephone interview with Morris Dees, August 11, 2015.
55. Morris Dees, *A Lawyer's Journey: The Morris Dees Story* (Chicago: American Bar Association, 2001), 23.

56. See Michael Ezra, *The Economic Civil Rights Movement: African Americans and the Struggle for Economic Power* (New York: Routledge, 2013); Tomiko Brown-Nagin, *Courage to Dissent: Atlanta and the Long History of the Civil Rights Movement* (New York: Oxford University Press, 2011); and Robert E. Weems, *Business in Black and White: American Presidents and Black Entrepreneurs in the Twentieth Century* (New York: NYU Press, 2009), for more on African Americans, civil rights, and business practices. For more on Asians and the fight for property protections during the nineteenth century, see Erika Lee, *At America's Gates: Chinese Immigrants during the Exclusion Era, 1882–1943* (Chapel Hill: University of North Carolina Press, 2003), and Angelo N. Ancheta, *Race, Rights, and the Asian American Experience* (New Brunswick: Rutgers University Press, 1998).

57. Continuation of the Deposition of Louis Beam, vol. 2, May 3, 1981, 42, AF.

58. Ibid., 46.

59. Ibid., 43.

60. Ibid., 57, 77.

61. Deposition of Gene Fisher, May 2, 1981, 39, AF.

62. Ibid., 80, 82, 115.

63. Deposition of Tran Van Phu, May 5, 1981, 11, AF.

64. Ibid., 17.

65. Ibid., 10.

66. Ibid., 11.

67. Deposition of Nam Van Nguyen, May 5, 1981, 62, 86, AF.

68. Ibid., 86.

69. Ibid., 46.

70. Ibid., 34.

71. McDonald, Memorandum Opinion and Order, 5.

72. Deposition of Phuong Pham, May 8, 1981, 10, AF.

73. Deposition of Nguyen Luu, May 5, 1981, 8, AF.

74. Ibid., 8.

75. Deposition of Nam Van Nguyen, 62.

76. McDonald, Memorandum Opinion and Order, 5.

77. Yen Le Espiritu, *Asian American Panethnicity: Bridging Institutions and Identities* (Philadelphia: Temple University Press, 1993), 82–112.

78. McDonald, Memorandum Opinion and Order, 4.

79. Ibid., 5.

80. Ibid.

81. Dees, *Lawyer's Journey*, 23.

82. Glenn Lewis, "Uneasy Peace Predicted as Shrimping Season Nears," *Houston Post*, May 14, 1981, 24A.

83. Deposition of Nam Van Nguyen, 81.

84. Ibid., 86.

85. Jason Sokol, *There Goes My Everything: White Southerners in the Age of Civil Rights, 1945–1975* (New York: Vintage, 2007), 180–85, 188. See also Morton J. Horwitz, *The Transformation of American Law, 1870–1960* (New York: Oxford University Press, 1992), and Robert H. Wiebe, *Businessmen and Reform: A Study of the Progressive Movement* (New York: Ivan R. Dee, 1988) and *The Search for Order, 1877–1920* (New York: Hill and

Wang, 1966), for more information on business, economics, and trust law during the Progressive movement.

86. "Injunction Bars Action against Viet Shrimpers," *Houston Post*, May 12, 1981, 1.
87. Ibid.
88. Ibid.
89. Ibid.
90. "Shrimp Season's Opening Day One of the Quietest in Years," *Houston Post*, May 16, 1981, 7A.
91. Ibid.
92. Final Judgment, *Vietnamese Fishermen's Association v. The Knights of the Ku Klux*, June 9, 1982, 543 F. Supp. 198, 3.
93. Ibid., 12.
94. Ibid.
95. Ibid.
96. Ibid., 16.
97. Ibid., 17.
98. Ibid., 13.
99. Ibid., 24

CHAPTER 5

1. AAHOA, *25th Anniversary of Asian American Hotel Owners Association* (Atlanta: AAHOA, 2014), 23.

2. See Jefferson R. Cowie, *Capital Moves: RCA's Seventy-Year Quest for Cheap Labor* (New York: New Press, 2001); Nelson Lichtenstein, *The Retail Revolution: How Walmart Created a Brave New World of Business* (New York: Picador, 2010); Bethany Moreton, *To Serve God and Walmart: The Making of Christian Free Enterprise* (Cambridge: Harvard University Press, 2009); and Kevin Kruse, *One Nation under God: How Corporate American Invented Christian America* (New York: Basic Books, 2015), for more on business in the South in the post–World War II era as well as the connections between Christianity, the rise of the New Right, and corporatization.

3. See Howard Morgan, *The Hotel Industry in the United States: Small Business in Transition* (Tucson: Bureau of Business and Public Research, University of Arizona, 1964); John A. Jakle, Keith A. Sculle, and Jefferson R. Rogers, *The Motel in America* (Baltimore: Johns Hopkins University Press, 1996); and Warren James Belasco, *Americans on the Road: From Autocamp to Motel, 1910–1945* (Baltimore: Johns Hopkins University Press, 1997), for more on the history of the hotel/motel industry in the United States.

4. See Paul Groth, *Living Downtown: The History of Residential Hotels in the United States* (Berkeley: University of California Press, 1999); William P. Jones, *The March on Washington: Jobs, Freedom, and the Forgotten History of Civil Rights* (New York: Norton, 2013); Juliet E. K. Walker, *The History of Black Business in America: Capitalism, Race, and Entrepreneurship* (Chapel Hill: University of North Carolina Press, 2009); Robert E. Weems, *Desegregating the Dollar: African American Consumerism in the Twentieth Century* (New York: NYU Press, 1998); and Tom Lewis, *Divided Highways: Building the Interstate*

Highways, Transforming American Life (Ithaca: Cornell University Press, 2013), for more on black-owned businesses and discrimination.

5. AAHOA, *25th Anniversary*, 17.

6. See Pravin Sheth, *Indians in America: One Stream, Two Waves, Three Generations* (Jaipur, India: Rawat Publications, 2001); Shinder Thandi, "Migrating to Mother Country: South Asian Settlement and the Post-War Boom, 1947–1980," in *A South Asian History of Britain: Four Centuries of Peoples from the Indian Sub-Continent*, ed. Michael H. Fisher, Shompa Lahiri, and Shinder Thandi (Westport, Conn.: Greenwood Press, 2007), 32–56; Maritsa Poros, *Modern Migrations: Gujarati Indian Networks in New York and London* (Palo Alto: Stanford University Press, 2010); Vinay Lal, *The Other Indians: A Political and Cultural History of South Asians in America* (Los Angeles: UCLA Asian American Studies Center, 2008); Usha Jain, *The Gujaratis of San Francisco* ((New York: AMS Press, 1989); Arthur Helweg and Usha Helweg, *An Immigrant Success Story: East Indians in America* (Philadelphia: Temple University Press, 2001); Roger Daniels, *History of Indian Immigration to the United States: An Interpretive History* (New York: Asia Society, 1989); and Govind Bhatka, *Patels: A Gujarati Community History in the United States* (Los Angeles: UCLA Asian American Studies Center, 2000).

7. Padma Rangaswamy, *Namaste America: Indian Immigrants in an American Metropolis* (University Park: Pennsylvania State University Press, 2000), 3.

8. T. Green, "Foreigners Buying Up U.S. Motels," *Los Angeles Times*, May 29, 1977, C5.

9. See Pawan Dhingra, *Life behind the Lobby: Indian American Motel Owners and the American Dream* (Palo Alto: Stanford University Press, 2012); Hein Steerflek, "Gujarati Entrepreneurship: Historical Continuity against Changing Perspectives," *Economic and Political Weekly* 32 (1997): M2–M10; Rebecca Raijman and Marta Tienda, "Immigrants' Pathway to Business Ownership: A Comparative Ethnic Perspective," *International Migration Review* 34 (2000): 682–706; Anjali Sahay, "Indian Diaspora in the United States and Brain Gain: Remittances, Return, and Network Approaches," in *Sociology of Diaspora: A Reader*, edited by Ajaya Kumar Sahoo and Brij Maharah (New Delhi, India: Rawat Publications, 2007), 940–79; and Gary Hess, "The Forgotten Asian Americans: The East Indian Community in the United States," *Pacific Historical Review* 43 (1974): 576–96.

10. Author's telephone interview with Lee Duschoff, September 16, 2015. See also Edna Bonacich, "Making It in America: A Social Evaluation of the Ethics of Immigrant Entrepreneurship," *Sociological Perspectives* 30 (October 1987): 446–66; Michael Hout, "The Possibility of Community: How Indian American Motel Owners Negotiate Competition and Solidarity," *Journal of Asian American Studies* 12 (2009): 321–46; Ivan Light, *Ethnic Enterprise in America: Business and Welfare among Chinese, Japanese, and Blacks* (Berkeley: University of California Press, 1972); Jimmy Sanders and Victor Nee, "Immigrant Self-Employment: The Family as Social Capital and the Value of Human Capital," *American Sociological Review* 61 (1996): 231–49; and Arthur Sakamoto, Kimberly Goyette, and Chang Hwan Kim, "Socioeconomic Attainments of Asian Americans," *Annual Review of Sociology* 35 (2009): 255–76, for more on historical and sociological approaches to Indian business tactics and experiences.

11. Author's telephone interview with H. P. Rama, Monday, October 6, 2015.

12. AAHOA, *25th Anniversary*, 18–19.

13. "Workers Drill with Sentra Test Cars," *Nashville Tennesseean*, February 8, 1985, 11.

14. Sheng-Mei Ma, *The Deathly Embrace: Orientalism and Asian American Identity* (Minneapolis: University of Minnesota Press, 2000), 77–81; Helen Zia, *Asian American Dreams: The Emergence of an American People* (New York: Farrar, Straus and Giroux, 2001), 59, 63–65, 72–73, 80–81.

15. Interview with Duschoff.

16. Leslie Bow, *Partly Colored: Asian Americans and Racial Anomaly in the Segregated South* (New York: NYU Press, 2011), 120, 142.

17. Interview with Rama.

18. Ibid.

19. Ibid.

20. Tunku Varadarajan, "A Patel Cartel?," *New York Times*, July 4, 1999, 17.

21. Interview with Rama.

22. Ibid.; AAHOA, *25th Anniversary*, 21.

23. Varadarajan, "Patel Cartel?," 17.

24. Interview with Rama.

25. Ibid.

26. AAHOA, *25th Anniversary*, 21.

27. Interview with Duschoff; interview with Rama.

28. See Lisa Mar, *Brokering Belonging: Chinese in Canada's Exclusion Era, 1885–1945* (New York: Oxford University Press, 2010); Victoria M. Wolcott, *Remaking Respectability: African American Women in Interwar Detroit* (Chapel Hill: University of North Carolina Press, 2001); Eiichiro Azuma, *Between Two Empires: Race, History, and Transnationalism in Japanese America* (New York: Oxford University Press, 2007); and Evelyn Brooks Higginbotham, *Righteous Discontent: The Women's Movement in the Baptist Black Church, 1880–1920* (Cambridge: Harvard University Press, 1994), for more on respectability politics in history and in different ethnic and racial communities.

29. Interview with Mike Leven, August 12, 2015.

30. Ibid.; AAHOA, *25th Anniversary*, 20.

31. Interview with Rama.

32. Ibid.

33. Ibid.

34. Interview with Duschoff.

35. Ibid.

36. Ibid.

37. AAHOA, *25th Anniversary*, 22.

38. Interview with Duschoff.

39. "Our History: An Overview," *AAHOA Annual Report* (2014), 46.

40. Interview with Duschoff.

41. AAHOA, *25th Anniversary*, 25; "Our History," 46.

42. Interview with Rama.

43. Ibid.

44. Ibid.

45. Ibid.

46. Interview with Leven.

47. AAHOA, *25th Anniversary*, 22.

48. Ibid.
49. Author's telephone interview with Ravi Patel, September 16, 2015.
50. Interview with Leven.
51. Interview with Patel.
52. Interview with Duschoff.
53. AAHOA, *25th Anniversary*, 21.
54. Ibid., 29; interview with Duschoff.
55. Interview with Rama.
56. Ibid.
57. AAHOA, *25th Anniversary*, 23.
58. Interview with Duschoff.
59. Interview with Rama.
60. AAHOA, *25th Anniversary*, 30; "Our History," 47.
61. AAHOA, *25th Anniversary*, 22.
62. Interview with Rama.
63. AAHOA, *25th Anniversary*, 28.
64. Ibid. See also David W. Koch, "The Proposed 'Small Business Franchise Act of 1999': The End of Franchising as We Know It?" (paper presented at the Federal Bar Association Annual Convention, Cleveland, Ohio, September 22, 2000), for an example of arguments presented against the act.
65. AAHOA, *25th Anniversary*, 32.
66. Ibid., 33.
67. Interview with Rama.
68. Interview with Leven.

CONCLUSION

1. Damien Cave, "In Florida, an Initiative Intended to End Bias Is Killed," *New York Times*, November 5, 2008, A22.
2. Ibid.; Rasha Madkour, "Amendment 1 Targets Florida's Anti-Asian Land Law," *Tampa Tribune*, October 18, 2008.
3. Karan Mahajan, "The Two Asian Americas," *New Yorker* (October 21 2015), http://www.newyorker.com/books/page-turner/the-two-asian-americas (accessed December 11, 2015).
4. "Asian Americans Intervene in Georgia Voting Rights Lawsuit," July 29, 2010, http://aaldef.org/press-releases/press-release/asian-americans-intervene-in-georgia-voting-rights-lawsuit.html (accessed December 20, 2015).
5. R. G. Ratcliffe, "Texas Lawmaker Suggests Asians Adopt Easier Names," *Houston Chronicle*, April 8, 2009, http://www.chron.com/news/houston-texas/article/Texas-lawmaker-suggests-Asians-adopt-easier-names-1550512.php (accessed December 20, 2015).
6. Lisa Lowe, *Immigrant Acts: On Asian American Cultural Politics* (Durham: Duke University Press, 1996), 8.
7. Derrick A. Bell Jr., "*Brown v. Board of Education* and the Interest-Convergence Dilemma," *Harvard Law Review* 93 (1980): 523–25.

SELECT BIBLIOGRAPHY

ARCHIVAL SOURCES

Austin, Texas
  Austin History Center
    Austin Smith Papers
    Wong Family Papers
  Dolph Briscoe Center for American History, University of Texas at Austin
    Vietnamese Oral History Project
Cleveland, Mississippi
  Delta State University Special Collections
    Chinese Oral Histories
Jackson, Mississippi
  Mississippi Department of Archives and History
    Loewen (James W.) Collection
      G. P. Rice et al. vs. Gong Lum and Martha Lum, 1924, case 24773, series 6, box 16951
Little Rock, Arkansas
  Arkansas Studies Institute
    Miscellaneous Files on Japanese Internment
    War Relocation Authority Personal Narratives
Montgomery, Alabama
  Southern Poverty Law Center
    Vietnamese Fishermen's Association v. The Knights of the Ku Klux Klan case files
Morrow, Georgia
  Georgia Archives
    State of Georgia v. Fortunatio Annunciatio, Fulton County Superior Court, Case Number 37315, Supreme Court Criminal Appeal Case Files, 1917–1990, Record Group 92/1/3
    Georgia Central Register of Convicts, 1913–1952, A–G, 4, and P–Z, 18

Princeton, New Jersey
　　Seeley G. Mudd Manuscript Library, Princeton University
　　　　American Civil Liberties Union Records, Carliner Records (box 1106)
Richmond, Virginia
　　Portsmouth Circuit Court
　　　　Han Say Naim v. Ruby Elaine Naim, Record Number 4386 case files
　　Virginia State Law Library
　　　　Brief of the Commonwealth of Virginia (Naim Case)

PERIODICALS

Afro-American	Ocala Banner
Atlanta Constitution	Ocala Evening Star
Augusta Chronicle	Opelousas Star-Progress
Coschocton Tribune	Pensacola Journal
Donaldson Chief	Punta Gorda Hardware
Gainesville Daily	Rice Belt Journal
Gainesville Twice-a-Week	Rohwer Outpost
Geneva Daily Times	Saint Landry Clarion
Houston Post	Saint Tammany Farmer
Jacksonville Star	Shreveport Caucasian
Madison New Enterprise	Tampa Tribune
McGehee Times	Thomasville Times Enterprise
New York Times	

PUBLISHED PRIMARY SOURCES

Biennial Report of the Attorney General. Anti-Jap Law. Little Rock, Ark., 1944. Chap. 3, "Aliens, S."

Clayton, Powell. The Aftermath of the Civil War in Arkansas. New York: Neale Publishing Company, 1915.

Laws of Florida. General Index to House Bills and Joint Resolutions. 1926.

Official Journal of the Proceedings of the Constitutional Convention of the State of Louisiana. Baton Rouge: Ramires-Jones Printing Company, 1922.

SECONDARY SOURCES

Ancheta, Angelo N. Race, Rights, and the Asian American Experience. New Brunswick: Rutgers University Press, 1998.

Anderson, William G. "Early Reaction in Arkansas to the Relocation of Japanese in the State." Arkansas Historical Quarterly 23 (Autumn 1964): 196–211.

Azuma, Eiichiro. Between Two Empires: Race, History, and Transnationalism in Japanese America. New York: Oxford University Press, 2007.

Baldoz, Rick. The Third Asiatic Invasion: Migration and Empire in Filipino America, 1898–1946. New York: NYU Press, 2011.

Beatty, Bess. "The Loo Chong Case in Waynesboro: A Case of Sinophobia in Georgia." *Georgia Historical Quarterly* 67 (1983): 35–48.

Bell, Derrick A. "*Brown v. Board of Education* and the Interest-Convergence Dilemma." *Harvard Law Review* 93 (1980): 518–33.

Bhatka, Govind. *Patels: A Gujarati Community History in the United States*. Los Angeles: UCLA Asian American Studies Center, 2000.

Borstelmann, Thomas. *The 1970s: A New Global History from Civil Rights to Economic Inequality*. Princeton: Princeton University Press, 2013.

Botham, Fay. *Almighty God Created the Races: Christianity, Interracial Marriage, and American Law*. Chapel Hill: University of North Carolina Press, 2009.

Bow, Leslie. *Partly Colored: Asian Americans and Racial Anomaly in the Segregated South*. New York: NYU Press, 2011.

Brattain, Michelle. "Miscegenation and Competing Definitions of Race in Twentieth-Century Louisiana." *Journal of Southern History* 71 (2005): 558–621.

Bronstein, Daniel. "Segregation, Exclusion, and the Chinese Communities in Georgia, 1850–1940." In *Asian Americans in Dixie: Race and Migration in the South*, edited by Khyati Y. Joshi and Jigna Desai, 107–30. Champaign: University of Illinois Press, 2013.

Brooks, Charlotte. *Alien Neighbors, Foreign Friends: Asian Americans, Housing, and the Transformation of Urban California*. Chicago: University of Chicago Press, 2009.

———. *Between Mao and McCarthy: Chinese American Politics in the Cold War Years*. Chicago: University of Chicago Press, 2015.

Brundage, W. Fitzhugh. *Lynching in the New South: Georgia and Virginia, 1890–1930*. Champaign: University of Illinois Press, 1993.

Burnett, Christian Duffy, and Burk Marshall, eds. *Foreign in a Domestic Sense: Puerto Rico, American Expansion, and the Constitution*. Durham: Duke University Press, 2001.

Chan, Kit Mui L. "The Chinese-Americans in the Mississippi Delta." *Journal of Mississippi History* 35 (1973): 29–35.

Chan, Sucheng. *The Vietnamese American 1.5 Generation: Stories of War, Revolution, Fight, and New Beginnings*. Philadelphia: Temple University Press, 2006.

Chan, Sucheng, and Madeline Y. Hsu. *Chinese Americans and the Politics of Race and Culture*. Philadelphia: Temple University Press, 2008.

Cheng, Cindy I-Fen. *Citizens of Asian America: Democracy and Race during the Cold War*. New York: NYU Press, 2013.

Chin, Gabriele, Cindy Hwang Chiang, and Shirley S. Park. "The Lost *Brown v. Board of Education* and Immigration Law." *North Carolina Law Review* 91 (2013): 1657–98.

Churchill, Malcolm. "Louisiana History and Early Filipino Settlement: Searching for the Story." *Bulletin of the American Historical Collection* 27 (1999): 25–32.

Cohen, Lucy M. *Chinese in the Post–Civil War South: A People without a History*. Baton Rouge: Louisiana State University Press, 1999.

Cowie, Jefferson R. *Capital Moves: RCA's Seventy-Year Quest for Cheap Labor*. New York: New Press, 2001.

———. *Stayin' Alive: The 1970s and the Last Days of the Working Class*. New York: New Press, 2011.

Daniels, Roger. *History of Indian Immigration to the United States: An Interpretive History*. New York: Asia Society, 1989.

———. *The Politics of Prejudice: The Anti-Japanese Movement in California and Struggle for Japanese Exclusion*. Berkeley: University of California Press, 1999.

Dees, Morris. *A Lawyer's Journey: The Morris Dees Story*. Chicago: American Bar Association, 2001.

Delgado, Richard. "*Naim v. Naim*." *Nevada Law Review* 12 (2012): 526–31.

Dhingra, Pawan. *Life behind the Lobby: Indian American Motel Owners and the American Dream*. Palo Alto: Stanford University Press, 2012.

Dorr, Gregory Michael. "Principled Expediency: Eugenics, *Naim v. Naim*, and the Supreme Court." *American Journal of Legal History* 42 (1998): 119–59.

Dorr, Lisa Lindquist. *White Women, Rape, and the Power of Race in Virginia, 1900–1960*. Chapel Hill: University of North Carolina Press, 2004.

Egerton, Douglas R. *The Wars of Reconstruction: The Brief, Violent History of America's Most Progressive Era*. New York: Bloomsbury Press, 2014.

Espana-Maram, Linda. *Creating Masculinity in Los Angeles's Little Manila: Working-Class Filipinos and Popular Culture, 1920s–1950s*. New York: Columbia University Press, 2006.

Espiritu, Yen Le. *Asian American Panethnicity: Bridging Institutions and Identities*. Philadelphia: Temple University Press, 1993.

Fujita-Rony, Dorothy. *American Workers, Colonial Power: Philippine Seattle and the West, 1919–1941*. Berkeley: University of California Press, 2002.

Ganschow, Thomas. *The Chinese in Augusta: A Historical Sketch*. Self-published, 1996.

Guglielmo, Thomas. *White on Arrival: Italians, Race, Color, and Power in Chicago, 1890–1945*. New York: Oxford University Press, 2003.

Helweg, Arthur, and Usha Helweg. *An Immigrant Success Story: East Indians in America*. Philadelphia: Temple University Press, 2001.

Hess, Gary. "The Forgotten Asian Americans: The East Indian Community in the United States." *Pacific Historical Review* 43 (1974): 576–96.

Higginbotham, Evelyn Brooks. *Righteous Discontent: The Women's Movement in the Baptist Black Church, 1880–1920*. Cambridge: Harvard University Press, 1994.

Horwitz, Morton J. *The Transformation of American Law, 1870–1960*. New York: Oxford University Press, 1992.

Howard, John. *Concentration Camps on the Home Front: Japanese Americans in the House of Jim Crow*. Chicago: University of Chicago Press, 2008.

Hsu, Madeline Y. *Dreaming of Gold, Dreaming of Home: Transnationalism and Migration between the United States and South China*. Palo Alto: Stanford University Press, 2000.

———. *The Good Immigrants: How the Yellow Peril Became the Model Minority*. Princeton: Princeton University Press, 2015.

Jacobson, Matthew Frye. *Whiteness of a Different Color: European Immigrants and the Alchemy of Race*. Cambridge: Harvard University Press, 1999.

Jain, Usha. *The Gujaratis of San Francisco*. New York: AMS Press, 1989.

Jakle, John A., Keith A. Sculle, and Jefferson R. Rogers. *The Motel in America*. Baltimore: Johns Hopkins University Press, 1996.

Joshi, Khyati Y., and Jigna Desai. "Discrepancies in Dixie." In *Asian Americans in Dixie: Race and Migration in the South*, edited by Khyati Y. Joshi and Jigna Desai, 1–11. Champaign: University of Illinois Press, 2013.

Jung, John. *Chopsticks in the Land of Cotton: Lives of Mississippi Delta Chinese Grocers*. New York: Yin and Yang Press, 2011.

Jung, Moon-Ho. *Coolies and Cane: Race, Labor, and Sugar in the Age of Emancipation*. Baltimore: Johns Hopkins University Press, 2008.

Ken, Sally. "The Chinese Community of Augusta, Georgia, from 1873–1971." *Richmond County History* 4 (1972): 51–60.

Kennedy, Randall. *Interracial Intimacies: Sex, Marriage, Identity, and Adoption*. New York: Vintage, 2004.

Kluger, Richard. *Simple Justice: The History of* Brown v. Board of Education *and the Struggle for Equality*. New York: Vintage, 2004.

Kramer, Paul. *The Blood of Government: Race, Empire, the United States, and the Philippines*. Durham: Duke University Press, 2006.

Kruse, Kevin. *One Nation under God: How Corporate America Invented Christian America*. New York: Basic Books, 2015.

Lai, Him Mark. "Lue Gim Gong: Wonder Grower." *East/West* (1973): 5–7.

Lal, Vinay. *The Other Indians: A Political and Cultural History of South Asians in America*. Los Angeles: UCLA Asian American Studies Center, 2008.

Lassiter, Matthew D. *The Silent Majority: Suburban Politics in the Sunbelt South*. Princeton: Princeton University Press, 2007.

Lee, Erika. *At America's Gates: Chinese Immigrants during the Exclusion Era, 1882–1943*. Chapel Hill: University of North Carolina Press, 2003.

Lichtenstein, Nelson. *The Retail Revolution: How Walmart Created a Brave New World of Business*. New York: Picador, 2010.

Loewen, James W. *The Mississippi Chinese: Between Black and White*. Long Grove, Ill.: Waveland Press, 1988.

Lowe, Lisa. *Immigrant Acts: On Asian American Cultural Politics*. Durham: Duke University Press, 1996.

Lui, Mary Ting Yi. *The Chinatown Trunk Mystery: Murder, Miscegenation, and Other Dangerous Encounters in Turn-of-the-Century New York City*. Princeton: Princeton University Press, 2005.

Ma, Sheng-mei. *The Deadly Embrace: Orientalism and Asian American Identity*. Minneapolis: University of Minnesota Press, 2000.

Mar, Lisa. *Brokering Belonging: Chinese in Canada's Exclusion Era, 1885–1945*. New York: Oxford University Press, 2010.

Matsuda, Mari J., Charles R. Lawrence III, Richard Delgado, and Kimberlè Williams Crenshaw. *Words That Wound: Critical Race Theory, Assaultive Speech, and the First Amendment*. New York: Westview Press, 1993.

Matsumoto, Valerie. "'What's Love Got to Do with It': The Politics of Rape and Marriage in the California Supreme Court's 1948 *Perez v. Sharp* Decision." *OAH Magazine of History* 18 (2004): 31–34.

McGuire, Danielle. *At the Dark End of the Street: Black Women, Rape, and Resistance—A New History of the Civil Rights Movement from Rosa Parks to the Rise of Black Power*. New York: Vintage, 2010.

Moon, Krystyn. *Yellowface: Creating the Chinese in American Popular Music and Culture*. New Brunswick: Rutgers University Press, 2004.

Moran, Rachel F. *Interracial Intimacy: The Regulation of Race and Romance*. Chicago: University of Chicago Press, 2003.

Morgan, Howard. *The Hotel Industry in the United States: Small Business in Transition*. Tucson: Bureau of Business and Public Research, University of Arizona, 1964.

Ngai, Mae M. *Impossible Subjects: Illegal Aliens and the Making of Modern America*. Princeton: Princeton University Press, 2006.

———. *The Lucky Ones: One Family and the Extraordinary Invention of Chinese America*. New York: Houghton Mifflin Harcourt, 2010.

O'Brien, Robert W. "Status of the Chinese in the Mississippi Delta." *Social Forces* 19 (1941): 386–90.

Odem, Mary E. *Delinquent Daughters: Protecting and Policing Adolescent Female Sexuality in the United States, 1885–1920*. Chapel Hill: University of North Carolina Press, 1995.

Omi, Michael, and Howard Winant. *Racial Formation in the United States: From the 1960s to the 1990s*. New York: Routledge, 1994.

Park, John S. W. *Elusive Citizenship: Immigration, Asian Americans, and the Paradox of Civil Rights*. New York: NYU Press, 2004.

Pascoe, Peggy. *What Comes Naturally: Miscegenation Law and the Making of Race in America*. New York: Oxford University Press, 2011.

Patterson, James T. *Brown v. Board of Education: A Civil Rights Milestone and Its Troubled Legacy*. New York: Oxford University Press, 2002.

Perlstein, Rick. *Nixonland: The Rise of a President and the Fracturing of America*. New York: Scribner, 2009.

Pfaelzer, Jean. *Driven Out: The Forgotten War against Chinese Americans*. Berkeley: University of California Press, 2007.

Poros, Maritsa. *Modern Migrations: Gujarati Indian Networks in New York and London*. Palo Alto: Stanford University Press, 2010.

Quan, Robert Seto. *Lotus among the Magnolias*. Jackson: University Press of Mississippi, 2007.

Raijman, Rebecca, and Marta Tienda. "Immigrants' Pathway to Business Ownership: A Comparative Ethnic Perspective." *International Migration Review* 34 (2000): 682–706.

Rangaswamy, Padma. *Namaste America: Indian Immigrants in an American Metropolis*. University Park: Pennsylvania State University Press, 2000.

Richardson, Heather Cox. *The Death of Reconstruction: Race, Labor, and Politics in the Post–Civil War North*. Cambridge: Harvard University Press, 2004.

Sahay, Anjali. "Indian Diaspora in the United States and Brain Gain: Remittances, Return, and Network Approaches." In *Sociology of Diaspora: A Reader*, edited by Ajaya Kumar Sahoo and Brij Maharah, 940–79. New Delhi, India: Rawat Publications, 2007.

Salyer, Lucy E. *Laws Harsh as Tigers: Chinese Immigrants and the Shaping of Modern Immigration Law*. Chapel Hill: University of North Carolina Press, 1995.

Sánchez, Sieglinde Lim de. "Crafting a Delta Chinese Community: Education and Acculturation in Twentieth-Century Southern Baptist Missionary Schools." *History of Education Quarterly* 43 (2003): 74–90.

Sanders, Jimmy, and Victor Nee. "Immigrant Self-Employment: The Family as Social Capital and the Value of Human Capital." *American Sociological Review* 61 (1996): 231–49.

Sandmeyer, Elmer. *The Anti-Chinese Movement in America*. Champaign: University of Illinois Press, 1991.

Shepherd, Tev. *The Chinese of Greenville, Mississippi*. Self-published, 1999.
Sheth, Pravin. *Indians in America: One Stream, Two Waves, Three Generations*. Jaipur, India: Rawat Publications, 2001.
Smith, Calvin C. "The Response of Arkansas to Prisoners of War and Japanese Americans in Arkansas, 1942–1945." *Arkansas Historical Quarterly* 53 (1994): 340–64.
Sohoni, Deenesh. "Unsuitable Suitors: Anti-Miscegenation Laws, Naturalization Laws, and the Construction of Asian Identities." *Law and Society Review* 41 (2007): 586–618.
Sokol, Jason. *There Goes My Everything: White Southerners in the Age of Civil Rights, 1945–1975*. New York: Vintage, 2007.
Steerflek, Hein. "Gujarati Entrepreneurship: Historical Continuity against Changing Perspectives." *Economic and Political Weekly* 32 (1997): M2–M10.
Takaki, Ronald. *Strangers from a Different Shore: A History of Asian Americans*. New York: Little, Brown, 1998.
Tang, Irwin A. *Asian Texans: Our Histories and Our Lives*. New York: It Works Publishing, 2008.
Thandi, Shinder. "Migrating to Mother Country: South Asian Settlement and the Post-War Boom, 1947–1980." In *A South Asian History of Britain: Four Centuries of Peoples from the Indian Sub-Continent*, edited by Michael H. Fisher, Shompa Lahiri, and Shinder Thandi, 32–56. Westport, Conn.: Greenwood Press, 2007.
Varzally, Allison. *Making a Non-White America: Californians Coloring outside Ethnic Lines, 1925–1955*. Berkeley: University of California Press, 2008.
Vu, Roy. "Natives of a Ghost Country: The Vietnamese in Houston and Their Construction of a Postwar Community." In *Asian Americans in Dixie: Race and Migration in the South*, edited by Khyati Y. Joshi and Jigna Desai, 165–89. Champaign: University of Illinois Press, 2013.
Tsai, Shih-shan Henry. "Chinese in Arkansas." *Amerasia Journal* 8 (1981): 1–18.
Wallenstein, Peter. *Tell the Court I Love My Wife: Race, Marriage, and Law—An American History*. New York: St. Martin's Griffin, 2004.
Weems, Robert E. *Business in Black and White: American Presidents and Black Entrepreneurs in the Twentieth Century*. New York: NYU Press, 2009.
———. *Desegregating the Dollar: African American Consumerism in the Twentieth Century*. New York: NYU Press, 1998.
Weise, Julie M. *Corazón de Dixie: Mexicanos in the U.S. South since 1910*. Chapel Hill: University of North Carolina Press, 2015.
Winter, Robert M. "Rosedale Presbyterians and the Mississippi Chinese: Changing Concepts of Equality in an Aristocratic Southern Town." *Journal of Presbyterian History* 78 (2000): 32–47.
Wolcott, Victoria M. *Remaking Respectability: African American Women in Interwar Detroit*. Chapel Hill: University of North Carolina Press, 2001.
Wong, K. Scott. *Americans First: Chinese Americans and the Second World War*. Cambridge: Harvard University Press, 2005.
Wu, Ellen. *The Color of Success: Asian Americans and the Origins of the Model Minority*. Princeton: Princeton University Press, 2013.
Zia, Helen. *Asian American Dreams: The Emergence of an American People*. New York: Farrar, Straus and Giroux, 2001.

INDEX

Adamo, Samuel, 181–83
Adkins, Homer, 63–64, 100
African Americans: and the civil rights movement, 1–3, 21, 26, 150, 179, 234, 235; relations of with Chinese Americans in Mississippi, 1–3, 83, 85, 101; shared discriminatory experiences of with Asian Americans, 3; and Reconstruction, 9–10; replacement of with Chinese labor, 11–12, 19; tensions of with Asian Americans, 21, 23; and citizenship, 29, 77, 116; compared to Japanese Americans, 38, 40, 51, 68; and school segregation, 75, 81–82, 90, 152; relations of with Chinese Americans in Georgia, 104, 111; deprivation of legal rights of, 117; and interracial relations, 123–24; compared to Filipinos, 125, 129; and World War II, 155; relations of with Asian Americans post–World War II, 156; and the Ku Klux Klan, 186; relations of with Indian Americans, 203. *See also* Hoteliers
Alamo Bay, 159
Alcorn, William, Jr., 86, 89–91
Alexander, Robert, 169
Allen, E. M., 60
Almond, J. Lindsey, Jr., 144
Ambia, Subia "Amby," 114; arrival in Atlanta, 118–20; relations with Frances Hutcheson and Rosa Mae Clower, 122, 125–27; attempt at retrial, 127; sentencing of, 128
American Civil Liberties Union, 144. *See also* Carliner, David
American Fishermen's Association (AFA), 181
American Hotel and Lodging Association, 211, 215, 221, 223, 225–26
American Legion, 31–32, 42
American-owned-and-operated campaign, 205–6, 208–11, 215–16, 219, 221, 224–27, 231
Angell Treaty, 144
Annunciatio, Fortunatio, 24, 114–15; rights as a colonial subject, 116, 129, 131–33, 137; arrival in Georgia, 118–19; interactions with Rosa Mae Clower and Frances Hutcheson, 121–22, 126; sentencing of, 128, 137; illegal search and seizure of, 131–33; and Han Say Naim, 141, 154–55, 234. *See also State of Georgia v. Fortunatio Annunciatio*
Anti-alien land laws: Supreme Court rulings on, 6, 69, 145; in Arkansas, 20; "aliens ineligible for citizenship," 23, 28, 41, 45, 47–48, 53–55, 57, 65–66, 232–33; in the South, 23, 29, 42, 113, 188, 213, 234; and Japanese, 28; in California, 42, 45, 81; in Louisiana, 43; and Louisiana constitution, 47–49; in Florida, 51–53;

and Florida constitution, 53–55;
in multiple states, 54; in Texas, 56, 58;
in Arkansas, 59–62, 65–67.
See also Incarceration of Japanese
Americans
Aplin, Billy, 168, 181
Aplin, Rudy, 168–69
Applegate, W. H., 60, 61, 68
Applegate v. Luke, 60–62
Arkansas: Chinese laborers in, 4, 11, 13,
15–16, 19, 22; Civil War in, 13; cotton in,
13; and need for agricultural labor, 13;
Reconstruction in, 13; immigrants in,
13–14; rights for laborers and immigrants
in, 15; and Japanese Americans, 45;
property rights in constitution of, 54,
59; Arkansas Supreme Court, 60–62;
in World War II, 62–63; and school
segregation, 79, 97; General Act 249,
59. *See also* Anti-alien land laws; Lum
Jung Luke; Incarceration of Japanese
Americans
Arkansas Valley Immigration Company, 15
Arnold, Dr. W. A., 130
Asian American Hotel Owners Association
(AAHOA), 25, 196, 233; and the Indo-
American Hospitality Association,
217; formation of, 217–19; as a civil
rights organization, 219–21, 230–31;
and the American Hotel and Lodging
Association, 221; relationship with Days
Inn, 222; early strategies of, 223–24;
activism of, 226–29; and the South, 229.
See also American-owned-and-operated
campaign
Asiatic Exclusion League, 31
Association of Immigration and
Nationality Lawyers, 149
Association on American Indian
Affairs, 149
Atlanta, Ga., 3, 24–26, 129; Chinese
Americans in, 105, 108; Filipinos in,
119–20, 124–25, 135–37; and yo-yo
craze, 119–20; growing Asian American
population of, 157; and AAHOA,
196, 214–16, 218, 220–23, 226; and the
New South, 197. *See also State of
Georgia v. Fortunatio Annunciatio*
Augusta, Ga.: Chinese Americans in, 4,
102–6; school segregation in, 23, 103, 105,
107–10; National Chinese Benevolent
Association chapter of, 106; First Baptist
Church Chinese school in, 105; and
Richmond County School District, 110;
relations between African Americans
and Chinese Americans in, 110–11

Barnett, Evelyn, 126, 133
Bass, E. E., 83, 97
Baton Rouge, La., 34, 44, 46
Beam, Louis, 159, 173–75, 177–79, 180–84,
187, 189–93
Berg, David, 190
Bilbo, Theodore, 100, 112
Birmingham, Ala., 13, 199
Black Codes, 9
Boca Raton, Fla., 35–36, 53
Boiling v. Sharpe, 145
Bolivar County, Miss., 71, 85–87, 89–90
*Bond, State Superintendent of Education v.
Tij Fung*, 72, 94–96
Boston, Mass., 213–14
Boykin, John, 127
Brewer, Brewer, and McGeeHee, 86
Brewer, Earl, 91
Brown v. Board of Education: and Chinese
Americans, 2, 23, 71–72, 81, 90–92, 97;
and school segregation in the South, 73,
112–13; and *Naim* case, 147, 149–53.
See also *Lum v. Rice*
Buchannan, Archibald, 145
Buffalo, Tenn., 201
Burke, Walter, 47
Burlingame Treaty, 15, 87, 94–97
Buy-American campaign, 203, 205

California: Chinese in, 10, 17–18, 57, 89,
145; and the "Chinese Problem," 17;
Japanese in, 28, 30–32, 37–38, 44, 73,
106; anti-alien land laws in, 41–42, 45,

48–49, 52, 59, 61, 66, 69, 80; Filipinos in, 120; Vietnamese refugees in, 161–62, 185; Indian Americans in, 195, 200–201
Camp Pendleton (Calif.), 161
Camp Puller (Tex.), 192
Canada, 32
Candler, Asa G., Jr., 125
Carliner, David, 116, 141–49, 153
Carter, James, 161
Casterline, Leslie "Lee," 165, 171–72, 187
Catholic Church, 161, 163, 185
Cendant Corporation, 228
Chapel Hill, N.C., 197
Chappius, William, 46
Chick-fil-A, 198
Chin, Vincent, 203–4
China: treaties with United States, 24, 71–72, 87, 94, 95, 96, 141, 144, 146; and World War II, 66, 68, 98, 100–101, 109, 148; and Cold War, 157
Chinese Americans: in Georgia, 4, 23, 72, 102–4, 106–8, 110; in Mississippi, 4, 82, 83, 84–85, 89, 98, 102; in the South, 5, 20, 23, 29, 97, 148; as laborers in Arkansas, 8, 20, 22; on the West Coast, 17; and antimiscegenation laws, 20, 105; and school segregation, 23, 71, 72, 81–82, 84, 89–91, 95, 103, 106–8, 110, 112; in Texas, 57–58; in Arkansas, 60, 66; treatment of compared with Japanese Americans, 68, 100, 112; and "Chineseness" and ethnic identity, 71, 77, 87, 92, 99, 101, 102, 103, 107–9, 111, 113; in Kentucky, 76. See also *Bond, State Superintendent of Education v. Tij Fung*; *Lum v. Rice*; *Naim v. Naim*; Pong Dock
Chinese Exclusion Act, 18, 27, 38, 66, 77, 80–81, 87, 96, 104, 106, 144, 155
Chinese Labor Convention, 13
Chinese mission schools, 97
"Chinese problem," 17
Chinese sailors. See Naim, Han Say
Chong, William Loo, 104–5
Christianity, 27
Cincinnati, Ohio, 76

Citizenship: and Asian Americans, 6, 7, 21, 23, 26, 29, 55; and the Fourteenth Amendment, 9, 144, 150–51, 154; and African Americans, 11, 112, 116; and Chinese Americans, 16–17, 71, 77–79, 86, 88, 92, 95–97, 112–13, 140–43, 146, 152–53; and Japanese Americans, 34, 39–40, 65; and Filipinos, 118, 129, 138. See also Anti-alien land laws
Civil Rights Act of 1964, 1, 209, 212, 215, 218, 229
Civil War, 1, 8, 10–11, 13, 15, 19, 21, 23, 30, 33, 38, 40, 59, 68, 103, 116, 158, 180, 196
Clark, Frank, 51–54
Clark, William, 35
Clarksdale Baptist Church (Miss.), 99
Clayton, Powell, 13–16
Clearwater Creek, Tex., 182
Clements, Bill, 166, 172, 177
Cleveland, Miss., 1, 100, 102, 156
Cleveland, Ohio, 197
Clower, Rosa Mae, 114, 117, 120–23, 126–32, 136–38
Coahoma County, Miss., 94, 96
Coast Guard, 165–68, 172
Coble, Howard, 227
Collins, David, 178–79
Collins, Joe, 173, 178–79
Colonialism. See Filipino Americans
Comfort Inn, 198, 209
Congress of Racial Equality, 20
Contracts. See *Vietnamese Fishermen's Association v. Knights of the Ku Klux Klan*
Convergent interests, 234–35
Coolies, 10–11, 17
Corpus Christi, Tex., 57–58
Cotton, 9, 11, 12, 13, 15–16, 33–34, 45–46, 59, 63–65
Coudert, Frederic R., 129
Covert, Carl, 166
Covington, Ky., 75–76
"Crab feud," 168
Cracraft, Brewer, 60
Crisp, Charles R., 136
Crowley, La., 43

Cruz, Jose, 125
Cumming v. Richmond County Board of Education, 92
"Curry palaces," 203, 205–6, 208, 216, 225

Dade County, Fla., 36
Dallas, Tex., 57, 169, 179, 197
Daniels, Paul W., 34
Day Law, 75
Days Inn, 196, 198, 208–9, 213–25 passim
Dean, Gregory, 166, 172
Dees, Morris, 179–81, 187–92
Deindustrialization, 197–99
DeLand, Fla., 27
Democratic Party: in Arkansas, 9–10, 14; and Chinese, 15, 17–18; and Japanese, 31, 41, 47, 51–52
Desai, Kanjibhai, 200
Desha County, Ark., 64
Detroit, Mich., 197, 203
Discrimination: and Asian Americans, 3, 5–7, 20–26, 28–29, 32, 58, 71, 106, 113, 144, 196; legal, 67–69, 116, 118, 134, 138, 149, 153–55, 157, 235; in education, 73, 87, 97; and African Americans, 101; social, 102, 106, 179; difference of from prejudice, 197, 206, 209, 212, 219, 230, 231, 234; entrepreneurial, 202, 204, 207, 210–11, 215–16, 218, 230. *See also* Filipino Americans; Indian Americans; Vietnamese Americans
Double V Campaign, 101
Doyle, Paul, 177
Dublin, Miss., 72, 93–96
DuPont Manual Training High School (Lexington, Ky.), 70, 74–75
Durham, N.C., 197
Durton, Harold, 152
Duschoff, Lee, 214–17, 219–22, 224–25, 230
Dykes, Jonathan, 45–49

Education. *See* School segregation
Eglin Air Force Base (Fla.), 161
Elaine, Ark., 59–60, 93
El Camp, Tex., 164

Elizabeth City, N.C., 139
El Paso, Tex., 57
Ethnicity. *See* Identity
European immigrants, 13–14, 17, 47, 80

Fair Housing Act of 1968, 202
Farm Security Administration, 62
Filipino Americans, 3–5, 8, 19; and miscegenation, 20, 24, 106, 123; and school segregation, 23, 70, 72–76, 78; and colonialism, 74, 117–18, 120, 124, 125, 129, 133–35, 13; "little brown brothers," 117; white perceptions of sexuality of, 136; and World War II, 155. *See also* Annunciatio, Fortunatio
First District School (Covington, Ky.), 76
Fisher, Gene, 173, 175, 178, 181
Flagler, Henry, 35–36
Flores, Pedro, 119
Florida: and Japanese Americans, 4, 22–23, 32, 35–39, 64, 229; convict labor in, 9; and Chinese Americans, 27; anti-alien land amendment, 28–29, 42, 49–55, 58, 69, 232–33; and school segregation, 74, 79; and Filipinos, 120–21; and Vietnamese refugees, 161
Florida East Coast Rail Road, 35–37
Florida Southern Settlement and Development Organization, 52
Forbes, Walter, 228
Ford, Gerald, 161, 175
Fort Chaffee (Ark.), 161
Fort Indiantown Gap (Pa.), 161
Fort Meyers, Fla., 51
Fourteenth Amendment of the U.S. Constitution, 6, 11, 15, 24, 29, 42, 48, 61–62, 77, 86–87, 89, 91–93, 95–97, 116–17, 129, 133, 144–46, 150, 178–80, 186
Fourth Amendment of the U.S. Constitution, 132
Franchises: hotel, 196, 198–99; and discrimination, 208–9, 213. *See also* Indian Americans; Small Business Franchise Bill
Frank, Leo, 125, 136

Freeman, Miller, 41
Frix, Gladys, 125
Fulcher, Denise, 104
Fulton County, Ga., 116–18, 120, 128, 134, 137–38
Fung, Joe Tij, 72, 94–96

Galveston Bay, Tex.: and Vietnamese refugees, 25, 159, 162–63, 179, 194; and fishing industry, 25, 188, 194; and Ku Klux Klan, 158, 172, 180, 183, 190, 193; Bruce Springsteen song about, 160. *See also* Vietnamese Americans
Garner, Charles, 38, 50
Garnett, James, 77
Gary, Ind., 197
Gentlemen's Agreement, 32, 40, 73, 96
Georgia: and convict labor, 9; Chinese Americans in, 23, 72, 102–4, 106, 109; and school segregation, 105, 107–8, 110, 113; and miscegenation law, 105–6, 123–24; relations between African Americans and Chinese Americans in, 111; and Filipino Americans, 114, 117–18, 120, 125; and punishment for rape, 124–25, 137, 128; and the New South, 195; and Indian Americans, 206. *See also* Annunciatio, Fortunatio; Filipino Americans
Georgia State Penitentiary, 115, 128, 137
Global South, 197–98
Gong Lum, Jeu, 2, 20, 26, 71–72, 81, 84–94, 97, 99–103, 108, 111–12, 229, 233
Great Depression, 114
Greensboro, S.C., 139
Greenville, Miss., 83, 97–102
Greenville, S.C., 201
Grenada, Miss., 1–2
Gujarat, India, 200, 208, 224
Gulf of Mexico: Vietnamese refugees in, 24, 162–63; and rice industry, 33–34

Hamlett, Barksdale, 77
Han Say Naim v. Ruby Elaine Naim, 24, 115, 139, 142–43. *See also* Naim, Han Say; *Naim v. Naim*

Harrison, Benjamin, 18
Highland Park, Mich., 203
Hirabayashi v. United States, 6
Holiday Inn, 208, 213
Hoteliers: impact of World War II on, 198–99; African American, 199; "accidental," 201–2, 204. *See also* American-owned-and-operated campaign; Indian Americans
Houston, Tex.: and Chinese Americans, 12, 57; and Vietnamese Americans, 25, 158–59, 163–69, 168, 177, 185; and Japanese Americans, 33–34; and Ku Klux Klan, 173; Federal District Court of, 178, 194
Huets, Henry, 188
Hutcheson, Frances, 114, 120–22, 126–31, 133
Hutchins, Ala., 60
Hyundai, 203

Identity (and Asian Americans): otherness, 4, 7, 29, 72, 76, 101, 204, 208, 235; Oriental, 4, 20–22, 24, 70–71, 73–76, 80, 83–84, 86, 101, 106, 110; yellow, 5, 8, 20, 22, 37, 43, 70, 93, 124, 155; interstitial, 5, 19, 25, 26, 49, 70, 93, 118, 167; colored, 5–6, 22–23, 51, 74, 75–76, 78–79, 81–86, 90–93, 94–98, 108, 110–11, 115–16, 124; noncolored, 6, 21, 71–72, 79, 85–86, 88–89, 91, 99–102, 106–7, 109, 111; Malay, 24, 70, 123–24, 141; "brown," 52, 75, 79, 124; Mongolian, 75–80, 88, 93, 98, 102, 104–6, 123
Illegal search and seizure. *See* Annunciatio, Fortunatio
Immigration Act of 1917, 80
Immigration and Nationality Act of 1952, 142, 155
Immigration and Nationality Act of 1965, 22, 24, 156, 157, 160–61, 167, 200
Imperialism. *See* Filipino Americans
Incarceration of Japanese Americans, 6, 62–68
Indian Americans: activism of, 5, 6, 202, 203, 211–12, 218–20, 229, 231; perceptions

of, 8, 204, 206, 214–15; and de facto discrimination, 20, 201, 219–20, 222, 230; as hoteliers, 25, 201; and World War II, 155; post-1965 migration of, 157, 200; and property insurance discrimination, 196, 207, 211, 219, 222, 230; and the New South, 197, 202, 210; and model minority, 204–5, 212; and Patel monopoly, 208; and discrimination in franchising, 209, 214, 219, 222, 230. *See also* American-owned-and-operated campaign; Asian American Hotel Owners Association
Indian independence (from Britain), 200
Indo-American Hospitality Association, 25, 216, 217, 222
Interracial relations: interracial activism, 21, 196, 220; sexual 23–24, 79, 101–2, 104, 106, 115–16, 123–25, 129, 139–42, 148–52, 160. *See also* Miscegenation laws; *Naim v. Naim*
Interstate highways, 195–98
Inumara, Tetsutaro, 34

Jacksonville, Fla., 35, 38, 50–52, 55, 79, 121
Jackson v. State, 140
Japanese American Citizens League, 149
Japanese Americans: in the South, 3, 33, 40, 44, 58, 106, 157, 204, 211, 233; perceptions of, 4, 8, 25, 29, 31, 37; activism of, 5, 211; on the West Coast, 24, 30, 42–43; in Florida, 35–39, 55; in Louisiana, 45–49, 59; and school segregation, 72–73, 79, 112; and Chinese Americans, 100; and World War II, 155. *See also* Anti-alien land laws; Incarceration of Japanese Americans; Yamato Colony, Fla.; Yellow peril
Jennings, William Sherman, 50
Jerome, Ark., 64–67, 100
Jewish Anti-Defamation League, 147
Jim Crow, 4–7, 19–24, 29, 49, 51, 70, 72–73, 75, 77, 80, 85, 87, 91, 93–94, 97, 102, 199; school segregation, 105–11, 114–18; miscegenation, 134, 138, 140, 149, 150, 153–55
Jones, Terry, 169
Junior Mechanics League of America, 110

Kellam, Floyd, 139, 142–43
Kemah, Tex., 159, 163, 173, 178–79, 185, 187–88, 190, 192–93
King, Martin Luther, Jr., 199
Kito, H., 35
Knapp, Seamann A., 33
Knights of Labor, 17
Knox, Rush, 90
Korean Americans, 26, 148–49, 220
Korematsu v. United States, 6
Korokan, 50–51
Ku Klux Klan, 8, 25, 104, 158–59, 172–73, 177–79, 183, 191–93

Labor: and Asian Americans, 7–8; in the post–Civil War South, 9–10; and Japanese Americans, 30–32, 34, 38–39, 43–44, 50, 52–53, 58, 63–64, 68; and Filipinos, 118, 120; and post-1965 immigrants, 156; and Vietnamese Americans, 162, 167, 169, 175, 186; and deindustrialization, 197; and Indian Americans, 200, 203. *See also* Chinese Americans
Lamberth, Ruby Elaine (Naim), 42, 152–53. *See also Han Say Naim v. Ruby Elaine Naim*
Land Ordinance Act of 1785, 95
Leasing land. *See* Anti-alien land laws
LeBlanc, Lou, 171
Legislative activism. *See* Indian Americans
L'Engle, Claude, 52
Leon County, Fla., 53
Leven, Michael, 212–17, 219–22, 224, 230–31
Levy, Herb Monte, 144, 146–49
"Little brown brothers": origins of term, 75, 117, 118, 249n5; in the South, 134
"Long civil rights movement," 3–4, 20–21, 23
Louise, Miss., 98, 100
Louisiana: Asian Americans in, 4, 22, 29; Chinese Americans in, 11–12, 14–17, 19, 28, 57; Japanese Americans in, 23, 33–35, 40, 43–44, 64, 229; Vietnamese Americans in, 25, 159, 162, 169, 175, 178; alien land laws of, 42, 44–46, 59;

278 *Index*

constitutional convention of, 46, 48;
constitutional amendment of, 47–49,
53–54, 58; school segregation in, 79
Louisville, Ky., 70, 74–76, 78–79
Loving v. Virginia, 140
Luce-Celler Act, 199
Lue Gim Gong, 27–28, 35, 68
Lum, Berda, 2, 71, 82, 84–85
Lum, Martha, 71, 82, 84–87, 89–97, 101.
See also *Lum v. Rice*
Lum Jung Luke, 20, 58–62, 180, 233–34
Lum v. Rice, 71, 86–93, 95
Lun, Joe Tin, 72, 93–97, 111–12

Mackenzie, Timothy, 53
Macon, Ga.: Chinese Americans in, 4, 40, 109
Madison County, Fla., 37–38
Malays. See Identity
Manchuria, 98, 109
Matagorda Bay, Tex., 163, 168
McDonald, Gabrielle Kirk, 178, 183, 186–87, 189–93
McLaurin v. Oklahoma, 2
Meiji Dynasty, 30
Memphis Convention, 11, 13
Messer, Henry, 107
Metropole. See Filipino Americans
Mexican Americans, 7, 112–13, 139
Miami, Fla., 35, 53, 55
Michigan, 138, 161, 163, 203, 227
Microtel, 213
Mid-South Indemnity Association, 25, 211, 216
Minnesota, 41–42, 161
Miscegenation laws: and Chinese Americans, 20, 79, 91, 101, 138, 150; and Asian Americans, 23–24, 80, 116, 117, 123, 140–41, 154, 212; and Filipino Americans, 20, 118, 124–25; in Mississippi, 91, 147; in Georgia, 102, 105–8, 124, 110; in Virginia, 115, 139, 142–43; in North Carolina, 139; in Alabama, 140. See also *Naim v. Naim*
Mississippi: African Americans in, 1; Chinese Americans in, 2–5, 20, 58–59, 81–83, 85–86, 99, 111, 120; Chinese laborers in, 11, 15, 18–19, 28; school segregation in, 20, 23, 72, 79, 81–84, 87–90, 92–93, 100, 102, 107, 110, 156; Vietnamese Americans in, 25, 159, 162; Japanese Americans in, 33, 45; Chinese schools in, 97–99; miscegenation law of, 103, 147–48; Mexican Americans in, 112–13
Mississippi Delta, 1, 12, 15, 58, 62, 71, 81, 103–4, 110
Model Land Company, 35–36
Model minority. See Identity
Moon, L. W., 139
Moore, Amzie, 1–3, 5, 26
Moore, Virlyn B., Sr., 128, 131, 134, 136–37
Mortgage purchase agreements, 201–2

Naim, Han Say, 115, 138–39. See also *Naim v. Naim*
Naim v. Naim, 116, 142–54 passim, 233
Nashville, Tenn., 201, 206–7, 210–11, 224
Nasternak, Thé Nguyen, 163–64
Natchez, Miss., 44
National Association for the Advancement of Colored People, 20, 149
National Chinese Benevolent Association, 106
Native Americans, 7, 20, 75, 181, 217
Nativism, 22, 193, 203. See also Xenophobia
Naturalization Act of 1906, 28, 93
Nebraska, 41–42, 79
Negro Motorist Green Book, 199
New Orleans, La.: Filipino Americans in, 3, 119; Chinese Americans in, 12–13, 72, 103; Italians in, 34; Japanese Americans in, 49, 79
New South: Chinese labor in, 11; Japanese Americans in, 32, 40; post World War II, 196–97, 202
Nguyen, Chinh Van L., 168
Nguyen, Hai Trong, 163
Nguyen, Luu, 183–84
Nguyen, Nam "Colonel Nam" Van, 175, 182–84
Nguyen, Nghai Van, 164

Nguyen, Sau Van, 168
Nguyen, Tuyen, 169–70
Nissan, 203
Nixon, Richard, 164, 175
Norfolk, Va., 115, 138, 142
Norrell, William F., 63
North Carolina, 24, 115, 123, 139, 143, 195, 197, 202, 215–16, 227

Oikee, Chozo, 39
Orderly Departure Program, 161
Ordinance 245 (La.), 46
Oregon, 28, 41–42, 63, 106
Orientalism, 119, 124, 204, 207, 235
Orlando, Fla., 53
Orr, Kim, 12
Oyama v. State of California, 6
Ozawa v. United States, 93

Pace v. Alabama, 139
Palacios, Tex., 162–63
Palm Beach, Fla., 53
Panethnicity, 4, 20, 21, 221
Parker, John, 46
Patel, Asvlin, 223
Patel, Mike, 226–27
Patel, Ravi, 216–17, 220–21, 223–25, 230
Patel, Shankur "Big Sam," 211
Patel, Vilpesh, 201
Patel hotels. *See* Indian Americans
Pattni, Harish, 195, 201
Pattni, Harry, 202–3
Payne, Neal, 192
Pennsylvania, 13, 161–62
Pensionados, 73–73. *See also* Filipino Americans
Perez v. Sharp, 139
Phagan, Mary, 125
Pham, Huong Thi, 172
Pham, Phuong, 183–84
Philippines, 73–74, 117, 119, 131–36, 161
Phillips County, Ark., 60–61
Poll tax, 88, 95
Pong Dock, 76–81; African American reaction to, 79

Porterfield v. Webb, 61
Port Lavaca, Tex., 163, 169, 185
Portsmouth, Va., 115, 139–40, 142, 144–45, 151, 153
Post–civil rights, 22, 25, 186, 209–10, 220, 229–30
Pounds, George, 126–27, 130, 132
Presbyterian New Covenant, Tex., 177
Property. *See* Anti-alien land laws
Pulaski County, Ark., 15
Punta Gorda, Fla., 39

Quality Inn, 198

Rabkin, Sol, 147–49
Racial Integrity Act of 1924, 123, 139, 143–46, 149–53
Raggsdale, C. B., 65–66
Railroads. *See* Chinese Americans
Raleigh, N.C., 197
Rama, H. P., 201–6, 208–9, 212–18, 222–26, 229–30
Rape. See *State of Georgia v. Fortunatio Annunciatio*
Reconstruction, 1, 8–9, 11, 13–14, 16, 20, 25, 32, 38, 46, 51, 67, 175, 186
Refugee Assistance Act of 1975, 161
Regional Parks and Wildlife Department, Tex., 166
Religion. *See* Chinese Americans; Vietnamese Americans
Republican Party: Radical Republicans, 8; in Arkansas, 13, 15, 16, 17, 59. *See also* Reconstruction
Rice: and Japanese Americans in Louisiana, 23, 34–35, 40, 43, 45–46; post Civil War, 33
Richmond County, Ga., 105–8, 110
Richmond Hill Plantation (Ga.), 64
Roberto Alvarez v. the Board of Trustees of the Lemon Grove School District, 112
Rockingham, N.C., 195, 202
Rockport, Tex., 163, 166, 171, 173
Rohwer, Ark., 62–67, 100
Roosevelt, Theodore, 32, 73

Rosedale, Miss., 2, 81–82, 85, 93, 100
Rosedale Consolidated High School (Miss.), 71, 84, 86–91, 101
Route 1, 199
Route 90, 199
Rowland, W. M., 109
Russo-Japanese War, 31, 50
Rust Belt, 197
Ruthenberg, Leon, 169–70

Saigon, Vietnam, 160–61, 185
Sakai, Joseph, 35–36, 38–39
San Antonio, Tex., 33, 57, 58, 159
San Antonio Bay, Tex., 163, 168, 171
Sands hotel and casino (Las Vegas, Nev.), 213
San Francisco, Calif., 27, 31, 73, 89, 93, 200–201
Santa Fe, Tex., 163, 173, 179
Savannah, Ga.: Chinese Americans in, 4, 104–5, 108; Filipino Americans in, 119
School segregation: and Asian Americans, 2–4, 20, 23, 73; on the West Coast, 31; and Filipino Americans, 70, 74–78; and Chinese Americans, 70–72, 78–81; in Augusta, 103–10. *See also* Augusta, Ga.; *Brown v. Board of Education*; *Lum v. Rice*
Seabrook, Tex., 158–59, 163, 166, 175–79, 185, 188, 190–93
Seabrook-Kemah Fishermen's Coalition, 178
Seadrift, Tex., 163, 165, 167–70, 172
Sei Fujii v. California, 6, 145
Sexuality. *See* Filipino Americans; *Naim v. Naim*
Seymour, Paul, 126–27, 130–34
Sherman Anti-Trust Act, 178, 180, 189–90
Sicilano, Richard, 177
Silent Majority, 164
Silverman, Henry, 214–17, 219–21, 223–25, 228, 230
Sing Lee, 76
Sixteenth Section Institution, 95–96
Slavery. *See* Reconstruction
Sluss, Homer O., 77

Small Business Franchise Bill, 227–28
Smith, Willis B., 65
South: civil rights narrative of, 3, 5–7, 19–21; Asian American demographics of, 3–4; definition of, 21–22. *See also* New South
Southern Christian Leadership Conference, 20
Southern Poverty Law Center, 25, 159, 179–81, 193
Spanish-American War, 74
Sprague, Lester, 169
SS *Lipari*, 138
Stanfield, James, 178
State of Georgia v. Annunciatio Fortunatio, 24, 128–37. *See also* Annunciatio, Fortunatio
Stephens, E. A., 117, 130, 134–37
St. Landry Parish, La., 35
St. Louis, Mo., 12–13, 74
St. Malo, La., 3
St. Tammany Parish, La., 44
Student Nonviolent Coordinating Committee, 20
Subia, Ambia "Amby," 114; arrival in Atlanta, 118–20; relations with Frances Hutcheson and Rosa Mae Clower, 122, 125–27; attempt at retrial, 127; sentencing of, 128
Sun Belt, 197–98
Supreme Court of the United States, 24, 140–41, 145–46, 147, 151–53 (Naim); *Lum v. Rice*, 2, 71–72, 91–93, 99, 107; and Japanese American incarceration, 6; and alien land laws, 6, 21, 69; and citizenship, 24; *Brown v. Board of Education*, 81
Swearingen, Van C., 52
Sweatt v. Painter, 2

Taft, William Howard, 49, 92, 117
Takamine, Jokichi, 33
Takenouchi, Masahi, 34
Tallmadge, Eugene, 154
Tallulah Apartments (Atlanta, Ga.), 114, 117, 126, 128
Taylor, James, 44–45

Index   281

Tennessee: Chinese laborers in, 11, 19; Indian Americans in, 25, 196, 201, 203, 207, 210–11, 213, 216; school segregation in, 79

Tenth Amendment of the United States Constitution, 96, 146

Terrace v. Thompson, 61

Texas: Asian Americans in, 4, 22, 29; Chinese laborers in, 13, 19, 57–59, 129; as part of the South, 21; Japanese Americans in, 22–23, 33–35, 40; alien land law of, 41, 42, 56; Ku Klux Klan in, 158, 162, 172, 173–74, 178–79, 186, 192; fishing industry in, 159, 188; Galveston Bay towns and cities, 163; and Klan calling card, 173; Indian Americans in, 195; recent immigration policy of, 235. *See also* Vietnamese Americans

Texas Civil Statute 5780, 191

Texas Conference of Churches, 177

Texas Emergency Reserves, 190–93

Texas Knights of the Ku Klux Klan, 158, 173

Till, Emmett, 1

Timmerman, N. D., 99

Toyota, 203

Trammel, Park, 52

Tran Van Phu, 181–82

Treaty of Guadalupe Hidalgo, 112

Trinity Bay, Tex., 158

Turner, Joe, 128–30, 132–34, 137

Twelve Points of Fair Franchising, 226–28

Uganda, 206

Union Parish, La., 45

United Nations, 145, 161

United States Civil Rights Commission, 169

United States Code 42, 187

United States Department of Agriculture, 33

United States Department of State, 161

United States v. Bhagat Singh Thind, 93

United States v. Wong Kim Ark, 6, 77

Universal Declaration of Human Rights, 186

Vandergriff, Bommy, 169

Veterans: World War II, 148; Vietnam War, 167

Victoria, Tex., 171

Vietnamese Americans: perceptions of, 4, 8, 25; legal activism of, 5, 19–20, 159–60; in Galveston Bay fishing industry, 7, 25, 159, 162–63, 165, 167–68, 171, 194, 196; post-1965 immigration of, 22, 157; in the Midwest, 24; on the West Coast, 24; Ku Klux Klan intimidation of, 158–59, 172–77, 192–93; refugee resettlement of, 161–64; relations of with white Texans, 164–68, 170–72; and crab feud, 168–69. *See also Vietnamese Fishermen's Association v. Knights of the Ku Klux Klan*

Vietnamese Fishermen's Association v. Knights of the Ku Klux Klan, 178–92 passim

Vietnam War, 22, 24, 157, 159, 160, 162, 167, 169, 171, 175, 185

Virginia: miscegenation law of, 24, 115–17, 123, 138–40, 142–46, 149–50; Supreme Court of Appeals of, 143–46, 151–53

Walton, Sam, and Walmart, 198

War Relocation Authority, 62–65

Washington (state), 17, 28, 41–42, 61, 80, 106

Washington, D.C., 21, 32, 51, 65, 115, 118, 142–43

Wasserman, Jack, 149

Waynesboro, Ga., 104

Welsh, La., 34

West Coast: Chinese Americans on, 1, 11, 12, 17–20, 61, 81–82, 84, 103–4; Asian American activism on, 4–6, 11, 21, 22; Japanese Americans on, 23, 28, 30, 31–35, 40–43, 47, 49–50, 53, 62, 66, 80, 100; Vietnamese Americans on, 24; school segregation on, 73; Filipino Americans on, 118, 129; Indian Americans on, 195, 201–2

Westminster v. Mendez, 112

Whitaker, Eli B., 62

Whiteness. *See* Identity

Williams, Frank B., 65

Williams, Guy E., 67

Williams, John Sharp, 18
Wilson, Billy, 170
Wolfe, Laura Anne, 140
Wong, Fred, 57–58
Wong, Katherine, 81–82
World War I, and Japanese Americans, 23, 45–46, 53
World War II: changing perceptions of Asian Americans in, 68–69, 99, 100–101, 110–13, 148, 154–56, 235; and repeal of Chinese Exclusion Act, 144; and economic development in the South, 196–99; Indian Americans and, 200, 208; Asian American activism in, 21. *See also* Chinese Americans; Incarceration of Japanese Americans

Xenophobia, 5, 26, 28, 165, 167, 175, 193–94, 203, 206

Yamato Colony, Fla., 36–40, 55
Yates, Steve, 171
Yellow (racial identity). *See* Identity
Yellow peril, 8; and Japanese Americans, 40, 43, 51; and Chinese Americans, 98; and transformation to model minority, 155
Yick Wo v. Hopkins, 6, 93, 145, 151
Yigh, Jong Len, 140
Yingling, Charles, 60
Yo-yo, 114, 117, 119, 120–21

Zamarripa, Kymberli, 162

www.ingramcontent.com/pod-product-compliance
Lightning Source LLC
Chambersburg PA
CBHW031800220426
43662CB00007B/480